Pro Oracle GoldenGate for the DBA

Bobby Curtis

⟨IOUG⟩
Independent oracle users group

Apress®

Pro Oracle GoldenGate for the DBA

Bobby Curtis
Winston, Georgia
USA

ISBN-13 (pbk): 978-1-4842-1180-9   ISBN-13 (electronic): 978-1-4842-1179-3
DOI 10.1007/978-1-4842-1179-3

Library of Congress Control Number: 2016950854

Managing Director: Welmoed Spahr
Lead Editor: Jonathan Gennick
Development Editor: Douglas Pundick
Technical Reviewer: Alex Fatkulin
Editorial Board: Steve Anglin, Pramila Balan, Laura Berendson, Aaron Black, Louise Corrigan, Jim DeWolf, Jonathan Gennick, Robert Hutchinson, Celestin Suresh John, Nikhil Karkal, James Markham, Susan McDermott, Matthew Moodie, Natalie Pao, Gwenan Spearing
Coordinating Editor: Jill Balzano
Copy Editor: Teresa F. Horton
Compositor: SPi Global
Indexer: SPi Global
Artist: SPi Global
Cover Designer: Anna Ishchenko

Distributed to the book trade worldwide by Springer Science+Business Media New York, 233 Spring Street, 6th Floor, New York, NY 10013. Phone 1-800-SPRINGER, fax (201) 348-4505, e-mail orders-ny@springer-sbm.com, or visit www.springer.com. Apress Media, LLC is a California LLC and the sole member (owner) is Springer Science + Business Media Finance Inc (SSBM Finance Inc). SSBM Finance Inc is a Delaware corporation.

For information on translations, please e-mail rights@apress.com, or visit www.apress.com.

Apress and friends of ED books may be purchased in bulk for academic, corporate, or promotional use. eBook versions and licenses are also available for most titles. For more information, reference our Special Bulk Sales–eBook Licensing web page at www.apress.com/bulk-sales.

Any source code or other supplementary material referenced by the author in this text is available to readers at www.apress.com. For detailed information about how to locate your book's source code, go to www.apress.com/source-code/.

Printed on acid-free paper

This book is dedicated to my family, who keeps me going and supports me through all the endeavors that I choose to pursue. I love you, Patty, Cole, Patrick, and Addison! Thank you for motivating me when I needed it. Now back to our busy baseball schedules!

About IOUG Press

*IOUG Press is a joint effort by the **Independent Oracle Users Group (the IOUG)** and **Apress** to deliver some of the highest-quality content possible on Oracle Database and related topics. The IOUG is the world's leading, independent organization for professional users of Oracle products. Apress is a leading, independent technical publisher known for developing high-quality, no-fluff content for serious technology professionals. The IOUG and Apress have joined forces in IOUG Press to provide the best content and publishing opportunities to working professionals who use Oracle products.*

Our shared goals include:

- Developing content with excellence
- Helping working professionals to succeed
- Providing authoring and reviewing opportunities
- Networking and raising the profiles of authors and readers

To learn more about Apress, visit our website at **www.apress.com**. Follow the link for IOUG Press to see the great content that is now available on a wide range of topics that matter to those in Oracle's technology sphere.

Visit **www.ioug.org** to learn more about the Independent Oracle Users Group and its mission. Consider joining if you haven't already. Review the many benefits at www.ioug.org/join. Become a member. Get involved with peers. Boost your career.

www.ioug.org/join

Apress®

Contents at a Glance

Contents

About the Author

Bobby L. Curtis, EMBA

Bobby L. Curtis is an Oracle ACE Director specializing in database monitoring and data integration technologies, both aimed at making usability simpler. Currently, he is working as an Infrastructure Principle at Accenture Enkitec Group (AEG; http://www.accenture.com/enkitec), focused on implementations and migrations of databases while providing monitoring solutions for these environments. He currently participates in many user groups including the Independent Oracle User Group (IOUG), Oracle Development Tools User Group (ODTUG), Georgia Oracle User Group (GaOUG), and the Rocky Mountains Oracle User Group (RMOUG).

Bobby holds a bachelor's degree in Information Systems and an Executive Masters of Business Administration from Kennesaw State University. He lives with his wife and three children in Douglasville, GA. He can be followed on Twitter at @dbasolved and his blog is at http://dbasolved.com.

About the Technical Reviewer

Alex Fatkulin is a master of the full range of Oracle technologies. His mastery has been essential in addressing some of the greatest challenges his customers have met.

Alex draws on years of experience working with some of the world's largest companies, where he has been involved with almost everything related to Oracle databases, from data modeling to architecting high-availability solutions to resolving performance issues of extremely large production sites.

Alex has a bachelor's degree in computer science degree from Far Eastern National University in Vladivostok, Russia. He is also an Oracle ACE and a proud OakTable member.

Acknowledgments

In writing this book there have been a lot of ups and downs, start overs, and doubts if I would ever finish; however, with the support and encouragement of friends and family, it is finally done. A huge special thanks has to go to one of my coworkers, Shane Borden, who helped me out when I needed it. Shane was instrumental in getting this book over the finish line. Thanks, Shane!

Thanks also to the Oracle Data Integration team, especially Joseph deBuzna, who provided input along the way when I would ask silly questions about the product. This assistance is very much appreciated and I hope to continue our discussions in the future.

Foreword

Too often the best consultants are too busy fielding insane customer requests with equally insane timelines, which would bring 99 percent of other consultants to their knees, and making them a reality. They do this by working late into the night, testing, testing, testing, and finding creative ways to ultimately satisfy their customers. They don't have the bandwidth to stop in the middle of all this and post responses to forums, turn what they learned into helpful blog posts, and definitely not to create comprehensive books. But in that elite 1 percent there are some that still rise above the rest and somehow find the time to contribute to the greater community. Bobby Curtis is one of those people.

A few years back when I first met Bobby, we began working together on a few projects. I quickly realized he was also the author of the blog dbasolved.com, which turns up often on my own Internet searches. After working with him, reading his blog more critically, and presenting with him at Oracle Open World, there is no doubt in my mind that he is truly a multitalented professional. When Bobby, who has implemented real-world replication with various technologies at least 100 times, asked me to write the foreword to this book, I did not hesitate to agree.

In this, his fourth book, *Pro Oracle GoldenGate for the DBA,* Bobby is tackling what I believe to be his biggest writing challenge to date: database replication and integration. It's a technology with nearly limitless use cases and in the last ten years or so, the technology industry has really caught on. Gone are the days where we would have to explain what database replication is. Instead we're explaining how to do it; how to stream real-time database changes into JMS, Kafka, Spark, Hive, HDFS, and the like; how to set up multimaster with conflict detection and resolution; and how to validate data consistency between heterogeneous systems. It really is a new era and Bobby's book is the most ambitious in this space yet. His writing style is clear and concise, presenting the world's most popular database replication technology—Oracle GoldenGate—to you, the reader, with usable examples taken from his vast experience.

This is the first book on Oracle GoldenGate to walk the reader through tuning the capture and apply (extract and replicate) components that are now integrated into the Oracle database. It's the first such book to walk you through the new drag-and-drop and wizard-based configuration utility called Oracle GoldenGate Studio. When you consider one of Bobby's previous books was about Oracle Enterprise Manager, it's no surprise that he also does an excellent job covering how to monitor Oracle GoldenGate using several methods.

Written in plain English, *Pro Oracle GoldenGate for the DBA* has something for new and seasoned users alike. There are a lot of exciting enhancements we have planned for Oracle GoldenGate and as it evolves over time I'll be looking forward to the updated versions of this book.

—Joseph deBuzna
Director of Oracle GoldenGate Product Management
June 2016

CHAPTER 1

■ ■ ■

Installation, Upgrade, and Removal

Oracle GoldenGate is a great tool for migrations, real-time replications, and data integration projects. For a tool that is great on so many levels, it does change over time. This is evident with the way Oracle GoldenGate has changed between the releases from 11g to 12c. In the past, Oracle GoldenGate was simply installed by unzipping the binaries to the location where it needed to be installed. With the latest release of Oracle GoldenGate 12c, this has changed; Oracle now provides an Oracle Universal Installer (OUI) for installation. This chapter covers how to install Oracle GoldenGate using the OUI that is packaged with Oracle GoldenGate 12c (12.1.2.0), how to use the same OUI to upgrade to a minor patch version (12.1.2.1), and how to remove the software if desired.

Selecting the Correct Version

When you first start looking into Oracle GoldenGate, you realize that there are numerous variations of this product. This is due to the heterogeneous nature of Oracle GoldenGate. How do you know what version of Oracle GoldenGate is supported for your platform? Sadly, Oracle doesn't make information this easy to find, but you can find it if you know where to look within the Oracle ecosystem. The easiest place to start is on the Oracle Technology Network (OTN) in the Middleware section. There you can find many of the base products, especially Oracle GoldenGate. Before you download Oracle GoldenGate, you should consult the certification matrix provided on OTN or the matrix on the My Oracle Support (MOS) site. The certification matrix on the OTN can be found at the top of the Downloads tab for Oracle GoldenGate as a hyperlink (Figure 1-1).

Figure 1-1. *Certification matrix for Oracle GoldenGate location*

© Bobby Curtis 2016
B. Curtis, *Pro Oracle GoldenGate for the DBA*, DOI 10.1007/978-1-4842-1179-3_1

Clicking the hyperlink will open the Fusion Certification page; there you will need to look for GoldenGate 12c in the Oracle Fusion Middleware 12c Certifications product area (Figure 1-2). Then under Generally Available System Configurations, open the spreadsheet for Oracle Fusion Middleware 12c (12.1.2).

Product Area	Generally Available System Configurations
Oracle Fusion Middleware 12c Certifications - 12.1.x	• System Requirements and Supported Platforms for WebLogic Server 12c (12.1.1) (xls) • System Requirements and Supported Platforms for Oracle Fusion Middleware 12c (12.1.2) (xls) • System Requirements and Supported Platforms for Oracle Fusion Middleware 12c (12.1.3) (xls)

Figure 1-2. *Oracle Fusion Middleware 12c Certifications*

The corresponding spreadsheet will be saved to your desktop and can be opened using Microsoft Excel or a similar tool. Once open, there is a tab at the bottom labeled GoldenGate. This page in the spreadsheet allows you to compare product and release to database vendor and database versions (Figure 1-3).

Oracle GoldenGate Certification Matrix 12c (12.1.2.0.*)

This document covers the following product releases for Oracle GoldenGate: ○
- Oracle GoldenGate 12c (12.1.2.0.0, 12.1.2.0.1, 12.1.2.0.2, 12.1.2.1.0, 12.1.2.1.1)
- Oracle GoldenGate Director 12c (12.1.2.0.0, 12.1.2.0.1)

Oracle GoldenGate

Product	Release	Processor Type	OS Version	OS Update Typ	OS Updat	Run Mc	Database Vendor
Oracle GoldenGate	12.1.2.1.1+	HP-UX Itanium	11.31	Update	12+	64	Oracle Database
Oracle GoldenGate	12.1.2.1.1+	IBM AIX on POWER Systems (64-bit)	6.1	Technology Level	7+	64	Oracle Database
Oracle GoldenGate	12.1.2.1.1+	IBM AIX on POWER Systems (64-bit)	7.1	Technology Level	1+	64	Oracle Database
Oracle GoldenGate	12.1.2.1.1+	Linux x86-64	Oracle Linux 5	Update Level	6+	64	IBM DB2
Oracle GoldenGate	12.1.2.1.1+	Linux x86-64	Oracle Linux 5	Update Level	6+	64	IBM DB2 Connect
Oracle GoldenGate	12.1.2.1.1+	Linux x86-64	Oracle Linux 6	Update Level	1+	64	IBM DB2
Oracle GoldenGate	12.1.2.1.1+	Linux x86-64	Oracle Linux 6	Update Level	1+	64	IBM DB2 Connect
Oracle GoldenGate	12.1.2.1.1+	Linux x86-64	Red Hat Enterprise Linux 5	Update Level	6+	64	IBM DB2
Oracle GoldenGate	12.1.2.1.1+	Linux x86-64	Red Hat Enterprise Linux 5	Update Level	6+	64	IBM DB2 Connect
Oracle GoldenGate	12.1.2.1.1+	Linux x86-64	Red Hat Enterprise Linux 6	Update Level	1+	64	IBM DB2
Oracle GoldenGate	12.1.2.1.1+	Linux x86-64	Red Hat Enterprise Linux 6	Update Level	1+	64	IBM DB2 Connect
Oracle GoldenGate	12.1.2.1.1+	Oracle Solaris on SPARC (64-bit)	10	Update	9+	64	IBM DB2
Oracle GoldenGate	12.1.2.1.1+	Oracle Solaris on SPARC (64-bit)	11	Update	0+	64	IBM DB2
Oracle GoldenGate	12.1.2.1.1+	Oracle Solaris on x86-64 (64-bit)	10	Update	9+	64	IBM DB2
Oracle GoldenGate	12.1.2.1.1+	Oracle Solaris on x86-64 (64-bit)	11	Update	0+	64	IBM DB2
Oracle GoldenGate	12.1.2.1.1+	IBM AIX on POWER Systems (64-bit)	6.1	Technology Level	7+	64	IBM DB2
Oracle GoldenGate	12.1.2.1.1+	IBM AIX on POWER Systems (64-bit)	6.1	Technology Level	7+	64	IBM DB2 Connect
Oracle GoldenGate	12.1.2.1.1+	IBM AIX on POWER Systems (64-bit)	7.1	Technology Level	1+	64	IBM DB2
Oracle GoldenGate	12.1.2.1.1+	IBM AIX on POWER Systems (64-bit)	7.1	Technology Level	1+	64	IBM DB2 Connect
Oracle GoldenGate	12.1.2.1.1+	Microsoft Windows x64 (64-bit)	2012	Service Pack	0+	64	IBM DB2
Oracle GoldenGate	12.1.2.1.1+	Microsoft Windows x64 (64-bit)	2008 R2	Service Pack	0+	64	IBM DB2
Oracle GoldenGate	12.1.2.1.1+	Microsoft Windows x64 (64-bit)	2008 R2	Service Pack	0+	64	IBM DB2 Connect
Oracle GoldenGate	12.1.2.1.1+	Linux x86-64	Oracle Linux 5	Update Level	6+	64	Teradata
Oracle GoldenGate	12.1.2.1.1+	Linux x86-64	Oracle Linux 6	Update Level	1+	64	Teradata
Oracle GoldenGate	12.1.2.1.1+	Linux x86-64	Red Hat Enterprise Linux 5	Update Level	6+	64	Teradata
Oracle GoldenGate	12.1.2.1.1+	Linux x86-64	Red Hat Enterprise Linux 6	Update Level	1+	64	Teradata
Oracle GoldenGate	12.1.2.1.1+	Oracle Solaris on SPARC (64-bit)	10	Update	9+	64	Teradata
Oracle GoldenGate	12.1.2.1.1+	Oracle Solaris on SPARC (64-bit)	11	Update	0+	64	Teradata

▶ | Menu | System | Client | Database | WebServer | Interop | ID&Access | ODI Source-Target | GoldenGate | Document Control | +

Figure 1-3. *Oracle GoldenGate Certification Matrix*

Once you identify the version of Oracle GoldenGate that is needed, you can either go back to OTN or to EDelivery (http://edelivery.oracle.com) to download the software needed for your environment.

■ **Note**   Access to EDelivery requires a valid customer support identifier (CSI) and a My Oracle Support login.

At this point, you should have identified what version of the software you need to use for your Oracle GoldenGate setup. Once you have identified the software, take a few minutes to download your software and stage it on the servers where it will be installed. With the software staged, let's take a look at how to install Oracle GoldenGate 12c. This chapter walks through how to install Oracle GoldenGate on an Oracle Enterprise Linux platform. This is the simplest platform on which to install Oracle GoldenGate and to demonstrate the process.

Installing Oracle GoldenGate 12c

Installation of Oracle GoldenGate is by far one of the simplest Oracle installs. In the past, the installation consisted of downloading and extracting a zip file in the desired directory and running a few commands to build subdirectories and process groups for replication. That is an oversimplified explanation, but it shows how simple the process was. With the latest release of Oracle GoldenGate 12c (12.1.2.0), Oracle has provided a new graphical installation process in the form of the OUI, which performs the initial steps of the installation for you. Using OUI, Oracle is placing Oracle GoldenGate 12c into the same installation, patching, and deinstall model as its many other products, creating a universal approach to the installation process for Oracle GoldenGate.

After you download the Oracle GoldenGate software, it should be staged in a temporary location from which it can be run. The staging location should have enough space to extract the file; this can be the universal temp directory or another directory of your choosing. For example:

```
[oracle@ggtest1 /]$ cd /tmp[oracle@ggtest1 tmp]$ ls -ltrtotal 343924-rwxrwx--- 1 oracle
vboxsf 352172376 Mar 18 10:20 121210_fbo_ggs_Linux_x64_shiphome.zip
```

Once the software is staged, it needs to be extracted. After that, all the files needed for installation will be available to you. In the following command, the usage of the -d option specifies that the software should be installed in the same directory where the file is stored.

```
[oracle@ggtest1 tmp]$ unzip ./121210_fbo_ggs_Linux_x64_shiphome.zip -d.
```

After the file is extracted, you will see a directory named fbo_ggs_Linux_x64_shiphome. Under this directory is a subdirectory called Disk1. In the Disk1 directory, you will find the runInstaller to initialize the OUI.

■ **Note**   Just like any other time you have used OUI, the installer will run using X Windows. Ensure that X Windows is configured before running the installer. You also have the option to run the OUI in silent mode.

Execute the OUI using the runInstaller command:

```
[oracle@ggtest1 Disk1]$ ./runInstaller &
```

After you execute runInstaller, the OUI should start (Figure 1-4) and bring you to the first page of the Install Wizard. Notice that the installer now provides two options for installing Oracle GoldenGate. The first option is for installing Oracle GoldenGate for Database 12c and the second option is for Oracle Database 11g. Oracle provides these two options because Oracle GoldenGate 12c can be used with two different versions of Oracle Database. The minimum version of Oracle Database that is supported is Oracle Database 11gR2 (11.2.0.1) and up to the latest version of the Oracle Database 12c (12.1.0.2). The installation option you choose here determines which Oracle libraries the Oracle GoldenGate binaries will look for when starting.

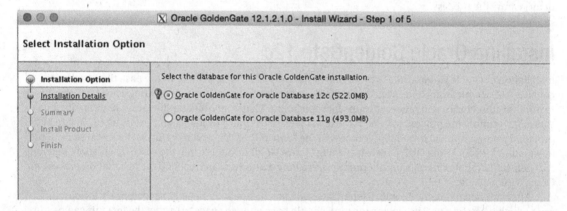

Figure 1-4. *Oracle GoldenGate Install Wizard Step 1 of 5*

■ **Note**   Oracle GoldenGate 12c (12.1.2.x) works with Oracle Database 11g (11.2.0.x) and Oracle Database 12c (12.1.0.x).

Select the version of Oracle GoldenGate that you want to install based on the database platform that will use Oracle GoldenGate for extraction or apply processes. After making your selection, move on with the installation.

The next step in the installation is to provide the location where the software will be installed. By default, the installer places the binaries in the user home directory, but this is not a good place to install the binaries. A better option would be to use Oracle Flexible Architecture (OFA) for your software location. By using OFA, you establish a directory structure that will allow you to keep a separate version of the Oracle GoldenGate software on the same machine. A path like /u01/app/oracle/product/12.1.2.0/ogghome_1 could be a valid and flexible OFA compliant path for installation.

Make the necessary changes to the software location to match your environment, hopefully using an OFA standard. Figure 1-5 shows the choice I made when installing GoldenGate for this book.

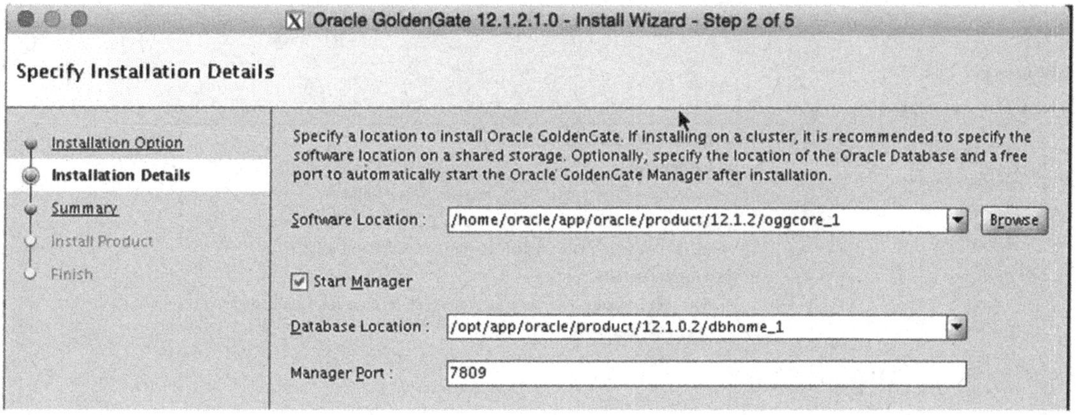

Figure 1-5. *Oracle Install Wizard Step 2 of 5*

After specifying your software location, notice that there is a Start Manager check box. The OUI will automatically set up the manager process for the Oracle GoldenGate environment. This check box is the indicator that the manger should be started once installed. The next two text boxes on the screen have to do with the location of the database that Oracle GoldenGate will run against and what port the manager process should be assigned to and listen on. Make changes as needed and then proceed with the installation.

■ **Note** The Database Location will be populated with more than one Oracle Database Home if more than one exists. Ensure that you select the correct database location.

The default port for the manager process is 7809. This is fine, buts I find it best practice to change the port number to something much higher to prevent any other process from interfering with communication of the manager process. I typically use a port like 15000, which ensures that no known process will be in the port range for Oracle GoldenGate.

With the software location set, database home selected, and port number assigned, the Install Wizard will move to the Summary screen (Figure 1-6). This screen provides all the details on what will be installed, how much space will be required, and additional details for the installation. There is also an option to save your settings to a response file. The response file, if saved, can be used to install future Oracle GoldenGate intsances by means of a silent install.

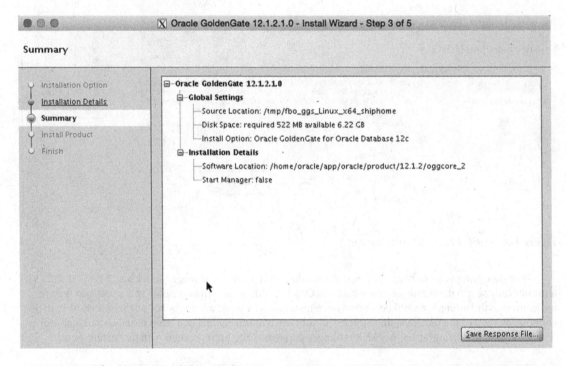

Figure 1-6. *Oracle Install Wizard Step 3 of 5*

After confirming that everything is correct and saving a response file, if desired, click Install to begin the installation. Once the installation begins, it will take five minutes or less to install (Figure 1-7). You can use the Details button, if needed, to review each step of the installation process.

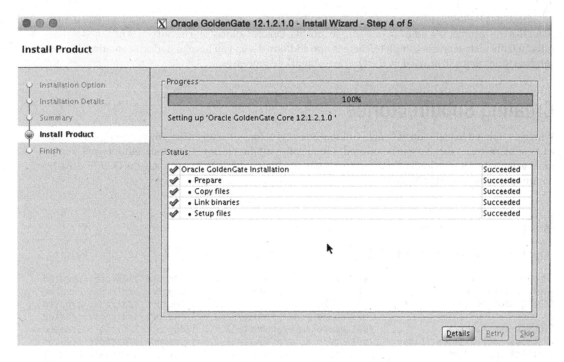

Figure 1-7. *Oracle Install Wizard Step 4 of 5*

Finally, when the installation is complete, the Install Wizard moves to the Finish screen (Figure 1-8). On this screen there is really nothing to do, so just exit out of the Install Wizard.

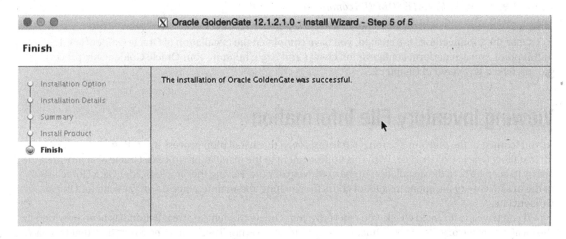

Figure 1-8. *Oracle Install Wizard Step 5 of 5*

Once this is done, you have successfully installed Oracle GoldenGate on your Linux system. It might seem like the installer is a little fat for a simple tool like Oracle GoldenGate because it is installed so fast. Although the installation is complete, there is one additional step you have to perform: creating the required subdirectories that will be used by the Oracle GoldenGate processes.

Creating Subdirectories

With a completed installation of Oracle GoldenGate 12c, before you can create any process groups there are a few subdirectories that have to be created. Creating the subdirectories is pretty straightforward. You just need to start the Oracle GoldenGate Service Command Interface (GGSCI) and issue the CREATE SUBDIRS command, as illustrated in Figure 1-9.

```
GGSCI (db12cgg.acme.com) 1> create subdirs

Creating subdirectories under current directory /u01/app/oracle/product/12.2.0.1/oggcore_3

Parameter files              /u01/app/oracle/product/12.2.0.1/oggcore_3/dirprm: created
Report files                 /u01/app/oracle/product/12.2.0.1/oggcore_3/dirrpt: created
Checkpoint files             /u01/app/oracle/product/12.2.0.1/oggcore_3/dirchk: created
Process status files         /u01/app/oracle/product/12.2.0.1/oggcore_3/dirpcs: created
SQL script files             /u01/app/oracle/product/12.2.0.1/oggcore_3/dirsql: created
Database definitions files   /u01/app/oracle/product/12.2.0.1/oggcore_3/dirdef: created
Extract data files           /u01/app/oracle/product/12.2.0.1/oggcore_3/dirdat: created
Temporary files              /u01/app/oracle/product/12.2.0.1/oggcore_3/dirtmp: created
Credential store files       /u01/app/oracle/product/12.2.0.1/oggcore_3/dircrd: created
Masterkey wallet files       /u01/app/oracle/product/12.2.0.1/oggcore_3/dirwlt: created
Dump files                   /u01/app/oracle/product/12.2.0.1/oggcore_3/dirdmp: created
```

Figure 1-9. *Using the CREATE SUBDIRS command*

Once the subdirectories are created, you have completed the installation of Oracle GoldenGate 12c. At this point, you can perform configuration checks and begin building your Oracle GoldenGate process groups, which is covered in Chapter 2.

Viewing Inventory File Information

As you learned in the previous section, Oracle improved the installation process by adding OUI as the means for installing Oracle GoldenGate. With this improvement to the installation process, Oracle also provided the ability to keep track of the installation in the oraInventory file. Having the Oracle GoldenGate Home listed in the oraInventory file opens up a lot of doors for patching and maintenance down the road for Oracle GoldenGate.

If you have the desire to check, you can verify your Oracle GoldenGate installation has been provided in the local oraInventory file. If your Oracle GoldenGate home is not listed, you need to confirm that you had the proper Oracle base provided prior to installation. This is going to be important as Oracle releases patches and major releases in the future.

Listing 1-1 shows the contents of the oraInventory file that was created during installation. As you can see, there is an Oracle Database 12c installation on the machine. You can also tell that there are two separate Oracle GoldenGate homes. This information is critical because you can now use tools like OPatch to check patchset and garner various other information from the installation with minimal effort.

Listing 1-1. Contents of oraInventory File

```
<?xml version="1.0" standalone="yes" ?>
<!-- Copyright (c) 1999, 2011, Oracle. All rights reserved. -->
<!-- Do not modify the contents of this file by hand. -->
<INVENTORY>
<VERSION_INFO>
  <SAVED_WITH>11.2.0.3.0</SAVED_WITH>
  <MINIMUM_VER>2.1.0.6.0</MINIMUM_VER>
</VERSION_INFO>
<HOME_LIST>
<HOME NAME="OraDB12Home1" LOC="/opt/app/oracle/product/12.1.0.2/dbhome_1" TYPE="O" IDX="1"/>
<HOME NAME="OraHome1" LOC="/opt/app/oracle/product/12.1.2/oggcore_1" TYPE="O" IDX="2"/>
<HOME NAME="OraHome2" LOC="/home/oracle/app/oracle/product/12.1.2/oggcore_2" TYPE="O"
IDX="3"/>
</HOME_LIST>
<COMPOSITEHOME_LIST>
</COMPOSITEHOME_LIST>
</INVENTORY>
```

Upgrading Oracle GoldenGate

Upgrading Oracle GoldenGate has always been quite simple. With past releases of Oracle GoldenGate, to perform an upgrade, you simply backed up your binaries and then overwrote them with the latest version. Starting with Oracle GoldenGate 12c, the process of an upgrade is still simple. The only difference now is that you have an OUI to guide you through the process.

If you are upgrading Oracle GoldenGate from an 11g version to a 12c version, there are a few changes that happen with regard to the trail files associated with the replication process that needs to be accounted for in the process; however, for an upgrade from 12.1.2.0 to 12.1.2.1 this is not a concern. This section focuses on how to upgrade Oracle GoldenGate 12c from 12.1.2.0 to 12.1.2.1 using the OUI.

■ **Note** Before running the installers, ensure that all Oracle GoldenGate processes have been stopped. Use the `ps -ef` command to verify there are not processes running.

Just like the installation process, the installer needs to be run using the `runInstaller` command. For example:

```
[oracle@ggtest1 tmp]$ cd fbo_ggs_Linux_x64_shiphome/Disk1/
[oracle@ggtest1 Disk1]$ ./runInstaller &
```

This will kick off the Install Wizard and bring you back to the screen to select what version of the database Oracle GoldenGate will use (Figure 1-10).

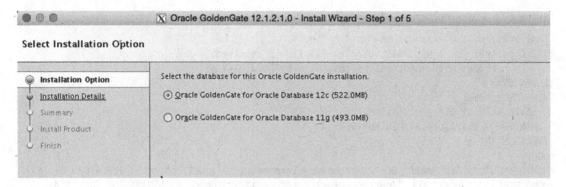

Figure 1-10. *Oracle Install Wizard Step 1 of 5 (upgrade)*

Although this is an upgrade, you still need to select what version of the database Oracle GoldenGate will run against. After selecting the database type, move on to the installation details.

On the Specify Installation Details screen (Figure 1-11) make sure you select the current Oracle GoldenGate home. This ensures that you overwrite the binaries that are in that location.

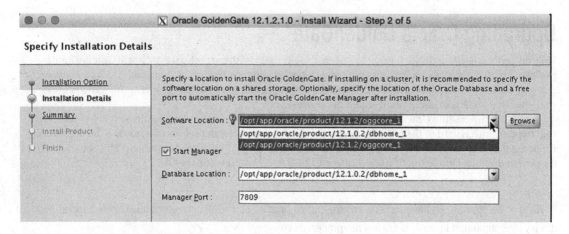

Figure 1-11. *Oracle Install Wizard Step 2 of 5 (upgrade)*

■ **Note**   Make sure you change the port number for the manager before moving forward with the upgrade. If you do not, the manager parameter file (`mgr.prm`) will be updated with the port number listed on the screen.

After selecting the correct software location for the upgrade, the Install Wizard moves on to the Summary screen (Figure 1-12). Just like installing the software, the Summary screen shows what is going to occur. Although this screen doesn't say anything about an upgrade being performed, the OUI will overwrite the binaries in the directory.

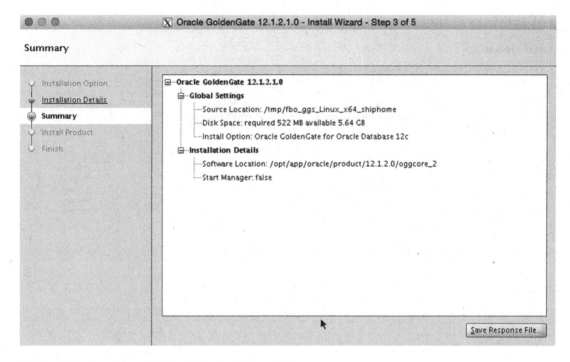

Figure 1-12. *Oracle Install Wizard Step 3 of 5 (upgrade)*

After verifying everything is correct for the upgrade, the installer will proceed to overwrite the binaries and upgrade them to the latest version of Oracle GoldenGate. The progress bar on the Install Product screen (Figure 1-13) will indicate how the upgrade is going and where it is at in the process. Below the status screen there is a Details button that can be used to access more information about what is being done.

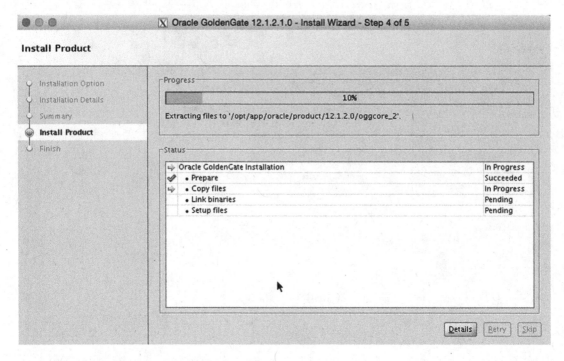

Figure 1-13. *Oracle Install Wizard Step 4 of 5 (upgrade)*

Once the binaries have been upgraded, the progress bar will reach 100 percent and the Install Wizard will move to the Finish screen (Figure 1-14). On this screen, you can complete the upgrade by clicking Finish.

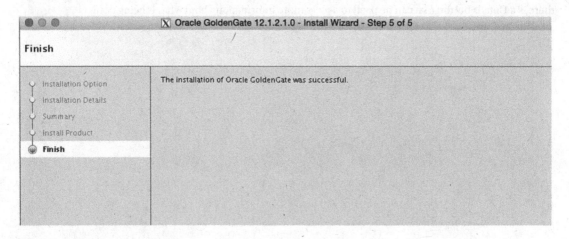

Figure 1-14. *Oracle Install Wizard Step 5 of 5 (upgrade)*

After the upgrade is done the next thing you want to verify is that Oracle GoldenGate comes up with the correct version. In the previous example, you were upgrading from Oracle GoldenGate 12.1.2.0 to Oracle GoldenGate 12.1.2.1. If the upgrade was successful, when executing the GGSCI, the header should indicate that it is running as version 12.1.2.1, as shown in this example.

```
[oracle@ggtest1 oggcore_2]$ ./ggsci

Oracle GoldenGate Command Interpreter for Oracle
Version 12.1.2.1.0 OGGCORE_12.1.2.1.0_PLATFORMS_140727.2135.1_FBO
Linux, x64, 64bit (optimized), Oracle 12c on Aug 7 2014 10:21:34
Operating system character set identified as UTF-8.

Copyright (C) 1995, 2014, Oracle and/or its affiliates. All rights reserved.

GGSCI (ggtest1.acme.com) 1>
```

Once you verify that everything is running as version 12.1.2.1 of Oracle GoldenGate, you can install your process groups or turn everything in the environment back on.

■ **Note** Because the upgrade was moving from a lower version of Oracle GoldenGate 12c to a current version, there was nothing you needed to do with the trail files. If you would have upgraded from an older version of Oracle GoldenGate to Oracle GoldenGate 12c, there would have been some conversion of trail files before existing process groups would restart.

Removing Oracle GoldenGate

There are occasions when you will want to remove Oracle GoldenGate from the systems where it is running. As simple as it was to install Oracle GoldenGate, is just as easy to remove it from a system. There are two primary ways of removing Oracle GoldenGate from a system:

1. Using the OUI deinstall option (the safe way)

2. Hacking the oraInventory file (the not so safe way)

Both of these methods will remove Oracle GoldenGate from your system. Let's take a look at how you can remove Oracle GoldenGate.

■ **Note** Prior to Oracle GoldenGate 12c, you just had to delete the directory, which is not the case with Oracle GoldenGate 12c.

Oracle Universal Installer Deinstall Option

Just like the installation of Oracle GoldenGate 12c, you can remove the software using a similar process. To deinstall Oracle GoldenGate 12c using the OUI deinstall option, you need to access the software from the home directory you want to remove. In the following example, Oracle GoldenGate home 3 will be removed.

```
[oracle@ggtest1 bin]$ pwd
/u01/app/oracle/product/12.2.0.1/oggcore_3/oui/bin[oracle@ggtest1 bin]$ ./runInstaller
-silent -deinstall "REMOVE_HOMES=/u01/app/oracle/product/12.2.0.1/oggcore_3"
Starting Oracle Universal Installer…

Checking swap space: must be greater than 500 MB.  Actual 2156 MB  Passed
Preparing to launch Oracle Universal Installer from /tmp/OraInstall2016-03-23_01-18-08AM.
Please wait ...[oracle@db12cgg bin]$ Oracle Universal Installer, Version 11.2.0.3.0 Production
Copyright (C) 1999, 2011, Oracle. All rights reserved.

Starting deinstall

Deinstall in progress (Wednesday, March 23, 2016 1:18:13 AM EDT)
........................................................... 100% Done.

Deinstall successful
```

At this point, you have successfully removed Oracle GoldenGate from your system. You will notice that runInstaller was run from the $OGG_HOME/oui/bin directory. This is the directory that the OUI creates under the home directory for OUI purposes. This is the cleanest way you can remove Oracle GoldenGate from any system.

Hacking the oraInventory File

The second way to remove Oracle GoldenGate from a system is basically a hacking session of the inventory files. This should only be done by administrators who understand the structure of the inventory files because if you corrupt your inventory file, you can corrupt every piece of Oracle software that is on your system and prevent these applications from being patched in the future.

1. Now with the risk just explained, to remove Oracle GoldenGate 12c from a system using the hacking method; there are two steps required to achieve the removal: Remove Oracle GoldenGate entry from oraInventory.

2. Remove the Oracle GoldenGate binaries.

To remove the Oracle GoldenGate entries from oraInventory, you need to locate the inventory.xml file. This file is typically in the $ORACLE_BASE/oraInventory/ContextXML/ directory. Once the inventory.xml file is located, it needs to be edited. The following example highlights what you should look for in the inventory.xml file specific to Oracle GoldenGate.

```
<?xml version="1.0" standalone="yes" ?>
<!-- Copyright (c) 1999, 2011, Oracle. All rights reserved. -->
<!-- Do not modify the contents of this file by hand. -->
<INVENTORY>
<VERSION_INFO>
  <SAVED_WITH>11.2.0.3.0</SAVED_WITH>
```

```
<MINIMUM_VER>2.1.0.6.0</MINIMUM_VER>
</VERSION_INFO>
<HOME_LIST>
<HOME NAME="OraDB12Home1" LOC="/opt/app/oracle/product/12.1.0.2/dbhome_1" TYPE="O" IDX="1"/>
<HOME NAME="OraHome1" LOC="/opt/app/oracle/product/12.1.2.0/oggcore_2" TYPE="O" IDX="2"/>
</HOME_LIST>
<COMPOSITEHOME_LIST>
</COMPOSITEHOME_LIST>
</INVENTORY>
```

In that example, you would want to remove the entry that has the name OraHome1. This is the location of the binaries for the Oracle GoldenGate home that will be removed.

■ **Note**   Before making any edits to `inventory.xml`, you should make a backup of the file.

Once the `inventory.xml` file has been edited, you can remove the directory where the binaries are. The simplest way of doing this is to run a recursive remove (`rm -rf`) command for the directory as shown here.

```
[oracle@ggtest1 ~]$ cd /opt/app/oracle/product/
[oracle@ggtest1 product]$ rm -rf ./12.1.2.0
```

At this point, you should not have any Oracle GoldenGate items on your system. If you have any Oracle GoldenGate processes running, you can kill these processes with using a standard command, such as `kill`.

Summary

In this chapter, we took a look at how Oracle GoldenGate 12c is installed using the OUI, how to use the OUI to perform an upgrade, and how to remove the binaries from the server using the OUI and manual processes. These items are just the basic tasks to prepare Oracle GoldenGate 12c for use or removal on any system on which you will run Oracle GoldenGate. After reviewing this chapter, you should be able to install Oracle GoldenGate 12c in a way that allows you to have an organized environment. In the chapters that follow, you build on this chapter by creating additional items in the framework of an Oracle GoldenGate 12c environment.

CHAPTER 2

■ ■ ■

Architecture

In Chapter 1, you took a look at how to install, upgrade, and remove Oracle GoldenGate. This chapter builds on your knowledge of Oracle GoldenGate by taking a look at the Oracle GoldenGate architecture and the components that are involved in this architecture. You should achieve a foundational understanding of the components used within the Oracle GoldenGate architecture. Then you will take a quick look at some of the tools and utilities used in running Oracle GoldenGate.

Before you dive into the components that make Oracle GoldenGate, you need to understand that Oracle GoldenGate is a replication technology used to move data among many different platforms. The ability to replicate between different platforms is what makes Oracle GoldenGate the only heterogeneous tool that is used not only for replication, but data integration and migrations. There are many different architectures that can be configured with the flexibility that Oracle GoldenGate provides while providing high-volume data replication in real time.

Architectures

One of the primary advantages with Oracle GoldenGate is the many architectures or use cases that this software can address. There are some common architectures that every organization implements depending on their requirements for replication. In this section, you take a look at the most common architectures that are used.

Unidirectional Replication

The simplest and most common replication architecture for Oracle GoldenGate is the unidirectional replication architecture. This architecture is used to replicate data from a single source system to one or more remote target systems. Gaining a foundational understanding of this architecture will provide the basis that will be used as you start reviewing the more complex architectures that Oracle GoldenGate can provide. Figure 2-1 illustrates this architecture.

Figure 2-1. *Unidirectional replication architecture*

© Bobby Curtis 2016

B. Curtis, *Pro Oracle GoldenGate for the DBA*, DOI 10.1007/978-1-4842-1179-3_2

A unidirectional architecture consists of the core processes that are used in Oracle GoldenGate. These processes consist of the extract (capture) process, the data pump process, and the replicate (delivery) process. In between these processes are proprietary binary files called trail files. The trail files are used to store the captured transactions.

Bidirectional (Active-Active) Replication

Building on the simplicity of the unidirectional replication architecture is the bidirectional (active-active) replication architecture. The bidirectional architecture is used to keep both the source and target systems in sync with data coming from both locations. Figure 2-2 illustrates how this architecture looks conceptually.

Figure 2-2. *Bidirectional replication architecture*

There are a few reasons for using a bidirectional architecture. The most common use case for a bidirectional architecture is during migrations when you are looking to upgrade your database systems. By using a pseudo-failback replication from the target, you can migrate your database and applications with a near-zero downtime approach. The pseudo-failback replication coming from the target side allows you to capture transactions and have an avenue to downgrade, if needed, without losing any transactions. The second use case for which people have been using bidirectional architecture for is a high-availability or disaster recovery solution. Although Oracle GoldenGate does not fall into Oracle's disaster recovery category, many organizations have been using it this way due to the read/write functionality it allows. With the onset of cloud technologies, a bidirectional replication can be used to move data into and out of public or private cloud architectures.

■ **Note**   Do not confuse high availability with Oracle GoldenGate with disaster recovery technology such as Oracle Data Guard. These two technologies are similar but they are used for different purposes.

Real-Time Data Warehousing

In today's fast-paced business world, data warehousing is critical to many organizations. Data is a valuable commodity that is used by decision makers and affects every aspect of business. Oracle GoldenGate is positioned to be one of the best tools for consolidation where data is a concern. Oracle GoldenGate can be used to consolidate data from many heterogeneous platforms down to a single data warehouse. This capability effectively allows organizations to take data from any platform and perform data integration techniques and analysis from a single source of truth. Figure 2-3 provides a better conceptual view of this architecture.

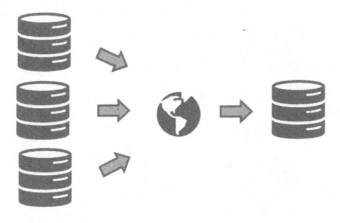

Figure 2-3. *Consolidation replication architecture*

With the ability to capture, transform, and apply data into a single source of truth database like a data warehouse, Oracle GoldenGate can be leveraged against other Oracle tools, allowing for a more robust integration process. Tools like Oracle Data Integrator can be leveraged alongside of Oracle GoldenGate to transform the data as the data is loaded into a data warehouse. Additionally, consolidation with Oracle GoldenGate can be extended to capture data from flat files, allowing a greater range of consolidation efforts from multiple sources.

As more and more organizations start to explore big data technology for decision making, Oracle GoldenGate can be used to consolidate data onto platforms like Hadoop. Using Oracle GoldenGate with big data will open up many more opportunities for organizations. At this point in the book, just be aware that Oracle GoldenGate can be used with current big data technologies.

Real-Time Data Distribution

Oracle GoldenGate is a good tool for consolidating data from multiple sources to a single source of truth; it is just as good at distributing data to remote locations. In a data distribution architecture, Oracle GoldenGate takes data or subsets of data and ships that data to target databases that reside in different geographical regions. This approach allows for organizations to segregate data based on what is required for different lines of business or locations. Figure 2-4 illustrates how this architecture looks when implemented.

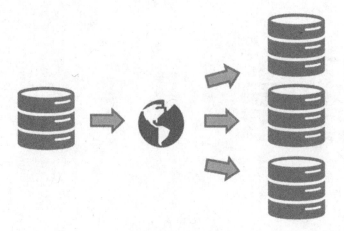

Figure 2-4. *Data distribution architecture*

By using a data distribution architecture, an organization can ensure that the correct geographical locations get the data that they require. This architecture also provides some sense of security for the data because the data being shipped is based on filters, within Oracle GoldenGate, that prevent data from being shipped to the wrong location. Overall, the data distribution architecture allows you to take a single source of truth and share the data based on predefined requirements for remote locations.

Data Distribution via Messaging

Data distribution via messaging is similar to the data distribution architecture previously discussed; the only difference is in how data is actually shipped to the geographical locations. This architecture uses flat files for data distribution. Using flat files, Oracle GoldenGate can ensure that data can be captured and shipped to any type of system. Most systems that this architecture supports are various database types, office applications such as Microsoft Excel, and larger systems running on a big data framework. Figure 2-5 illustrates this architecture.

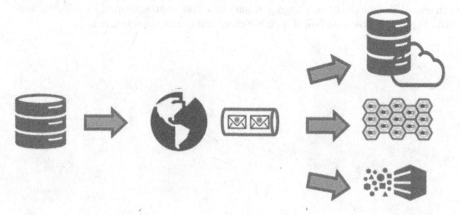

Figure 2-5. *Data distribution via messaging architecture*

As you can see, there are many different architectures in which Oracle GoldenGate can be used. The architectures highlighted in this chapter are just the tip of the iceberg. Oracle GoldenGate is such a flexible product that almost any type of architecture can be built for a wide range of use cases. This is the reason most organizations, after purchasing and exploring what it can do, start to find different business requirements that Oracle GoldenGate can address, leading to enterprise-wide adaptation of Oracle GoldenGate.

To understand where you can go with Oracle GoldenGate, you will need to take a closer look at what makes up these architectures. The simplest way of doing this is to use the unidirectional use case and dissect that to gain better understanding. Figure 2-6 shows the unidirectional use case in more detail.

Figure 2-6. *Detail of the unidirectional architecture*

You can see in Figure 2-6 is that there are a few different processes that are taking place. Starting from the left of Figure 2-6, you see the capture process, then trail files followed by a pump process (extract; more on this shortly). On the remote side, you see additional trail files feeding into a delivery process for applying to the target database. These processes make up the core of Oracle GoldenGate and allow for the product to be flexible and scalable no matter the environment. Let's take a closer look at these processes.

Understanding System Change Numbers

Now that you understand a few of the different architectures, getting an understanding of the system change number (SCN) is important. Oracle GoldenGate uses the SCN on an Oracle database to identify where the transactions are within the replication process. This number is also used when instantiating the replication process, so it is a very important piece of information to gather after setting up the capture process.

■ **Note**   The Oracle GoldenGate documentation uses the term change system number (CSN) in places. This means the same thing as SCN when using Oracle databases. Other databases like Microsoft SQL Server and MySQL will use a similar number. Consult your documentation for what you will need to use.

Finding the System Change Number in Oracle

Within an Oracle database, finding the SCN is quite simple. This information can be found in the V$DATABASE view or by using the DBMS_FLASHBACK package on the source database. Recording this number after starting the capture process will ensure that you have a consistent point to pull data from for instantiation purposes using Oracle Export Data Pump. Here's are the queries you can use to pull this information:

```
SQL> select current_scn from v$database;
```

```
SQL> select dbms_flashback.get_system_change_number from dual;
```

Once you have the SCN, this number should be used with Oracle Export Data Pump to ensure you get a consistent read of the data that needs to be imported into the target system. Any transactions that are captured after the SCN will be placed in the trail files. All data that is exported while using the SCN will be handled by Oracle Export Data Pump. Once this data is imported to the target system along with transactions from the Oracle GoldenGate processes, you will have a complete set of data with a near-zero downtime approach on the target system.

■ **Note** The GV$DATABASE view can also be used if using Oracle Real Application Cluster (RAC).

GoldenGate Processes

What makes Oracle GoldenGate so flexible and scalable are the processes that are used to capture, transmit, and deliver data in a heterogeneous environment. These processes coupled with trail files for storing the transactions between processes can be configured to provide a robust environment. This section looks at each of the processes and how they are used within an Oracle GoldenGate environment.

Manager Process

The manager process is not the most talked about process in the Oracle GoldenGate environment; however, it can be considered the brains of the process operation. The manager is responsible for many different parts within the environment. This is the one process that must be running, and remain running, on every system within a replication environment. Because it has to remain running on every system, the manager process is responsible for the following functions:

- Start and restart of Oracle GoldenGate processes

- Starting of dynamic processes

- Maintaining port numbers for processes

- Trail file management

- Event, error, and threshold reports

One manager process can control many different types of Oracle GoldenGate processes. This allows for central management of all things related to Oracle GoldenGate from a single home structure.

■ **Note** If running in a Microsoft Windows environment, the manager process can be configured to run as a service.

Collector Process

The collector process is a background process that runs on the delivery (target) side when online change synchronization is active. Collector processes are needed to ensure that the following tasks are performed:

- Connection requests from a remote extract to manager can be scanned and bound to available ports. Then assign the port number to the requesting extract via the manager process.

- Receive extracted transactions that are sent by the extract and write them to the trail file.

When a network connection is requested, the manager process automatically starts the collector process so there is no need for Oracle GoldenGate users to interact with the collector process. Because the collector can only receive information from only one extract, this means that there will be one collector started for each extract started. The collector process is terminated when the extract process is terminated.

Capture Process

The extract process of Oracle GoldenGate is used to perform change data capture from the source database. The extract is used to synchronize data that is read from the online transaction log (in Oracle the online redo logs) or the associated archive logs. The data that is extracted, when configured for change synchronization, from the source database is then stored until it receives either a commit or rollback. On a commit, the extract persists the transaction to disk where it is stored in a series of files known as a trail file. Committed transactions will be stored in a trail file in sequentially organized transaction units. Once transactions are persisted to disk in a trail file, the transaction can be shipped using standard TCP/IP protocols.

■ **Note**   Trail files do not have to be shipped in all cases. Trail files can be consumed on the same local system or trail files can be shared via a shared file system such as Network File System (NFS).

There are two ways that an extract can be configured:

1. *Initial load*: The extract (captures) a current, static set of data directly from a source object. This is often referred to as a special run.

2. *Change synchronization*: The source data is synchronized with another set of data.

The initial load extract is used to perform static data set loads directly over the network. This process is normally considered a special run type of process. It is only intended to help get static data loaded into the target system and then stop running once that is complete. The change synchronization extract is your standard extract that allows you to synchronize data between the source and target. This is the most common type of extract that is used in most architectures. Both ways of using an extract are valid, but you will mostly likely use one over the other during normal operations.

Just as there are two ways of configuring the extract, there are two types of extract (capture) processes. The first is the classic capture, which is the basic version of Oracle GoldenGate capturing data. The second is the integrated capture. This version of the capture process takes the fundamental capture process from the operating system level and places it more in line with the database for replication purposes for Oracle databases. Both types of extract processes can be configured as either an initial load or change synchronization process. The following sections take a closer look at these two capture processes.

Classic Capture

The classic capture process is the default capture process for all Oracle GoldenGate setups. This type of capture process is controlled from the GGSCI utility but is closely managed from the operating system layer. This means that when there are problems, such as performance, the items needed to identify what is occurring have to come from the operating system level. Tools such as *sar, mpstat, iostat,* and *free* can be used to help diagnose what is occurring on the operating system and within Oracle GoldenGate.

The classic extract (capture) process also has a memory requirement that most people do not know of. Like any other process running on a machine, the process has to have a memory location from which to run. By default, the classic capture process will take between 25 and 55 MB of memory. This memory requirement ensures that data can be captured in an efficient way. Keep this in mind as you start building your Oracle GoldenGate environments.

Integrated Capture

The integrated capture process is relatively new for Oracle GoldenGate. Integrated capture was introduced with GoldenGate release 11.2.0.2. At the time, integrated extract was only supported on Oracle Database versions 11.2.0.3 or later. Using an integrated capture requires the process to be registered with the Oracle Database. This allowed the capture process to interact with the log miner processes in the database.

■ **Note**   Integrated capture only works with Oracle Database versions 11.2.0.3 or later.

To really understand the integrated capture process, you need to take a closer look at the log miner processes inside of the Oracle Database. Figure 2-7 shows you the architecture for this type of process from a high level.

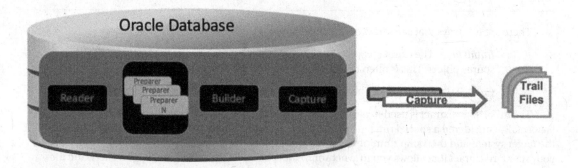

Figure 2-7. *Integrated capture process*

Looking at the image in Figure 2-7, you can tell there are a few internal database processes that are used to make the integrated process run. These processes are a part of the log miner configuration within the Oracle Database.

The log miner server is broken up into the following processes, which you will look at briefly:

- *Reader*: Used to read the online redo logs and split these files into sections to be scanned.

- *Preparer(n)*: Used, in parallel if needed, to read the scanned regions of the online redo logs and prefilter the transactions.

- *Build*: Merges redo records identified by the preparer process and preserves them by SCN.

- *Capture*: Formats the redo records and places them into a logical change record (LCR), which places transactions into the local trail files.

As you can see, the integrated process is a bit more complicated than the classic process. Both processes have their benefits, although Oracle's plan is to move toward the integrated process. Depending on the database platform and version, the classic process still has a place in the Oracle GoldenGate framework.

■ **Note**   The System Global Area (SGA) requires the `streams_pool_size` to be set for better performance.

Data Pump Process

The data pump group is a secondary extract group that is used to help ship data across network. Although a data pump is another extract group similar to the capture process, don't confuse the two. The main purpose of the data pump process is to ship trail files across the network to the remote target system.

■ **Note**   Best practice is to rename the trail file when it reaches the target system.

If the data pump, if shipping trail files, is not configured, the primary extract group will write directly to the remote trail file.

With the data pump process being mostly used for shipping trail files across the network, why would you want to use a data pump process? The single, largest advantage of using a data pump process within your Oracle GoldenGate architecture is that a data pump helps protect against network failures. This ability to protect the captured transactions from being lost is huge for many business reasons. If your network were to have an outage, there are two scenarios that can occur:

1. With a network outage, the data pump process will continue to collect the trail files generated by the primary capture process and store them until the network is restored.

2. If you are not using local trail files and only writing remote trail files, i the case of a network outage, the primary extract will fail. Once the network is restored, the primary extract can be restored with no loss of transactions.

These scenarios highlight why many organizations need to ensure that network discussions are a part of the planning sessions for Oracle GoldenGate.

Unlike the capture process, the data pump does not have more than one configuration that you can use; classic mode is the only configuration available. The associated footprint that the data pump takes is much smaller than the classic capture process, but it still requires memory to run. Remember in most cases, the data pump process is used to ship trail files across the network.

Delivery Process

The delivery process is the apply process within an Oracle GoldenGate environment. The delivery process is responsible for reading the trail files and applying the transactions found in chronological order. This ensures that the data is applied in the same order it was captured (SCN order). Until recently, there was only one version of the delivery process, the classic replicate. Starting in Oracle GoldenGate 12c (12.1.2.0), there are now three distinct versions of the replicate:

- Classic
- Coordinated
- Integrated

Each of these modes provides some sort of benefit, depending on the database to which it is being applied. Oracle is pushing everyone to a more integrated approach; however, you have to be on database version 11.2.0.4 at a minimum.

Classic Delivery

The classic delivery process is the default delivery process for basic Oracle GoldenGate configurations. This type of delivery process is managed from the operating system layer. Just like the classic capture process, this means when there are problems, such as performance, the items needed to identify what is occurring have to come from the operating system level.

This version of the delivery process also has a memory requirement that mirrors the classic capture process. Like any other process running on a machine, it has to have a memory location to run. By default, the classic delivery process will take between 25 and 55 MB of memory. This memory requirement is needed to sure that data is organized and processed in an efficient way.

Coordinated Delivery

The coordinated delivery process is similar to the classic delivery process. The difference here is that the coordinated delivery process will spin up slave processes that are coordinated by a master delivery process. The purpose of the coordinated delivery process is to help split up the delivery process. The parallel process the coordinated delivery uses can be applied to large transactions as well as small transactions.

Integrated Delivery

The integrated delivery process has been introduced with the release of Oracle GoldenGate 12c. This type of delivery brings the ability for an Oracle database to ingest large amounts of transactions without dependence on specialized functions to help split the data into manageable groupings. This approach tracks the dependencies between transactions and applies the transactions based on primary key, foreign key, or unique key constraints, as they are processed.

Just like the integrated capture process, to get a better understanding of how this delivery process works, you need to take a closer look at the log miner architecture (Figure 2-8). Within the database, the following processes are used to ingest the transactions that are coming from the trail files:

- Receiver

- Preparer

- Coordinator

- Apply(n)

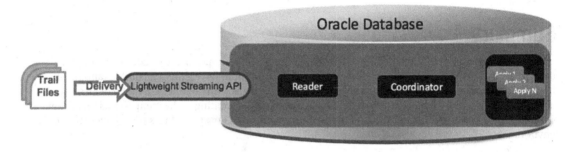

Figure 2-8. *Integrated delivery process*

Each of one of these internal processes has a specific function for applying the transactions to the database.

- *Reader*: This is the inbound server that computes the dependencies among the transactions in the trail files based on constraints defined at the target database (PK, UK, FK). Data Definition Language (DDL) and barrier transactions are maintained and managed automatically.

- *Coordinator*: This ensures that all records are maintained in the order of transaction and then passes the record on to the apply processes.

- *Apply(n)*: These are the processes that apply the records to the database in order of SCN; however, transactions that do not have interdependencies can be safely executed and committed out of order to achieve faster throughput. Parallelism of the apply processes is determined by the amount of records and the load on the receiving database.

■ **Note**   Just like the integrated capture process, the `streams_pool_size` needs to be configured to ensure proper performance.

Trail Files

In many of the architectural images in this chapter, there is an image labeled "trail files." What exactly are trail files? They are Oracle GoldenGate-specific binary files used to ship transactions within the Oracle GoldenGate architecture. These files support the continuous extraction and replication of database changes by storing records of captured changes temporarily on disk. Trail files can exist on a source system, known as local trail files. They can also be stored on the target system, known as remote trail files. By using trail files as storage, Oracle GoldenGate supports data accuracy and fault tolerance. The usage of trail files also allows you to keep Oracle GoldenGate processes independent of each other. This gives you greater flexibility within your Oracle GoldenGate framework and more control over how data is processed and delivered.

Summary

This chapter looked at a few architectures that Oracle GoldenGate supports, the different type of processes that are needed to run a robust replication environment. You should have gained an understanding of how these processes work. You were briefly told what trail files are. With an understanding of all these architectures, processes, and files, you should have a good understanding of the components that go into an Oracle GoldenGate environment. Chapter 3, will walk you through how to build a simple Oracle GoldenGate environment.

CHAPTER 3

■ ■ ■

Basic Replication Configuration

This chapter takes a look at a few of the items needed to configure an Oracle GoldenGate environment. These items include getting an understanding of the profiler, parameter files, a better understanding of trail files, and how to approach doing an initial load of data. Later in the chapter, you take a look at how to set up a unidirection replication between two Oracle databases. This chapter also points out various commands that you might need to use when configuring your environment.

Now that you have gained an understanding of how to install Oracle GoldenGate and the many different replication architectures, you are ready to configure and begin to replicate data in your environment. This chapter covers how to set up unidirectional replication between two Oracle databases so you can gain an understanding of what is involved to establish replication. It also discusses how to prepare the database for replication, configure and establish replication processes (extract, data pump, and replicat) and initial load of data.

Profiler

In preparing an Oracle database for replication with Oracle GoldenGate, you will need to identify anything within the database that might not be able to be replicated. For this purpose, Oracle has created an Oracle GoldenGate Profiler. The profiler is intended to query the database of all the nondefault users to identify the current configuration and any unsupported data types or data types that might need special attention. The latest profiler script can be located on My Oracle Support.

■ **Note** My Oracle Support Notes 1298562.1 and 1296168.1 providethe scripts for all schemas or single-schema profiling.

Run Profiler

Once you have downloaded the profiler from My Oracle Support (MOS), running it is quite simple. All you need is access to SQL*Plus and SYSDBA access. Listing 3-1 provides a glimpse at how the script is run.

Listing 3-1. Running Profiler

```
$ sqlplus / as sysdba
SQ> @full-DB_CheckOracle_07082015sql
```

After the profiler has gathered all the information it requires from the database, an output file will be produced with the results. Review the output file and verify there is nothing of concern that you need to address before setting up replication. Listing 3-2 provides an example of what the profiler report looks like for an older version of the Oracle database.

Listing 3-2. Profiler Output

```
------ System Info:

DateTime:
-------------------
10-24-2014 12:50:02

BANNER
-----------------------------------------------------------------
Oracle Database 10g Enterprise Edition Release 10.2.0.5.0 - 64bi
PL/SQL Release 10.2.0.5.0 - Production
CORE    10.2.0.5.0    Production
TNS for IBM/AIX RISC System/6000: Version 10.2.0.5.0 - Productio
NLSRTL Version 10.2.0.5.0 - Production

NAME      LogMode       SupLog: PK  UI  For FK  All Created
--------- ------------- -------- --- --- --- --- --- -------------------
TEST1234  ARCHIVELOG    NO       NO  NO  NO  NO  NO  10-03-2010 15:45:32

PLATFORM_NAME
--------------------------------------------------------------------------------------
AIX-Based Systems (64-bit)

------ Objects stored in Tablespaces with Compression are not supported in the current
release of OGG

------ Distinct Object Types and their Count By Schema:

OWNER            OBJECT_TYPE            TOTAL
---------------  ---------------------  ----------
TSMSYS           TABLE                       1
TSMSYS           INDEX                       1
ORACLE_OCM       JOB                         2
EDS              TABLE                     158
VPDADM           FUNCTION                    5
EDS              FUNCTION                    2
EDS              TRIGGER                    40
EPHARM           TRIGGER                     2
FDB_2            TABLE                     244
EAS              TABLE                      12
CS_CLINICAL      TABLE                      22
SBMO             TYPE                        1
MDS              SEQUENCE                    1
DIB3_AUX         TABLE                       8
VPDADM           PROCEDURE                   2
MDS              PROCEDURE                   1
WL_CPR_REGLOG    SYNONYM                     6
REGISTRATION_LO  PACKAGE                     1
```

Starting with Oracle Database 11g (11.2.0.4) and later versions, the Oracle GoldenGate Profiler script has been replaced with a database view, DBA_GOLDENGATE_SUPPORT_MODE. From this database view, you can query what schemas and objects will not be supported with Oracle GoldenGate. Figure 3-1 shows that there are schemas and tables that are not supported.

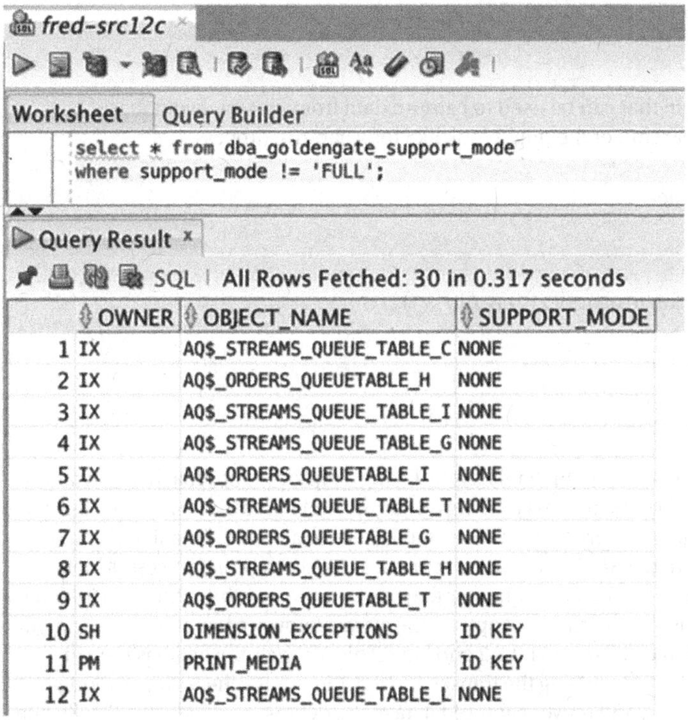

Figure 3-1. *Output from DBA_GOLDENGATE_SUPPORT_MODEs*

Notice that Owner IX has a few objects that are not supported by Oracle GoldenGate, indicated by the NONE value in the SUPPORT_MODE column. If all columns in the table were supported by Oracle GoldenGate, the SUPPORT_MODE column would indicate this with a value of FULL. When you see a value of ID KEY, this means that the identity column of the object can be used in replication configurations.

At this point, you should understand how to confirm if your database, schemas, or both can be replicated for Oracle GoldenGate. For database versions that are older than 11.2.0.4, you should use the profiler scripts that Oracle provides. If databases are version 11.2.0.4 or newer, you should use the DBA_GOLDENGATE_SUPPORT_MODE view to look at what is supported.

Additionally, although you have focused on Oracle databases in this chapter, the profiler scripts also support the heterogeneous platforms that Oracle GoldenGate supports. These profiler scripts can be found in My Oracle Support using the MOS notes provided earlier.

Parameter Files

Part of the configuration process in setting up Oracle GoldenGate is establishing the parameter files for each of the processes within the environment. The parameter files are simple text files that can be edited with any text editor. These files can also be precreated before creating the required processes within Oracle GoldenGate from the GGSCI.

Parameter files are the runtime brains within the Oracle GoldenGate environment. The settings that are placed in the parameter files tell Oracle GoldenGate what to capture from the source, where to ship the data, and how to apply the data to the target side. In small environments, you might have as few as two parameter files to worry about. In larger environments, the number of parameter files can increase dramatically depending on the needs of the environment and architecture.

Extract Parameter File

Let's take a look at a simple parameter file that can be used to capture data from an Oracle database. Listing 3-3 provides a view into what a parameter file might look like for a capture process.

Listing 3-3. Simple Extract Parameter File

```
EXTRACT E_HR
USERID ggate, PASSWORD ggate
SETENV (ORACLE_HOME="/u01/app/oracle/product/11.2.0/db_3")
SETENV (ORACLE_SID="tst12c")
TRANLOGOPTIONS DBLOGREADER
 EXTTRAIL ./dirdat/bt
TABLE HR.*;
```

The way that Oracle GoldenGate processes parameter files is by taking a top-down approach. If you take the same approach, you can understand what the process is doing on startup and replication. In Listing 3-3, you can see that this is for a capture process named E_HR, uses a user named ggate to access the database, and sets up the environment to access the tst12c database. After the environment is set, the capture process is looking to read from the transaction log. TRANLOGOPTIONS is the parameter that controls the way the extract will interact with the database transaction log. By using the DBLOGREADER option, the extract knows to use a new application programming interface (API) that is available in Oracle 11.2.0.2 and later. This API uses the database server access to mine the redo and archive logs. After accessing the transaction log, the extract checks for any long-running transactions on a 30-minute interval, and moves captured data to the defined local trail file. Finally, the capture process captures all Data Manipulation Language (DML) coming from tables in the HR schema.

■ **Note**   The CHECKPARAMS parameter can be used for all processes. This parameter allows you to check the syntax of the parameter file before replication starts. Although CHECKPARAMS is available to use with the parameter file, starting in Oracle GoldenGate 12c (12.2), there is a new checkprm utility.

Data Pump Parameter File

Just like the extract parameter file, the data pump parameter file provides similar information. The distinct difference here is that the data pump process is used to ship the trail file and captured transactions to a remote location on the network. Listing 3-4 provides a view of how simple the data pump parameter file can be.

Listing 3-4. Data Pump Parameter File

```
-- Verifies parameter file syntax. COMMENT OUT AFTER TESTING.
CHECKPARAMS
EXTRACT P_HR
PASSTHRU
RMTHOST 172.16.15.132, MGRPORT 15000, COMPRESS
RMTTRAIL ./dirdat/rt
TABLE HR.*;
```

■ **Note**   Starting in Oracle GoldenGate 12c (12.2), the PASSTHRU parameter is deprecated due to metadata being shipped in the trail files.

When reading this parameter file, you can tell that an extract process is set up as a data pump when you see the parameter PASSTHRU. If the PASSTHRU parameter is not included, then the extract will operate as a normal extract. Additionally, in the parameter file you will see where the trail files and transactions are shipped to with the remote host (RMTHOST) parameters. As part of the RMTHOST parameter, you need to tell the data pump how to connect to the remote server with the MGRPORT option with port number. Finally, the COMPRESS option forces the data packets to be compressed across the network. The RMTTRAIL parameter tells Oracle GoldenGate to create a new trail file on the remote side, containing data and transformations, when they are shipped. The data pump needs to know what data is being shipped.

■ **Note**   The MGRPORT is the port of the manager process on the target side. The number can be different for every manager.

Replicat Parameter File

The replicat parameter file is the parameter file that tells Oracle GoldenGate what to apply. It provides the mapping command that links the incoming transactions to the targeted tables. In active-active or multimaster environments, this file is where you would configure conflict detection and resolution (CDR) to help resolve conflicts as they occur. Listing 3-5 displays a simple apply file for a replicat process.

Listing 3-5. Replicat Parameter File

```
REPLICAT R_HR
SETENV (ORACLE_HOME="/u01/app/oracle/product/11.2.0/db_3")
SETENV (ORACLE_SID="tst12cr")
USERID ggate, PASSWORD ggate
map HR.*, target HR.*;
```

Just like the extract parameter file, the replicat parameter file needs to set up the environment that is needed to connect to an Oracle database. You then need to provide a username and password to interact with the database. In older versions of Oracle GoldenGate, the parameter ASSUMETARGETDEFS is used to correlate the metadata structure between source and target if the tables match. If the metadata of tables are different, then this parameter needs to be replaced with a SOURCEDEF file that supports the mapping. At the end of the file, you see the map statement. This statement maps the incoming transactions to the target side.

Manager Parameter File

The manager process is the process that keeps track of all the other processes in the Oracle GoldenGate environment. Out of all the processes, this parameter file is the simplest to configure. Listing 3-6 shows how simple it is.

■ **Note**   Notice you do not need to name the manager. In Oracle GoldenGate environments, the manager process has a default name of MGR, so the parameter file has to be named MGR.prm.

Listing 3-6. Manager Parameter File

```
PORT 15000
```

Listing 3-6 shows a simple parameter file for the manager process. The only thing required in the manager parameter file is the port number that the manager will listen on. This allows Oracle GoldenGate instances to connect with each other and write trails files. Additionally, as mentioned earlier, the manager process is used to keep track of items like events, up or down status of processes, and errors that occur. To make better use of the items that the manager keeps track of, the parameter file can be expanded on. Listing 3-7 shows a detailed version of the manager parameter file with additional details.

Listing 3-7. Detailed Manager Parameter File

```
PORT 15000
DYNAMICPORTLIST 15010-15035
PURGEOLDEXTRACTS ./dirdat/*, USECHECKPOINTS, MINKEEPDAYS 2
AUTORESTART ER *, RETRIES 6, WAITMINUTES 2, RESETMINUTES 30
LAGCRITICALSECONDS 30
LAGREPORTMINUTES
```

In this version of the manager parameter file, you see there are more parameters added to tell the manager what to do with old trail files (PURGEOLDEXTRACTS), when to restart (AUTORESTART) the other processes if they are terminated abnormally, and when to check for lag (LAGCRITITCALSECONDS/LAGREPORTMINUTES). You will also notice there is a parameter to use dynamic ports. The DYNAMICPORTLIST parameter is used to help Oracle GoldenGate communicate beyond firewalls if needed and limits port allocations to specific ranges for communication. This is helpful, because Oracle GoldenGate will grab random unused ports otherwise.

Trail Files

Chapter 2 touched on the concept of trail files, the files that Oracle GoldenGate uses to store committed transactions that are captured. On the capture side of the environment, the trail file is considered the local trail file because it is on the capture side of the setup. The local trail file is created by the capture process and then referenced by the data pump process for shipping. As the file is shipped, the data pump process creates the remote trail file at the target location. The apply process will then read the remote trail file to process the transactions on the target database.

Sizing and Retention of Trail Files

Sizing of the trail files is always a question that comes up when building an Oracle GoldenGate environment. By default, the size of a trail file will be 50 MB. For many environments, this size is too small, so how do you effectively size the trail files for your environment? Once they are sized, how do you retain them in the case of disasters?

Here are a few recommendations that can be followed:

1. Make the size the same as archive logs.

2. Identify the size and frequency of redo log switches and use that as a guide.

3. Monitor lag and trail file switch, based on size, and readjust as needed.

4. Retention of trail files should be handled similar to retention of archive logs.

To address the first two recommendations, the best way to look at this is to use the same rules that you would apply when looking at the database. If the database archive logs are configured at intervals to switch up to four times per hour, then your trail files should be sized similarly. By keeping the archive log switching and the trail file switching the same, you will ensure proper retention of the trail files along with cutting down on network bandwidth.

As for the third recommendation, your trail files should be on average between 10 percent and 30 percent of the archive log sizes if you are replicating everything. This value should be smaller if you are only doing a few schemas or less.

After you have sized the trail files, you should be following the same process for retaining them as you would use for your database. Prior to Oracle GoldenGate 12c (12.2), retaining trail files was critical, especially on the target side. With the release of Oracle GoldenGate 12c (12.2), the data pump process keeps track of the trail files that are shipped and created on the target side based on the checkpoints. If there is a need to recover the remote trail files, you just need to clear the trail files from the target side and then stop and restart the data pump process. This will re-create the remote trail files that you need for processing.

Obey Files

Obey files are files that you create to run against an Oracle GoldenGate environment. The content of an obey file is a sequenced set of Oracle GoldenGate commands that can be run from a single file. Listing 3-8 provides an example of an obey file that is used to create a capture and data pump process.

Listing 3-8. Obey File Example

```
--Adds Extract process
ADD EXTRACT E_HR, TRANLOG, BEGIN NOW

--Adds local trail file
ADD EXTTRAIL ./dirdat/lt, EXTRACT E_HR, megabytes 1000

--Adds Data Pump Process
ADD EXTRACT P_HR, EXTTRAILSOURCE ./dirdat/lt

--Adds remote trail file
ADD RMTTRAIL ./dirdat/rt, EXTRACT P_HR, megabytes 1000
```

You will notice in Listing 3-8 that all the commands have to do with adding the processes to Oracle GoldenGate. Obey files are created for setting up environments and they can be created for any command you would like to run within the Oracle GoldenGate environment.

Until now, you have taken a look at the profiler that is run against an Oracle database to see if there is anything you need to worry about before setting up your replication environment. You have also taken a look at the different parameter files that are needed for the components of the replication environment. Now, let's take a look at how to put these pieces together in a simple replication environment.

Unidirectional Configuration

The simplest configuration that can be done with Oracle GoldenGate is the unidirectional or one-way replication. This architecture is used for moving data from one database to another, mostly in migrations or reporting architectures with Oracle GoldenGate. To set up unidirectional replication, there are a series of steps that have to be completed. These steps are broken down into three distinct categories:

1. Prerequisites.

2. Instantiation.

3. Apply.

The largest of these categories is the prerequisites category. For many Oracle GoldenGate architectures, this is where you will spend a bulk of your time until replication is started. By spending your time on the prerequisites, you will ensure that the capture process is done correctly and captures all the required data. This will make the overall replication process simpler and cleaner.

Prerequisites

As mentioned previously, the prerequisites are the part of the Oracle GoldenGate configuration on which you will spend a good bit of time. Some of the steps in the prerequisites will also be done on the target (apply) side of the configuration as well. The prerequisites cover several areas of database configuration for replication, including these:

1. Archive Log mode

2. Logging modes (supplemental logging/force logging)

3. GoldenGate Parameter

4. GoldenGate Users

5. GoldenGate Extract Parameters   .

6. Trandata (table supplemental logging)

7. Building Extract (Capture)

8. Building Data Pump (Shipping)

Following these prerequisites, you should be able to have your unidirectional replication up and running in no time.

Enable Archive Log Mode

With any Oracle database, the recoverability of the database is based on the data that can be recovered. Oracle provides for recoverability of the database using the online redo logs and archive logs. By default, Oracle uses online redo logs in No Archive Log mode to provide a minimal form of recoverability for transactions during rollback operations. Although this is good, it is not valid for Oracle GoldenGate operations against an Oracle database. An Oracle database needs to be placed into Archive Log mode for recoverability purposes and archiving purposes.

■ **Note** For more information on archive log items, refer to the Oracle documentation at http://docs.oracle.com/database/121/ADMIN/archredo.htm#ADMIN11332

To enable Archive Log mode within the Oracle Database, follow these steps:

1. Shut down the database.

   ```
   $ sqlplus / as sysdba
   SQL> shutdown immediate
   ```

2. Mount the database.

   ```
   SQL> startup mount;
   ```

3. Alter the database.

   ```
   SQL> alter database archivelog;
   ```

4. Open the database.

   ```
   SQL> alter database open;
   ```

5. Verify that the database is in Archive Log mode.

   ```
   SQL> archive log list;
   ```

Enable Supplemental Logging

Within the Oracle database framework, the redo log files are used for instance recovery and media recovery when there is a failure. Data that are needed for recovery are automatically recorded to the redo logs; however, supplemental logging expands on the logging of columns within a table. By default on an Oracle database installation, supplemental logging is not enabled, meaning that if a column is not changed, it is not going to make it into the redo.

■ **Note** Supplemental logging, at a minimum, must be enabled before the log files can be used with LogMiner.

By turning on supplemental logging at the database level, you are ensuring that the database is logging the minimal amount of data needed for recovery. Oracle GoldenGate leverages this supplemental logging to ensure that transactions can be captured and used. Later in this chapter, we look at how Oracle GoldenGate allows you to enable supplemental logging at the table level using schematrandata or trandata. For now, know that supplemental logging at the database level has been enabled for use with Oracle GoldenGate. To turn on supplemental logging, the SQL statement in Listing 3-9 should be run against the database.

Listing 3-9. Enable Supplemental Logging

```
SQL> alter database add supplemental log data;
```

After enabling supplemental logging within the database, verify that it was enabled by looking at the SUPPLEMENTAL_LOG_DATA_MIN column in the V$DATABASE view using the SQL in Listing 3-10.

Listing 3-10. SQL to Verify Supplemental Logging

```
SQL> select supplemental_log_data_min from v$database;
```

The output from SQL to check if supplemental logging is enabled will return a YES value if it is enabled (Listing 3-11).

Listing 3-11. SQL Output for Supplemental Logging

```
SQL> col supplemental_log_data_min format a30;
SQL> select supplemental_log_data_min from v$database;
SUPPLEMENTAL_LOG_DATA_MIN
------------------------------
YES
```

Once supplemental logging is enabled, the minimal amount of columns needed to track the change will be captured and recorded to the redo logs.

Enable Force Logging

Unlike supplemental logging, force logging is used to ensure all changes in the database except changes to temporary tablespaces and temporary segments are captured. Force logging does exactly what is refers to: It forces the capture of changes within the database. This setting takes precedence over and is independent of any logging options set for individual tablespaces and individual database objects.

For Oracle GoldenGate, force logging is good because it ensures that all changes are captured regardless of tablespace or object that needs to be captured. Coupled with supplemental logging, all SQL transactions performed against the database will be captured and recorded to the redo logs.

■ **Note**   Force logging mode can have performance effects on the database.

To enable force logging at the database level, use the SQL shown in Listing 3-12.

Listing 3-12. Enable Force Logging

```
SQL> alter database force logging;
```

After force logging has been enabled, it can be checked using the FORCE_LOGGING column of the V$DATABASE view (Listing 3-13).

Listing 3-13. Checking for Force Logging

```
SQL> select force_logging from v$database;

            FORCE_LOGGING
            ---------------------------------------
            YES
```

With force logging enabled, the database is now configured to ensure that all transaction types are captured to the redo logs. This will be critical to ensuring that all transactions are captured by Oracle GoldenGate.

Enable GoldenGate Parameter

Starting with Oracle Database 11g (11.2.0.4 or later), to use Oracle GoldenGate a new parameter needs to be enabled. This parameter is a Boolean parameter that tells the database that Oracle GoldenGate is going to be used to perform replication within the database framework.

To show the default settings of this parameter, issue a show parameter command from the SQL plus prompt as illustrated in Listing 3-14.

Listing 3-14. Checking for GoldenGate Parameter

```
SQL> show parameter goldengate

NAME                                 TYPE        VALUE
------------------------------------ ----------- ----------------
enable_goldengate_replication        boolean     FALSE
```

Notice that the default setting for the parameter is set to FALSE. To change this setting, an ALTER SYSTEM command needs to be issued. Changing this parameter can be done dynamically and requires no bouncing of the database, as illustrated in Listing 3-15.

Listing 3-15. Enable the Database to Use Oracle GoldenGate Replication

```
SQL> alter system set enable_goldengate_replication=true scope=both;
```

After enabling the database, it can be verified by using the SHOW PARAMETER command (Listing 3-16):

Listing 3-16. Verifying GoldenGate Parameter

```
SQL> show parameter goldengate;

NAME                                    TYPE        VALUE
--------------------------------------- ----------- --------------------
enable_goldengate_replication           boolean     TRUE
```

The next step in the prerequisites is to create the user that will be used to manage the Oracle GoldenGate environment. This user is a standard Oracle database user and will need to be created on both the source and target databases.

Create a GoldenGate User

Before building out the GoldenGate environment for a unidirectional implementation, you first have to have a database user that will be referred to as the GoldenGate user. This user will be used for Oracle GoldenGate to interact with the database. This user is a standard database user with a few special permissions to ensure that replication can be performed.

The simplest way to create a user is to use the defaults that the Oracle database provides. An example of creating the GoldenGate user is provided in Listing 3-17.

Listing 3-17. Creating the GoldenGate User

```
create user GGATE
identified by ggate
default tablespace USERS
temporary tablespace TEMP
quota unlimited on USERS
account unlock
/
```

As you can tell, creating the GoldenGate user is quite simple. In any GoldenGate configuration, this user needs to be created on both sides of the replication environment to ensure that GoldenGate users are easily identified and controlled between environments.

Granting Permissions to GoldenGate Users

GoldenGate users require a set of permissions to ensure that replication activities can perform for any updates, inserts, deletes, and Data Definition Lanuague (DDL) changes. These permissions are granted by using grant and revoke statements as needed with the Oracle ecosystem. Table 3-1 illustrates the permissions need for the GoldenGate user.

If you are building your GoldenGate user on 11.2.0.4 or later databases, you have the option to use the DBMS_GOLDENGATE_AUTH.GRANT_ADMIN_PRIVILEGE procedure. This procedure grants all the same permissions that are discussed in Table 3-1.

Table 3-1. *Permissions for Oracle GoldenGate Users*

Permission	Purpose
Create session	Allows GoldenGate user to create a session
Resource	Allows GoldenGate user to create database objects
Connect	Allows GoldenGate user to connect to database
Select any dictionary	Allows GoldenGate user to view the data dictionary
Flashback any table	Allows GoldenGate user to perform flashback operations on a table
Select any table	Allows GoldenGate user to select from any table
Select on dba_clusters	Allows GoldenGate user to read DBA_CLUSTERS
Execute on dbms_flashback	Grants GoldenGate user permission to flashback procedures
Select any transaction	Allows GoldenGate user to select any transaction
Lock any table	Allows GoldenGate user to lock any table
Insert any table	Allows GoldenGate user to insert any table
Update any table	Allows GoldenGate user to update any table
Delete any table	Allows GoldenGate user to delete any table
Create table	Allows GoldenGate user to create tables in their own schema

■ **Note** Many of these privileges are also covered in the DBMS_STREAMS_AUTH package; however, it appears that they don't always take through the package so granting them directly through SQL might be easier.

Once the GoldenGate user is created and privileges are granted, this is all that is needed within the database at this time. Verify that the user works by logging in from SQL*Plus or some other SQL utility. Figure 3-2 demonstrates that logging in with the GoldenGate user was successful.

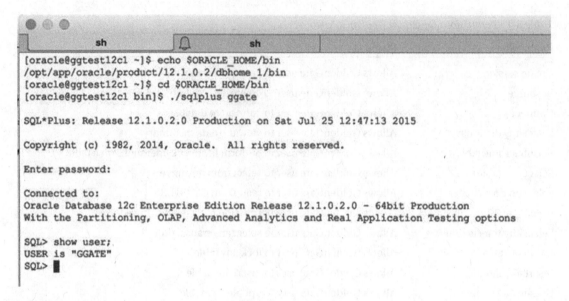

```
[oracle@ggtest12cl ~]$ echo $ORACLE_HOME/bin
/opt/app/oracle/product/12.1.0.2/dbhome_1/bin
[oracle@ggtest12cl ~]$ cd $ORACLE_HOME/bin
[oracle@ggtest12cl bin]$ ./sqlplus ggate

SQL*Plus: Release 12.1.0.2.0 Production on Sat Jul 25 12:47:13 2015

Copyright (c) 1982, 2014, Oracle.  All rights reserved.

Enter password:

Connected to:
Oracle Database 12c Enterprise Edition Release 12.1.0.2.0 - 64bit Production
With the Partitioning, OLAP, Advanced Analytics and Real Application Testing options

SQL> show user;
USER is "GGATE"
SQL>
```

Figure 3-2. *Logging in as GGATE*

After validating that the GoldenGate user works, it is time to move on to setting up the Oracle GoldenGate processes.

Building Source GoldenGate Environment

Now that the database is configured to be used with Oracle GoldenGate, the next step is to build the source side of the replication environment. As discussed earlier, you will need a parameter file for each of the processes on the source side. These processes consist of a manager process, an extract (capture) process, and the data pump process.

■ **Note**   The parameter files can be created ahead of time with any text-based editor.

To begin working on the parameter files, you need to access the Oracle GoldenGate environment. To do this, navigate to the Oracle GoldenGate home directory where Oracle GoldenGate is installed.

■ **Note**   To make this easier, setting the Oracle GoldenGate information in /etc/oratab will enable quick setup for accessing the Oracle GoldenGate binaries.

To access the binaries, change directories to $OGG_HOME. As you navigate to the binaries also make sure that Oracle Home ($ORACLE_HOME) is set to the database binaries needed to support replication. See Listing 3-18.

Listing 3-18. Navigating to GoldenGate Home

```
[oracle@ggtest12c1 ~]$ env | grep _HOME
OGG_HOME=/opt/app/oracle/product/12.1.2/oggcore_1
ORACLE_HOME=/opt/app/oracle/product/12.1.0.2/dbhome_1
[oracle@ggtest12c1 ~]$ cd $OGG_HOME
[oracle@ggtest12c1 oggcore_1]$
```

■ **Note**   If working from the command line a lot, it might be a good option to look into rlwrap. This tool allows you to store a command history that can be toggled through using the arrow keys on the keyboard. See http://utopia.knoware.nl/~hlub/uck/rlwrap/.

After accessing the Oracle Home for GoldenGate, call the GGSCI utility to take you into the GoldenGate environment. Before you build any GoldenGate processes, it is a good idea to create the table-level supplmental log groups needed for GoldenGate by running either schematrandata or trandata once you log in to the database using the GoldenGate user you configured. The next section looks at how to add these options.

Adding SCHEMATRANDATA or TRANDATA

There are two types of trandata that can be used within Oracle GoldenGate. Both types do the same thing, but one is more specific to the schema level and the other is more specific to the database level. Both approaches can be used with enabling trandata, though. This section explains what each type of trandata is used for and why you should understand the use of it.

SCHEMATRANDATA

When you use SCHEMATRANDATA to enable schema-level supplemental logging for tables, logging will act on all of the current and future tables in an associated schema. This option automatically logs a superset of available keys that Oracle GoldenGate requires for row identification. This option is valid for both classic and integrated capture modes with Oracle GoldenGate.

ADD SCHEMATRANDATA provides the following benefits:

- Enables Oracle supplemental logging for new tables created with the CREATE TABLE command.

- Updates supplemental logging information for tables affected by an ALTER TABLE to add or drop columns.

- Updates supplemental logging for tables that are renamed.

- Updates supplemental logging for tables where unique or primary keys are added or dropped.

An additional benefit of using ADD SCHEMATRANDATA is that by default it logs the key columns of a table in the following order of priority:

1. Primary keys.

2. If there are no primary keys, all unique indexes will be used for the table, including those that are disabled, unusable, or invisible. Additionally, foreign keys will be used for row dependency.

3. If the prior two are not available, the all scalar columns of the table will be logged.

TRANDATA

When you have a need to capture the transaction information from the transaction records, then it is time to use ADD TRANDATA. ADD TRANDATA is valid for specific databases like, IBM DB2, DB2 LUW, DB2 z/OS, MS SQL Server, and a few others, including the Oracle Database. This option expands on the information captured during the extraction process. Oracle recommends that force logging be enabled along with minimal supplemental logging at the database level when using Oracle GoldenGate.

Now that you have an understanding of the difference between ADD SCHEMATRANDATA and ADD TRANDATA, you will need to add it to database configuration through Oracle GoldenGate. To do this, you need to log in to the Oracle Database as the GoldenGate user through GGSCI. The steps for this process are outlined here.

1. Access the GGSCI.

```
[oracle@ggtest12c1 dirprm]$ $OGG_HOME/ggsci

Oracle GoldenGate Command Interpreter for Oracle
Version 12.1.2.1.0 OGGCORE_12.1.2.1.0_PLATFORMS_140727.2135.1_FBO
Linux, x64, 64bit (optimized), Oracle 12c on Aug  7 2014 10:21:34
Operating system character set identified as UTF-8.

Copyright (C) 1995, 2014, Oracle and/or its affiliates. All rights reserved.

GGSCI (ggtest12c1.acme.com) 1>
```

2. Log in as the GoldenGate database user.

```
GGSCI (ggtest12c1.acme.com) 1> dblogin userid ggate password ggate
Successfully logged into database.

GGSCI (ggtest12c1.acme.com as ggate@src12c) 2>
```

3. Run the desired TRANDATA option. In our case we will use SCHEMATRANDATA because this an Oracle-to-Oracle setup.

```
GGSCI (ggtest12c1.acme.com as ggate@src12c) 4> add schematrandata scott

2015-07-25 14:06:26 INFO OGG-01788 SCHEMATRANDATA has been added on schema scott.

2015-07-25 14:06:26 INFO OGG-01976 SCHEMATRANDATA for scheduling columns has been
added on schema scott.

GGSCI (ggtest12c1.acme.com as ggate@src12c) 5>
```

Now you have everything in place that needs to be done to successfully configure the database. The next tasks you need to tackle are building the capture and data pump processes. The following sections describe how to edit parameter files and build the processes needed to make Oracle GoldenGate work.

Edit Parameter Files

Before you can edit any parameter files, you need to be in the Oracle GoldenGate Home directory. Once you are in the $OGG_HOME directory, start the GGSCI and issue the EDIT PARAMS command. This command is used to edit the parameter files associated with the processes running in the GoldenGate environment.

The steps to edit a parameter file from within Oracle GoldenGate are as follows:

1. Start GGSCI.

    ```
    [oracle@ggtest12c1 ~]$ cd $OGG_HOME
    [oracle@ggtest12c1 oggcore_1]$ ./ggsci

    Oracle GoldenGate Command Interpreter for Oracle
    Version 12.1.2.1.0 OGGCORE_12.1.2.1.0_PLATFORMS_140727.2135.1_FBO
    Linux, x64, 64bit (optimized), Oracle 12c on Aug  7 2014 10:21:34
    Operating system character set identified as UTF-8.

    Copyright (C) 1995, 2014, Oracle and/or its affiliates. All rights reserved.

    GGSCI (ggtest12c1.acme.com) 1>
    ```

2. Edit the desired parameter file. Parameter files are named the same as the group or process name.

    ```
    GGSCI (ggtest12c1.acme.com) 1> edit params esrc1
    ```

3. Enter the desired parameters, starting a new line with each parameter statement.

    ```
    EXTRACT ESRC1
    USERID ggate, PASSWORD <pwd>
    TRANLOGOPTIONS DBLOGREADER
    SETENV (ORACLE_HOME="/opt/app/oracle/product/12.1.0.2/dbhome_1")
    SETENV (ORACLE_SID="src12c")
    WARNLONGTRANS 1h, CHECKINTERVAL 30m
    EXTTRAIL ./dirdat/lt
    TABLE SCOTT.EMP;
    ```

The steps just listed are an example of editing a parameter file for an extract (capture) process. The same steps can be followed for any of the Oracle GoldenGate processes. At this point, if you were to execute an INFO ALL command from GGSCI, notice that the only process listed is the manager (MGR) process (Figure 3-3). This is due to GoldenGate's ability to allow simple file edits without the processes being in place. Allowing you to edit from within GGSCI ensures that the parameter files are located in the dirprm subdirectory under Oracle GoldenGate.

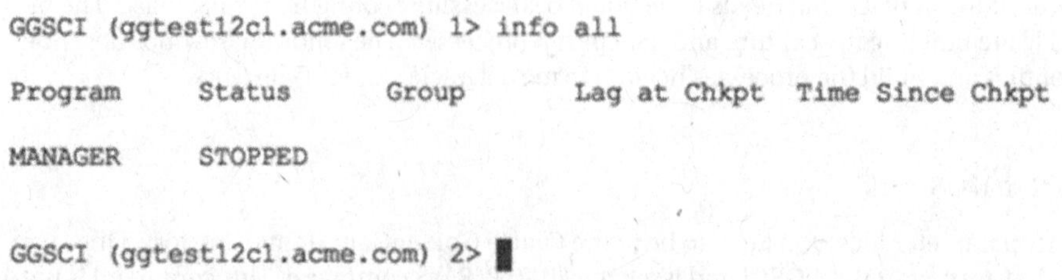

```
GGSCI (ggtest12c1.acme.com) 1> info all

Program      Status      Group        Lag at Chkpt  Time Since Chkpt

MANAGER      STOPPED


GGSCI (ggtest12c1.acme.com) 2> ▮
```

Figure 3-3. *GGSCI with only MGR process adding the extract (capture) process*

For anything in Oracle GoldenGate to work, you need to have a way of capturing the data that changes within the database. This is achieved by using an extract process; you might also hear the extract process called the capture process. There are two types of capture processes, commonly referred to as classic and integrated capture processes. For the simplicity of a unidirectional setup, we look at how to add a classic extract (capture) process.

In the previous section, you saw how to edit a parameter file from within the GGSCI. If you saved the file after editing, you should see a parameter file named esrc1.prm in the $OGG_HOME/dirprm directory.

■ **Note**   Although I use numbers at the end of my process group names, it is not best practice to do this because the report files that are generated and associated with the process could be overwritten due to the number at the end.

Notice in the dirprm directory there are two other parameter files, jagent.prm and mgr.prm (see Figure 3-4). Ignore these parameter files for now, as they are used by other processes within Oracle GoldenGate.

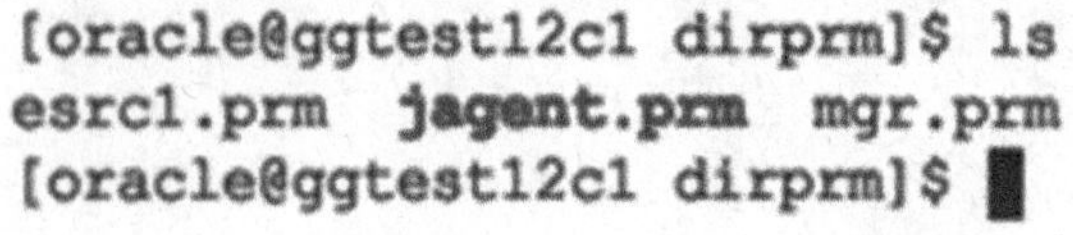

```
[oracle@ggtest12c1 dirprm]$ ls
esrc1.prm  jagent.prm  mgr.prm
[oracle@ggtest12c1 dirprm]$ ▮
```

Figure 3-4. *dirprm with parameter files*

To add the extract process to Oracle GoldenGate, you need to run two commands (Listing 3-19) within GGSCI.

Listing 3-19. Adding an Extract Process

```
GGSCI> add extract esrc1, tranlog, begin now
GGSCI> add exttrail ./dirdat/lt, extract esrc1, megabytes <size>
```

These two add commands will add a classic extract named esrc1 with a local trail file in the $OGG_HOME/dirdat directory using the prefix lt (Figure 3-5).

```
Oracle GoldenGate Command Interpreter for Oracle
Version 12.1.2.1.0 OGGCORE_12.1.2.1.0_PLATFORMS_140727.2135.1_FBO
Linux, x64, 64bit (optimized), Oracle 12c on Aug  7 2014 10:21:34
Operating system character set identified as UTF-8.

Copyright (C) 1995, 2014, Oracle and/or its affiliates. All rights reserved.



GGSCI (ggtest12c1.acme.com) 1> add extract esrc1, tranlog, begin now
EXTRACT added.


GGSCI (ggtest12c1.acme.com) 2> add exttrail ./dirdat/lt, extract esrc1, megabytes 50
EXTTRAIL added.


GGSCI (ggtest12c1.acme.com) 3> info all

Program     Status      Group      Lag at Chkpt  Time Since Chkpt

MANAGER     STOPPED
EXTRACT     STOPPED     ESRC1      00:00:00      00:00:21


GGSCI (ggtest12c1.acme.com) 4> █
```

Figure 3-5. GGSCI after adding extract

Although the classic extract has been added, before you can start the process the underlying tables that will be replicated require additional configuration. This additional configuration is called TRANDATA. Adding TRANDATA ensures that all the tables that will be replicated have the required supplemental logging enabled. The settings that are added when running TRANDATA can be viewed when you look at the tables directly. They will have a supplemental log group added with a log name that is prefixed with a GG. This is an indicator that GoldenGate has turned on TRANDATA for the table. Once TRANDATA has been added to the tables that GoldenGate will capture from, you can start the process and verify that the local trail file is produced in the $OGG_HOME/dirdat directory.

■ **Note**   I typically wait to start the extract (capture) process until I have built the data pump process. I do this to make sure that my network on the target side works and ensure that trail files can be shipped over the network.

Starting the Extract

With everything in place, you should now be able to start the extract and begin capturing transactions into the local trail files located in the dirdat subdirectory.

To start the extract, issue the following command:

```
GGSCI (ggtest12c1.acme.com as ggate@src12c) 9> start extract esrc1
```

Once the extract has started, it can be confirmed using the INFO ALL command.

```
GGSCI (ggtest12c1.acme.com as ggate@src12c) 10> info all
Program     Status     Group      Lag at Chkpt  Time Since Chkpt
MANAGER     RUNNING
EXTRACT     RUNNING    ESRC1      00:00:00      00:00:01
```

After confirming that the extract has started, you can exit GGSCI and verify the trail file was created in the $OGG_HOME/dirdat directory, as illustrated in Listing 3-20.

Listing 3-20. Confirming Local Trail Files

```
GGSCI (ggtest12c1.acme.com as ggate@src12c) 11> exit
[oracle@ggtest12c1 dirprm]$ cd ../dirdat
[oracle@ggtest12c1 dirdat]$ ls -ltr
total 4
-rw-r-----. 1 oracle oinstall 1437 Jul 25 14:53 lt000000
```

With the extract started, you can now focus on creating the data pump process.

Extract (Data Pump) Process

With the capture process running, you are capturing any transactions that are occurring in the database at the time they are committed. This means that transactions are going into the local trail file in the order in which they are committed and ready to be shipped to the remote server in the architecture. To facilitate the shipping of the trail files, you need to create another extract that is commonly known as the data pump process.

The data pump process is a standard extract that is configured as a pass-through for shipping of the trail files. What makes this process different from a standard capture extract is that the parameter file is using a parameter called PASSTHRU to ensure that the trail file is shipped through the process to the remote location without any additional overhead. Listing 3-21 shows you what a data pump file looks like.

Listing 3-21. Data Pump Parameter File

```
EXTRACT PSRC1
PASSTHRU
RMTHOST 10.10.1.12, MGRPORT 15000, COMPRESS
RMTTRAIL ./dirdat/rt
TABLE SCOTT.EMP;
```

Others things to be aware of in the data pump parameter file are the address for the remote host (RMTHOST) and the manager port (MGRPORT) number. The RMTHOST parameter tells GoldenGate what server to access for shipping of trail files. The MGRPORT parameter tells the extract what manager process or port to connect to on the remote host. These parameters ensure that network traffic occurs between source and target systems.

■ **Note** Although the PASSTHRU parameter is used to ship trail files without affecting them, there are times when you will want to interact with the trail file while shipping. In that case, the PASSTHRU parameter can be turned on and off using PASSTHRU and NOPASSTHRU.

Adding the Extract (Data Pump) Process

Adding the extract (data pump) process is done using the same methodology that is used when adding a capture (extract) process. You first have to edit the parameter file and make sure it is in the $OGG_HOME/dirprm directory, then add the process using GGSCI commands. The following steps will help you add a data pump process to your configuration.

1. Edit the parameter file.

    ```
    GGSCI (ggtest12c1.acme.com) 5> edit params psrc1
    ```

2. Add the extract (data pump) to the architecture through GGSCI. Notice that the extract is looking at the local trail files that the capture extract uses.

    ```
    GGSCI (ggtest12c1.acme.com) 6> ADD EXTRACT PSRC1, EXTTRAILSOURCE ./dirdat/lt
    ```

3. Tell the extract (data pump) where to write the remote trail file. This is where the extract is sending the trail file along with renaming it on the remote side. Notice that the size of the remote trail file matches that of the local trail file.

    ```
    GGSCI (ggtest12c1.acme.com) 7> ADD RMTTRAIL ./dirdat/rt, EXTRACT PSRC1, megabytes 50
    ```

Starting the Data Pump (Extract) Process

Once the process is added to the GGSCI environment, it can be reviewed and verified by issuing an INFO ALL command just as you did with the extract process previously. This lists all the processes associated with GoldenGate on the local server. Listing 3-22 provides sample output.

Listing 3-22. Output After Adding Data Pump

```
GGSCI (ggtest12c1.acme.com) 8> info all
Program     Status     Group     Lag at Chkpt  Time Since Chkpt
MANAGER     RUNNING
EXTRACT     RUNNING    ESRC1     00:00:00      00:00:01
EXTRACT     STOPPED    PSRC1     00:00:00      00:02:32
```

You will notice that the data pump is not started yet. To start the data pump, you need to issue the START EXTRACT command because data pumps are still extracts, just configured as a pass-through to allow for trail file shipping. Listing 3-23 shows how to start a data pump process.

Listing 3-23. Starting Data Pump

```
GGSCI (ggtest12c1.acme.com) 9> start extract psrc1
Sending START request to MANAGER ...
EXTRACT PSRC1 starting
```

Once the process has started, it can be verified again using the INFO ALL command within GGSCI. Once the data pump is up successfully, you should be able to check the $OGG_HOME/dirdat directory on the remote host as shown in Figure 3-6.

```
[oracle@ggtest12c2 oggcore_1]$ cd dirdat
[oracle@ggtest12c2 dirdat]$ ls
rt000000
[oracle@ggtest12c2 dirdat]$ █
```

Figure 3-6. Verifying that the remote trail file is in $OGG_HOME/dirdat (remote)

Now with the source side of the architecture running, capturing, and shipping transactions, you are almost finished setting up a unidirectional replication. Before you can complete the replicat configuration, though, you need to instantiate the environment. Let's take a look at that now.

Instantiation

The instantiation process is the process used to load a copy of static source data into the target database. This process captures a point-in-time snapshot of the data, and Oracle GoldenGate maintains the consistency by applying captured transactional data while the static data are loaded. Once instantiation is complete, Oracle GoldenGate will maintain the synchronization state throughout ongoing transactional changes.

Oracle GoldenGate provides three initial load methods specifically for Oracle databases:

1. Oracle Data Pump.

2. Direct Build Load to SQL*Loader.

3. Load from an Input File to SQL*Loader.

The most common approach for instantiation with an Oracle database is to use Oracle Data Pump, so we review this approach here in place of the other two approaches. Using this method, you start the extract, data pump, and replicat at the SCN at which the copy was made. This ensures that any transactions that were copied prior to that SCN are skipped to avoid collisions from integrity violations.

To instantiate using Oracle Data Pump, you need to have the extract and data pump running. Once the extract has been running for a few minutes, you can begin the export process with Oracle Data Pump. The key thing to remember is that you have to use the export data pump parameter FLASHBACK_SCN.

■ **Note** FLASHBACK_SCN tells the Oracle database to make a consistent copy of all the data from that point in time.

The FLASHBACK_SCN parameter is very important to the instantiation process. This is the same number that you will use to start the replicat once the import of the static data is complete. An example of a parameter file for Oracle Data Pump Export is provided in Listing 3-24.

Listing 3-24. Export Data Pump Paramter Files

```
DUMPFILE="expdp_%U.dmp"
LOGFILE="expdp.log"
DIRECTORY=EXPORTS
PARALLEL=4
JOB_NAME='EXPDP_GG_FULL_SCOTT'
SCHEMA=SCOTT
COMPRESSION=ALL
CONTENT=ALL
FLASHBACK_SCN=1891898
```

■ **Note**   To grab the SCN to be used after starting the extract, issue the following SQL:

```
Select current_scn from v$database;
```

With `FLASHBACK_SCN` set in the export data pump parameter file, the export can be run and later imported into the target database. Once the data are imported on the target side, you can begin working on the replicat process.

Apply (Replicat) Process

With the import complete, you can now create an apply (replicat) process that will process all the transactions that are stored in the trail files on the remote system. Adding a replicat process is just like adding your extracts earlier. The replicat is responsible for reading the remote trail files and applying the data found in chronological order. This ensures that the data are applied in the same order in which they were captured.

Just like the capture process, the replicat process has a few different modes in which it can be configured:

1. Classic.

2. Coordinated.

3. Integrated.

Any one of these modes can be used with any type of extract process because they represent different types of processes with the data. Because you have been reviewing the classic mode processes in this chapter, let's stay with a classic mode replicat.

Just like the other Oracle GoldenGate processes, the replicat process uses a parameter file that needs to be configured. The parameter file can be created through GGSCI using the `EDIT PARAMS` command. Listing 3-25 is an example of what a replicat parameter file could look like.

Listing 3-25. Replicat Parameter File

```
REPLICAT RTGT1
SETENV (ORACLE_HOME="/opt/app/oracle/product/12.1.0.2/dbhome_1")
SETENV (ORACLE_SID="tgt12c")
USERID ggate, PASSWORD ggate
ASSUMETARGETDEFS
DISCARDFILE ./dirrpt/RTGT1.dsc, append, megabytes 500
map SCOTT.EMP, target SCOTT.EMP;
```

■ **Note**   There are two things to notice in this parameter file. The first is the clear text password for the GoldenGate user. This is only shown as an example; you should be using the new USERALIAS option in GoldenGate. The second is the DISCARDFILE. Starting in GoldenGate 12c (12.2), the discard file is automatically created for you if you do not specify one.

You will notice in the example that there are some similarities to the extract (capture) process and some differences. In this parameter file, the parameters ASSUMETARGETDEFS, DISCARDFILE, and MAP are telling the replicat process what it needs to do. The ASSUMETARGETDEFS parameters lets the replicat process know that the table structure on both sides (source and target) should be the same. DISCARDFILE is where the replicat process should place any transactions that have errors out of the apply process. Finally, the MAP parameter is doing the mapping between the transactions in the trail files and the target tables on the target system.

These basic parameters allow you to replicate data between the SCOTT.EMP table on the source system and the SCOTT.EMP table on the target system. The MAP parameter can do a few more things, but they are not covered here because this is just a basic configuration.

Adding the Apply (Replicat) Process

Just like the other processes, adding the apply (replicat) process is done from the GGSCI. The primary difference comes when the replicat is started. Let's walk through adding the apply (replicat) process now.

1. Edit the parameter file.

    ```
    GGSCI (ggtest12c2.acme.com) 2> edit params rtgt1
    ```

2. Add a checkpoint table for the replicat to keep track of applied transactions.
    Notice that you have to log in to the database from GGSCI and then run ADD
    CHECKPOINTTABLE. If the checkpoint table name is configured in the ./GLOBALS
    file, then GoldenGate uses that name instead of the default table name.

    ```
    GGSCI (ggtest12c2.acme.com) 1> dblogin userid ggate password ggate
    Successfully logged into database.

    GGSCI (ggtest12c2.acme.com as ggate@rmt12c) 2> add checkpointtable

    No checkpoint table specified. Using GLOBALS specification (ggate.checkpoint)…

    Successfully created checkpoint table ggate.checkpoint.
    ```

3. Add the apply (replicat) to the architecture through GGSCI. Notice that the
    replicat is looking at the location of the remote trail files that were created earlier
    by the data pump process.

    ```
    GGSCI (ggtest12c2.acme.com as ggate@rmt12c) 3> add replicat RTGT1, exttrail ./
    dirdat/rt
    REPLICAT added.
    ```

At this point, when you do an INFO ALL, you should see the manager process and the replicat process in the GGSCI as illustrated in Listing 3-26. Now, you are ready to start the replicat.

Listing 3-26. GGSCI Output After Adding Replicat

```
GGSCI (ggtest12c2.acme.com as ggate@rmt12c) 4> info all
Program     Status      Group      Lag at Chkpt  Time Since Chkpt
MANAGER     RUNNING
REPLICAT    STOPPED     RTGT1      00:00:00      00:03:07
```

Starting the Apply (Replicat) Process

Although at this point you can start the apply (replicat) process and start replicating transactions, you need to pause for a minute. Earlier we discussed the SCN. Besides using the SCN for extracting the static data from the source, you need to use it here when starting the apply (replicat) process. This ensures that the replicat process is started at a point in time when transactions are not conflicting with each other and failing transactional integrity.

■ **Note** If using Oracle Database 11.2.0.4 or later, ensure that enable_goldengate_replication is set to true.

To start the apply (replicat) process, you need to issue a command similar to the one shown in in Listing 3-27.

Listing 3-27. Starting Replicat

```
Start replicat rtgt1, [ aftercsn || atscn ] [ SCN ]
```

When running this command with the SCN you gathered earlier, the process attempts to start the replicat from that point in time. Let's start the replicat now.

1. Issue start replicat with current_scn.

    ```
    GGSCI (ggtest12c2.acme.com as ggate@rmt12c) 5> start replicat rtgt1, aftercsn
    1891898
    ```

2. Once the command is run, you can check the status of the replicat by issuing INFO ALL and monitoring the start of the replicat.

    ```
    GGSCI (ggtest12c2.acme.com) 10> info all

    Program     Status      Group      Lag at Chkpt  Time Since Chkpt

    MANAGER     RUNNING
    REPLICAT    RUNNING     RTGT1      00:00:00      00:00:00
    ```

At this point, you should now be replicating transactions in a single direction between the source and target databases. This can be verified by doing any type of DML against the source database, in the schema being replicated, and seeing the changes reflected on the target side after a commit has occurred.

Summary

In this chapter, you took a look at some of the basics to building a functional replication environment using Oracle GoldenGate. As you read through this chapter, you were provided with a walk-through of how to build a unidirectional replication, which is the basic replication between two Oracle databases using the classic approach. The beauty of Oracle GoldenGate is that this classic approach can be used for just about any type of database and is the basis of the many different architectures that Oracle GoldenGate supports. With the skills gained here, you should be able to implement a solid replication environment to support your data distribution needs.

CHAPTER 4

■ ■ ■

Tuning Oracle GoldenGate

At this point, you have seen a few different types of unidirectional replication configured; after all, Oracle GoldenGate is a heterogeneous replication tool. Although you can now move data between different environments, the speed at which transactions are replicated might need to be improved. There are a few things that need to be considered when looking to improve the performance of replication between sites. In keeping with the theme of replication, we look at how to improve performance using the Oracle database as both the source and target replication environment.

Different Types of Tuning

To tune the replication that Oracle GoldenGate provides in an Oracle environment, you will need to have an environment set up with the minimal requirements as outlined in Chapter 3. This ensures that the database settings are all in place. Outside of the minimal requirements, you have to understand the different types of replication processes that Oracle GoldenGate provides. These different process types will require different approaches to tuning. Table 4-1 lists the different types of processes that are supported by Oracle GoldenGate.

Table 4-1. Oracle GoldenGate Process Types

Process Types	Tuning Approach
Classic	Classic processes will require more insight into what the operating system and GoldenGate processes are doing.
Integrated	Integrated processes will be more database-based tuning and primarily related to Oracle databases.

With either tuning approach you could use with an Oracle GoldenGate environment, there are different workflows of items that should be reviewed and tuned. Figure 4-1 illustrates a top-down source-to-target approach for tuning, the top-down waterfall method. This method can be used for both the classic and integrated processes. The tools that are illustrated in Figure 4-1 can be and often are used on both sides of the replication environment.

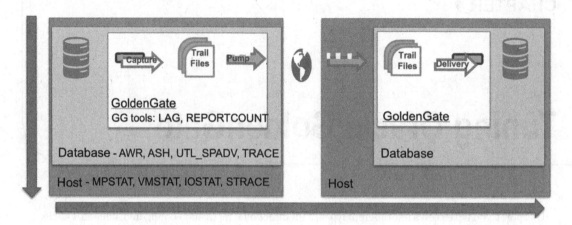

***Figure 4-1.** Top-down waterfall method*

The top-down waterfall method is a form of source-to-target methodology used to troubleshoot where performance issues are occurring in the Oracle GoldenGate environment. To effectively use this approach for tuning, the Oracle GoldenGate processes have to be configured to report on any latency and how many transactions have been processed by the associated processes. Then the database layer and the operating system layer will use standardized Oracle and non-Oracle tools for capturing performance data. These tools include the performance-related tools found in the Oracle Database (Automatic Workload Repository [AWR] and Active Session History [ASH] reports) and the operating system is going to use the tools to identify what the underlying system is doing.

■ **Note** Oracle's AWR and ASH reports require you to have access to Oracle's Diagnostic and Tuning packs before you can use this. This is a paid option for the Oracle Enterprise Edition Database. Statspack is still available for use with the Oracle Standard Edition Database.

Now let's take a look at the different approaches for tuning where you will use these different tools to identify performance problems and how they can be remedied.

Classic Process Tuning

The simplest form of replication with Oracle GoldenGate is using classic processes. These processes consist of an extract, a secondary extract (data pump), and a replicat. Each one of these processes has to be looked at for tuning when problems arise. As mentioned in the previous section, the simplest way to troubleshoot an Oracle GoldenGate environment is to use the top-down waterfall method.

■ **Note** The top-down waterfall method is an approach to identifying problems within Oracle GoldenGate by starting at the capture level and working down through the replication to the apply process.

One of the most important things to understand is that when replicating with classic processes, tuning will be a combination of Oracle GoldenGate and the host operating systems. For this reason, identifying and knowing the tools needed for tuning is important to every GoldenGate administrator.

Tools for Tuning

In keeping with the top-down waterfall method of tuning, there are different types of tools that can be used to help you tune the environment. You will find it easier to understand if you break down the tools by categories and what each of the categories is used for. These tools are designed to help you identify bottlenecks across the replication environment. These categories of tools are as follows:

1. GoldenGate tools.

2. Database tools.

3. Operating system tools.

GoldenGate Tools

The tools that Oracle GoldenGate provides come in a mix of parameters and reports that can be used during the operation of GoldenGate processes. Let's take a look at the parameters that are available for reporting on latency within the replication environment, then we'll examine the reporting options that are available.

Monitoring Latency or Lag Events

When it comes to replicating transactions, the speed at which the transactions are processed is critical. What prevents the speed of the replication is latency (or lag) in the environment, which could be caused by anything within the replication environment. Oracle GoldenGate provides three parameters that can be used within the manager parameter (mgr.prm) file to help troubleshoot latency events, listed in Table 4-2.

Table 4-2. *Latency Event Monitoring*

Parameter Info	Example
LAGINFO [SECONDS	MINUTES	HOURS]	LAGINFOSECONDS 5
LAGREPORT [MINUTES	HOURS]	LAGREPORTMINUTES 5
LAGCRITICAL [SECONDS	MINUTES	HOURS]	LAGCRITCALSECONDS 5

■ **Note** The information obtained from the LAG parameters will be reported in the Oracle GoldenGate error file (ggserr.log).

Each one of these lag parameters performs a specific function when monitoring for lag events in the environment. In reviewing Table 4-2, you will notice that these events can be checked any number of seconds, minutes, or hours. The function of each of these parameters is listed in Table 4-3.

Table 4-3. *Latency Event Parameters Definitions*

Parameter	Definition
LAGINFO	Specifies a lag threshold that is considered critical and generates a warning to the error log.
LAGREPORT	Sets an interval for reporting lag time to the error log.
LAGCRITICAL	Specifies a lag threshold that is considered critical and generates a warning to the error log.

Now that you know what and how these parameters are used, you can add them to the manager parameter (mgr.prm) file. They will not take effect until the manager process is restarted. After restarting the manager process, depending on the thresholds that were set, you will start seeing messages in the GoldenGate error log (ggserr.log). With the parameters set to monitor latency in your environment, let's take a look at what reports are available to you within the Oracle GoldenGate environment.

Reporting Transactional Statistics

With Oracle GoldenGate processing transactions you will want to know how many transactions are being captured or applied within the environment. To do this, Oracle provides a parameter that can be used in both the extract and the replicat parameter files. This parameter is REPORTCOUNT, which provides statistical information on the number of transactions that have been processed for the given process. This information is then retained in the report file for the associated extract or replicat process.

■ **Note**   The associated report file is normally located in $OGG_HOME/dirrpt and named similar to the parameter file.

An example of the parameter to be used in an extract or replicat parameter file is illustrated in Listing 4-1.

Listing 4-1. REPORTCOUNT Example

```
Syntax:
REPORTCOUNT EVERY [ # ] [ SECONDS | MINUTES | HOURS ], RATE

Actual usage:
REPORTCOUNT EVERY 5 SECONDS, RATE
```

The REPORTCOUNT parameter can be added anywhere in the parameter file, and then the process must be restarted. Depending on the time frame you specified, the report file in $OGG_HOME/dirrpt will start recording the amount of records processed while the process is running. The records processed are recorded as a cumulative number that is reported. At the end of the line, you will see the rate and the associated delta that Oracle GoldenGate is keeping track of. You can clearly see this information by tailing the associated report file. Figure 4-2 shows the associated output when using REPORTCOUNT in your parameter files.

```
2015-08-22 15:58:01  INFO     OGG-01517  Position of first record processed Sequence :
              48 records processed as of 2015-08-22 15:59:20 (rate 9,delta 9)
             123 records processed as of 2015-08-22 15:59:25 (rate 11,delta 14)
             203 records processed as of 2015-08-22 15:59:31 (rate 12,delta 12)
             308 records processed as of 2015-08-22 15:59:37 (rate 13,delta 18)
             384 records processed as of 2015-08-22 15:59:42 (rate 14,delta 14)
             464 records processed as of 2015-08-22 15:59:47 (rate 14,delta 15)
             559 records processed as of 2015-08-22 15:59:53 (rate 14,delta 16)
             618 records processed as of 2015-08-22 15:59:59 (rate 13,delta 9)
             696 records processed as of 2015-08-22 16:00:04 (rate 14,delta 14)
             708 records processed as of 2015-08-22 16:00:09 (rate 12,delta 2)
             773 records processed as of 2015-08-22 16:00:15 (rate 12,delta 11)
             818 records processed as of 2015-08-22 16:00:21 (rate 12,delta 7)
             882 records processed as of 2015-08-22 16:00:26 (rate 12,delta 12)
             957 records processed as of 2015-08-22 16:00:31 (rate 12,delta 14)
            1017 records processed as of 2015-08-22 16:00:36 (rate 12,delta 11)
            1080 records processed as of 2015-08-22 16:00:42 (rate 12,delta 11)
            1154 records processed as of 2015-08-22 16:00:48 (rate 12,delta 11)
            1197 records processed as of 2015-08-22 16:00:56 (rate 11,delta 5)
            1270 records processed as of 2015-08-22 16:01:03 (rate 11,delta 10)
            1293 records processed as of 2015-08-22 16:01:10 (rate 11,delta 3)
            1373 records processed as of 2015-08-22 16:01:16 (rate 11,delta 12)
            1424 records processed as of 2015-08-22 16:01:22 (rate 11,delta 9)
            1495 records processed as of 2015-08-22 16:01:27 (rate 11,delta 14)
            1546 records processed as of 2015-08-22 16:01:34 (rate 11,delta 7)
            1639 records processed as of 2015-08-22 16:01:39 (rate 11,delta 18)
            1684 records processed as of 2015-08-22 16:01:45 (rate 11,delta 7)
            1781 records processed as of 2015-08-22 16:01:51 (rate 11,delta 14)
            1852 records processed as of 2015-08-22 16:01:56 (rate 11,delta 13)
            1920 records processed as of 2015-08-22 16:02:01 (rate 11,delta 13)
            1968 records processed as of 2015-08-22 16:02:07 (rate 11,delta 9)
            2041 records processed as of 2015-08-22 16:02:12 (rate 11,delta 13)
            2119 records processed as of 2015-08-22 16:02:17 (rate 11,delta 14)
            2205 records processed as of 2015-08-22 16:02:24 (rate 11,delta 13)
            2277 records processed as of 2015-08-22 16:02:29 (rate 11,delta 13)
            2352 records processed as of 2015-08-22 16:02:34 (rate 11,delta 14)
```

Figure 4-2. REPORTCOUNT output

With the reporting parameter in place for the extracts and replicats, you will see the number of transactions processed based on the monitor period requeted. Now that processes are reporting what they are processing, you can start looking at the tools used at the database layer to reveal any tuning problems.

Database Tools

Although you have access to operating system tools for turning, this only gives you so much information. Depending on the performance issue, you might need to dig into the databases to see what is happening there. Just like tuning any database, you will need to tune for response times. Understanding and tuning for response time can be an effective way of addressing slowness within the database on either side of the replication environment. Remember that this is where you should be looking at the AWR or ASH reports for performance bottlenecks.

▪ **Note**   Oracle's AWR and ASH reports require you to have access to Oracle's Diagnostic and Tuning packs. This is a paid option with Oracle Enterprise Edition Database.

Tuning for response time can be time consuming and there are many different approaches to this type of tuning. There are a number of resources available to reference and learn from; however, Oracle provides a few good resources right within the database. In newer versions of the Oracle Database, you can use AWR to help identify waits and other events that are affecting response time and later replication timing. One area you would need to look at is the replication statistics that Oracle provides in the AWR reports. Starting in Oracle Database 12c (12.1.0.1), Oracle has updated the AWR report with detailed information related to Oracle GoldenGate. Figure 4-3 shows you the section of the AWR report that contains this information.

Replication Statistics (GoldenGate, XStream)

- Replication System Resource Usage
- Replication SGA Usage
- GoldenGate Capture
- GoldenGate Capture Rate
- GoldenGate Apply Reader
- GoldenGate Apply Coordinator
- GoldenGate Apply Server
- GoldenGate Apply Coordinator Rate
- GoldenGate Apply Reader and Server Rate
- XStream Capture
- XStream Capture Rate
- XStream Apply Reader
- XStream Apply Coordinator
- XStream Apply Server
- XStream Apply Coordinator Rate
- XStream Apply Reader and Server Rate
- Table Statistics by DML Operations
- Table Statistics by Conflict Resolutions
- Replication Large Transaction Statistics
- Replication Long Running Transaction Statistics

Back to Top

Figure 4-3. *Replication statistics in the AWR report*

After reviewing what is in the AWR and ASH reports, you might need to look deeper into the environment and see if anything has changed. The Automatic Database Diagnostic Manager [ADDM] report can yield valuable information on what might have changed in the environment. Once all these items have been reviewed, if there are still performance problems, you will need to see what is occurring at the operating system level.

Operating System Tools

There are a few tools that you will need to use when tuning Oracle GoldenGate processes. You might think that operating system tools are not needed; however, Oracle GoldenGate works closely with the operating system, especially with the classic processes. Many of these tools are at the operating system level because most of the performance issues will be seen at the operating system level. The tools that are used from the operating system will depend on the operating system used in the replication environment. Table 4-4 displays the most common tools used for a majority of UNIX and Linux environments.

Table 4-4. *UINX and Linux Tuning Tools*

Tool	Description
top	Provides a dynamic, real-time view of running a system.
mpstat	Writes to STDOUT the activities for each available processor. Global average activities among all processors will be reported.
vmstat	Reports information about processes, memory, paging, block I/O, traps, and CPU activity.
iostat	Monitors system I/O device loading by observing the time the devices are active in relation to their average transfer rates.

■ **Note** For Microsoft Windows environments, tools like PerfMon can be used to monitor the performance of Oracle GoldenGate processes.

Tuning the Classic Processes

In most Oracle GoldenGate implementations, a single extract, secondary extract, and replicat can process transactions. Depending on the type of transactions, amount of transactions, and type of transactions, you might find that you need to run multiple processes in parallel to help distribute the transaction load. This could occur on either side of the replication environment. An architecture that uses multiple processes would look something like Figure 4-4.

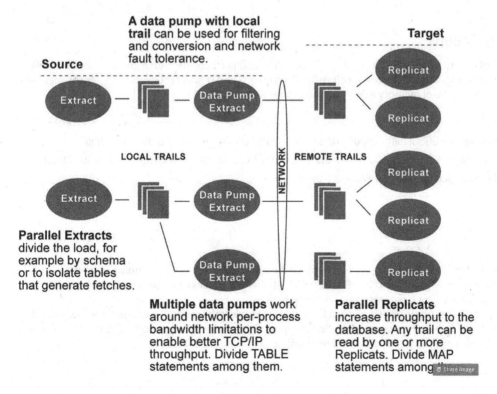

Figure 4-4. *Standard Oracle tuning of Oracle GoldenGate*

Considerations When Using Multiple Process Groups

Although you can configure multiple process groups, you must be aware of the following considerations before doing so:

1. Maintaining data integrity.

2. Number of groups.

3. Memory.

4. Isolating process-intensive tables.

These considerations will have affect on the performance of the system as well.

Maintaining Data Integrity

Not every workload has the option of being partitioned across multiple process groups and keeping the atomicity of the transaction intact. Before splitting transactions up into multiple process groups, you must ensure that the transactional dependencies of one group will never have dependencies on objects in another process group, transactional or otherwise.

■ **Note**   If tables do not have foreign keys (FKs) or updates on primary keys (PKs), you might be able to use multiple processes if keeping related DML in the same process stream.

Number of Groups

The number of concurrent extract and replicat process groups that can be used on a given system depends on how much memory the system has or can spare. Each extract and replicat process needs approximately 25 MB to 55 MB or more of memory to process related transactions.

■ **Note**   Although the GGSCI fully supports up to 5,000 concurrent extracts and replications, it is recommended to stay at 300 or less to ensure the environment can be managed effectively. The number of groups can be controlled by using the MAXGROUP parameter.

Memory

As pointed out when discussing number of groups for the extract and replicat, the amount of memory needed for each is somewhere between 25 MB and 55 MB for each process. The system must also have available swap space for each process it will be running.

A quick way to determine what size swap is needed is to look at the report file and find the line PROCESS VM AVAIL FROM OS (min). Once you find this in the report file, round it to the nearest gigabyte and then multiply by the number of processes that will be running.

Isolating Process-Intensive Tables

In using multiple process groups, you can break out the tables that have a tendency to interfere with normal processing and contribute to a high latency rate. To do this, different parameters need to be set in either the extract or replicat parameter files.

For the extract, statistics on the fetching of records can be done by using the STATS EXTRACT command at the GGSCI or including STATOPTIONS REPORTFETCH in the parameter file. This command or parameter will retrieve the details on tables that are taking the most time for the extract to fetch information from. Once those tables are identified, you can move them to their own extract processes.

For the replicat when running in classic mode, it can be a source of performance bottlenecks because it is a single-threaded process that is processing SQL from the associated trail file as regular SQL. Due to this, the replicat might take longer to process transactions that have larger or long-running transactions, heavy volume, a very large number of columns changing, and line-of-business (LOB) data, providing that transactional integrity can be maintained.

■ **Note** In classic mode, I determined that if a table has LOB data and can be broken out, it should be.

Using Parallel Replicat Groups on the Target System

This example takes a look at one configuration where you are using more than one replicat to process transactions. The steps provided here show how you would add a replicat to an existing Oracle GoldenGate environment for replication.

Adding New Trails from the Extract

To add more replicats to the target system, you first need to break the data out to independent trail files coming from the primary extract. To do this, you need to use the ADD EXTTRAIL command in GGSCI to associate the number of trail files to use.

■ **Note** Another approach is to repartition the workload among the replicats. The downside to this approach compared to the approach being discussed is that the replicats need to read through large amounts of data because everything is in a single trail file.

Source Steps

1. Stop all extract processes.

    ```
    GGSCI (ggtest12c1.acme.com) 12> stop extract *

    Sending STOP request to EXTRACT ESRC1 ...
    Request processed.

    Sending STOP request to EXTRACT PSRC1 ...
    Request processed.
    ```

2. Add a new trail file to the primary extract.

   ```
   GGSCI (ggtest12c1.acme.com) 13> ADD EXTTRAIL ./dirdat/la, EXTRACT ESRC1,
   megabytes 50
   EXTTRAIL added.
   ```

3. Add a new remote trail file to the secondary extract (data pump).

   ```
   GGSCI (ggtest12c1.acme.com) 14> ADD RMTTRAIL ./dirdat/ra, EXTRACT PSRC1,
   megabytes 50
   RMTTRAIL added.
   ```

4. Edit the parameter files for the primary extract and data pump to allocate what tables go which trail file. This is done by adding the EXTTRAIL parameter in the primary extract file and the RMTTRAIL parameter in the data pump parameter file.

   ```
   Primary Extract:
   GGSCI> edit params esrc1

   --CHECKPARAMS
   EXTRACT ESRC1
   USERID ggate, PASSWORD ggate
   TRANLOGOPTIONS DBLOGREADER
   SETENV (ORACLE_HOME="/opt/app/oracle/product/12.1.0.2/dbhome_1")
   SETENV (ORACLE_SID="src12c")
   WARNLONGTRANS 1h, CHECKINTERVAL 30m
   WILDCARDRESOLVE IMMEDIATE
   EXTTRAIL ./dirdat/lt;
   TABLE SOE.ADDRESSES;
   TABLE SOE.CARD_DETAILS;
   TABLE SOE.CUSTOMERS;
   TABLE SOE.INVENTORIES;
   TABLE SOE.LOGON;
   EXTTRAIL ./dirdat/la;
   TABLE SOE.ORDER_ITEMS;
   TABLE SOE.ORDERENTRY_METADATA;
   TABLE SOE.ORDERS;
   TABLE SOE.PRODUCT_DESCRIPTIONS;
   TABLE SOE.PRODUCT_INFORMATION;
   TABLE SOE.WAREHOUSES;

   Secondary Extract (Data Pump):
   GGSCI> edit params psrc1
   ```

```
EXTRACT PSRC1
PASSTHRU
RMTHOST 10.10.1.12, MGRPORT 15000, COMPRESS
RMTTRAIL ./dirdat/rt
TABLE SOE.ADDRESSES;
TABLE SOE.CARD_DETAILS;
TABLE SOE.CUSTOMERS;
TABLE SOE.INVENTORIES;
TABLE SOE.LOGON;
RMTTTRAIL ./dirdat/ra;
TABLE SOE.ORDER_ITEMS;
TABLE SOE.ORDERENTRY_METADATA;
TABLE SOE.ORDERS;
TABLE SOE.PRODUCT_DESCRIPTIONS;
TABLE SOE.PRODUCT_INFORMATION;
TABLE SOE.WAREHOUSES;
```

5. Restart the extracts.

```
GGSCI> start extract esrc1
GGSCI> start extract psrc1
```

Target Steps

On the target system, you need to create a new replicat that will read the additional trail file.

1. Add new replicat.

```
GGSCI (ggtest12c2.acme.com) 2> ADD REPLICAT rsrc2, EXTTRAIL ./dirdat/ra
REPLICAT added.
```

2. Start both replicats (using a wildcard in this case).

```
GGSCI (ggtest12c2.acme.com) 4> start replicat *

Sending START request to MANAGER ...
REPLICAT RSRC1 starting

Sending START request to MANAGER ...
REPLICAT RSRC2 starting
```

Once both of the replicats have started running, you will now have a successful implementation of a parallel replicat architecture for a unidirectional configuration. These steps are only a small part of what can be done with Oracle GoldenGate classic processes for tuning at the process level.

Network Tuning

Often when setting up Oracle GoldenGate, people do not think about what needs to be tuned in the network layer. Network tuning is just as important as tuning the individual Oracle GoldenGate processes. Tuning the network is important, and in many cases you might not have to do too much. If you understand this, you can understand and validate what your network administrators are telling you when it comes to network performance.

In the next couple of sections, you are going to look at how you can identify and tune Oracle GoldenGate for your network.

Detecting Any Network Bottlenecks

There is a series of steps that you have to perform to identify if there are any bottlenecks in your network. These steps are performed from within Oracle GoldenGate and help you identify what is going on.

1. To view the ten most recent extract checkpoints, issue the following command:

    ```
    GGSCI> info extract <group>, showch 10
    ```

2. In the output, look for the line that is identified by Write Checkpoint #1.

    ```
    Primary Extract:
    Write Checkpoint #1

      GGS Log Trail

      Current Checkpoint (current write position):
        Sequence #: 4
        RBA: 2003288
        Timestamp: 2015-08-22 17:01:29.056322
        Extract Trail: ./dirdat/lt
        Trail Type: EXTTRAIL

    Data Pump:
    Write Checkpoint #1

      GGS Log Trail

      Current Checkpoint (current write position):
        Sequence #: 9
        RBA: 386089
        Timestamp: 2015-08-22 17:13:00.521146
        Extract Trail: ./dirdat/rt
        Trail Type: RMTTRAIL
    ```

3. This should be done for both the primary extract and the data pump. Once you have identified the latest checkpoint, make note of the sequence number (logfile number), the RBA number, and the timestamp.

4. Validate that the information you just recorded is due to the extract generating checkpoints. This applies to the data pump process as well.

5. Issue an INFO EXTRACT command to check the sequence number, RBA, and timestamp. Do these match the latest checkpoint or are they incremented forward? If they are incremented forward, then the replicat needs to be validated.

6. Validate the replicat by issuing the following command:

```
GGSCI> SEND REPLICAT <group>, STATUS
Sending STATUS request to REPLICAT RSRC1 …
  Current status: At EOF
  Sequence #: 9
  RBA: 386089
  0 records in current transaction
```

What you are looking for on the replicat is if the process is at the EOF marker or if it is still processing transactions. If it was still processing transactions, then there would potentially be a network bottleneck that needs to be addressed. To dig deeper and verify if there is a bottleneck in the network, you can use the GETTCPSTATS option of the SEND EXTRACT command to get current statistics on the network.

Workaround for Bandwidth Issues

In an chapter 3, we looked at the different processes in the Oracle GoldenGate architecture. One of the processes was the secondary extract, or data pump; this process can also be used in parallel to work around any potential bottleneck issues. The added benefit of using data pump is that the primary extract can focus on just capturing the transactions while the data pump is responsible for the TCP/IP interaction.

Compressing Data for Bandwidth Reduction

Within the data pump process, you have to specify where the remote server is by using the RMTHOST parameter. There are a few options that can be used with this parameter. Listing 4-2 provides a look at the options that are available for this parameter. The option needed for reducing bandwidth is the COMPRESS option.

Listing 4-2. Parameters for the RMTHOST Parameter

```
RMTHOST
{ host name | IP address}
[, COMPRESS]
[, COMPRESSTHRESHOLD]
[, ENCRYPT algorithm [KEYNAME key_name]]
{, MGRPORT port | PORT port}
[, CPU number]
[, PRI number]
[, HOMETERM device_name]
[, PROCESSNAME process_name]
[, PARAMS collector_parameters]
[, STREAMING | NOSTREAMING]
[, TCPBUFSIZE bytes]
[, TCPFLUSHBYTES bytes]
[, TIMEOUT seconds]
```

To set this parameter in the data pump file would look something like Listing 4-3. Notice in this example that the RMTHOST parameter is taking the hostname of the target system. You can also provide an IP address in place of the hostname; however, a properly run network should allow hostname resolution. The next option in this line assigns the proper manager port number. The manager port number tells the data pump where to connect on the target system. Finally, you are letting Oracle GoldenGate know that everything that is going to the remote system needs to be compressed, so Oracle GoldenGate keeps the packets small while shipping and helps in minimizing network bandwidth.

Listing 4-3. Correct Setting of RMTHOST

```
RMTHOST ggtest12c2.acme.com, MGRPORT 15000, COMPRESS
```

Although the compression option allows you to reduce the bandwidth, the benefits of using it should be weighed against any performance effects associated with the CPU on the source and target systems.

Increasing the TCP/IP Packet Sizes

Another way to help increase the bandwidth for Oracle GoldenGate is to set the TCPBUFSIZE option for the RMTHOST parameter. The TCPBUFSIZE option is used to control the size of the TCP socket buffer that the extract maintains. Increasing the size of this buffer allows Oracle GoldenGate to send larger packets to the target system.

Before increasing the size of TCPBUFSIZE, there are a few steps that should be followed to determine what size the buffer should be.

■ **Note**   The default buffer size is set to 1 MB. Generally, this is a good size for most networks.

To determine how to increase the TCP/IP buffer size, the following steps need to be performed and reviewed.

Sizing TCP/IP Buffer Size

1. From the source system, use the PING command to ping the target system from the command line.

    ```
    [oracle@ggtest12c1 ~]$ ping ggtest12c2.acme.com
    PING ggtest12c2.acme.com (10.10.1.12) 56(84) bytes of data.
    64 bytes from ggtest12c2.acme.com (10.10.1.12): icmp_seq=1 ttl=64 time=3.83 ms
    64 bytes from ggtest12c2.acme.com (10.10.1.12): icmp_seq=2 ttl=64 time=1.92 ms
    64 bytes from ggtest12c2.acme.com (10.10.1.12): icmp_seq=3 ttl=64 time=3.24 ms
    64 bytes from ggtest12c2.acme.com (10.10.1.12): icmp_seq=4 ttl=64 time=4.58 ms
    ^C
    --- ggtest12c2.acme.com ping statistics ---
    4 packets transmitted, 4 received, 0% packet loss, time 3883ms
    ```

2. Multiply the value of the network bandwidth. This example takes the highest RTT value (4.58 ms) for the network. If the bandwidth is 100 megabits per second, then the optimal buffer size is as follows:

```
4.58 ms = .00458 seconds
.00458 seconds * 100 megabits per second = .458 megabits
```

3. Dividing the result by 8 to determine the number of bytes yields the number of megabytes we would be sending with the current TCP/IP buffer.

```
.458 megabits / 8 = .05725 megabyte per second
```

If you were going to set TCPBUFSIZE, it would have to be in the format of bytes. The value to be set up would look like. .00005591. Because the default setting for TCPBUFSIZE is 1 MB (1000000), I would not set it in this case and let Oracle GoldenGate work as needed.

If you need to increase the buffer size for non-Windows systems, consult your system administrator and ask him or her to increase the default value on the source and target systems. This will allow Oracle GoldenGate to use the buffer you configure in TCPBUFSIZE, if greater than 1 MB.

Eliminating Disk I/O Bottlenecks

Just like other Oracle products, the disks that are used for different components need to be as fast as possible. Oracle GoldenGate can suffer from bottlenecks due to I/O activities if not configured correctly for the extract and replicat processes.

Each of the processes have I/O issues that need to be addressed as well, as follows:

1. Primary extract generates disk writes to a trail file and disk reads from the database that is the source.

2. Secondary extract (data pump) generates disk reads from the local trail file.

3. Each process will write a recovery checkpoint to the checkpoint file on a predetermined schedule.

As you can tell, there are wait events that need to be addressed throughout the life of the process. There are two different ways to address I/O issues within Oracle GoldenGate:

1. Improve I/O performance by system configuration.

2. Improve I/O performance within Oracle GoldenGate.

Improving I/O Performance by System Configuration

With any system, its speed is dependent on how fast the I/O subsystem is. If Oracle GoldenGate is having high I/O waits, then the I/O subsystem needs to be investigated. If possible, move the trail files to the fastest disks possible.

If the I/O subsystems are a redundant array of independent disks (RAID) configuration, this should be checked. Oracle GoldenGate writes data sequentially and using the right RAID configuration is critical. A RAID configuration of RAID 0+1 (striping and mirroring) is better than RAID 5 because checksums are used and that slows down I/O operations.

Improving I/O Performance Within Oracle GoldenGate

If you want to improve the I/O performance of Oracle GoldenGate from within GoldenGate itself, there are a few parameters for which you can try increasing the values. These parameters are highlighted in Table 4-5.

Table 4-5. *I/O Performance Parameters*

Parameter	Description
CHECKPOINTSECS	Parameter to control how often extract and replicat make their routine checkpoints.
GROUPTRANOPS	Parameter to control the number of SQL operations that are contained in the replicat transaction when operating in its normal mode. I/O is reduced by reducing the number of times the replicat executes to applies and has to write checkpoints to the checkpoint file and table.
EOFDELAY or EOFDELAYCSECS	Parameter to control how often extract, data pump, or replicat checks for new data after it has reached the end of the current data in its data source. I/O overhead is reduced by increasing the value of this parameter.

■ **Note**   The CHECKPOINTSECS and GROUPTRANOPS parameters are not valid for the integrated products of Oracle GoldenGate.

Managing Virtual Memory and Paging

Because Oracle GoldenGate only replicates committed transactions, each operation is stored in a managed virtual memory pool known as a *cache* until a commit or rollback is issued. To do this, Oracle GoldenGate uses a global cache as a shared resource of an extract or replicat process. This global cache is managed by the *cache manager* (CACHEMGR) and takes advantage of the memory management functions of the underlying operating system. By doing so, Oracle GoldenGate ensures that the processes work in the most sustained and efficient manner possible. To control the cache manager, the parameter CACHEMGR is used to control the amount of virtual memory and temporary disk space needed for caching uncommitted transactions being processed.

By default, the CACHEMGR parameter should not need to be set. Oracle GoldenGate will allocate as much virtual memory as it needs to manage the uncommitted transactions while a process is running. You can find the current values used by the cache manager by looking in the report files associated with the Oracle GoldenGate processes that have been started. If you begin to see excessive paging and the performance of critical processes is affected, the CACHESIZE option of the CACHEMGR can be used to reduce the size of virtual memory.

For the temporary directory being used, the CACHEDIRECTORY option can be used to provide a directory of allocated space to be used.

Applying Similar SQL Statements (Using Arrays)

By default, the replicat will process all transactions in a row-by-row fashion. At times this will affect performance, especially in a large transactional environment. As a workaround to this issue, Oracle GoldenGate provides a replicat parameter called BATCHSQL. This parameter is used by the replicat to increase performance of transactions being applied by identifying similar SQL statements and organizing them into arrays. The arrays of transactions can then be applied at an accelerated rate.

By using BATCHSQL, the improvements seen will also require more memory. To maintain optimum performance, the following BATCHSQL options are available:

```
BATCHESPERQUEUE
BYTESPERQUEUE
OPSPERBATCH
OPSPERQUEUE
```

Additionally, you can use the BATCHTRANSOPS option to tune the size of the array that BATCHSQL uses. This parameter controls the number of batch operations that can be grouped into a transaction before requiring a commit.

■ **Note**   The default setting for BATCHTRANSOPS for a nonintegrated replicat is 1,000. The default for an integrated replicat is 50.

Most of the time, using BATCHSQL is a good thing and can help with performance. There are occasions when BATCHSQL will cause more problems than solutions. Although this is a good parameter to include in the replicat parameter file, using it only when needed is the better approach.

Full Table Scan Due to Absence of Keys

At times there is a need to replicat a table that does not have a primary key; this means that Oracle GoldenGate would need to use the whole table structure as the reference point for updates and deletes that happen to the table. In exchange this could produce a full table scan on the table with the net effect of poor performance. To address this problem, the Oracle GoldenGate TABLE parameter can be extended to specify which columns should be used as the key on the table. Listing 4-4 provides an example of this.

Listing 4-4. Identifying Key Colums for a Table

```
TABLE soe.emp, KEYCOLS (first_name, last_name, date_of_birth, emp_id);
```

By specifying the table columns for Oracle GoldenGate to use, the transactions will be resolved against this pseudo-key for updates and deletes, in turn preventing a full table scan and helping with performance on the table.

Tuning Integrated Processes

Up until this point, our discussion has revolved around the Oracle GoldenGate classic processes, how to tune a classic configuration, and some general tuning items. What we take a look at now is how these concepts of tuning apply to the new integrated processes for Oracle GoldenGate that Oracle introduced starting in version 11.2.0.2 and later.

Starting in Oracle Database 11.2.0.3, Oracle introduced the integrated extract. This extract performs the same function as the classic extract in that it captures transactions from the Oracle database and stores them in a trail file. By using an integrated extract, you are telling the Oracle database that you want to use the internal log mining server to capture the transactions. Figure 4-5 provides a conceptual view of how the log miner looks inside of a source database.

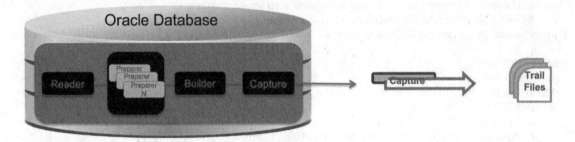

Figure 4-5. *Source log miner server*

If you look at Figure 4-5 closely, you will see that before the extract (capture) is done, the log miner has to read, prepare, and build the transaction in SCN order. The capture process then formats the transactions in logical change record (LCR) order before passing them to the extract for processing. Table 4-6 provides details of the functions of the log miner on a source system.

Table 4-6. *Log Miner Functions (Source System)*

Process	Purpose
READER	Reads log files and splits into regions.
PREPARER	Scans regions of log files and prefilters based on extract parameters.
BUILDER	Merges prepared records in SCN order.
CAPTURE	Formats LCR and passes to GoldenGate extract.

As the transactions make it to the capture part of the log mining server, the extract is requesting the LCR from the log mining server. Once received by the extract, it performs mapping and transformations of the transactions and then writes the transaction to the trail file.

On the receiving side of the replication process, Oracle introduced the integrated replicat with the release of Oracle GoldenGate 12.1.2, and it is supported in Oracle Database 11.2.0.4 and Oracle Database 12c (12.1.0.1 and later). The integrated replicat takes advantage of the parallel apply servers that are readily available in the Oracle database. Using this version of the replicat, there is no need to partition data. The added bonus is the replicat becomes simpler to manage because there is only one replicat to manage.

Just like the integrated extract, the integrated replicat relies on the log mining server to apply the transactions that are processed. In Figure 4-6, you can see how the replicat (delivery) reads the associated trail files. As it is reading the trail files, the integrated replicat is constructing the transactions to be applied by LCRs and then uses a lightweight streaming API to transmit the LCR to the database.

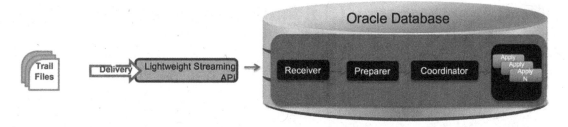

Figure 4-6. *Target log miner server*

Once the database receives the transactions, the receiver process reads the LCR. Once the LCR is read, the preparer process reviews the LCR to see if there are any dependencies between transactions. This means it looks for any primary keys, foreign keys, or unique keys and ensures that they are placed in the correct order. Then the coordinator ensures the order is maintained between the transactions. Finally, the applier begins to apply the transactions in the order specified. If there are any errors, the applier handles conflict detection and resolution (CDR) along with error handling. This process ensures that all transactions are applied successfully or handled as needed for the environment. Table 4-7 explains these processes in a bit more detail.

Table 4-7. *Log Miner Functions (Target System)*

Process	Purpose
RECEIVER	Reads LCRs.
PREPARER	Computes dependencies between transactions (primary keys, foreign keys, unique keys).
COORDINATOR	Maintains the order between transactions.
APPLIER	Applies transactions asynchronously, including CDR and error handling.

Tuning Tools for Integrated Processes

As listed earlier in this chapter, many of the parameters and solutions for tuning can be used when tuning the integrated processes. Oracle has either enhanced or provided additional tools that can be used for monitoring and seeking tuning opportunities.

Automatic Workload Repository Output

Starting in Oracle Database 12c (12.1.0.1 and later), Oracle has enhanced the AWR report to provide information related to the integrated processes. This information can be found in the Replication Statistics area of the report (Figure 4-7).

■ **Note**   AWR reports from Oracle Database 11g (11.2.0.x) will not have this option. This means if you are running integrated processes against an Oracle 11.2.0.3 or 11.2.0.4 database, AWR reports might not help you when it comes to Oracle GoldenGate.

Replication Statistics (GoldenGate, XStream)

- Replication System Resource Usage
- Replication SGA Usage
- GoldenGate Capture
- GoldenGate Capture Rate
- GoldenGate Apply Reader
- GoldenGate Apply Coordinator
- GoldenGate Apply Server
- GoldenGate Apply Coordinator Rate
- GoldenGate Apply Reader and Server Rate
- XStream Capture
- XStream Capture Rate
- XStream Apply Reader
- XStream Apply Coordinator
- XStream Apply Server
- XStream Apply Coordinator Rate
- XStream Apply Reader and Server Rate
- Table Statistics by DML Operations
- Table Statistics by Conflict Resolutions
- Replication Large Transaction Statistics
- Replication Long Running Transaction Statistics

Back to Top

Figure 4-7. *AWR Replication Statistics report area*

The AWR report provides valuable information on what the log miner server processes are doing and you can see what is causing the problem very quickly. Figure 4-8 shows a few of the output areas from a previously run AWR report.

GoldenGate Apply Coordinator Rate

- GoldenGate Apply Coordinator rate information ordered by Replicat Name and Apply Name in ascending order
- Apply name prefixed with a * indicates process (re)started between Begin and End snapshots

Replicat Name	Apply Name	Txns Received/sec	Txns Applied/sec	Txns Rolled Back/sec	Unassigned Complete Txn/sec	Total Errors/sec
REPI	OGG$REPI	14.51	13.69	0.00	0.80	0.00

GoldenGate Apply Reader and Server Rate

- GoldenGate Apply Reader and Server rate information ordered by Replicat Name and Apply Name in ascending order
- Apply name prefixed with a * indicates process (re)started between Begin and End snapshots
- Time Per Msg values are in centiseconds

Replicat Name	Apply Name	Reader LCRs/sec	Server LCRs Applied/sec	Server Dequeue Time/msg	Server Apply Time/msg	Total LCRs Retried/sec	Total Txn Retried/sec
REPI	OGG$REPI	59.19	55.85	0.52	0.00	0.00	0.00

GoldenGate Apply Server

- GoldenGate Apply Server statistics ordered by Replicat Name and Apply Name in ascending order
- Apply name prefixed with a * indicates process (re)started between Begin and End snapshots
- Columns suffixed with K,M,G,T,P are in multiples of 1000

Replicat Name	Apply Name	Server LCRs Applied	Server Dequeue Time(s)	Server Apply Time(s)	Total LCRs Retried	Total Txns Retried
REPI	OGG$REPI	150.6K	0.00	779.79	0	0

Figure 4-8. *AWR information for integrated processes*

Just as AWR is a valuable resource for tuning Oracle Database, it will become a valuable resource for tuning Oracle GoldenGate processes.

Streams Performance Advisor

The Streams Performance Advisor is another tool that Oracle has provided that works in helping identify what is going on under the covers of Oracle GoldenGate. Do not let the name of this tool fool you; it is a tool with which many streams administrators will be familiar. This is due to the fact that Oracle is slowly moving the core functionality of Oracle-to-Oracle replication with Oracle Streams into Oracle GoldenGate.

This advisor tool can be used for both the integrated extract and integrated replicat processes. It provides you with real-time statistics on what is occurring within the integrated environment. However, to use the Streams Performance Advisor, it needs to be installed in the database where the integrated processes are running.

Installing Streams Performance Advisor

To install the Streams Performance Advisor (see Listing 4-5), you need to run the utlspadv.sql script from the admin directory of the Oracle home. Before you can run the script, you will need to connect to the database as the Oracle GoldenGate user and ensure that the user has Execute permissions on the DBMS_LOCK and DBMS_STREAMS_ADVISOR_ADM packages. After granting access to the packages, the advisor can be installed by the GoldenGate user.

Listing 4-5. Install Streams Performance Advisior

```
[oracle@ggtest12c1 ~]$ cd $ORACLE_HOME/rdbms/admin
[oracle@ggtest12c1 admin]$ sqlplus / as sysdba
SQL*Plus: Release 12.1.0.2.0 Production on Sun Aug 23 14:14:31 2015
Copyright (c) 1982, 2014, Oracle.  All rights reserved.
Connected to:
Oracle Database 12c Enterprise Edition Release 12.1.0.2.0 - 64bit Production
With the Partitioning, OLAP, Advanced Analytics and Real Application Testing options
SQL> @utlspadv.sql
```

Once the Streams Performance Advisor is in place, you can run it against any running integrated process.

Understanding Streams Performance Advisor Output

When you run the Streams Performance Advisor, you will be presented with output that looks similar to the output in Listing 4-6. At first glance this might look like a lot of garbage that was collected; however, it is quite valuable information related to the performance of the integrated process.

Listing 4-6. Streams Performance Advisor Output

```
PATH 1 RUN_ID 1 RUN_TIME 2015-JAN-12 15:17:31 CCA Y
|<C> OGG$CAP_EXTI 31 31 0 LMR 99.7% 0% 0.3% "" LMP (2) 199.7% 0% 0.3% "" LMB 99.3% 0% 0.3%
"" CAP 99.7% 0% 0.3% "" |<Q> "GGATE"."OGG$Q_EXTI" 0.01 0.01 0 |<A> OGG$EXTI 0.01 0.01 0
|<B> NO BOTTLENECK IDENTIFIED
```

The highlighted letters and percentages coordinate to the architecture in the log miner. In Listing 4-6, from looking at this fact it is clear that the process being monitored is an integrated extract. The reader (LMR) process is idle 99.7 percent of the time. The preparer (LMP) is idle 199.7 percent of the time, and the last two processes in the log miner architecture are idle 99.3 percent and 99.7 percent of the time. This tells you that the extract process is running very efficiently and should not need any tuning.

> ■ **Note**   The Log Miner Preparer (LMP) process is being calculated based on the number of parallel threads needed, 100% × 2 = 200%.

Database Performance Views

Everything in Oracle Database has some sort of performance view. Oracle GoldenGate is no exception, especially when using integrated processes. Many of these views are new views created specifically for Oracle GoldenGate, and some of them are views that have been around for as long as Oracle Streams existed.

The views that are used for Oracle GoldenGate are classified into two categories, shown in Listing 4-7, and can be used as such. The first category is the runtime views. These views are used to give the DBA a view into what Oracle GoldenGate is doing throughout the life of the transaction. The second category of views is the configuration views. These views are used to take a look at what configurations are in place without having to go look at the parameter files.

Listing 4-7.   Database Views for GoldenGate

```
Runtime Views
V$GOLDENGATE_CAPTURE
V$GG_APPLY_RECEIVER
V$GG_APPLY_READER
V$GG_APPLY_COORDINATOR
V$GG_APPLY_SERVER
V$GOLDENGATE_TABLE_STATS
V$GOLDENGATE_CAPABILITIES
V$DBA_APPLY_ERRORS


Configuration Views
DBA_GOLDENGATE_PRIVILEGES
DBA_GOLDENGATE_SUPPORT_MODE
DBA_CAPUTRE
DBA_CAPTURE_PARAMETERS
DBA_GOLDENGATE_INBOUND
DBA_GG_INBOUND_PROGRESS
DBA_APPLY
DBA_APPLY_PARAMETERS
DBA_APPLY_REPERROR_HANDLERS
DBA_APPLY_HANDLE_COLLISIONS
DBA_APPLY_DML_CONF_HANDLERS
```

Many of the views that you will see in the database are related to Oracle Streams. If an administrator has scripts written for Oracle Streams Monitoring, those same scripts should be usable against an Oracle GoldenGate integrated setup as well.

Health Checks

Last among all the tools that are available for Oracle GoldenGate tuning are health checks. Health checks are available for many different version of Oracle GoldenGate, so to get an understanding of which script is needed for your environment, consult My Oracle Support Note 1448324.1.

Health checks provide information over a wide range of areas. The three areas of concern are the summary, analysis, and statistics. The summary gives an overview of the environment along with advice and warnings on potential issues with the configuration. In the analysis, the health check will compare configurations, provide performance recommendations, and provide additional detailed information on diagnostic purposes. The statistics section provides runtime information on Streams (GoldenGate) processing.

Summary

This chapter looked at what options you have for tuning an Oracle GoldenGate environment. You were giving basic concepts of tuning, what to look for, what tools are available for tuning, and tuning when it comes to classic and integrated processes. Regardless of the type of Oracle GoldenGate process you are using, there are some similarities in tuning. When you switch from classic to integrated processes, however, you are given a few more tools to help you identify bottlenecks within the database ecosystem. Using all the information that has been provided is vital to you understanding how your Oracle GoldenGate environment is running.

The next chapter looks at how to monitor your Oracle GoldenGate environment. There are many different ways you can monitor Oracle GoldenGate. Just like tuning a GoldenGate environment, you will have options for monitoring as well.

CHAPTER 5

■ ■ ■

Monitoring Oracle GoldenGate

Because Oracle GoldenGate is a heterogeneous replication tool, it lends itself to many unique and diverse environments. These unique environments require some sort of monitoring to ensure a healthy and well-oiled replicating environment. Traditionally monitoring tools provide common features, including graphical tools, for recording events and providing opportunities for analysis within the environment. This chapter takes a look at how you can monitor Oracle GoldenGate from the command line, using scripts, and what tools are available at a graphical layer. Many of these approaches are common in everyday environments.

■ **Note**   Many of the examples in this chapter are based on UNIX and Linux. You can make adjustments for Windows as needed.

Logs

Oracle GoldenGate provides a few logs that can be used to help monitor what is happening in the environment. These logs record events that happen at a global level, along with events at the processes level. There are three primary logs that are used within an Oracle GoldenGate environment: the error log, process reports, and the discard file.

GoldenGate Service Error Log

The GoldenGate Service error log (GGSERR.LOG) is used to keep track of errors that happen within the environment. This log is used to keep track of errors including the following:

- A historical record of GGSCI commands.
- Starting and stopping of processes.
- Processing that was performed.
- Errors that occurred.
- Information and warning messages.

Events that happen within the environment are stored in GGSERR.LOG in the sequence in which they occurred. Due to this fact, GGSERR.LOG is good for detecting the cause of an outage or problems with process.

To view GGSERR.LOG, you can use standard shell commands such as vi or cat to view the log file from the root of the GoldenGate directory. From within GGSCI, you are provided a wrapper command called VIEW GGSEVT, which provides a "more" approach to reviewing the GGSERR.LOG while within the Oracle GoldenGate environment.

B. Curtis, *Pro Oracle GoldenGate for the DBA*, DOI 10.1007/978-1-4842-1179-3_5

Process Reports

With GGSERR.LOG being used to view events within an environment at a global level, how can you see what is going on at the process level? This is done by reviewing the process reports associated with each of the extract or replicat processes. Process reports are used to help identify issues with a process. Depending on the process, you might see items as follows:

- Parameters in use.

- Table and column mappings.

- Database information.

- Runtime messages and errors.

- Runtime statistics for the number of operations processed.

Process report files are created for every extract, replicat, and manager process on startup. Process reports are helpful in diagnosing problems that occur during runtime events, invalid mapping syntaxes, SQL errors, and connection errors.

Just like GGSERR.LOG, you can view process report files from the command line using operating system tools like vi or cat while in the dirrpt subdirectory of GoldenGate base directory. Process report files can also be viewed from within GGSCI by using the VIEW REPORT command followed by the process group name.

■ **Note**   If a process fails without generating a report, the information can be seen on the terminal by issuing a command similar to this from the command line, not GGSCI:

```
Process paramfile path.prm
```

where Process is the extract or replicat, and path.prm is the fully qualified path to the parameter file. For example:

```
extract paramsfile /u01/app/oracle/product/12.1.2.0/12c/oggcore_1/dirprm/egg12c.prm
```

Discard File

Whenever a process is started with the start command through GGSCI, a discard file is created for the process. The discard file is used to capture information about Oracle GoldenGate operations that have failed. The information within the discard file can help you resolve data errors that could be preventing replication. Information that you will find in the discard file could include the following:

- Database error message.

- Sequence number of the data source (archive log) or trail file.

- Relative byte address of the record in the data source (archive log) or trail file.

- Details related to the discarded operation; that is, column values of a DML statement or text for a DDL statement.

The discard file will be found in the `dirrpt` subdirectory of the Oracle GoldenGate Home directory. The discard file can also viewed by using operating system commands like `vi` and `cat` or through GGSCI using the `VIEW REPORT` command. The maximum size of the discard file is 2 GB. The default size is 50 MB if no maximum size setting is provided when setting up a discard file. If the discard file exists at startup, it is purged before new data are written.

You can change the location of the discard file by using the `DISCARDFILE` parameter. Disabling the discard file can also be done using the `NODISCARDFILE` parameter. After the discard file is created, it needs to stay in the location where it was created to ensure that Oracle GoldenGate operates properly when processing has started.

Maintenance of Process Reports and Discard Files

During the startup of an Oracle GoldenGate process, the process report and discard file are aged. The aging of the process report and discard file is where the files are rolled over and archived before creating a new file. The aged files are identified by the sequence number, from zero through nine, that is appended to the end of the file.

If you would like to age the process report or the discard files on a schedule, this is accomplished by using the `REPORTROLLOVER` and `DISCARDROLLOVER`. These parameters ensure that the process report and discard file are aged at a predetermined interval. This is a handy approach to controlling the size of these files as well to preventing any process outages due to files being full.

No process will have more than ten aged files and one active process report or discard file. After the tenth aged file, the oldest is deleted on creation of a new report or discard file.

■ **Note**   A recommended best practice, if you want to keep older process reports or discard files, is to determine a backup schedule for these files.

Monitoring Within Oracle GoldenGate

Oracle GoldenGate comes with many different monitoring tools to help you identify what is going on within your environment. These tools all rely on either being run from the GGSCI or being embedded within the parameter files. The parameters that are used for monitoring are often the same ones used for performance tuning of the environment, as discussed in Chapter 4.

When monitoring Oracle GoldenGate from within the GGSCI, each process has a set of similar commands that can be used to view what is going on within that environment. If you were to enter a help command at the GGSCI prompt, you would get a Command Summary, providing a list of many different commands. From a monitoring perspective, the manager, JAgent, extract, and replicat provide command options for `INFO`, `STATS`, `STATUS`, `SEND`, and `LAG`. All of these options can aid in the monitoring of an Oracle GoldenGate environment.

INFO ALL Command

The simplest of these commands actually falls in the miscellaneous category because it doesn't require any process for it to run; this is the `INFO ALL` command. `INFO ALL` is used to get the current status of all processes running in the environment. The output of `INFO ALL` is displayed in Listing 5-1.

Listing 5-1. Info All Output (Target Side)

```
GGSCI (wilma.acme.com as ggate@rcv12c) 29> info all
Program     Status     Group      Lag at Chkpt  Time Since Chkpt
MANAGER     RUNNING
JAGENT      RUNNING
REPLICAT    RUNNING    RGG12C     00:01:27      00:00:01
```

If you look at Listing 5-1, you will notice that the replicat is running and that it has a lag of 1 minute and 27 seconds at the checkpoint. This means that the lag at checkpoint was a minute and a half ago. The next column, Time Since, shows the last time that the system checked on the checkpoint. In the output in Listing 5-1, the info all command is providing you with an overview of everything going on in the environment. If there were any issues, such as a process abending, you would immediately see it here.

STATS Command

Another useful command that can be run from the GGSCI prompt is the STATS command. This command, when run against an extract or replicat, will provide information on the type of transactions and number of rows that are occurring against the source or target tables.This command is executed by sending STATS [extract | replicat] [process name] from the GGSCI prompt. Listing 5-2 provides the output for one table when running STATS against the replicat.

Listing 5-2. Stats Against Replicat

```
GGSCI (wilma.acme.com as ggate@rcv12c) 32> stats replicat rgg12c

Sending STATS request to REPLICAT RGG12C ...

Start of Statistics at 2015-09-07 20:10:59.

Replicating from SOE.LOGON to SOE.LOGON:

*** Total statistics since 2015-09-07 20:04:58 ***
        Total inserts                          17477.00
        Total updates                              0.00
        Total deletes                              0.00
        Total discards                             0.00
        Total operations                       17477.00

*** Daily statistics since 2015-09-07 20:04:58 ***
        Total inserts                          17477.00
        Total updates                              0.00
        Total deletes                              0.00
        Total discards                             0.00
        Total operations                       17477.00

*** Hourly statistics since 2015-09-07 20:04:58 ***
        Total inserts                          17477.00
        Total updates                              0.00
        Total deletes                              0.00
        Total discards                             0.00
        Total operations                       17477.00
```

```
*** Latest statistics since 2015-09-07 20:04:58 ***
        Total inserts                          17477.00
        Total updates                              0.00
        Total deletes                              0.00
        Total discards                             0.00
        Total operations                       17477.00
```

As you can tell, the STATS command provides a lot of statistics for one table. The output of the command provides you with a total overall, daily, hourly, and then latest statistics. This is very useful information when you are trying to see what type of operations are occurring against your database tables. As you will notice in this example, this table was only getting inserts; however, if there were other data manipulations happening, those DML changes would be captured with the STATS command as well.

STATUS Command

The next command that you will use is the STATUS command. This command provides a status of the process that it is run against. Listing 5-3 provides the output of running this command against the replicat process.

Listing 5-3. Status of Replicat

```
GGSCI (wilma.acme.com as ggate@rcv12c) 33> status replicat rgg12c
REPLICAT RGG12C: RUNNING
```

In larger environments, this is a great command to use because you are focused on a single process and not the whole environment. Additionally, to make running this command simpler, you can remove the process type (i.e., Replicat) and just run the status command with the group name.

SEND Command

The SEND command is a helpful command if you want to know your runtime statistics. Normally, runtime statistics are sent at the conclusion of the run; however, SEND allows you to produce these statistics without waiting for the end of the run. Listing 5-4 illustrates what the command does from the GGSCI prompt.

Listing 5-4. SEND from GGSCI

```
GGSCI (wilma.acme.com as ggate@rcv12c) 47> send replicat rgg12c report

Sending REPORT request to REPLICAT RGG12C ...
Request processed.
```

In Listing 5-4, the request for runtime statistics was sent using the SEND command. The only thing that GGSCI provides for you is that the request was processed. The actual output, shown in Listing 5-5, was written by the process report file for the replicat.

Listing 5-5. SEND/Report Output

```
2015-09-07 20:32:07  INFO    OGG-01021  Command received from GGSCI: REPORT.

***********************************************************************
*                    ** Run Time Statistics **                       *
***********************************************************************

Last record for the last committed transaction is the following:

_____
Trail name : ./dirdat/ra000001
Hdr-Ind     :     E  (x45)    Partition  :    .  (x04)
UndoFlag    :     .  (x00)    BeforeAfter:    A  (x41)
RecLength   :    88  (x0058)  IO Time    : 2015-09-07 20:29:04.996716
IOType      :   115  (x73)    OrigNode   :  255  (xff)
TransInd    :     .  (x02)    FormatType :    R  (x52)
SyskeyLen   :     0  (x00)    Incomplete :    .  (x00)
AuditRBA    :        422      AuditPos   : 38376
Continued   :     N  (x00)    RecCount   :    1  (x01)

2015-09-07 20:29:04.996716 GGSKeyFieldComp    Len    88 RBA 11968769
Name: SOE.INVENTORIES
_____


Reading ./dirdat/ra000001, current RBA 11968949, 199728 records

Report at 2015-09-07 20:32:07 (activity since 2015-09-07 20:04:58)

From Table SOE.LOGON to SOE.LOGON:
      '#                   inserts:   48550
       #                   updates:       0
       #                   deletes:       0
       #                   discards:      0
From Table SOE.CUSTOMERS to SOE.CUSTOMERS:
       #                   inserts:    6627
       #                   updates:     724
       #                   deletes:       0
       #                   discards:      0
From Table SOE.ADDRESSES to SOE.ADDRESSES:
       #                   inserts:    7351
       #                   updates:       0
       #                   deletes:       0
       #                   discards:      0
From Table SOE.CARD_DETAILS to SOE.CARD_DETAILS:
       #                   inserts:    6627
       #                   updates:       0
       #                   deletes:       0
       #                   discards:      0
```

```
From Table SOE.ORDERS to SOE.ORDERS:
        #                       inserts:      17571
        #                       updates:      20730
        #                       deletes:          0
        #                       discards:         0
From Table SOE.ORDER_ITEMS to SOE.ORDER_ITEMS:
        #                       inserts:      45293
        #                       updates:        962
        #                       deletes:          0
        #                       discards:         0
From Table SOE.INVENTORIES to SOE.INVENTORIES:
        #                       inserts:          0
        #                       updates:      45293
        #                       deletes:          0
        #                       discards:         0


***********************************************************************
**                     Run Time Warnings                            **
```

As you can see, the current run of transactions are reported to the process report file. This is a handy way to see what is processing in near real time when someone asks about information related to processing.

LAG Command

The LAG command is a simple command to help you see what the lag is for the process that it is run against. It is important to understand what LAG means, depending on the process that it is running against.

Lag against the extract is defined as the difference in seconds between the time that the record was processed by the extract and the timestamp of the record in the data source. Lag against the replicat is defined as the difference in seconds between the time the last record was processed and the timestamp recorded in the trail file.

By using the LAG command, you can see how much lag there is depending on the process you are looking at. Listing 5-6 illustrates the LAG command against a replicat.

Listing 5-6. LAG Against a Replicat

```
GGSCI (wilma.acme.com as ggate@rcv12c) 50> lag replicat rgg12c

Sending GETLAG request to REPLICAT RGG12C ...
Last record lag 3 seconds.
```

In reviewing these simple command-line tools, you have gained the basics of being able to monitor Oracle GoldenGate from the GGSCI command-line interface. With any monitoring solution you might have to monitor Oracle GoldenGate, manual monitoring is by far less dynamic and more time consuming than any other. You might be asking yourself now, how can I build on to these commands to make monitoring easier?

That is a simple question to answer. Being that Oracle GoldenGate is mostly a command-line tool for replication, you can use scripts to monitor the environment in a more dynamic way. In many UNIX or Linux environments, you can write different types of scripts to meet your needs of administration. As for Windows environments, you can still do the same thing using DOS scripts or the new PowerShell interfaces. The fact of the matter is that Oracle GoldenGate monitoring can be scripted to make monitoring easier. The next section looks at how to monitor Oracle GoldenGate by using scripts to make administration easier.

Scripting Oracle GoldenGate

Although there is a lot of information that can be gained from the files you just reviewed and the commands that can be run from GGSCI, those items tend to require a lot of manual intervention with the environment. Like any good administrator, you should be trying to make your life easier by scripting out items in an automated fashion. Fortunately, Oracle GoldenGate easily lends itself to many different scripting languages.

By scripting out the commands used by Oracle GoldenGate, you can begin automating your interaction with GGSCI for such activities like startup, shutdown, failover, and information reporting on the processes. The simplest version of automating a GGSCI command is using an input file, as shown in Listing 5-7.

Listing 5-7. Input a Script to GGSCI

```
GGSCI < input_file
```

In Listing 5-7 shows that an input file is used and is passed to the GGSCI using the angle bracket. The input file is traditionally called an obey file. An obey file contains the commands that you wish to issue to the GGSCI. Having a series of obey files would help you speed up your interaction within the Oracle GoldenGate framework.

Although obey files are a great stepping stone to automating Oracle GoldenGate, there are still other ways to be more efficient with scripting. As mentioned earlier, just about any type of scripting language can be used to interact with Oracle GoldenGate. If you look at Listing 5-8, you can see that this script is a shell script and is used to get the information of the current Oracle GoldenGate environment.

Listing 5-8. Shell Script Example

```
#!/bin/sh
#
#Author: Bobby Curtis, Oracle ACE
#Copyright: 2013
#Title: info_all.sh
#

export ORACLE_SID=ora11g
export ORACLE_HOME=/opt/oracle/product/11.2.0.3.0/db_1
export ORACLE_BASE=/opt/oracle/product
export GGS_HOME=/opt/oracle/product/ggate
export PATH=$PATH:$HOME/bin:$ORACLE_HOME/bin:/usr/local/bin:/bin
export LD_LIBRARY_PATH=$ORACLE_HOME/lib

echo
echo "####################################################################"
echo `date +%d/%m/%Y\ %k:%M:%S`
echo
$GGS_HOME/ggsci <<EOF
info all
exit
EOF
```

In Listing 5-8, notice that the script has to have the environment set up before execution. This is accomplished by using a series of export commands to set the variables needed; this can be accomplished in many ways, and ideally you shouldn't hard-code this information into the script file. Then GGSCI can be run until end-of-file (EOF), in between issuing the INFO ALL command. When run against an active environment, the output would look exactly like the output if you call the command manually (Listing 5-9).

Listing 5-9. INFO ALL from Shell Script (Source System)

```
[oracle@fred Scripts]$ sh ./info_all.sh

##################################################################
14/09/2015 19:09:35

Oracle GoldenGate Command Interpreter for Oracle
Version 12.1.2.1.0 OGGCORE_12.1.2.1.0_PLATFORMS_140727.2135.1_FBO
Linux, x64, 64bit (optimized), Oracle 12c on Aug  7 2014 10:21:34
Operating system character set identified as UTF-8.

Copyright (C) 1995, 2014, Oracle and/or its affiliates. All rights reserved.

GGSCI (fred.acme.com) 1>
Program     Status      Group       Lag at Chkpt  Time Since Chkpt

MANAGER     RUNNING
JAGENT      RUNNING
EXTRACT     RUNNING     EGG12C      00:00:00      00:00:07
EXTRACT     RUNNING     PGG12C      00:00:00      00:00:09
```

Another example of getting the status or any other command with Oracle GoldenGate from the GGSCI prompt is using Perl. With Perl being a flexible scripting language, it can be used for many different purposes. In Listing 5-10, you can see that the Perl script is gathering information on all the statuses of the environment and then placing the status in a pipe (|) delimited format that can be used by other functions or programs.

■ **Note**   I have hard-coded the Oracle GoldenGate home in this example. You can customize these scripts to prevent the hard-coding and make things more flexible.

Listing 5-10. Perl Script for Gathering Environment Status

```
#!/usr/bin/perl -w
#
#
use strict;
use warnings;

#Static Variables
my $gghome = "/oracle/app/product/12.1.2/oggcore_1";

#Program
my @buf = `$gghome/ggsci << EOF
info all
EOF`;
```

```
foreach (@buf)
{
        if(/MANAGER/|||/JAGENT/|||/EXTRACT/|||/REPLICAT/)
    {
            no warnings 'uninitialized';
             chomp;
            my ($program, $status, $group, $lagatchkpt, $timesincechkpt) = split(" ");

            if ($group eq "")
            {
                    $group = $program;
            }

            if ($lagatchkpt eq "" || $timesincechkpt eq "")
            {
                    $lagatchkpt = "00:00:00";
                    $timesincechkpt = "00:00:00";
            }

            my ($hours, $minutes, $seconds) = split (/:/, $lagatchkpt);
            $lagatchkpt = ($hours*60*60)+($minutes*60)+($seconds);

            ($hours, $minutes, $seconds) = split (/:/, $timesincechkpt);
            $timesincechkpt = ($hours*60*60)+($minutes*60)+($seconds);

            print "$program|$status|$group|$lagatchkpt|$timesincechkpt\n";
    }
}
```

This script gathers all the information for the environment in memory and then calculates the lag times into whole numbers for easier reading. The benefit of this script is that now the output in Listing 5-11 can be used by other monitoring tools, such as Oracle Enterprise Manager, to provide updates on the status of Oracle GoldenGate processes.

Listing 5-11. Output from Perl Script

```
[oracle@fred Scripts]$ perl ./gg_metric_ext_am.pl
MANAGER|RUNNING|MANAGER|0|0
JAGENT|RUNNING|JAGENT|0|0
EXTRACT|RUNNING|EGG12C|0|2
EXTRACT|RUNNING|PGG12C|0|3
```

■ **Note**   The Perl script in Listing 5-10 can be used against many different monitoring tools, especially with Oracle Enterprise Manager in metric extensions.

With the scripts displayed in the examples you should see how easy it is to create scripts that can be used either as jobs or for general purposes to provide information on your Oracle GoldenGate environment, in the end freeing you up from manually executing commands from the command line. These approaches are a good start to automating your monitoring of Oracle GoldenGate; however, you can take it a step further and use a graphical interface to monitor the environment.

Graphical Tools for Monitoring

When you want to get down to monitoring Oracle GoldenGate with a graphical tool, there are two choices that Oracle provides. The first is the Oracle GoldenGate Monitor and the second is Oracle Enterprise Manager. You might be asking why Oracle has two graphical monitoring tools to do the same job. The short answer is because they can.

The much longer answer is that Oracle GoldenGate Monitor was the primary monitoring tool for GoldenGate prior to Oracle acquiring the technology. Oracle later started to build a plug-in for Oracle GoldenGate to be used with Oracle Enterprise Manager 12c. With the current direction of Oracle GoldenGate, the monitoring is becoming increasingly done by Oracle Enterprise Manager.

■ **Note** Both Oracle GoldenGate Monitor and Oracle GoldenGate plug-in are paid options for monitoring Oracle GoldenGate.

GoldenGate Management Agent

Before anything in the Oracle GoldenGate environment can be monitored, there is a requirement to have a management agent. This agent is a Java-based agent that uses Java Messaging Exchange (JMX) to communicate with other Oracle products.When enabled in the Oracle GoldenGate environment, this agent is seen and labeled as JAgent.

Before the JAgent can be used, it has to be installed and enabled within the environment. Once enabled, the JAgent will communicate with other products using ports 5555 (JMX) and 5550 (Remote Method Invocation [RMI]). To enable the JAgent, the ENABLEMONITORING parameter has to be placed inside of the GLOBALS file that is located in the Oracle GoldenGate Home directory.

■ **Note** Although the ENABLEMONITORING parameter will turn on the JAgent within the Oracle GoldenGate code, it will not work with Oracle GoldenGate 12c. To use the JAgent correctly with Oracle GoldenGate 12c, the JAgent has to be installed using the latest release of the JAgent that is downloaded with the 12.1.3.0 version of the Management Pack for Oracle GoldenGate.

After enabling the Oracle GoldenGate JAgent, it can be seen in the GGSCI environment by issuing an INFO ALL command (Listing 5-12).

Listing 5-12. Listing JAgent

```
GGSCI (fred.acme.com) 1> info all
Program     Status      Group       Lag at Chkpt  Time Since Chkpt

MANAGER     RUNNING
JAGENT      RUNNING
```

Notice in the output that the JAgent doesn't have lag information or a group name. This is due to the JAgent being similar to the manager process. The only reason to run a JAgent is to enable monitoring for the environment.

Oracle Enterprise Manager

With the JAgent installed, this opens up the opportunity to monitor an Oracle GoldenGate environment with Oracle Enterprise Manager 12c (OEM). OEM is the monitoring tool of choice for many organizations running Oracle due to OEM's ability to monitor the entire Oracle enterprise stack of hardware and software. This is accomplished using monitoring agents with plug-ins for various products. Oracle GoldenGate is one such product that has a plug-in that is used with OEM.

■ **Note**   The Management Pack for Oracle GoldenGate is required to monitor Oracle GoldenGate within OEM.

Oracle GoldenGate Plug-In

The Oracle GoldenGate plug-in is currently bundled with the Oracle GoldenGate Monitoring Management Pack that Oracle provides for monitoring Oracle GoldenGate. This management pack includes other monitoring tools, such as Oracle GoldenGate Monitor; however, the Oracle GoldenGate plug-in is the best option for monitoring Oracle GoldenGate.

To download the Oracle GoldenGate plug-in, you need to use the same process that is used for any other plug-in in the OEM framework. This consists of going through the Self Update options and downloading any new plug-ins that are available.

■ **Note**   This process, Setup ➤ Extensibility ➤ Self Update ➤ Check for Updates, will update everything in the software library. Once complete, you can locate the new plug-in under Setup ➤ Extensibility ➤ Plug-ins.

After the plug-in has been downloaded and applied to the software library within OEM (Figure 5-1), you can push the plug-in to the Oracle Management Server (OMS) and then out to the agents on the monitored hosts. Keep in mind that the management server will need to be restarted for the plug-in to take effect.

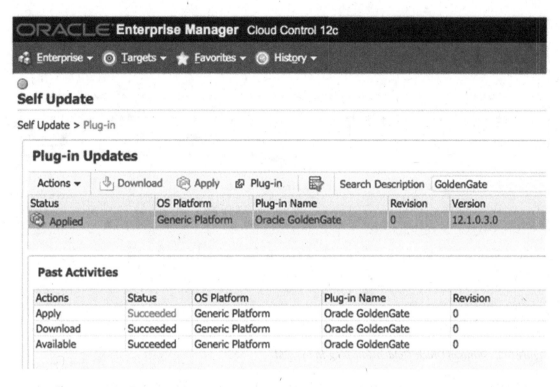

Figure 5-1. *Plug-in information*

After deploying the plug-in to the OMS, you can verify that everything is successful and the plug-in is applied by reviewing the plug-ins under the Setup menu. Figure 5-2 shows the plug-in as deployed on the OMS and to two agents where Oracle GoldenGate is running.

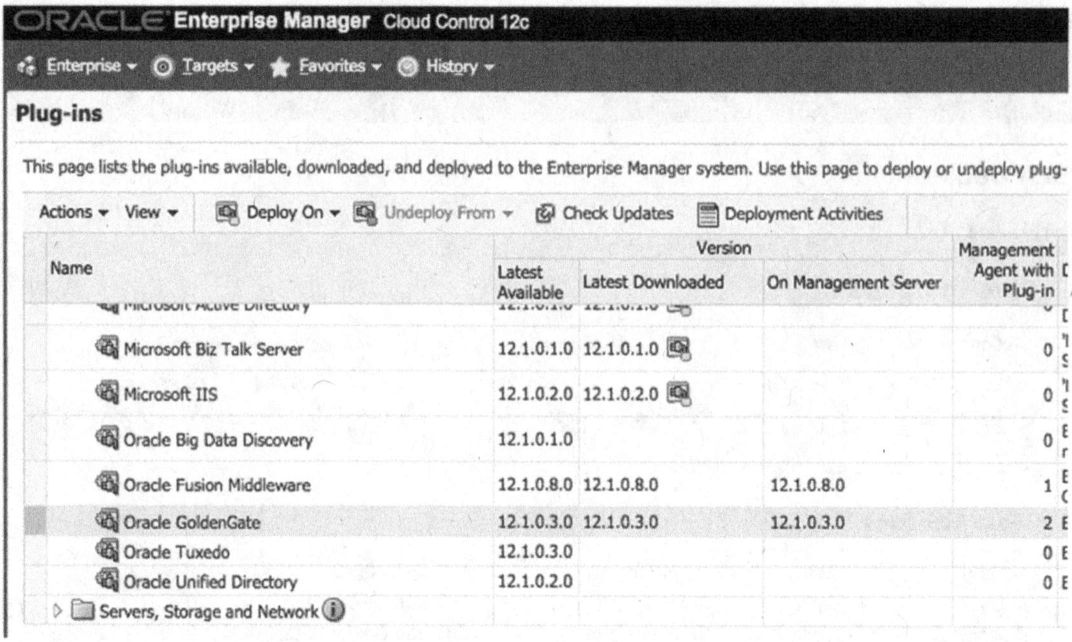

Figure 5-2. *Status of Oracle GoldenGate plug-in in OEM*

With the plug-in deployed on the OMS and to the management agents on the hosts where Oracle GoldenGate is running, you will be able to monitor Oracle GoldenGate with OEM. Even though the plug-in is deployed, there are still some additional steps that have to be configured before Oracle GoldenGate is ready to be monitored.

Oracle Java Agent (JAgent)

The Oracle GoldenGate Management Agent, the JAgent, is a Java-based agent that Oracle GoldenGate uses to communicate with monitoring tools. This agent is installed by default with the Oracle GoldenGate binaries, but it is hidden until it is activated through the GLOBALS file that is found in the Oracle GoldenGate Home directory.

There are two forms of the JAgent that can be used with Oracle GoldenGate. The first option is the JAgent that is installed with the Oracle GoldenGate binaries. Depending on the version of Oracle GoldenGate you are using, this JAgent will only work with the Oracle GoldenGate plug-in 12.1.0.1. Using this version of the JAgent will prevent you from enabling all the advanced features of the plug-in.

To get around this limitation, Oracle has published newer plug-ins for Oracle GoldenGate monitoring. These new plug-ins are release numbers 12.1.0.2 and 12.1.0.3. Both of these plug-ins are huge improvements over the 12.1.0.1 release. The only downside to these plug-ins is that they require a different, stand-alone JAgent, version 12.1.3.0. To get the new JAgent, you will need to download Oracle Data Integrator 12.1.3.0 binaries and install it from that binary set. The improvements in the plug-in are well worth having to download the new JAgent!

■ **Note** The new JAgent software can be downloaded from `http://www.oracle.com/technetwork/ middleware/data-integrator/downloads/index.html`

Functionality of the JAgent

At this point, if you know anything about OEM and the associated plug-ins, you might be asking why you need the JAgent to enable monitoring. In short, the JAgent is a leftover from other GoldenGate monitoring tools. The JAgent provides for communication between the OEM Agent and the Oracle GoldenGate environment. This is done by using JMX on Port 5555 and Java RMI on Port 5559. These two protocols allow for the JAgent to send near real-time updates of the Oracle GoldenGate environment to OEM through the associated management agent. Figure 5-3 illustrates the basic concept of what the JAgent is doing.

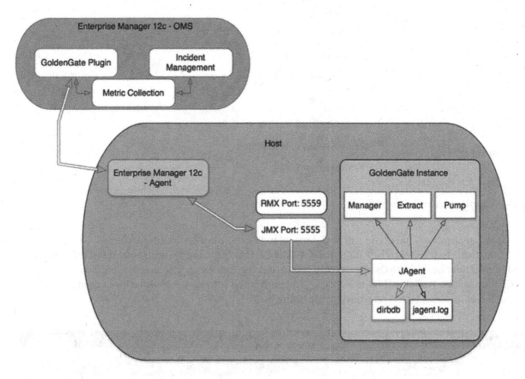

Figure 5-3. *JAgent communication with OEM*

As you can tell from Figure 5-3, the JAgent and the OEM Agent both are configured on the managed host. The OEM Agent is the only agent responsible for talking to the OMS and reporting on interactions with Oracle GoldenGate. The JAgent's whole process is to capture the data and metrics related to Oracle GoldenGate. Without the JAgent, monitoring with OEM will not be possible.

Configure Oracle GoldenGate Plug-In Within Oracle Enterprise Manager

With the Oracle GoldenGate plug-in installed on the OMS and the Oracle Management Agents, along with the JAgent installed and running on the host, you need to tell OEM how to communicate with both agents. To do this, you need to set up OEM to discover Oracle GoldenGate processes.

To discover Oracle GoldenGate processes from within OEM, you need to configure the Auto Discovery settings within OEM (Figure 5-4). This is done by following Setup ➤ Add Target ➤ Configure Auto Discovery.

Figure 5-4. *Configure Auto Discovery*

On the Setup Discovery page, you will find three tabs. The middle tab should be selected, which displays all the hosts that are currently monitored within the Oracle GoldenGate environment. From here, you need to select the host where Oracle GoldenGate is running. Once that is selected, the Discovery Modules button will be available (Figure 5-5). Clicking this button provides you with a list of modules that can be enabled or disabled based on what you are trying to do.

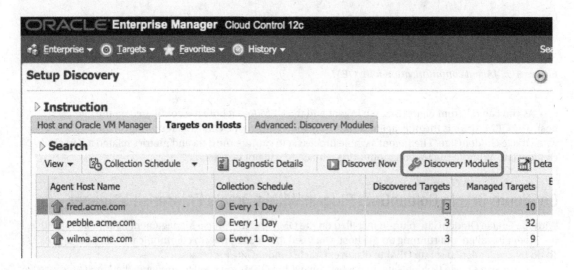

Figure 5-5. *Discovery Module button*

On the Discovery Modules page for the host you selected (Figure 5-6), you will see a list of modules that can be enabled or disabled by clearing the Enabled check box. These modules are driven by the plug-ins that are enabled on the host being monitored.

ORACLE **Enterprise Manager** Cloud Control 12c

Discovery Modules : fred.acme.com

Configure discovery modules and parameters on this host.

View ▼   ✎ Edit Parameters

Discovery Module	Enabled	Target Types	Discovery Parameters
GoldenGateDiscovery	☑	Oracle GoldenGate, Oracle GoldenGate Extract, Oracle ...	JAgent User Name=root, :
Oracle Cluster and High Availability Service	☑	Cluster, Oracle High Availability Service	
Oracle Database, Listener and Automatic Storage Mana...	☑	Database Instance, Listener, Pluggable Database	Enter Clusterware Home=
Oracle Fusion Middleware	☑	Oracle WebLogic Domain	Enter value of Middleware
Oracle Home Discovery	☑	Oracle Home	
Oracle Secure Backup Domain	☑	Oracle Secure Backup Domain	

Figure 5-6. *Discovery Modules page*

If you look closely at the discovery module for Oracle GoldenGate, you will see a column for Discovery Parameters. By highlighting the GoldenGateDiscovery module and clicking Edit Parameters, you will be able to edit the associated parameters to talk with the JAgent (Figure 5-7).

Edit Parameters: GoldenGateDiscovery   ✕

* JAgent User Name	root
* JAgent Password	
* JAgent RMI Port	5559
* Jagent Host Name	fred.acme.com

OK   Cancel

Figure 5-7. *Parameters to work with JAgent*

In the edit parameters for GoldenGateDiscovery, you will need to provide the username that the JAgent will use, the password associated with the user account, the port that the RMI will communicate on, and the host that is running Oracle GoldenGate. Much of this is filled in for you, but you need to confirm the information is correct and provide the valid password.

■ **Note**   These settings have to be configured at the host level for the JAgent first. The file where this has to be edited is in the $JAGENT_HOME/cfg/Config.properties file.

After providing the parameters to communicate with the JAgent, you have two options for discovery from the Setup Discovery page. You can either force a discovery by running the Discovery Now option or you can wait 24 hours to see if the Oracle GoldenGate processes are discovered.

Once the Oracle GoldenGate processes are discovered, they will appear in the Auto Discovery Results under Setup ➤ Add Target menu. From here, the Oracle GoldenGate processes can be promoted and monitored with OEM.

Monitoring Oracle GoldenGate

With the Oracle GoldenGate processes discovered within OEM, you can now monitor and manage each of the processes. Figure 5-8 shows all the processes that are currently being monitored. On this page, you can clearly see what is going on within the Oracle GoldenGate environment. All the metrics that you would normally get form the command line using GGSCI, you can quickly see here and diagnose if there is an issue.

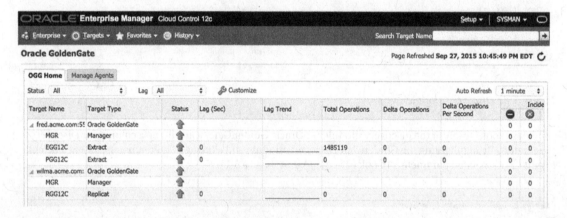

Figure 5-8. *Oracle GoldenGate processes being monitored*

■ **Note**   Before you can interact with any of the Oracle GoldenGate processes, you will need to set up Preferred Credentials for each of the processes under Setup ➤ Security ➤ Preferred Credentials.

Besides being able to quickly see what is going on with the Oracle GoldenGate environment, you have the ability to drill down into any one of the processes being monitored and look at a wide range of items for each process.

Starting and Stopping Oracle GoldenGate Processes

From the Oracle GoldenGate home page within OEM, you can easily stop and start any of the Oracle GoldenGate processes. This is done by highlighting one of the processes. Once a process is highlighted, a series of buttons appears at the top of the screen (Figure 5-9). These buttons represent the commands to start, stop, and kill a GoldenGate process.

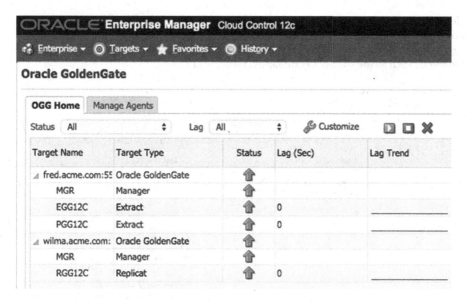

Figure 5-9. *Start, Stop, and Kill buttons*

These buttons are seen on any page that you have access to while interacting with the Oracle GoldenGate process. As noted earlier, these buttons will only appear if you have permissions on the target process and preferred credentials have been configured.

Drilling Down Into an Oracle GoldenGate Process

The real benefit of the Oracle GoldenGate plug-in comes with the ability to drill directly down into the process that is running. By drilling down into the process, you can get a more detailed view of what the Oracle GoldenGate process is doing, take a look at the logs associated with the process, and review the configuration of the processes. Figure 5-10 illustrates part of this drill-down process.

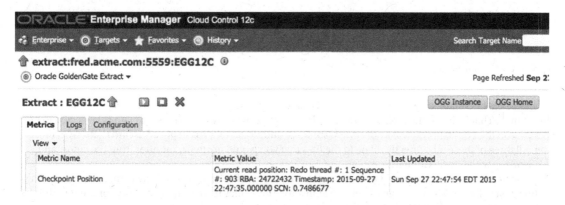

Figure 5-10. *Drilling down into an Oracle GoldenGate process*

97

As you can tell from Figure 5-10, once you drill down into the process, there are three tables that provide access to various information related to the process. The first tab is about metrics. This tab provides a wide range of details related to the process. These metrics provide similar information to that you would normally gain from GGSCI commands such as the statistics commands (Figure 5-11).

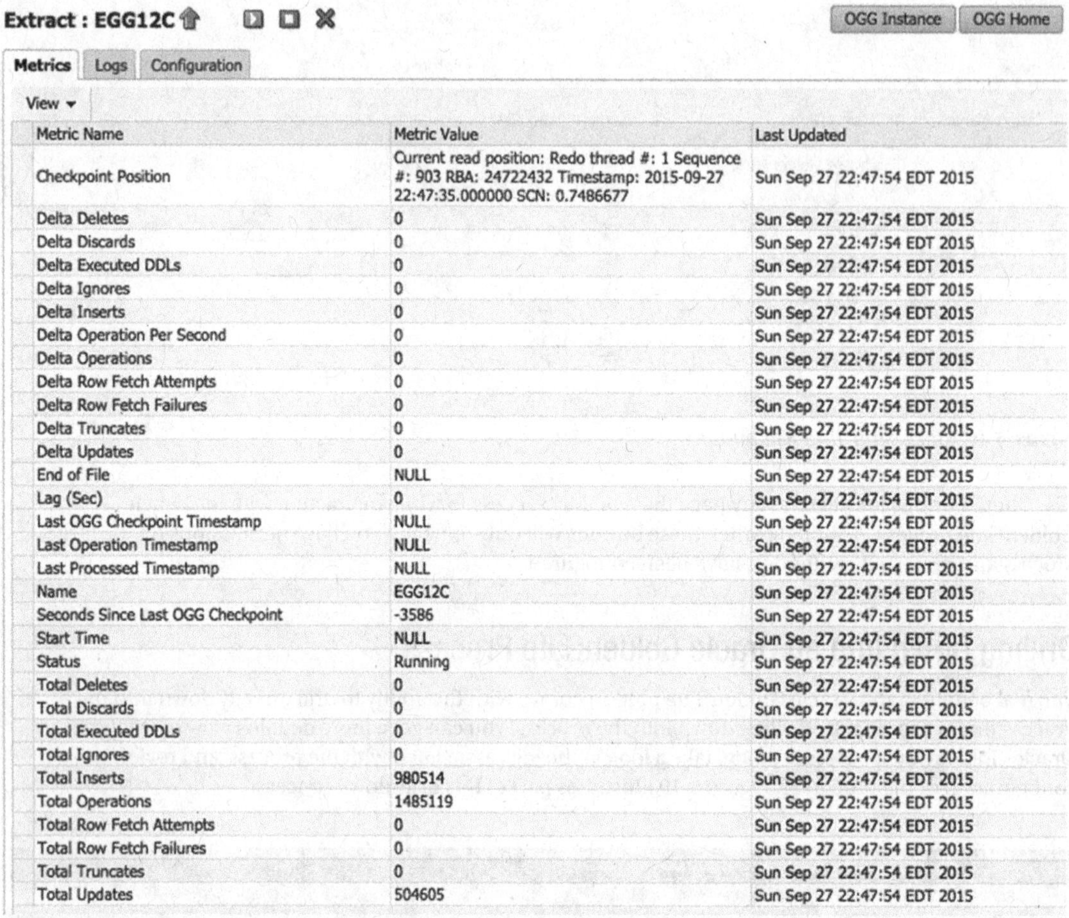

Extract : EGG12C ⬆   ▷ ▢ ✖   OGG Instance   OGG Home

Metrics Logs Configuration

View ▾

Metric Name	Metric Value	Last Updated
Checkpoint Position	Current read position: Redo thread #: 1 Sequence #: 903 RBA: 24722432 Timestamp: 2015-09-27 22:47:35.000000 SCN: 0.7486677	Sun Sep 27 22:47:54 EDT 2015
Delta Deletes	0	Sun Sep 27 22:47:54 EDT 2015
Delta Discards	0	Sun Sep 27 22:47:54 EDT 2015
Delta Executed DDLs	0	Sun Sep 27 22:47:54 EDT 2015
Delta Ignores	0	Sun Sep 27 22:47:54 EDT 2015
Delta Inserts	0	Sun Sep 27 22:47:54 EDT 2015
Delta Operation Per Second	0	Sun Sep 27 22:47:54 EDT 2015
Delta Operations	0	Sun Sep 27 22:47:54 EDT 2015
Delta Row Fetch Attempts	0	Sun Sep 27 22:47:54 EDT 2015
Delta Row Fetch Failures	0	Sun Sep 27 22:47:54 EDT 2015
Delta Truncates	0	Sun Sep 27 22:47:54 EDT 2015
Delta Updates	0	Sun Sep 27 22:47:54 EDT 2015
End of File	NULL	Sun Sep 27 22:47:54 EDT 2015
Lag (Sec)	0	Sun Sep 27 22:47:54 EDT 2015
Last OGG Checkpoint Timestamp	NULL	Sun Sep 27 22:47:54 EDT 2015
Last Operation Timestamp	NULL	Sun Sep 27 22:47:54 EDT 2015
Last Processed Timestamp	NULL	Sun Sep 27 22:47:54 EDT 2015
Name	EGG12C	Sun Sep 27 22:47:54 EDT 2015
Seconds Since Last OGG Checkpoint	-3586	Sun Sep 27 22:47:54 EDT 2015
Start Time	NULL	Sun Sep 27 22:47:54 EDT 2015
Status	Running	Sun Sep 27 22:47:54 EDT 2015
Total Deletes	0	Sun Sep 27 22:47:54 EDT 2015
Total Discards	0	Sun Sep 27 22:47:54 EDT 2015
Total Executed DDLs	0	Sun Sep 27 22:47:54 EDT 2015
Total Ignores	0	Sun Sep 27 22:47:54 EDT 2015
Total Inserts	980514	Sun Sep 27 22:47:54 EDT 2015
Total Operations	1485119	Sun Sep 27 22:47:54 EDT 2015
Total Row Fetch Attempts	0	Sun Sep 27 22:47:54 EDT 2015
Total Row Fetch Failures	0	Sun Sep 27 22:47:54 EDT 2015
Total Truncates	0	Sun Sep 27 22:47:54 EDT 2015
Total Updates	504605	Sun Sep 27 22:47:54 EDT 2015

Figure 5-11. *Metrics tab*

The next tab on the page is the Logs tab. This tab relies heavily on the JMX and RMI discussed earlier in the chapter. That is due to the direct interaction that the plug-in has with the files that you have access to on this tab. On the Logs tab, you will notice there are three additional tabs for Report, Discards, and GGS Error Log. All three of these tabs directly relate to the files that you would normally monitor from the command line working with Oracle GoldenGate.

The Report and Discards tabs provide access to the current file being used along with the ten previously archived files (Figure 5-12). This gives you the ability to browse files in an easy-to-use environment without having to go to the command line.

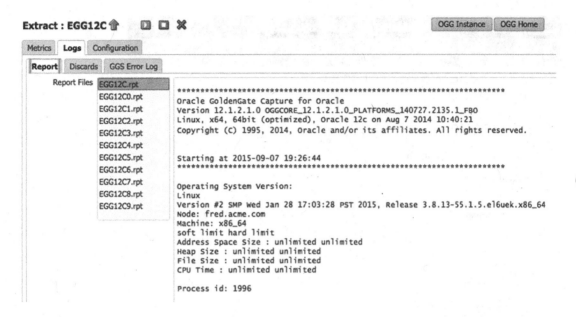

Figure 5-12. *Report tab*

The last of the subtabs provides access to the GoldenGate Service error log (GGSERR.log). Again, this tab provides the same benefits as the Report and Discards tabs. The additional benefit this tab provides is that you can download GGSERR.log if needed (bottom of screen). Figure 5-13 provides a look at the tab within OEM.

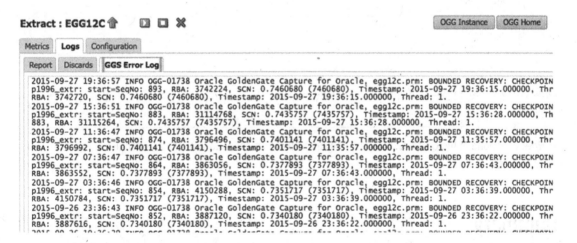

Figure 5-13. *GGS Error Log tab*

The last main tab under any of the processes is the Configuration tab. This tab provides you with access to view and edit the currently running process parameter file. Although this is simple to understand, it is a great feature along with the other features, because any changes that need to be made to a running process can be done from within OEM very quickly and then restarted. Figure 5-14 provides a look at the Configuration tab for an Oracle GoldenGate process.

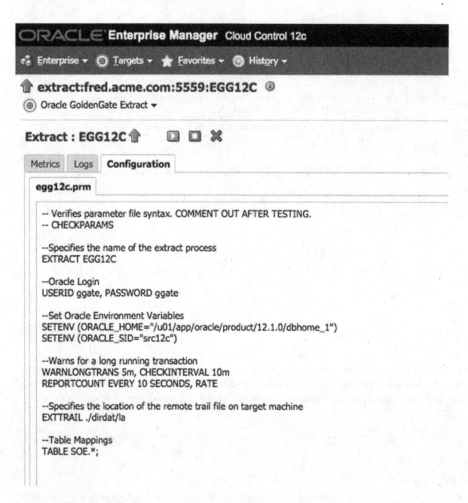

Figure 5-14. *Configuration tab for Oracle GoldenGate process*

■ **Note**   In none of the Oracle GoldenGate plug-ins is there an option to view the architecture of an environment.

Summary

This chapter has taken a look at how to monitor Oracle GoldenGate from a few different perspectives. By starting at the command line, you reviewed what files needed to be involved in your monitoring approaches. Then you looked how these files and processes can be monitored very quickly by using scripting to achieve a more automated type of monitoring. Finally, you reviewed the key areas of the Oracle GoldenGate plug-in that is used with OEM for monitoring in a graphical environment. No matter which approach you take for monitoring your Oracle GoldenGate environment, you should be able to identify a quick and easy method for monitoring using what has been discussed in this chapter. The next chapter builds on these monitoring options and looks at how the data being replicated can be validated from both a graphical and SQL approach.

CHAPTER 6

■ ■ ■

Data Verification

by Shane Borden

This chapter discusses the options for verification of data replicated by Oracle GoldenGate. We discuss how to install Veridata and create and execute comparison jobs using Veridata. Should you not own a license for the Veridata product, we discuss other options for data verification that could be as simple as a row count comparison or the execution of the DBMS_COMPARE package that is part of the database.

Veridata consists of several components. An application server (Veridata server) and an agent (Veridata agent) are installed on each database host to be compared. In addition, a database to create a very small schema is needed for the Veridata repository.

For the demonstration outlined in this chapter, the server topology will consist of the following:

- veridata.localdomain (application server)
    - Java Development Kit (JDK) 8
    - Oracle Fusion Middleware Infrastructure 12c (12.2.1.0)
    - Veridata Application Server 12c (12.2.1.0)
- orcl-vbox1.localdomain (source database)
    - JDK 8
    - Veridata Agent 12c (12.2.1.0)
    - Veridata Application Server Repository
- orcl-vbox2.localdomain (target database)
    - JDK 8
    - Veridata Agent 12c

The Veridata application server can be installed onto the same host as the database host, but for best performance, the application server should be installed on a separate host. Similarly, the Veridata agent could be colocated with the Veridata server, but best practice dictates that the Veridata agent should be installed as close to the database as possible to minimize network traffic.

© Bobby Curtis 2016
B. Curtis, *Pro Oracle GoldenGate for the DBA*, DOI 10.1007/978-1-4842-1179-3_6

Obtain Software

All software can be obtained from Oracle E-Delivery or via the Oracle Technology Network (OTN). This chapter discusses installation on Linux. If you are not installing on Linux, be sure to obtain the proper download for your operating system.

Oracle Fusion Middleware Infrastructure

This software is needed to run the Oracle GoldenGate Veridata Server. You can obtain the software under the Oracle ADF Downloads geading. Choose version 12.2.1.0 from http://www.oracle.com/technetwork/developer-tools/adf/downloads/index.html.

For this demonstration, it is important that you download the following version of the infrastructure, as there are many to choose from:

fmw_12.2.1.0.0_infrastructure_Disk1_1of1.zip

Oracle Java JDK 8

This software is needed to install and run the Veridata server, agent, and Fusion Middleware Infrastructure. You can obtain the software from http://www.oracle.com/technetwork/java/javase/downloads/jdk8-downloads-2133151.html.

For this demonstration, it is important that you download the following version file. Again, there are many versions to choose from: jdk-8u74-linux-x64.tar.gz

Oracle GoldenGate Veridata Server 12c/Veridata Agent 12c

This is the application software itself. This software performs the comparisons of data between two schemas. This software is obtained from http://www.oracle.com/technetwork/middleware/goldengate/downloads/index.html.

This demonstration requires fmw_12.2.1.0.0_ogg.jar. Be sure to download the correct version, as there are many to choose from.

After obtaining all of the required software, stage the files within /tmp on each host. Instructions on how to install the software follow later in in the chapter.

WebLogic and Veridata Server Basic Requirements

To install Veridata Server, you must first install the WebLogic Infrastructure Server. There are minimum server requirements for WebLogic and for the purposes of this installation demonstration, assume the following minimum requirements:

- 4 GB physical memory

- 4 GB swap configured

- JDK 1.8 or higher

- 3 GB disk space required for WebLogic

- Minimum of 500 MB database space for repository creation

Keep in mind that Veridata does not perform any of the data comparisons within the database itself, so it is very important that you take into account the data you will actually compare when sizing your Veridata application server. The server itself requires approximately 200 MB of fixed memory above and beyond that memory that will be used for data comparisons. For data comparisons that require more memory than is available, there must also be adequate disk space for that comparison.

A basic sizing formula can be used:

((Number of columns in the key + 1) * 4) + 16 + (comparison width of key columns)

where comparison width of key columns must be matched to one of formats shown in Table 6-1.

Table 6-1. *Formats Per the Installation and Configuration Guide*

Comparison Format	Data Size
Numbers	1 byte for each significant digit. Leading zeros and trailing zeros after the decimal point (e.g., the rightmost zeros in 1234.500) are not counted.
Timestamp	19 to 32 bytes depending on the fractional precision.
Date	10 bytes.
Time	8 to 18 bytes depending on the fractional precision.
String	1 to 4 bytes per character for the UTF-8 encoding of the Java agent. The NonStop agent and the Oracle C agent use the database native character set.
Binary	The bytes as stored in the database.

Example for an In-Memory Sort

The number "0123456789" stored in the only key column and if compared per the decimal float comparison format, would require:

((1 + 1) * 4) + 16 + 9 = 33 bytes of memory for each row

Because there is a source and target row, you must multiply this size requirement by 2, thus requiring 66 bytes for each row in this example. If this table had 15 million rows and each key column was representative of this size, the entire comparison for this table would require approximately 2 GB (in-memory sort requires 2.5 times more memory than the base requirement) of memory to accomplish an in-memory sort comparison correctly.

The other available sort modes include one disk pass and two disk pass. Adequate disk space is required to ensure that the other sort modes can be accommodated for the data sets that you plan to compare. For this example, a one disk pass would require approximately 72 MB of disk space, whereas a two disk pass would require approximately 10 MB of space. Other sort modes might require fewer resources, but it comes with a sacrifice of performance, so keep that in mind.

Veridata Agent Basic Requirements

Veridata Agent must be installed for each database that you wish to compare. For this example, we need two complete installations of the agent: one to retrieve source rows and the other to retrieve rows from the target.

For most platforms, the Java agent will meet data comparison requirements. There are only a few situations in which a C agent is required. Because most cases can use the Java agent, this demonstration focuses on that installation type.

The following are the minimum requirements:

- JDK 1.8 or higher must be available.

- 1 GB of RAM.

- 200 MB of disk space.

Preparing the Linux Operating System for WebLogic Infrastructure

Now that we have determined the minimum server requirements, we are ready to proceed with the installation of the WebLogic Application Tier. To successfully install WebLogic you must ensure that certain kernel parameters meet the minimum requirements before executing the OUI. At a minimum, you should set the kernel.shmmax value to the amount of memory present on the host. If the current value is larger, use the larger value:

```
kernel.shmmax = 4294967295
```

If necessary, update the kernel by executing the following command:

```
[root@veridata ~]# /sbin/sysctl -p
```

Creating WebLogic User and Groups

There are various user combinations that you can use to install the Veridata Application Server, but for most installations, using a standard user such as oracle will suffice. If the user does not currently exist, you can create the user with the following steps. The last step will prompt you to enter the password for the oracle user. Choose a password that is appropriate for your environment and record it for future reference. As the root user:

```
[root@veridata ~]# groupadd oinstall
[root@veridata ~]# useradd -g oinstall oracle
[root@veridata ~]# passwd oracle
```

Creating WebLogic Directory Structure

WebLogic and the applications that run via the WebLogic Server should be installed using a specific directory structure. The directory tree contains three sections:

- *Oracle Home:* Contains WebLogic binary files created during the installation process. Runtime processes will not write to this location.

- *Domain Home:* Contains the WebLogic files necessary to for one or more WebLogic Server instances that you will manage with a single Administration Server. Typically this directory should be created outside of the Oracle Home to ease the WebLogic upgrade process.

- *Application Home:* Contains the specific application files that will be managed by a WebLogic Administration Server. Typically this directory should also be created outside of the Oracle Home to ease the WebLogic upgrade process. Because Veridata is an integrated product that utilizes the WebLogic infrastructure, this directory is not needed.

For installation of Veridata Application Server the following directories will be used:

- *Oracle Base:* /u01/app/oracle

- *Oracle Home:* /u01/app/oracle/product/wlserver/12.2.1.0

- *Domain Home:* /home/oracle/config/domains/oggVeridata

As the oracle user, once you have decided on the following directories, create them as follows:

```
[oracle@veridata ~]$ mkdir -p /u01/app/oracle/product/wlserver/12.2.1.0
[oracle@veridata ~]$ mkdir -p /home/oracle/config/domains/oggVeridata
```

Install the JDK for WebLogic Infrastructure

As mentioned earlier, JDK 1.8 is needed for WebLogic to install and function properly. Based on your installation requirements, your environment might require multiple versions of a JDK to be present, so it might be best to install the JDK outside the default Java that is installed on your system.

Before you install the JDK, create the directory where you want the software to reside. For this example we use /u01/app/oracle/product/jdk.

```
[oracle@veridata ~]$ mkdir -p /u01/app/oracle/product/jdk
```

Once the directory is created, un-tar the file that was downloaded from OTN and placed on the veridata.localdomain server to this location:

```
[oracle@veridata tmp]$ tar xvfz jdk-8u74-linux-x64.tar.gz -C /u01/app/oracle/product/jdk/
```

Take note of the installation location, as we will need this for creating a JAVA_HOME environment variable.

Set Up Environment Variables for WebLogic Infrastructure

To make the install process and the administration of the server easier, some standard environment variables should be set up. To do this, place the following into your .bash_profile or equivalent.

```
ORACLE_BASE=/u01/app/oracle; export ORACLE_BASE
ORACLE_HOME=$ORACLE_BASE/product/wlserver/12.2.1.0; export ORACLE_HOME
JAVA_HOME=/u01/app/oracle/product/jdk/jdk1.8.0_74; export JAVA_HOME
DOMAIN_HOME=/home/oracle/config/domains/oggVeridata; export DOMAIN_HOME
```

If modification of the profile is not easily done in your environment, an alternative is to create another file that contains the variables so that they can be sourced in on demand.

Install WebLogic Infrastructure

Now that the environment is set up with the prerequisites, we can now install WebLogic Infrastructure.

As the oracle user, first, unzip the file that was downloaded from OTN or E-Delivery:

```
[oracle@veridata tmp]$ unzip -d /tmp fmw_12.2.1.0.0_infrastructure_Disk1_1of1.zip
```

Once the file has been unzipped, proceed with the installation by invoking the OUI:

```
[oracle@veridata ~]$ /u01/app/oracle/product/jdk/jdk1.8.0_74/bin/java -jar /tmp/
fmw_12.2.1.0.0_infrastructure.jar
Launcher log file is /tmp/OraInstall2016-03-08_08-14-23PM/launcher2016-03-08_08-14-23PM.log.
Extracting files...........................
Starting Oracle Universal Installer

Checking if CPU speed is above 300 MHz.    Actual 2194.858 MHz     Passed
Checking monitor: must be configured to display at least 256 colors.    Actual
16777216    Passed
Checking swap space: must be greater than 512 MB.    Actual 3967 MB    Passed
Checking if this platform requires a 64-bit JVM.    Actual 64    Passed (64-bit not required)
Checking temp space: must be greater than 300 MB.    Actual 27816 MB    Passed
Preparing to launch the Oracle Universal Installer from /tmp/OraInstall2016-03-08_08-14-23PM
```

Once the OUI starts, it will ask you to define the Inventory Directory and Operating System Group as displayed in Figure 6-1 and Figure 6-2.

Figure 6-1. *Oracle Universal Installer*

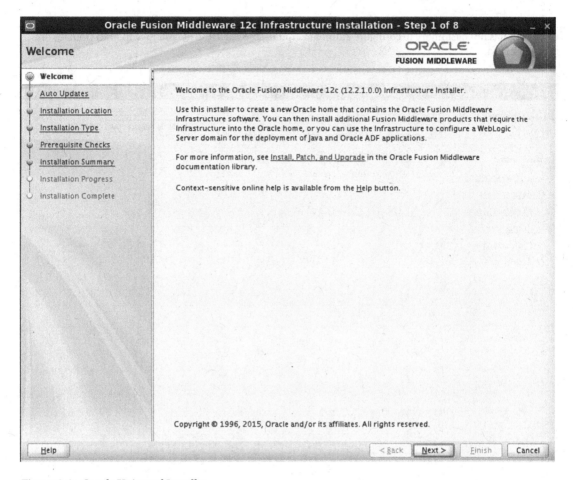

Figure 6-2. *Oracle Universal Installer*

You can accept the defaults and click OK.

The splash screen confirms the product and version that is being installed. There is no information to confirm or change on the screen shown in Figure 6-2, so click Next.

Next the OUI provides the ability to subscribe to automatic updates for this product (Figure 6-3). Generally, it is not customary to configure automatic updates, so leave the default to Skip Auto Updates and then click Next.

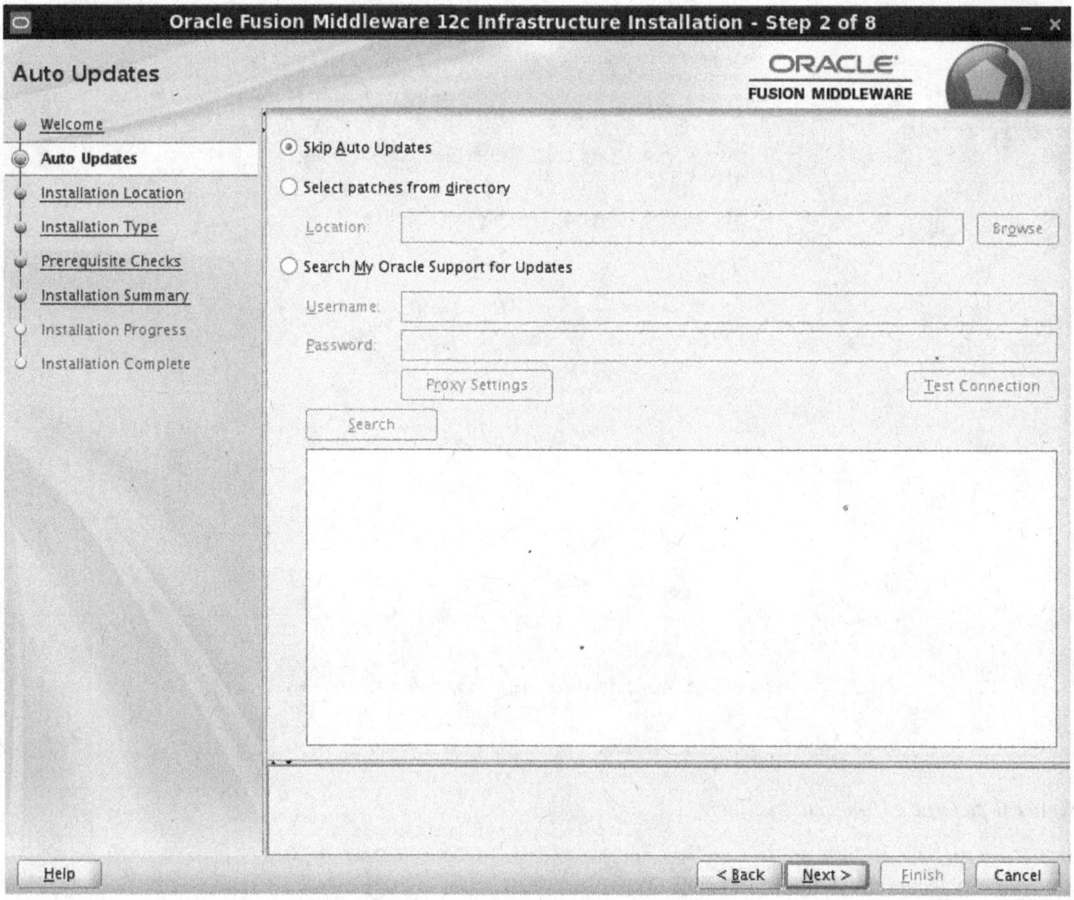

Figure 6-3. *Oracle Universal Installer*

In the next step, shown in Figure 6-4, update the Oracle Home location to the predetermined location as discussed earlier in this chapter. Once the information has been entered, click Next.

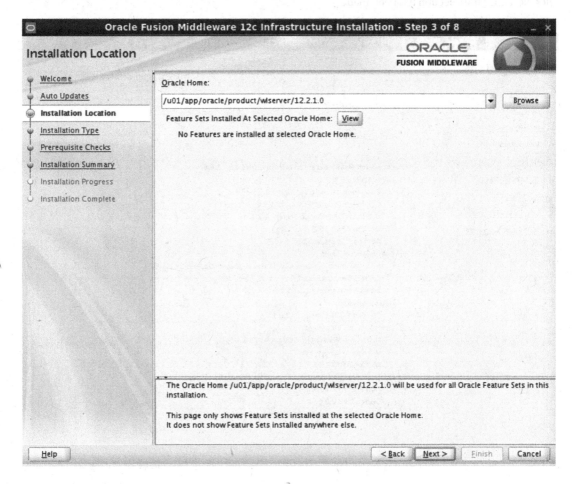

Figure 6-4. *Oracle Universal Installer*

The OUI now presents the option of what software should be installed (Figure 6-5). For this demonstration, there is no need to install Examples, so select the Fusion Middleware Infrastructure option. Click Next once the selection has been made.

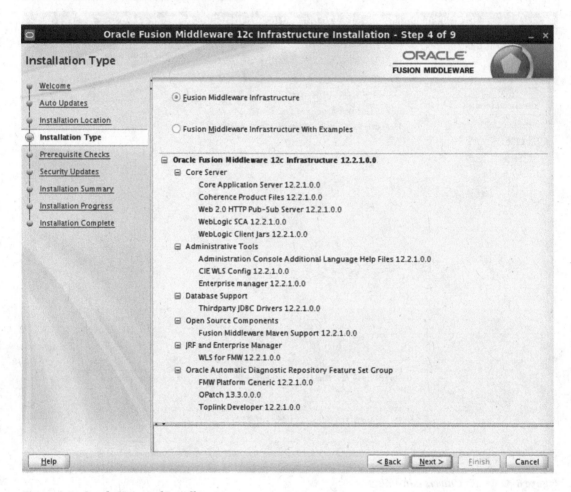

Figure 6-5. *Oracle Universal Installer*

At this point, the OUI will run a check to make sure that all prerequisites are met for the successful installation of this software. Should any prerequisite not pass the check, the OUI will present a notification and allow you to fix the error before proceeding, as illustrated in Figure 6-6. Once all checks are successful, click Next.

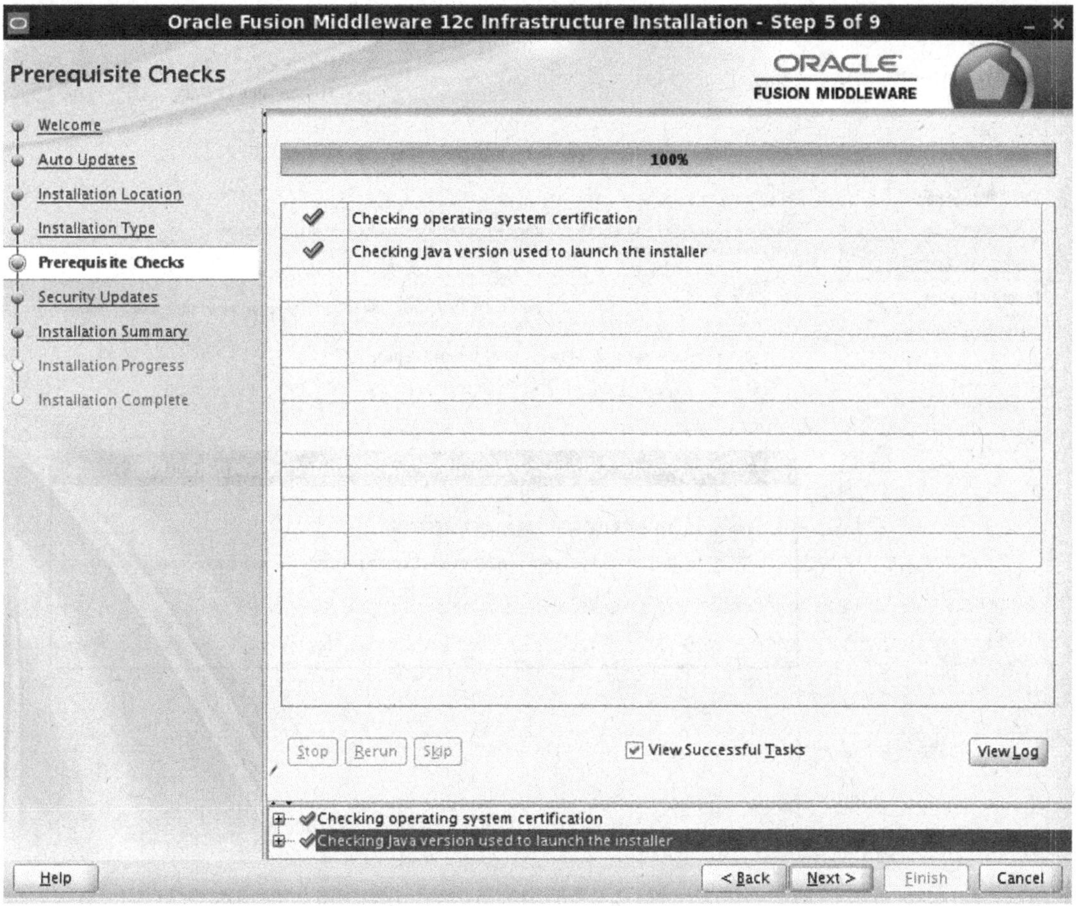

Figure 6-6. *Oracle Universal Installer*

Registration for Oracle Security Updates will then be presented by the OUI. Choose the option that is best suited for your installation. If you choose not to register, you will get a warning (Figure 6-7). Typically, it is also not customary to register for these updates at the individual product level. To proceed clear the check box, click Next, and acknowledge any warnings that might occur.

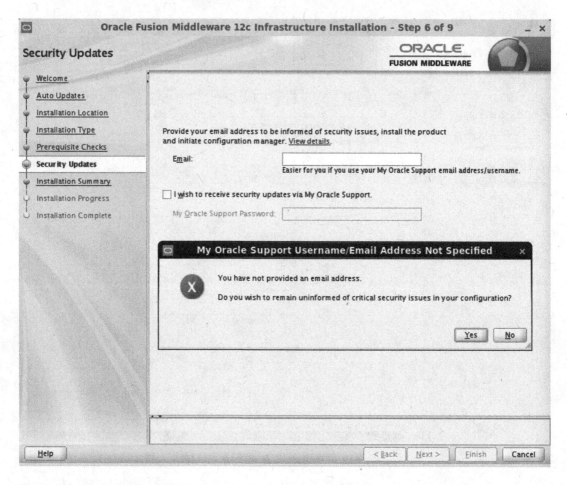

Figure 6-7. *Oracle Universal Installer*

A summary of the installation options is then presented by the OUI (Figure 6-8). If you need to do a rapid deployment at a later date, you can save a response file at this time. This response file can be used as input to the OUI to complete a "silent" installation should one need to occur in the future. Once you are satisfied with your options, click Install.

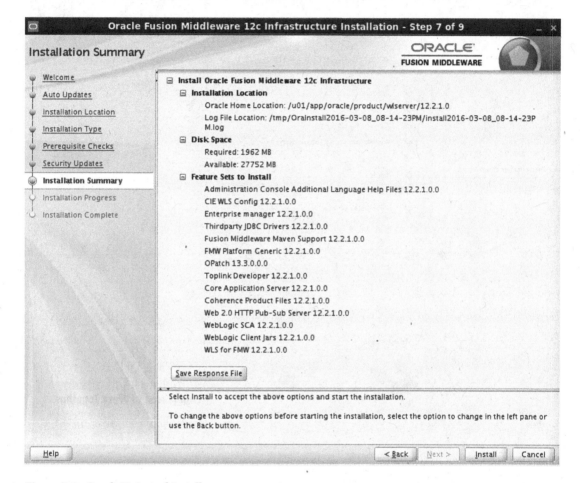

Figure 6-8. *Oracle Universal Installer*

A progress screen, similar to the one presented in Figure 6-9, will then be presented, providing updates for the individual steps of the installation. Once the installation is completed, you click Next.

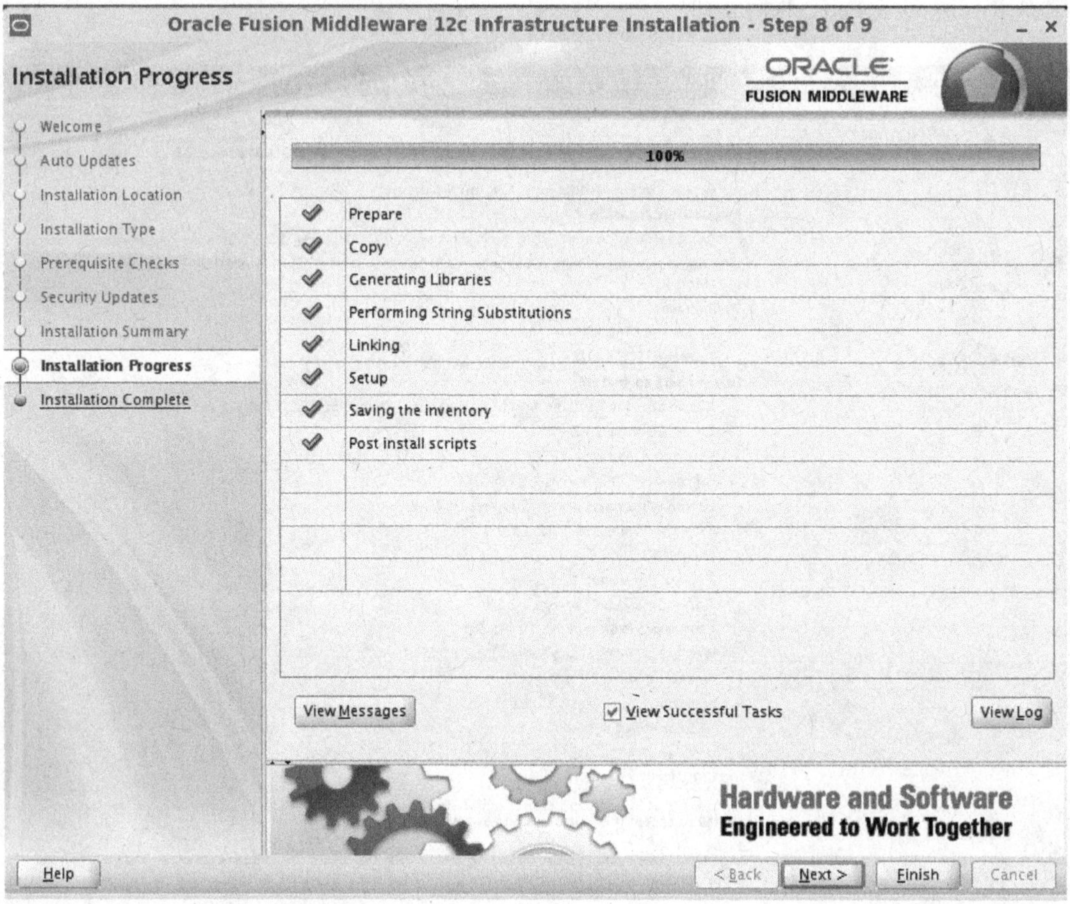

Figure 6-9. *Oracle Universal Installer*

The last screen (Figure 6-10) will be a summary of what was just installed. Make sure to take note of any pertinent information such as the ORACLE_HOME and log file location. At this time you can click Finish. The OUI for the WebLogic Infrastructure installation is now complete.

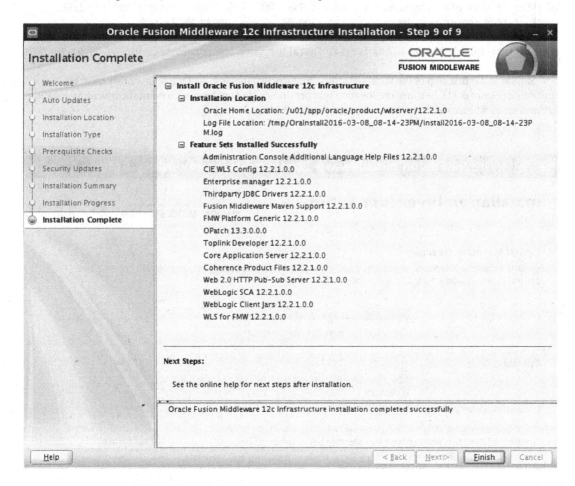

Figure 6-10. *Oracle Universal Installer*

Installing Oracle Veridata Server

Once WebLogic has been installed, then the Oracle Veridata Server can be installed. As the oracle user, you can start the installation program by locating the installation media (which was previously deployed in the temporary location you chose earlier). Invoke the OUI by executing the following command:

```
[oracle@veridata ~]$ /u01/app/oracle/product/jdk/jdk1.8.0_74/bin/java -jar /tmp/
fmw_12.2.1.0.0_ogg.jar

Extracting files.......
Starting Oracle Universal Installer
```

```
Checking if CPU speed is above 300 MHz. Actual 2194.858 MHz Passed
Checking monitor: must be configured to display at least 256 colors. Actual 16777216 Passed
Checking swap space: must be greater than 512 MB. Actual 3967 MB Passed
Checking if this platform requires a 64-bit JVM. Actual 64 Passed (64-bit not required)
Checking temp space: must be greater than 300 MB. Actual 30748 MB Passed

Preparing to launch the Oracle Universal Installer from /tmp/OraInstall2016-03-08_07-20-18PM
```

Similar to the first step of the WebLogic Infrastructure installation, the Oracle Inventory must be confirmed (Figure 6-11). Because the location was previously chosen, be sure to point the inventory location to the same location used in the prior step and then click Next.

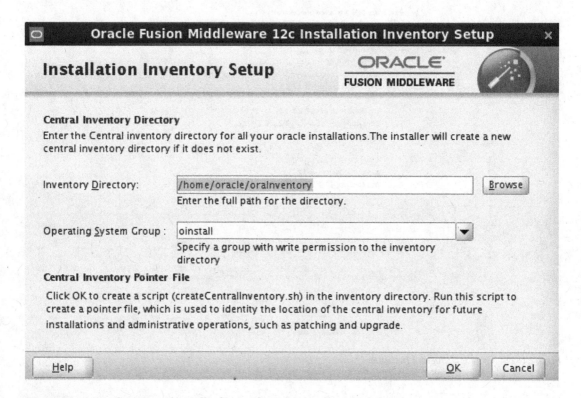

Figure 6-11. *Oracle Universal Installer for Oracle Veridata*

The splash screen shown in Figure 6-12 confirms the product and version that is being installed. There is no information to confirm or change on this screen, so click Next.

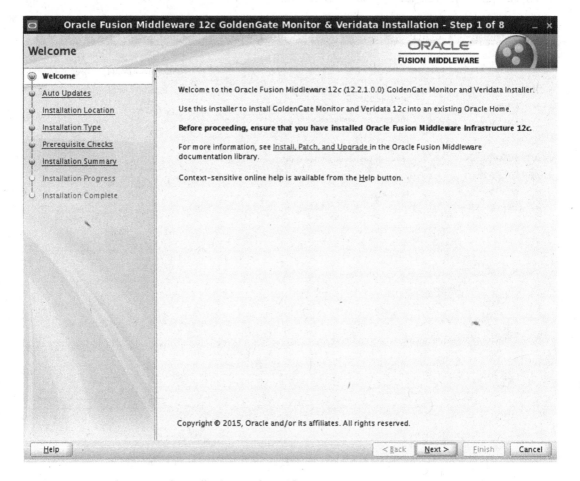

Figure 6-12. *Oracle Universal Installer for Oracle Veridata*

On the following screen, the OUI provides the ability to subscribe to automatic updates for this product (Figure 6-13). Generally, it is not customary to configure automatic updates. Leave the default set to Skip Auto Updates and then click Next.

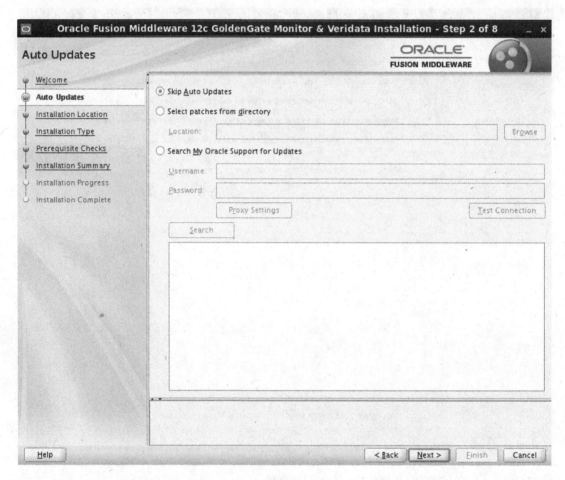

Figure 6-13. *Oracle Universal Installer for Oracle Veridata*

Update the Oracle Home location to the same as the Oracle Home used for the Fusion Middleware Infrastructure. The OUI should detect that installation and the path should be available to be chosen in the drop-down list. To confirm the proper selection, click View once the home is chosen. The OUI should display specifics of the Fusion Middleware Infrastructure installation similar to what is illustrated in Figure 6-13.

Next the OUI will ask you to provide an Oracle Home for the binaries. There is a drop-down list that will be populated with the Oracle Home of the WebLogic Server that is available for to use with Oracle Veridata as displayed in Figure 6-14. Once the Oracle Home setting is chosen and all information has been verified, click Next.

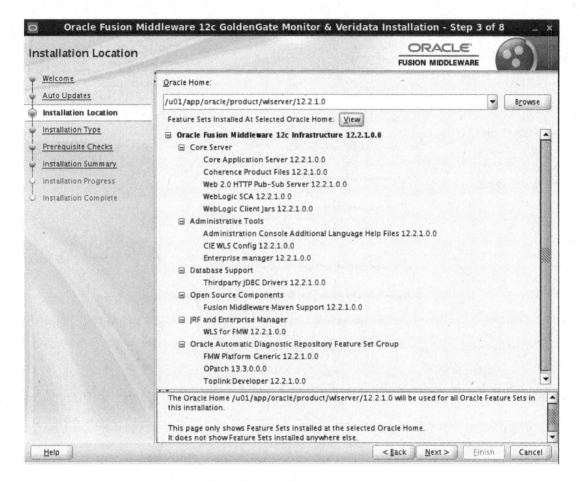

Figure 6-14. *Oracle Universal Installer for Oracle Veridata*

As stated earlier in the chapter, this demonstration uses a separate server for the Veridata Application Server from the Veridata Agent installation. Based on that topology, select the Oracle GoldenGate Veridata Server option as shown in Figure 6-15. After you have selected the component you want to install, click Next to confirm the proper installation has been selected.

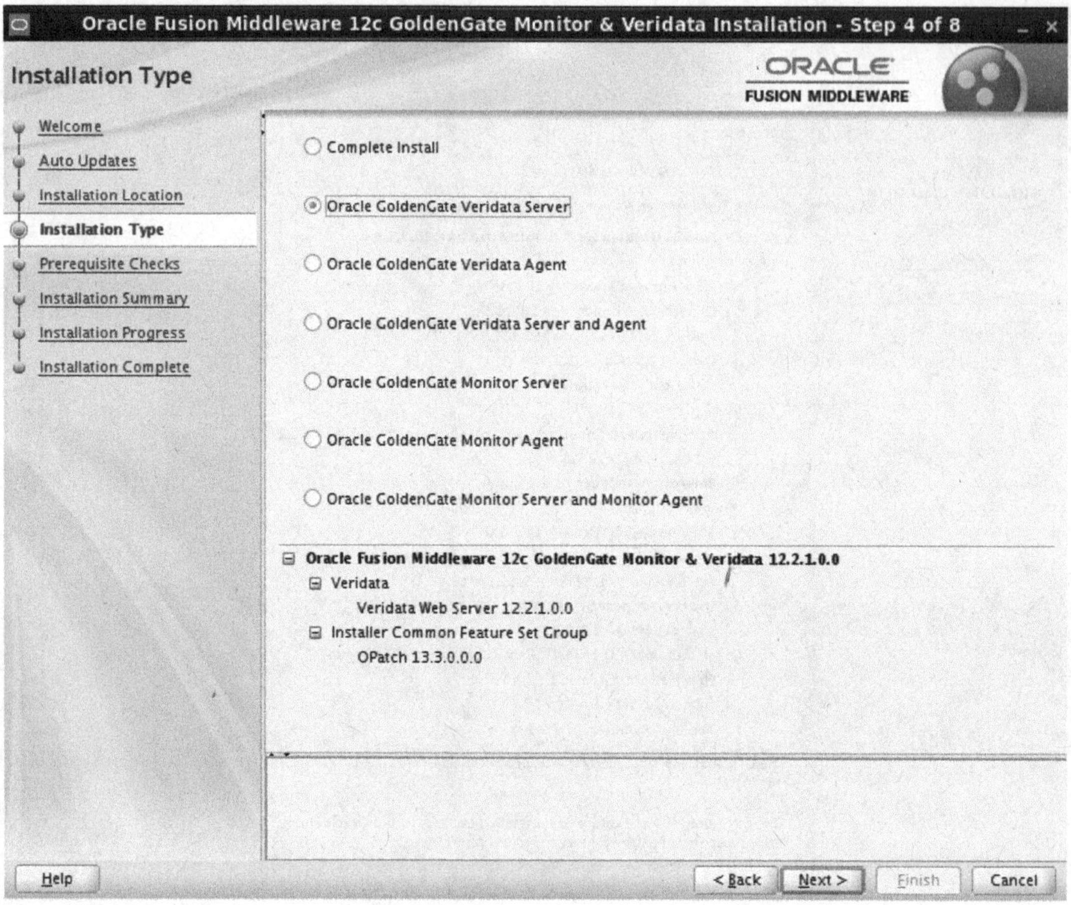

Figure 6-15. *Oracle Universal Installer for Oracle Veridata*

Next, the OUI will execute prerequisite checks needed for the installation of this software, as illustrated in Figure 6-16. Should any prerequisite not pass, the OUI will stop and allow correction of the issue. If all the prerequisites come back successful, click Next to move to the next screen in the OUI.

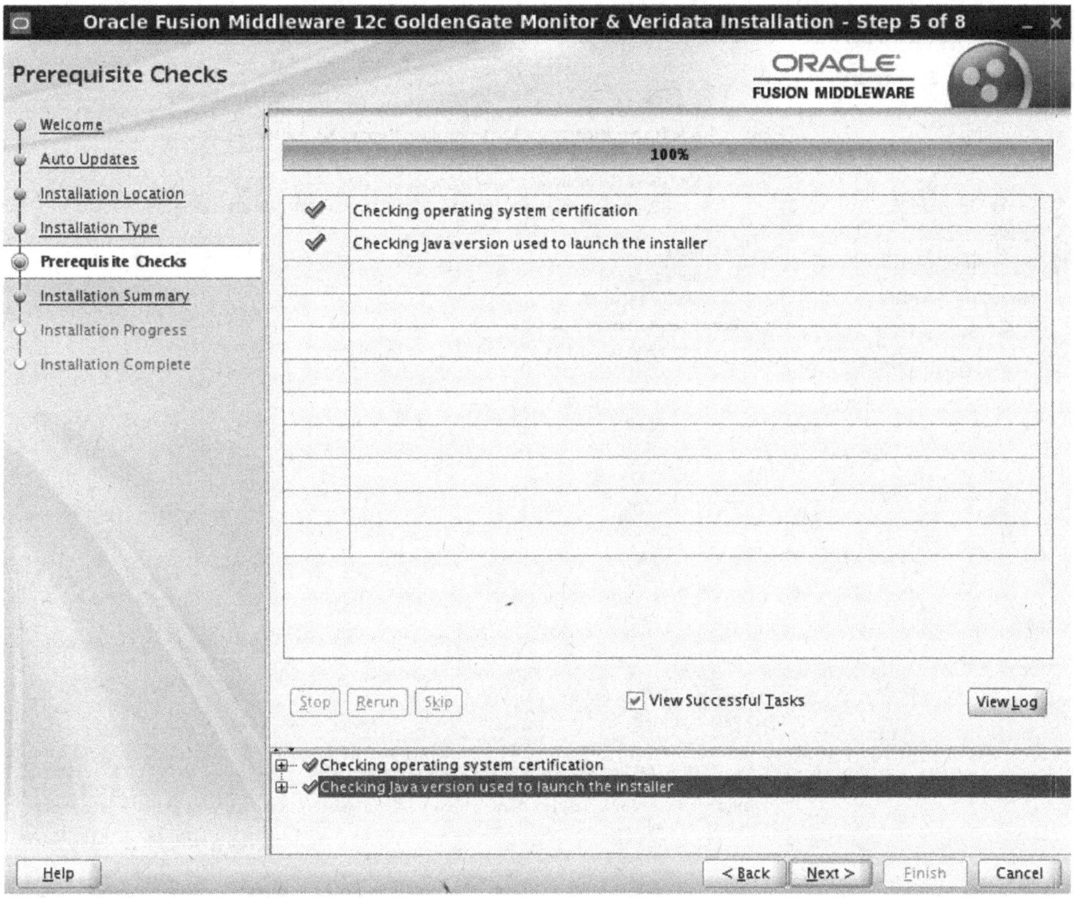

Figure 6-16. *Oracle Universal Installer for Oracle Veridata*

On the next screen (Figure 6-17), you will get a summary of your installation options. If you need to do a rapid deployment at a later date, you can save a response file at this time. Once you are satisfied with your options, click Install to begin the installation of Oracle Veridata into the Oracle WebLogic Server.

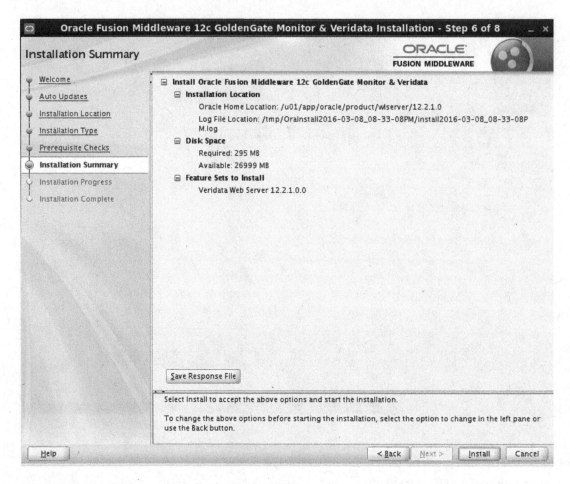

Figure 6-17. *Oracle Universal Installer for Oracle Veridata*

The OUI then presents a progress screen that details the individual parts of the installation and its relevant status, as displayed in Figure 6-18. If you would like to view the log file at this time, it is available to you via the OUI. Once you are satisfied with the installation and it is completed, you can click Next to go to the final screen in the OUI.

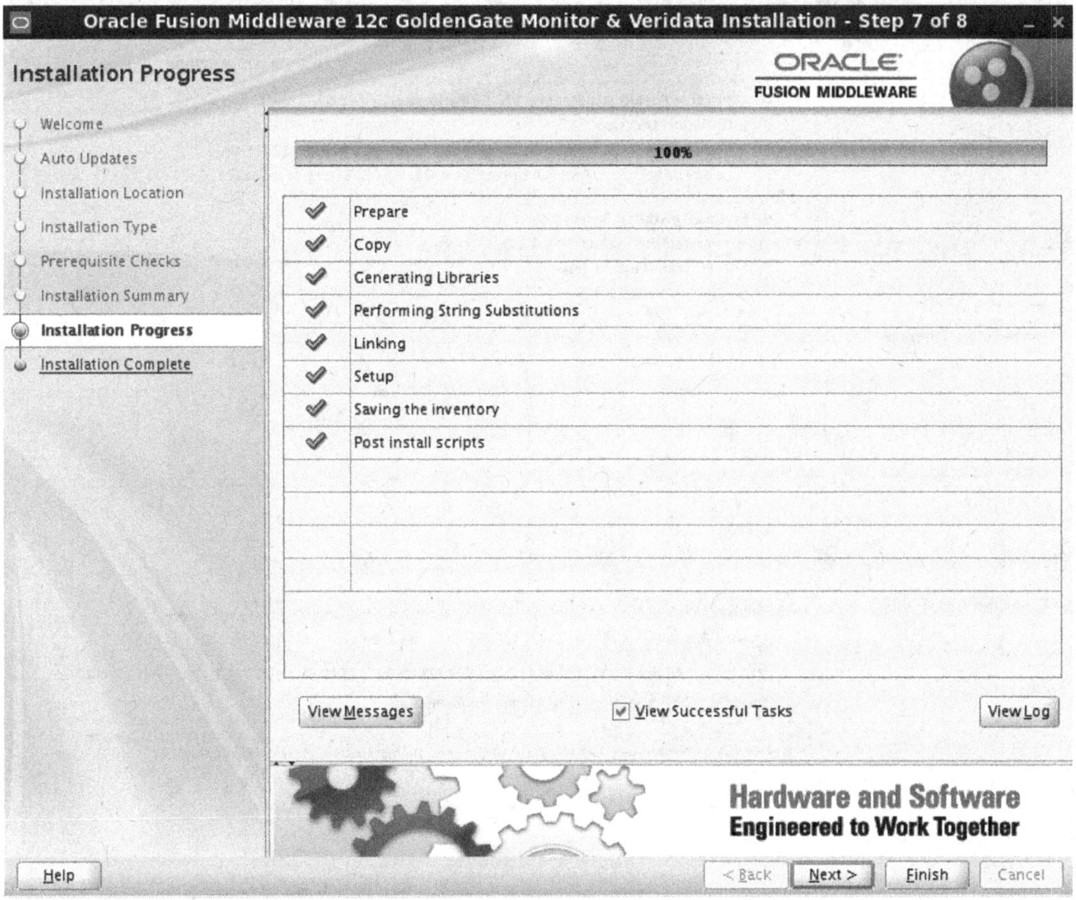

Figure 6-18. Oracle Universal Installer for Oracle Veridata

The last screen will be a summary of the installation (Figure 6-19). Be sure to take note of any pertinent information such as the ORACLE_HOME and log file locations for future reference. Click Finish to close the OUI and complete the installation.

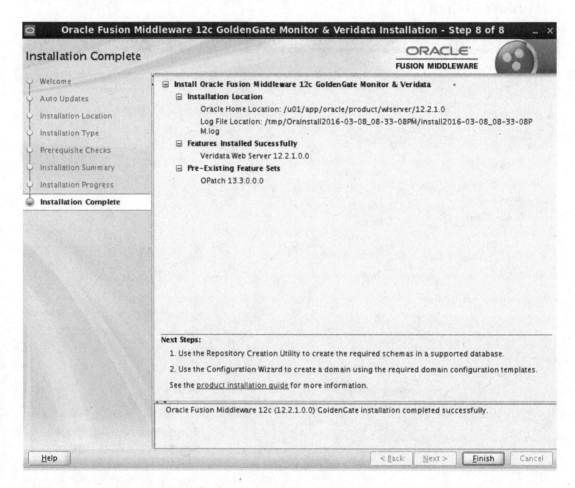

Figure 6-19. Oracle Universal Installer for Oracle Veridata

Configuration of the Oracle GoldenGate Veridata Repository Schema

The next step in the process of installing Oracle GoldenGate Veridata Server is the installation of the repository schemas. These schemas are needed to store connections, data mappings, and other configuration options needed by Veridata Server. If you are familiar with other Oracle Data Integration products, that framework also uses a similar approach to creating a repository. This repository can be configured to use DOracle Database, Oracle MySQL atabase, IBM DB2, or Microsoft SQL Server. Because multiple products can use these repositories, separate schemas should be given based on the products that will be housed in the repository.

Before starting, ensure that you have your JAVA_HOME set in your environment. This should already be set from the previous steps, but you can verify the setting by running this command:

```
[oracle@veridata ~]$ env | grep JAVA_HOME
```

If the JAVA_HOME is not set, set the variable:

```
[oracle@veridata ~]$ JAVA_HOME=/u01/app/oracle/product/jdk/jdk1.8.0_74; export JAVA_HOME
```

It is also important to verify that ORACLE_HOME is properly set to the WebLogic or Veridata home. To verify the setting run this command:

```
[oracle@veridata ~]$ env | grep ORACLE_HOME
```

If ORACLE_HOME is not set, set the variable:

```
ORACLE_HOME=/u01/app/oracle/product/wlserver/12.2.1.0; export ORACLE_HOME
```

To start the installation process, first navigate to the following directory:

```
$ORACLE_HOME/oracle_common/bin
```

Start the Repository Configuration Wizard by executing the following script:

```
On Unix:
./rcu

On Windows:
./rcu.cmd
```

The first screen of the repository creation studio should look familiar (Figure 6-20). Similar to the welcome screen encountered when installing Veridata Application Server, this is the first page of the Installation Wizard and is a general welcome screen that can be used to confirm general version information for the software you are about to install. At this point you can click Next and proceed with the next step of the installer.

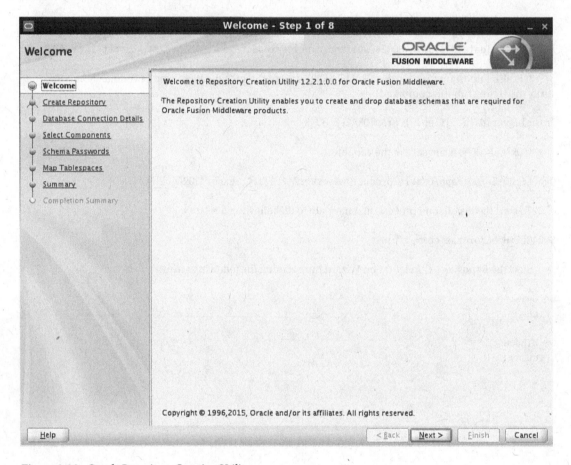

Figure 6-20. *Oracle Repository Creation Utility*

The next step (Figure 6-21) presents the options with which the repository can be built or dropped in the event that it has been chosen to deinstall the product. The wizard presents a few options to create the repository, one of which will create scripts to run in the event a DBA needs to run the task. Because this is a simple installation, the defaults are fine. The default options make the assumption that proper credentials have been received and that all connection information is available to the individial completing the installation. Click Next to proceed to advance the utility to the next screen.

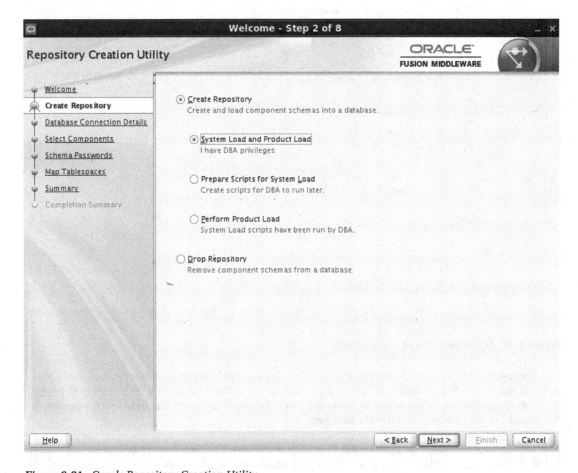

Figure 6-21. *Oracle Repository Creation Utility*

The next step in creating the repository is to provide the proper credentials and database connection information (Figure 6-22). In the Database Type drop-down list, choose the database vendor that will be used for the installation. Because the defaults are being assumed, choose Oracle Database. Remember that there are other choices, but there are different requirements should something other than Oracle Database be chosen. Be sure to enter the fully qualified host name, port, and database service. Next, enter either SYSDBA credentials or other DBA user credentials. Once the data has been entered, click Next.

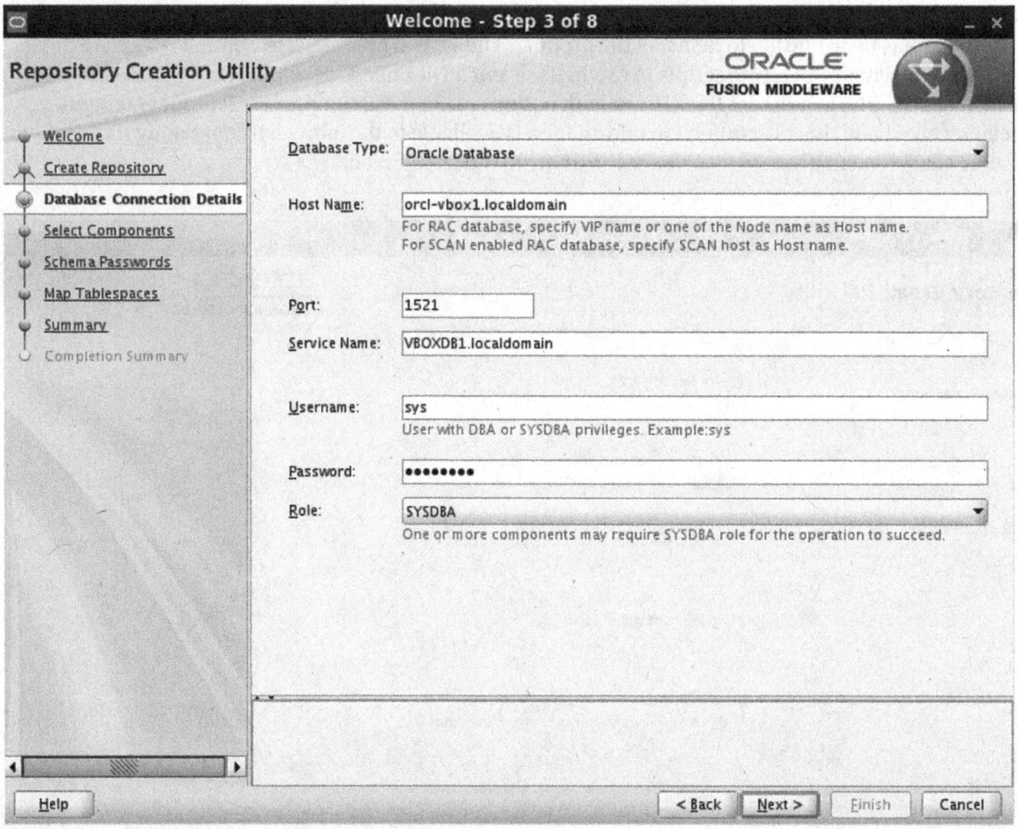

Figure 6-22. *Oracle Repository Creation Utility*

The installer will then test the connection to ensure that it is valid. As part of the connection check, this step will also verify a few prerequisites (Figure 6-23). Should any of these checks fail, the installer will prompt you as necessary so that the errors can be corrected. Once the wizard has given the signal that the operation has completed, click OK to proceed to the next step.

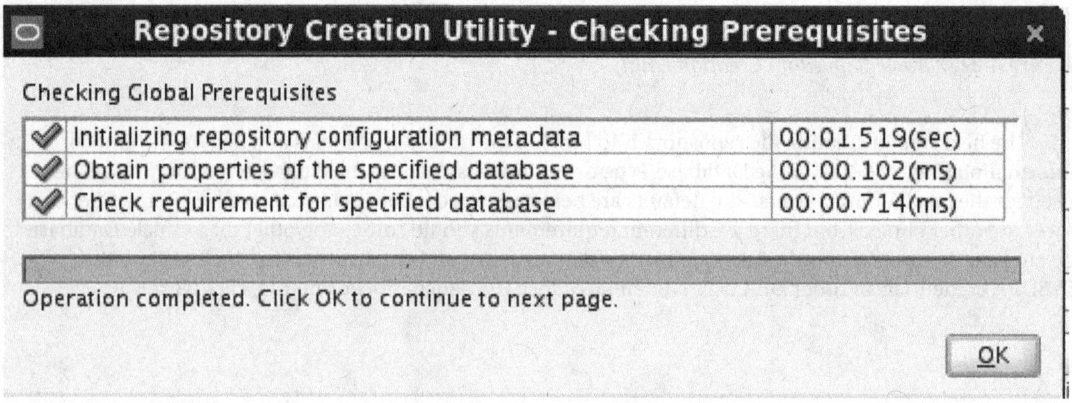

Figure 6-23. *Oracle Repository Creation Utility*

The next step, shown in Figure 6-24, involves naming of the Veridata repository schemas as well as choosing the correct components to install. Because Veridata is a specific product, it is preferable to assign a unique prefix to the Veridata repository schemas. In this demo, the OGGVDS prefix has been used to signify Oracle GoldenGate Veridata. Next it is time to choose the components that need to be installed. There are a few components that must be installed for Veridata. Because it has been chosen to install the repository on an Oracle Database, the following components are required:

- Oracle Platform Security Services (OPSS).

- Veridata Repository.

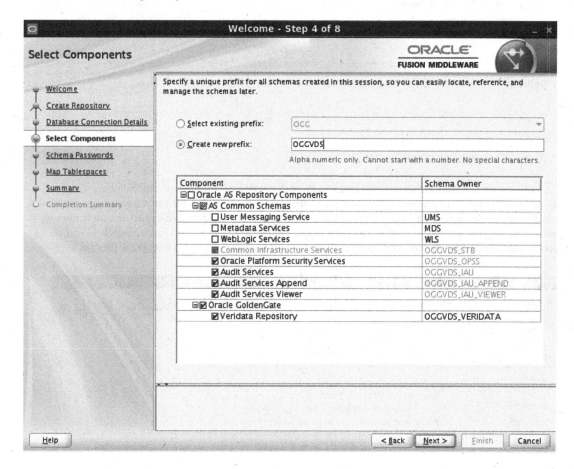

Figure 6-24. *Oracle Repository Creation Utility*

Other dependencies based on those two selections will be automatically selected.

Once the appropriate schema prefix and options have been verified, click Next to proceed to the next step. Prerequisite checks will then again execute and if there are any issues there will be a chance to correct them (Figure 6-25). Once the prerequisites have been checked successfully, click Next.

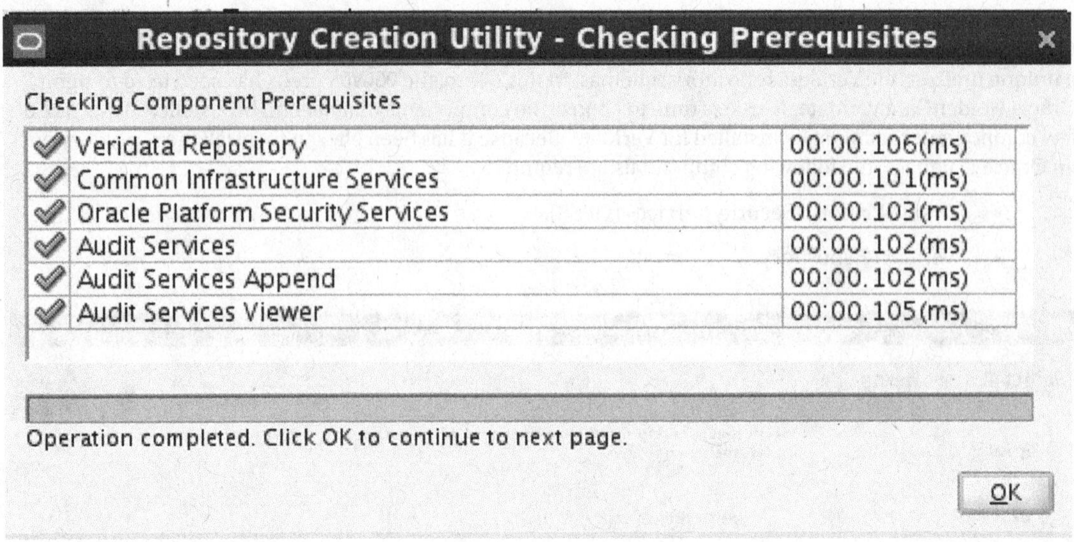

Figure 6-25. *Oracle Repository Creation Utility*

The screen that follows (Figure 6-26) asks you to set the passwords for the repository schemas that are about to be created. For purposes of this simple installation, use the default, which is to use the same password for all schemas. An alternative option is to provide a separate password for each schema. Ultimately, choose the option that best fits the installation. Once the password has been entered and confirmed, click Next to proceed to the next step. Be sure to remember this password, as it will be needed later in the process.

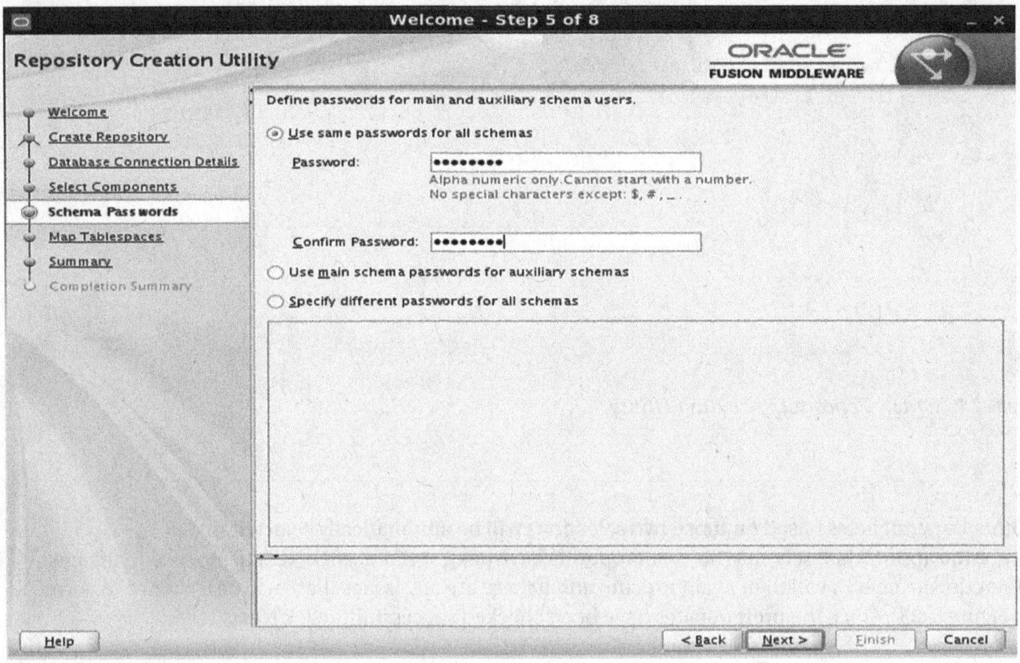

Figure 6-26. *Oracle Repository Creation Utility*

After setting the password you want to use for Veridata, the utility allows you to map tablespaces to each repository schema being created (Figure 6-27). This is where the data are actually stored within the database. The default will create several sets of tablespaces, both temporary and regular, that contain the schema prefix as part of the name. The defaults can be used or custom entries can be provided, depending on your needs. Because this is a simple installation, choose the defaults and then click Next to proceed to the next step.

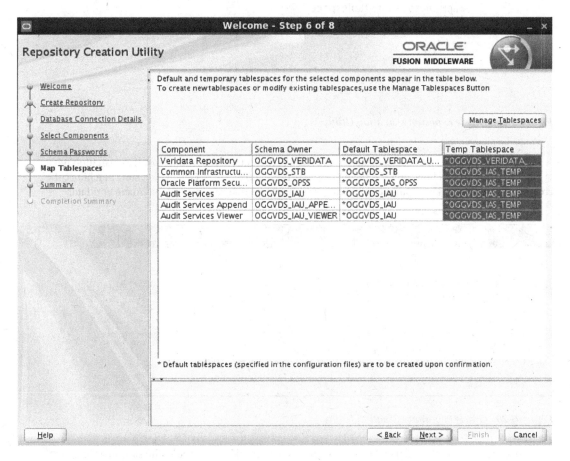

Figure 6-27. *Oracle Repository Creation Utility*

The dialog box shown in Figure 6-28 will then appear to signify that the tablespaces just specified will be created unless they already exist. Click OK to acknowledge the warning and the Installation Wizard will begin to build the tablespaces in the database.

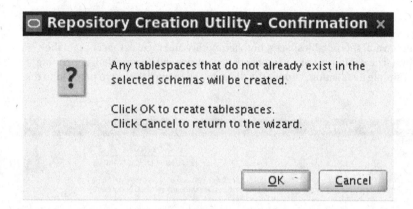

Figure 6-28. *Oracle Repository Creation Utility*

The utility provides a dialog box, shown in Figure 6-29, that will provide you with information related to what step it is on and how long it is taking to create these tablespaces. On smaller, slow machines, the creation time will be higher compared to enterprise machines that can be used for Oracle Veridata.

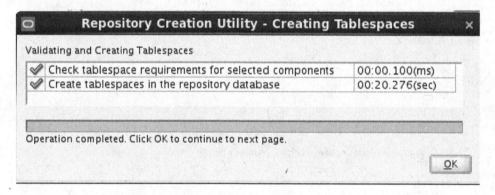

Figure 6-29. *Oracle Repository Creation Utility*

Once the creation of the tablespaces has completed, click OK to proceed to the summary screen (Figure 6-30). On the summary screen, you are able to confirm all of the previous selections before proceeding with the repository creation. Once all selections are confirmed, click Create to allow the wizard to create the repository.

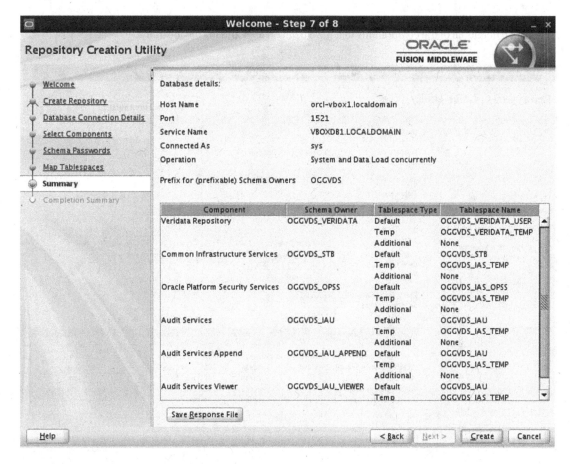

Figure 6-30. *Oracle Repository Creation Utility*

At this point, the utility will begin to build out the common framework of the repository. You are presented with a system load dialog box (Figure 6-31) that will provide output on the process.

Repository Creation Utility - System Load	
Repository System Load in progress.	
✔ Execute pre create operations	00:00.107(ms)
✔ Common Infrastructure Services	00:09.559(sec)
✔ Audit Services Append	00:09.252(sec)
✔ Audit Services Viewer	00:10.177(sec)
🕐 Audit Services	00:04.949(sec)
Oracle Platform Security Services	0
Veridata Repository	0
Execute post create operations	0

Figure 6-31. *Oracle Repository Creation Utility*

After all items have been created, the wizard will load the Completion Summary screen (Figure 6-32). This screen details all of the components that have been created and log file locations.

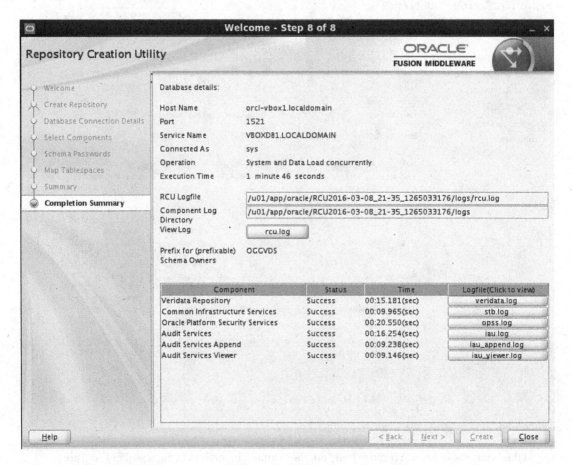

Figure 6-32. *Oracle Repository Creation Utility*

The Repository Creation Utility is now complete and you may can Close to exit the wizard. At this point, you will be able to log in to the database that houses the repository and review the metadata structure of the repository.

Configuring the Domain for Oracle GoldenGate Veridata Server

Becauses GoldenGate Veridata Server is a web application, a domain must be configured within the WebLogic instance in which to run the application. The domain includes the administration server, which is the central point from which you configure and manage all resources in the domain. It also includes an additional server instance called a managed server. This is the server where the Veridata application will be deployed.

As in previous steps, be sure that your JAVA_HOME and ORACLE_HOME variables are set. Once these variables are confirmed, you are ready to configure the domain. To begin configuring the domain, navigate to the following directory:

```
$ORACLE_HOME/oracle_common/common/bin
```

Then start the WebLogic Server Configuration Wizard by executing the following command:

```
On UNIX:
./config.sh

On Windows:
./config.cmd
```

On the introduction screen, shown in Figure 6-33, you will be asked to either create a new domain or upgrade an existing one. Beause this is a new installation, select Create a New Domain and then select the location that was defined earlier in this chapter. Remember, it is important at this point to locate your domain home outside of $ORACLE_HOME. Doing so will help you avoid issues should you need to upgrade or reinstall the software. Once the selections are confirmed, click Next to proceed to the next step.

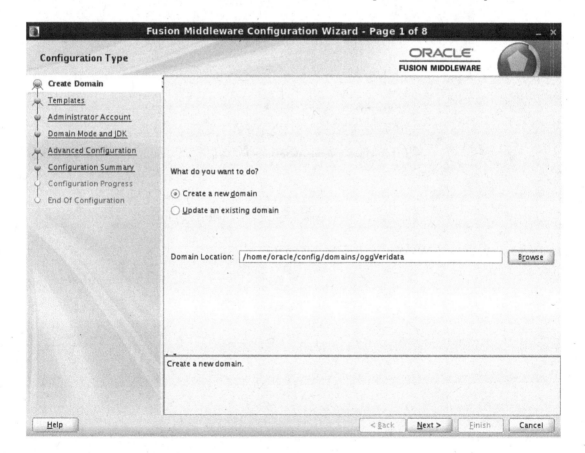

Figure 6-33. Oracle Fusion Middleware domain configuration

In the next step (Figure 6-34), make sure to create the domain by using the packaged product templates. The template that should be selected is Oracle GoldenGate. Once this selection is made, be sure to also make sure that the actual template Veridata Standard Weblogic Server Domain is selected. Selecting this template will ensure that all of the proper dependencies are also selected. Once the proper template has been selected, choose Next to proceed to the next step.

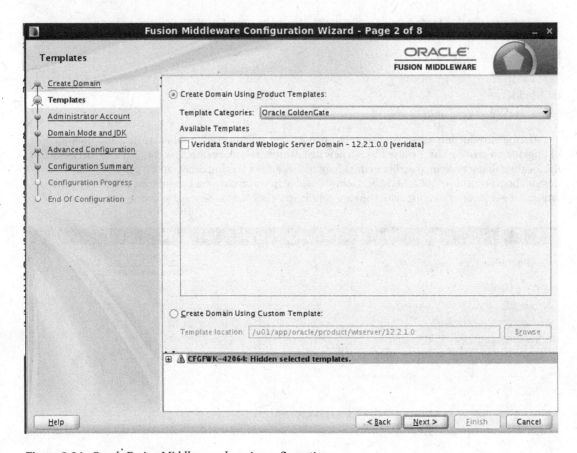

Figure 6-34. Oracle Fusion Middleware domain configuration

The next step, shown in Figure 6-35, is to select an administrator account for the domain. For this installation, using the default username of weblogic is appropriate. Be sure to enter an appropriate password for this administrator account and be sure to note this password for future reference. Once the selections are confirmed, click Next to proceed to the next step.

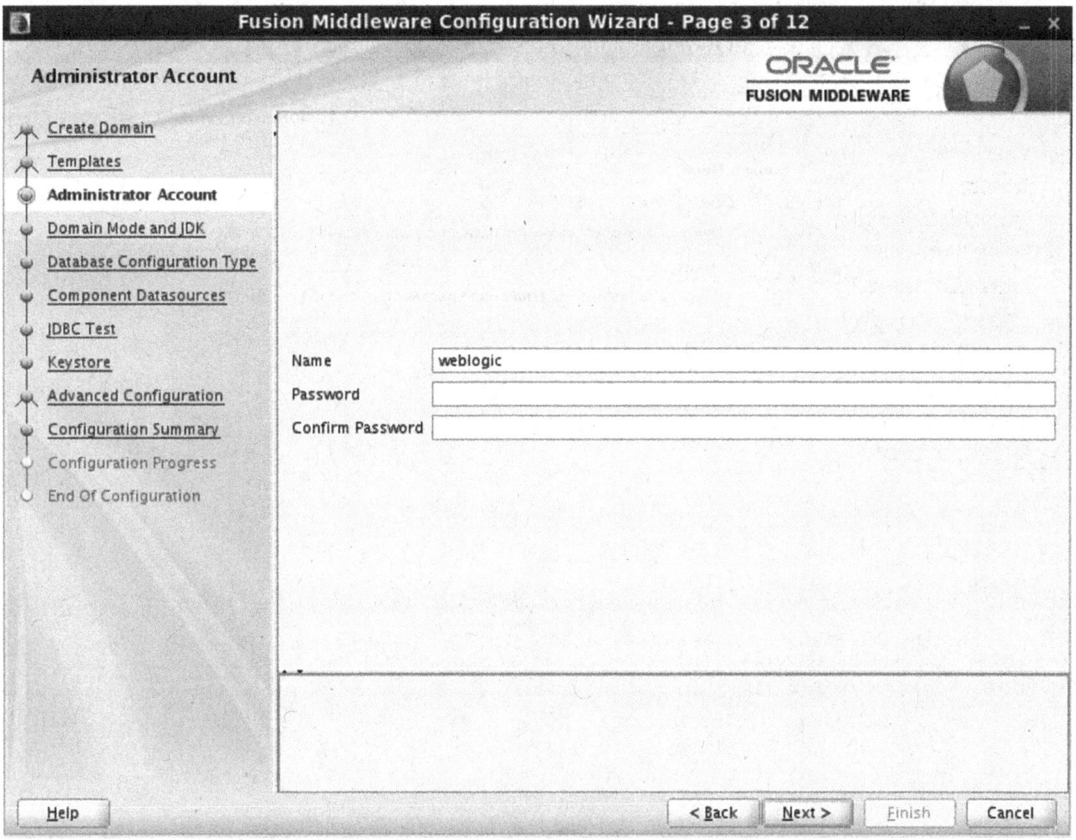

Figure 6-35. *Oracle Fusion Middleware domain configuration*

In the next step, depicted in Figure 6-36, you will select the Domain Mode and the appropriate JDK. For the highest level of security, Production mode should be selected. This mode will require a username and password to start the admin server as well as to deploy any new applications. For more advanced WebLogic users, the ability exists to configure a boot.properties file to avoid manually entering the username and password for server startup. We do not cover how to create this file in this book.

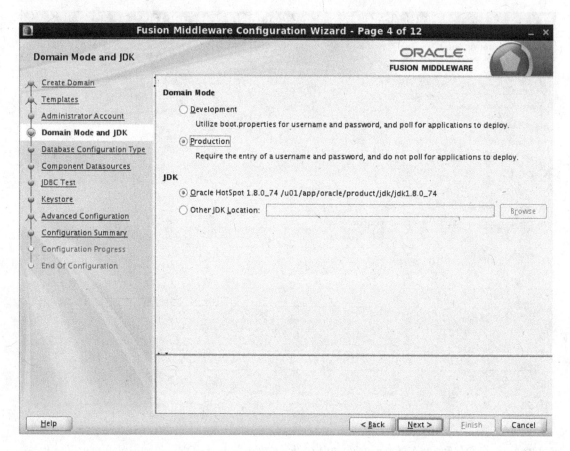

Figure 6-36. *Oracle Fusion Middleware domain configuration*

When choosing the JDK, be sure to select the option that correlates to the JDK that was installed earlier in the chapter. If that selection is not available, you can specify a JDK manually. After your selection has been confirmed, click Next to proceed to the next step.

Next, it is time to configure the database connection to the Veridata repository, which was created in the previous section. To begin configuration, select the RCU Data option. Once that selection has been made, the fields in which to enter the connection information will become available (Figure 6-37). Be sure that the Schema Owner field contains the correct schema. Based on the previous example, OGGVDS_STB would be used. Once the information is entered, click Get RCU Information to validate the connection and to gather data from the repository. Once the metadata have been validated, click Next to move to the next step.

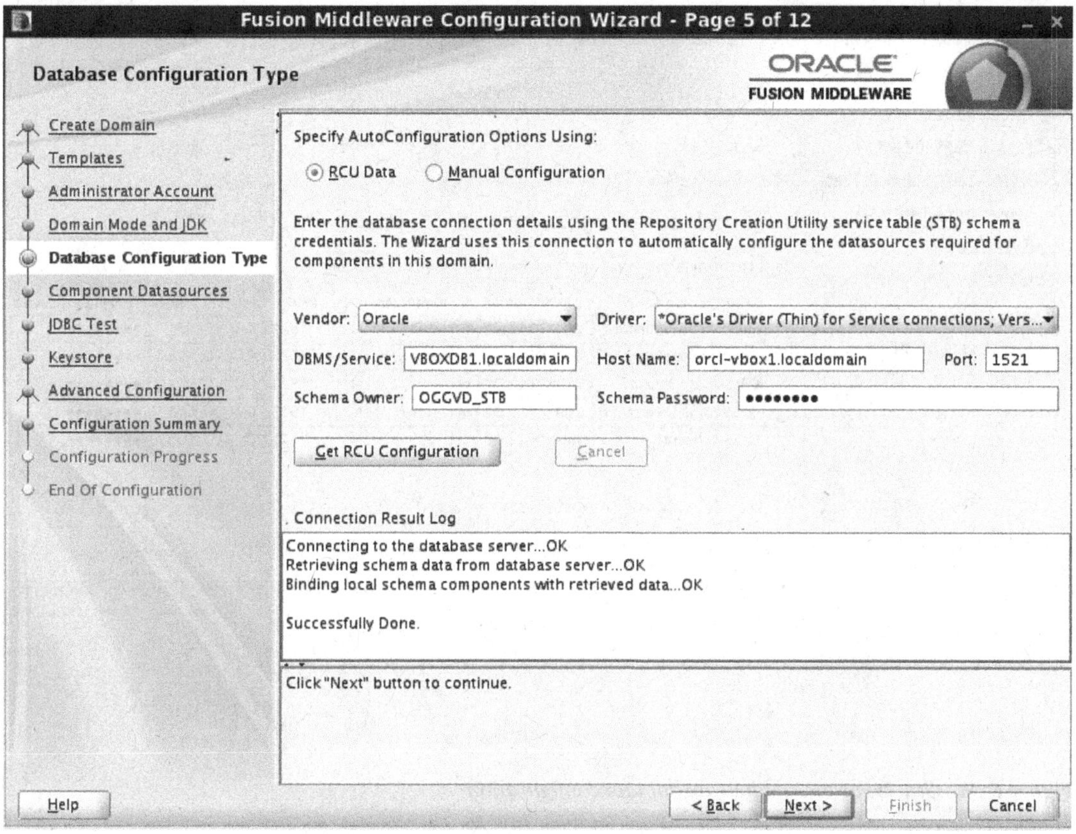

Figure 6-37. *Oracle Fusion Middleware domain configuration*

For the validation step (Figure 6-38), all that needs to be done is to validate the data that was retrieved from the Veridata repository. Because we used the defaults during the repository configuration step, there are no actions to take with this step, so click Next to proceed.

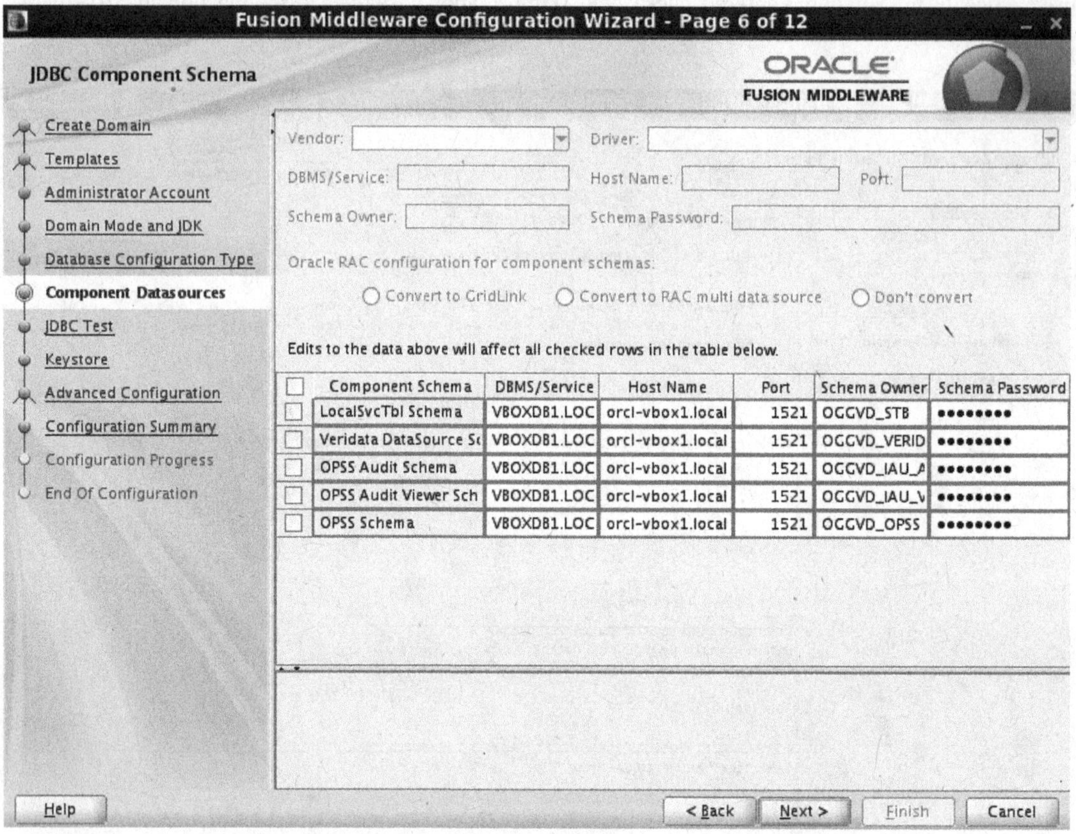

Figure 6-38. *Oracle Fusion Middleware domain configuration*

In the next step, the OUI will automatically validate the Java Database Connectivity (JDBC) connection based on the values stored in the Veridata repository (Figure 6-39). Once the automatic check has occurred and connection tests are verified to be successful, click Next to continue.

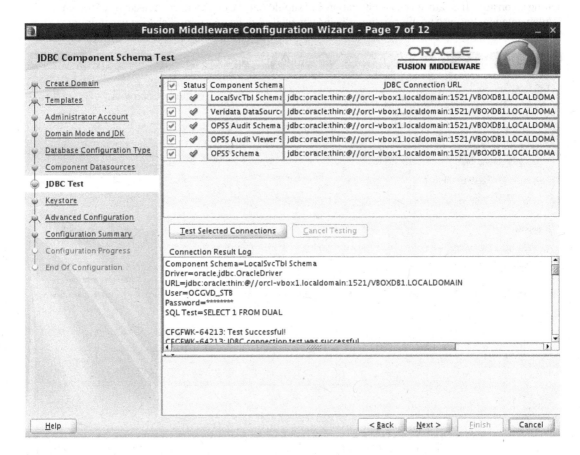

Figure 6-39. *Oracle Fusion Middleware domain configuration*

In the step shown in Figure 6-40, you set up the Keystore. Setup of the Keystore is most commonly used when using HTTPS to connect to the Veridata application server and agents. Because this is a simple installation, choose the defaults and continue. Setting up and using the Keystore in an enterprise setting is considered an advanced configuration and should only be changed when necessary for your implementation. Because no information is being changed with the Keystore, click Next to continue.

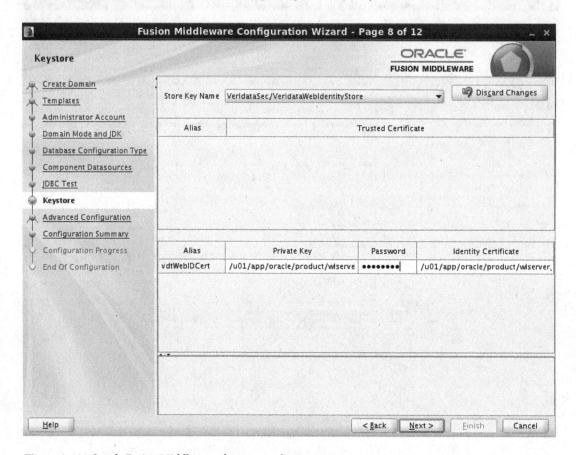

Figure 6-40. *Oracle Fusion Middleware domain configuration*

After setting up the Keystore, next you will be presented with advanced options (Figure 6-41) that must be selected to properly configure the topology. Select the following check boxes:

- Administration Server

- Node Manager

- Managed Servers, Clusters and Coherence

Once these selections are made, you will see additional screens pop up on the left menu bar. The next set of configuration steps addresses each of these three topics. Click Next to configure the administration server.

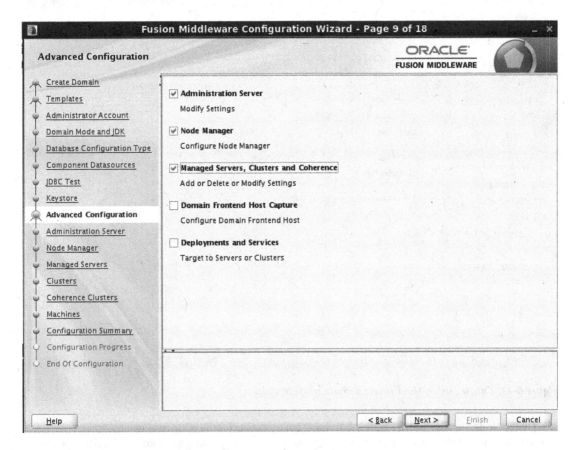

Figure 6-41. *Oracle Fusion Middleware domain configuration*

In this configuration, it is important to choose the proper attributes for the administration server. You can modify the Server Name field to represent something meaningful to your installation, but in this example, we leave it set to the default for purposes of this walkthrough (Figure 6-42). In the Listen Address field, be sure to choose the IP address on the host where the administration server will reside. In this case, the selection will be 192.168.56.203, which is the IP address of this server. Do not use All Local Addresses. You will also leave the default Listen Port, but in many installations, the default might not be used for various reasons, such as the port already being in use. Finally, do not specify any Server Groups for this administration server. Click Next to proceed to the Node Manager setup.

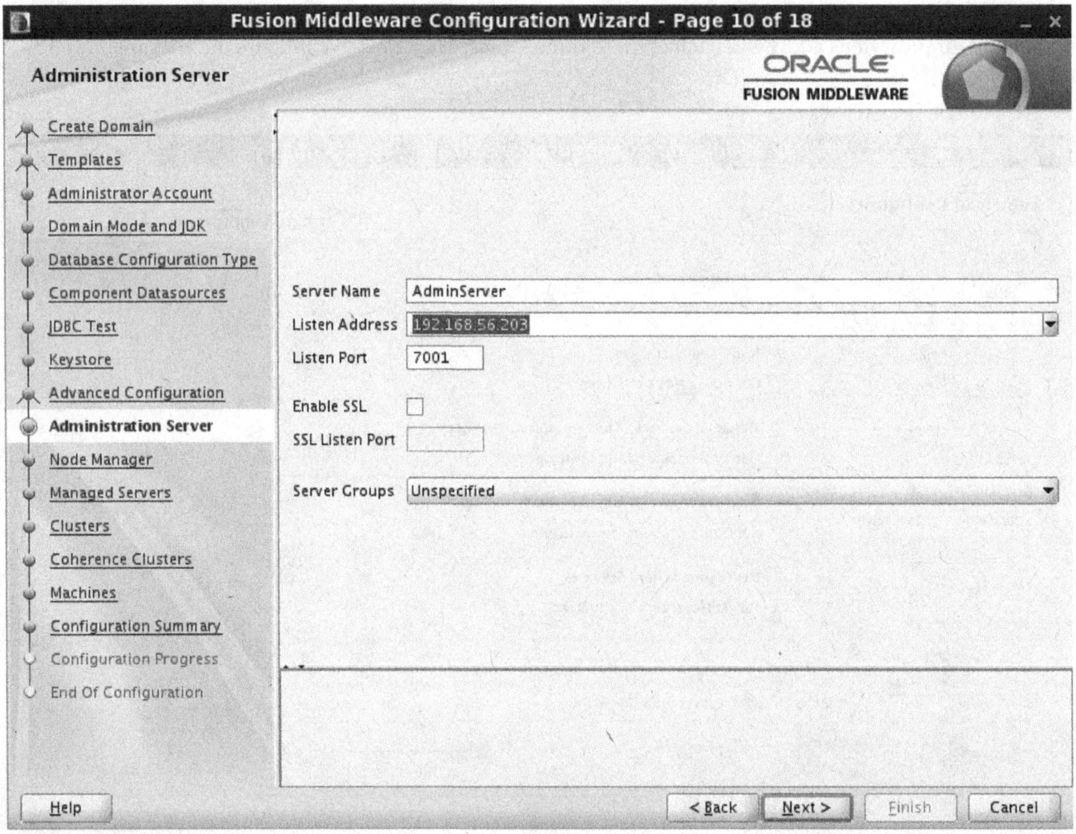

Figure 6-42. *Oracle Fusion Middleware domain configuration*

On the Node Manager page (Figure 6-43), some basic options for the node manager must be entered. For this installation, choose Per Domain Default Location and then enter any credentials that are appropriate for your installation. For purposes of this demonstration, we use the username nodemanager and then choose a password appropriate for the setting. Click Next to proceed to the Managed Servers page.

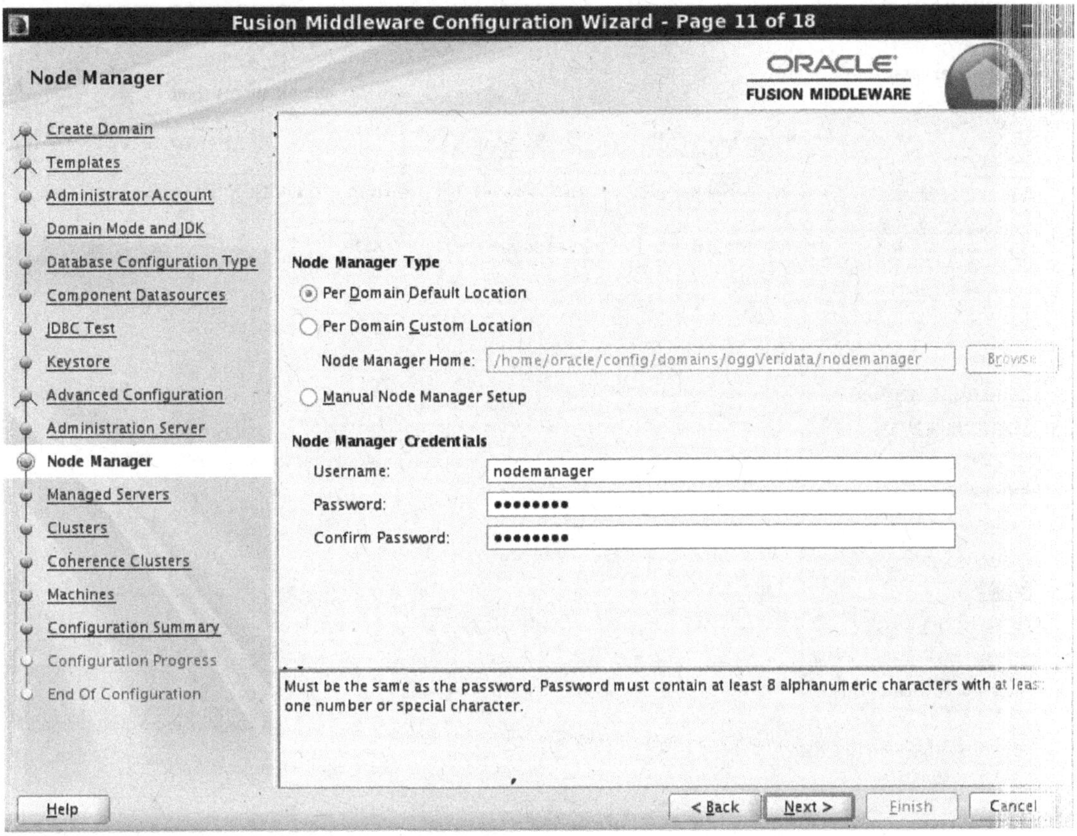

Figure 6-43. *Oracle Fusion Middleware domain configuration*

The Managed Servers page shown in Figure 6-44 represents configuration options specific to the Veridata application server. By default, the Server Name is set to VERIDATA_server1. You can change this to something meaningful to you, but for now, use the default. Remember, if you change any of the defaults, be sure to take note of them, as they will be needed in other steps of the setup. Next, choose the following options:

- *Listen Address*: Choose IP Address for this host (192.168.56.203).

- *Listen Port*: Leave as default (8803).

- *Server Groups*: Choose VERIDATA-MANAGED-SERVERS

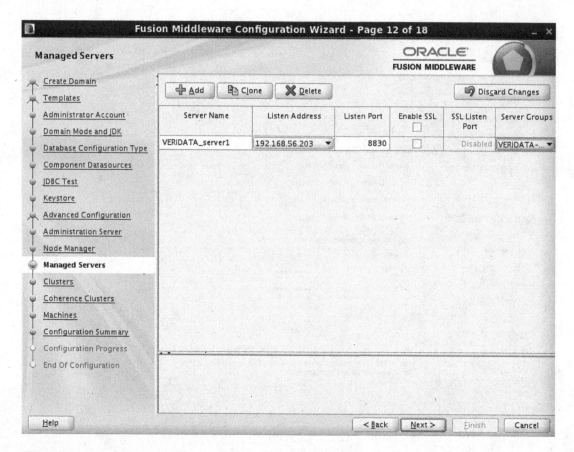

Figure 6-44. *Oracle Fusion Middleware domain configuration*

Server groups are useful in a clustered configuration where you can target certain applications and services to one or more servers by defining groups of resources. For this installation, there is only a single server so this group is a group of one.

At this point, be sure to take note of the IP Address and Listen Port settings, as well as any other values that were modified from the defaults. You will need this information to set up the Veridata agent later in the process. Click Next once the settings have been confirmed.

WebLogic clustering is implemented when multiple application servers are used for an application. Because there is only one application server for this Veridata installation, no changes are necessary for this step (Figure 6-45). Proceed by clicking Next.

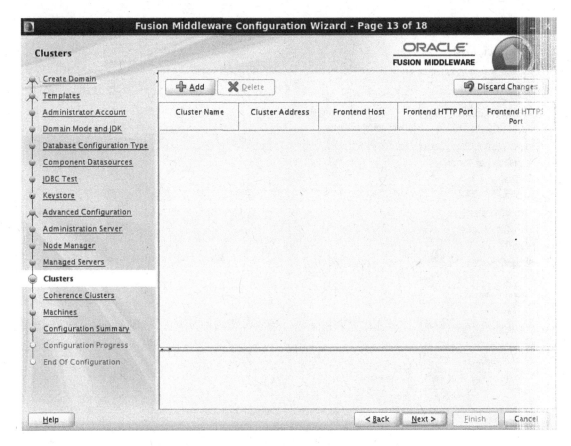

Figure 6-45. *Oracle Fusion Middleware domain configuration*

For this installation, the Coherence Clusters page, shown in Figure 6-46, requires no changes from the default settings. No changes are necessary due to the fact that coherence is not used for this Veridata installation. Proceed to the next step by clicking Next.

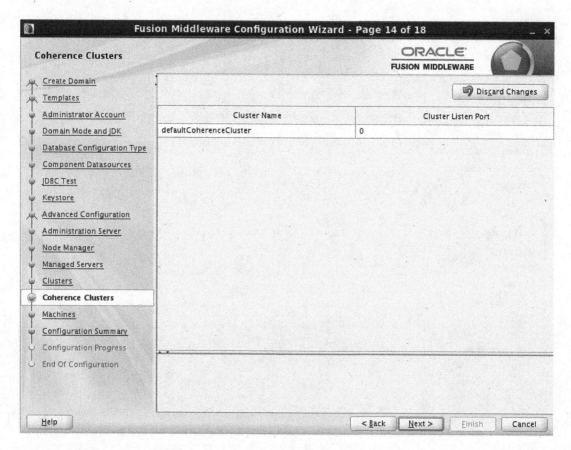

Figure 6-46. *Oracle Fusion Middleware domain configuration*

You can also dismiss the Machines page (Figure 6-47), as no changes are required here. Proceed to the Configuration Summary page by clicking Next.

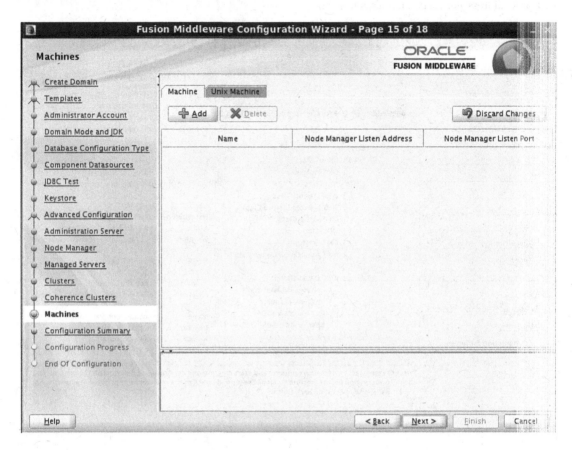

Figure 6-47. *Oracle Fusion Middleware domain configuration*

The Configuration Summary page, shown in Figure 6-48, confirms all of the previous selections that have been made. Be sure to thoroughly check all of the items on this page and take note of specific changes such as IP address, port, server names, and so on.

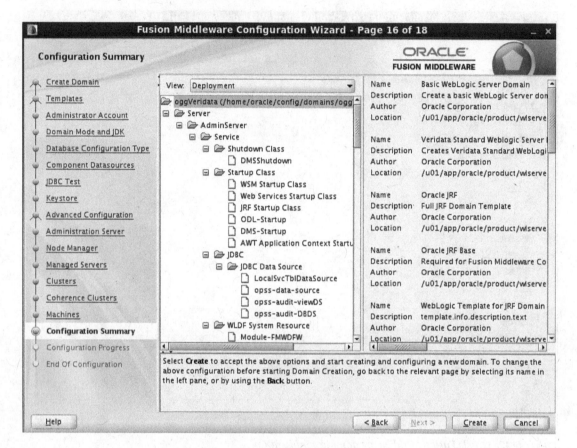

Figure 6-48. *Oracle Fusion Middleware domain configuration*

Once all of the entries have been confirmed, click Create to create the domain. The page that follows (Figure 6-49) shows the individual steps and progress in creating the domain. Click Next to proceed to the End Of Configuration screen.

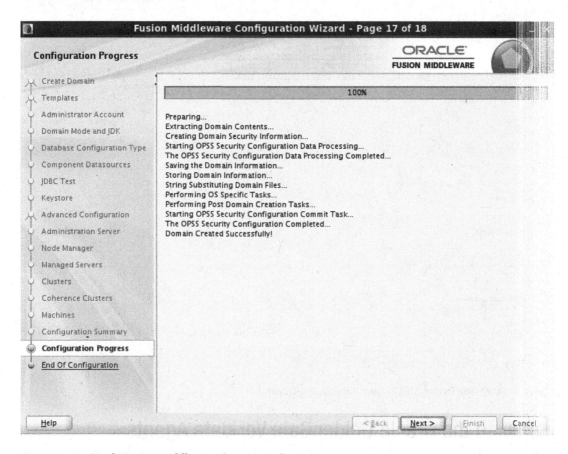

Figure 6-49. *Oracle Fusion Middleware domain configuration*

On this final screen (Figure 6-50), be sure to take note of the Domain Location and URL of the administration server that was just configured. Be sure to take note of both items, as they will be needed to start and log in to the server. Finally, click Finish to dismiss the wizard. The domain has been successfully created.

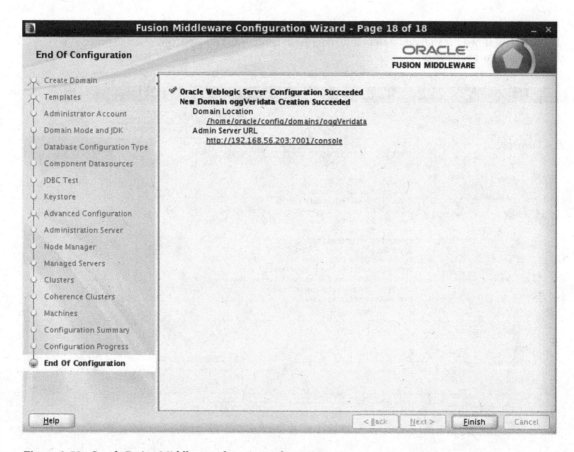

Figure 6-50. *Oracle Fusion Middleware domain configuration*

Installing the Oracle GoldenGate Veridata Agents

As discussed in the beginning of the chapter, most cases will use the Oracle GoldenGate Veridata Java Agent to compare two data sets. Only in very rare circumstances, such as NonStop, will you need to use the C agent.

One Oracle GoldenGate Veridata Agent must be installed for each database that contains data to be compared. For this demonstration, we need to install a minimum of two agents, one on the source and one on the target. Remember that an agent can retrieve data from multiple schemas from a single database but not on multiple instances or schemas on other hosts. If you have more than one database on a single host, an agent will be needed for each database, otherwise the agent configuration will need to be changed each time you wish to compare another database. If you are comparing data between two schemas in the same database or host, only one agent is needed.

Install the JDK for Oracle GoldenGate Veridata Agent

JDK 1.8 is also needed for the Veridata agent to function properly. Based on your installation and requirements for multiple versions of a JDK to be present, it might be best to install the JDK outside the default Java that is installed on your system.

The same installation media that was used to install the JDK for the Veridata application server can also be used for the installation of the Veridata agent. Assuming that the same installation media is available and present on the database server orcl-vbox1.localdomain, you can proceed with the installation. If the media is not available, follow the same download instructions found earlier in the chapter.

As you recall from when we previously installed the JDK for the application server, the installation location should be created prior to installation of the JDK. For this example we use /u01/app/oracle/product/jdk.

```
[oracle@orcl-vbox1 ~]$ mkdir -p /u01/app/oracle/product/jdk
```

Once the directory is created, un-tar the file that was downloaded from OTN to this location:

```
[oracle@orcl-vbox1 tmp]$tar xvfz jdk-8u74-linux-x64.tar.gz -C /u01/app/oracle/product/jdk
```

Take note of the installation location, so that you can set your JAVA_HOME environment variable properly. In addition to this environment variable, it is advisable to set a few others before the agent is installed and deployed.

To make the install process and the administration of the agent easier, some standard environment variables should be set up. Because this server also has a database instance running on it, it would be advisable to create a separate file such as ogg_agent_env and place these variables into that file. That way, this file can be sourced in and everything needed to administer the agent is set in the environment.

```
ORACLE_BASE= /u01/app/oracle; export ORACLE_BASE
JAVA_HOME=$ORACLE_BASE/product/jdk/jdk1.8.0_74; export JAVA_HOME
AGENT_BASE_DIR=$ORACLE_BASE/product/oggVeridataAgent/; export AGENT_BASE_DIR
AGENT_DEPLOY_HOME=$ORACLE_BASE/product/veridataAgentVBOXDB1; export AGENT_DEPLOY_HOME
```

Of course, if these variables do not interfere with other variables needed on this particular server, they can be placed into the .bash_profile or equivalent so that they are automatically sourced in on user login to the server.

Installing the Oracle GoldenGate Veridata Agent

At this point, now that the Veridata server is installed, you can proceed with the installation of the Veridata agent software on each database host that will be compared. As stated earlier in the chapter, our databases are running on orcl-vbox1 and orcl-vbox2. This example shows the installation for orcl-vbox1 and the steps can be repeated for the other host orcl-vbox2.

Before proceeding, you should decide on a location to install the software and precreate that location. As the oracle user, create the following directories:

```
[oracle@orcl-vbox1 ~]$ mkdir -p /u01/app/oracle/product/oggVeridataAgent/
[oracle@orcl-vbox1 ~]$ mkdir -p /u01/app/oracle/product/veridataAgentVBOXDB1
```

These directories represent the AGENT_BASE_DIR and AGENT_DEPLOY_HOME variables that were defined earlier in the process. Next, make sure the installation media (fmw_12.2.1.0.0_ogg.jar) is present on the host as necessary. Next, as the oracle user, start the installation program by locating the installation media and invoking the OUI by executing:

```
[oracle@orcl-vbox1 ~]$ /u01/app/oracle/product/jdk/jdk1.8.0_74/bin/java -jar /tmp/
fmw_12.2.1.0.0_ogg.jar
```

```
Extracting files.....
Starting Oracle Universal Installer
Checking if CPU speed is above 300 MHz. Actual 2194.986 MHz Passed
Checking monitor: must be configured to display at least 256 colors. Actual 16777216 Passed
Checking swap space: must be greater than 512 MB. Actual 3967 MB Passed
Checking if this platform requires a 64-bit JVM. Actual 64 Passed (64-bit not required)
Checking temp space: must be greater than 300 MB. Actual 15635 MB Passed

Preparing to launch the Oracle Universal Installer from /tmp/OraInstall2016-03-10_09-36-36PM
Log: /tmp/OraInstall2016-03-10_09-36-36PM/install2016-03-10_09-36-36PM.log
```

As the installer starts, it will look very familiar, as it is the very same wizard that installed the Veridata server software. Even though the steps are very similar, the step-by-step install instructions are illustrated in this section.

First, you will see the Welcome screen (Figure 6-51) that offers a summary of the Installation Wizard that has been invoked. Confirm that this is the correct version that you expect to be installed. Once the information is confirmed, click Next to proceed with the installation.

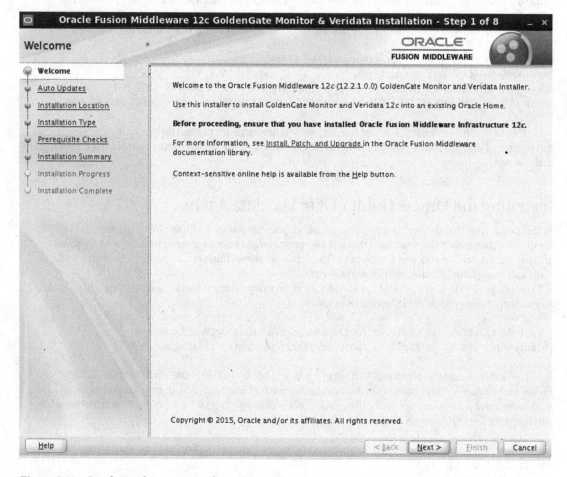

Figure 6-51. Oracle Veridata agent configuration

The next step will be to decide whether or not to subscribe to Auto Updates (Figure 6-52). Typically, this is something that is done manually, so select Skip Auto Updates. Once the selection has been confirmed, click Next to continue.

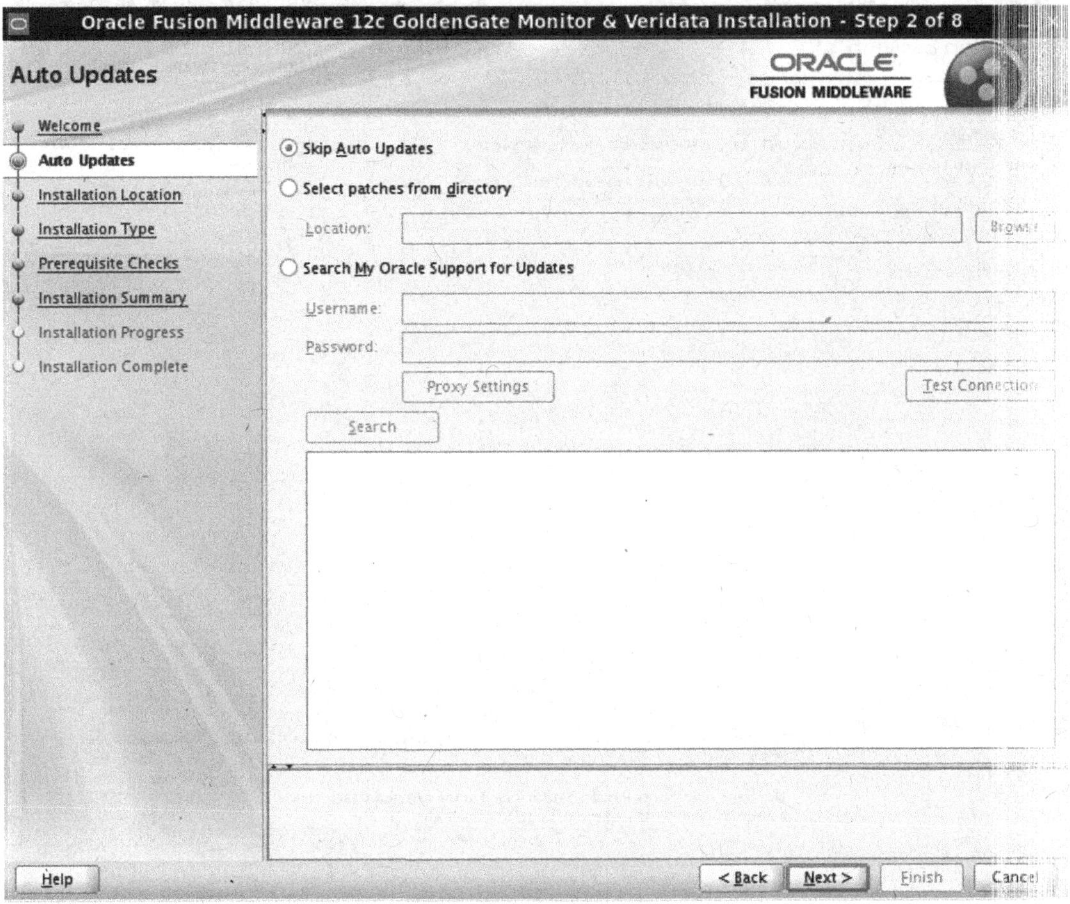

Figure 6-52. *Oracle Veridata agent configuration*

Next, select the software location that represents the AGENT_BASE_DIR that was precreated prior to starting the Installation Wizard (Figure 6-53). Once the software location is chosen, click Next to proceed.

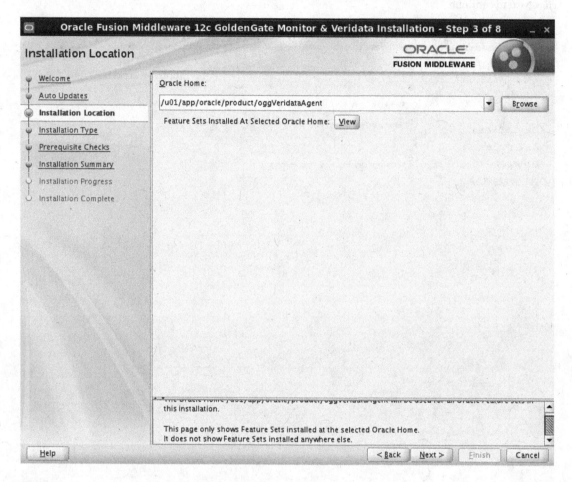

Figure 6-53. *Oracle Veridata agent configuration*

At this point, select the Oracle GoldenGate Veridata Agent option (Figure 6-54). Once that choice is made, a summary will appear at the bottom of the screen confirming which agent version will be installed. Once your choice is confirmed, click Next to proceed to the next step.

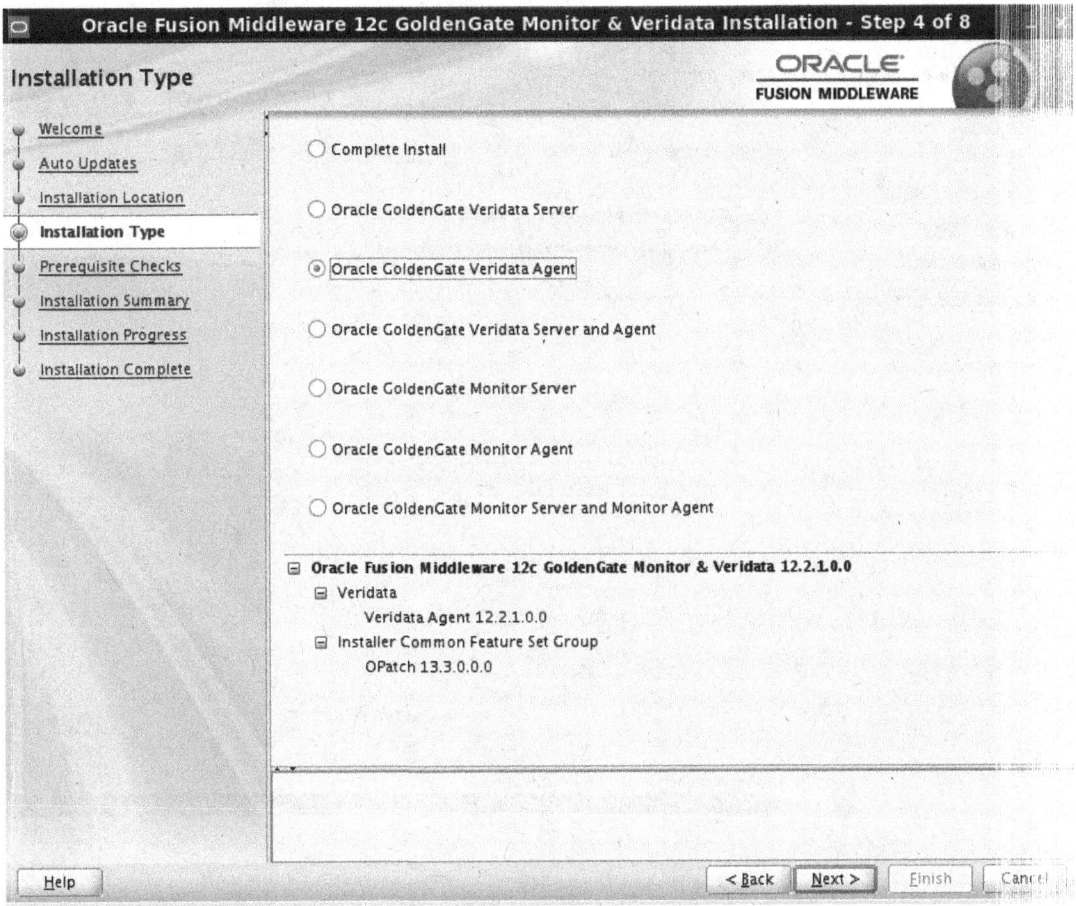

Figure 6-54. *Oracle Veridata agent configuration*

At this point, all prerequisite checks will be performed (Figure 6-55). If there are any issues to be corrected, a notification will occur. Should any of the prerequisite checks fail, you can correct them now. If the prerequisite check completes satisfactorily, click Next to proceed to the next step.

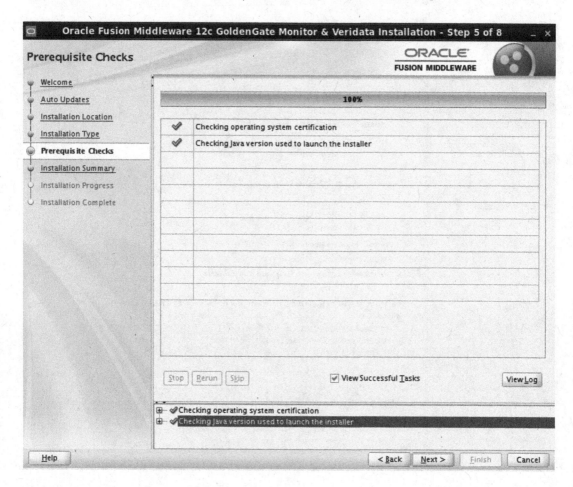

Figure 6-55. *Oracle Veridata agent configuration*

During this step, you are able to confirm all of your previous choices. Be sure to take the opportunity to note the ORACLE_HOME location as well as the location of the log files should you need to inspect them later. If the choices are appropriate, click Install to proceed (Figure 6-56).

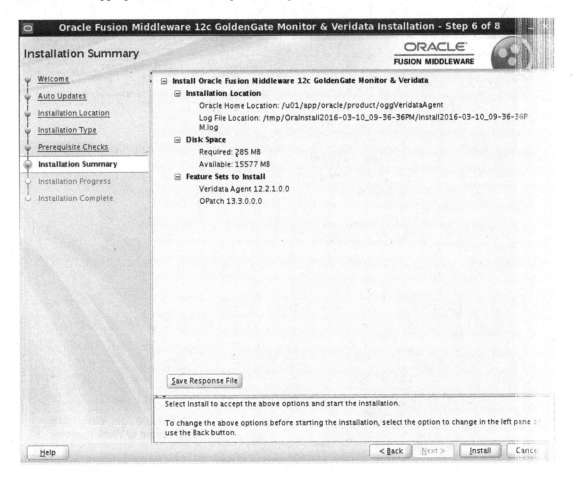

Figure 6-56. *Oracle Veridata agent configuration*

Once the software begins to install, you will be presented with the Installation Progress page shown in Figure 6-57. There is nothing specific to do here other than to monitor the installation. Once the software reports that the process is 100 percent complete, click Next to go to the Completion page.

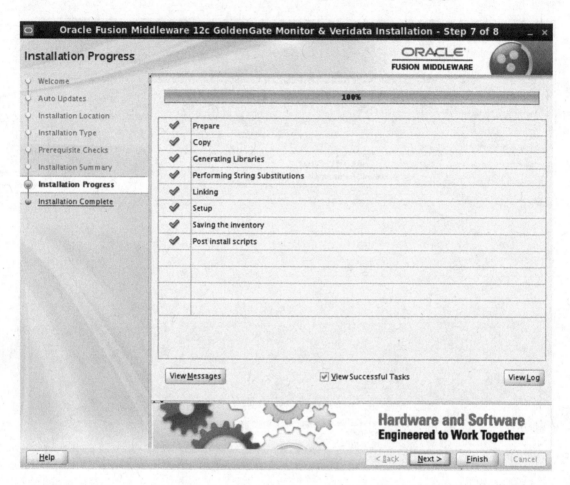

Figure 6-57. *Oracle Veridata agent configuration*

This last step, Figure 6-58, summarizes the actions of the Installation Wizard. Here you have another opportunity to take note of the ORACLE_HOME location as well as the location of the log files created during installation. Remember, you will need to reference the ORACLE_HOME for the agent during the agent deploy process.

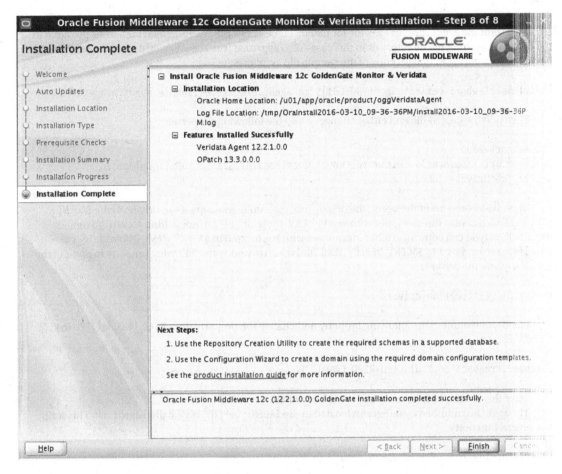

Figure 6-58. Oracle Veridata agent configuration

Deploying and Starting the Oracle GoldenGate Veridata Agent

Once the agent software is installed, it needs to be deployed and some basic configuration items adjusted. First, it is important to know the location where you want to deploy the agent. If you recall, we previously set up two locations, the AGENT_BASE_DIR (/u01/app/oracle/product/oggVeridataAgent) and the AGENT_DEPLOY_HOME (/u01/app/oracle/product/veridataAgentVBOXDB1). It is important to remember that you must deploy an agent for each instance running on the host. The only way to not deploy individual agents would be to manually modify configuration files each time you wanted to switch instances.

Before we proceed, be sure that the environment variables that were previously defined for the agent have been sourced in. To deploy the agent, execute the following steps:

```
[oracle@orcl-vbox1 ~]$ cd /u01/app/oracle/product/oggVeridataAgent/veridata/agent

[oracle@orcl-vbox1 agent]$ ./agent_config.sh /u01/app/oracle/product/veridataAgentVBOXDB1
```

This will write an instance of the agent to the specified directory.

Next, you need to configure the agent that was just deployed. To configure the agent, you first need to create and edit the agent.properties file for that instance. A sample agent.properties file is provided in the deployed agent home directory or in this case /u01/app/oracle/product/veridataAgentVBOXDB1. To begin the configuration, make a copy of the sample file as follows:

```
[oracle@orcl-vbox1 veridataAgentVBOXDB1]$ cp agent.properties.sample agent.properties
```

Then edit the copied file and either change or add the following properties:

```
server.port=7850
database.url=jdbc:oracle:thin:@orcl-vbox1.localdomain:1521:VBOXDB1.localdomain
server.jdbcDriver=ojdbc7.jar
```

In previous versions of the agent, the deploy process would also copy JDBC drivers to the $AGENT_DEPLOY_HOME/drivers directory, but with version 12.2, these drivers are not getting copied. To remedy this situation, you can copy the ojdbc7.jar driver, which is located in $AGENT_BASE_DIR/oracle_common/modules/oracle.jdbc/ to $AGENT_DEPLOY_HOME/drivers, or modify the following property to point to the location where the driver is.

```
server.driversLocation=drivers
```

Finally, uncomment the following property and change the property from READ_UNCOMMITTED to READ_COMMITTED.

```
database.transaction.isolation=READ_COMMITTED
```

Once this is complete, we are ready to start the agent.

The agent is controlled by one script located in the $AGENT_DEPLOY_HOME called agent.sh. This script has several functions:

```
start|run|stop|reloadLog|version|debug
```

We focus on using the start and stop functions of the script. If you do not have the luxury of manipulating this script from a scheduling tool, then you will have to remember to start the agent via a local session. To do this, execute the following command:

```
[oracle@orcl-vbox1 ~]$ $AGENT_DEPLOY_HOME/agent.sh start
```

All logs will be directed to the following location: $AGENT_DEPLOY_HOME/logs.

Starting the Veridata Application Server

Because the Veridata application server is an application within a WebLogic domain, we must first start the WebLogic administration server for that domain. To start the server, navigate to the DOMAIN_HOME where WebLogic was installed. As you recall from earlier in the chapter, that location is:

```
[oracle@orcl-vbox1 ~]$ cd /home/oracle/config/domains/oggVeridata
```

Once you have changed to that directory, start the WebLogic administration server by running the following command:

```
[oracle@orcl-vbox1 bin]$ ./startWebLogic.sh
```

If you recall, we configured the domain to be a production domain, so it will prompt you for the admin username and password. When we configured the WebLogic administration server, we used weblogic as the username and welcome1 as the password. To avoid this prompt, you will need to create a boot identity file. More information on this can be found in the "Administering Server Startup and Shutdown for Oracle WebLogic Server" documentation.

This command also starts the administration server as a foreground process. This might be fine for development or debugging purposes, but to start the server in the background and to ensure that it continues to run after you have exited your session, start the server the following way:

```
[oracle@orcl-vbox1 bin]$ nohup ./startWebLogic.sh > startWebLogic.log &
```

After looking at the log, and ensuring that the server has started properly, test the administration server URL for proper operation by navigating your browser to either of the following addresses. These addresses were presented to you on the final summary page when you created the domain.

```
http://192.168.56.203:7001/console
```

or

```
http://veridata.localdomain:7001/console
```

Once on the splash page (Figure 6-59), to log in, enter the admin username and password that you configured during the WebLogic administration server installation. In our case, the username was weblogic and the password is welcome1.

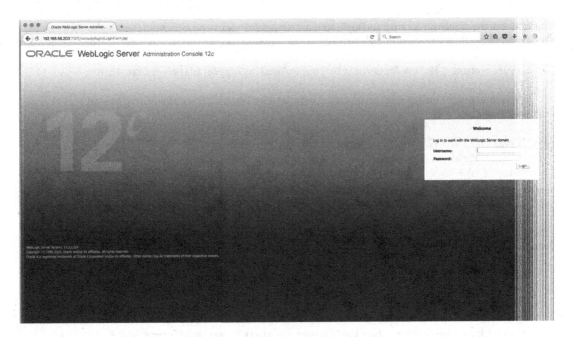

Figure 6-59. WebLogic administration server

After logging in, you should see the administration server Home Page, which should look similar to Figure 6-60.

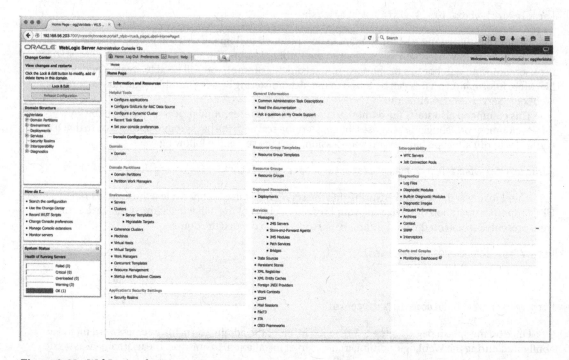

Figure 6-60. *WebLogic administration server*

Now that the admin server is up and login tests are successful, we can proceed with starting the Veridata application server. To start, simply change to the Veridata managed server bin directory, which, in our case is this:

```
[oracle@orcl-vbox1 ~]$  cd /home/oracle/config/domains/oggVeridata/veridata/bin
```

In this directory, there is a start script called veridataServer.sh. This script is used to start the managed server.

```
[oracle@veridata bin]$ ./veridataServer.sh
Usage : VeridataServer(.sh/.cmd)(start/stop) [SERVER_NAME] [ADMIN_URL]
[Optional] SERVER_NAME   : Veridata Managed Server Name to Start or Stop.
                         : Default Veridata Managed Server Name is : VERIDATA_server1
[Optional] ADMIN_URL     : Veridata Domain Admin Server URL
                         : Default is : t3://192.168.56.203:7001

[oracle@veridata bin]$ ./veridataServer.sh start
```

This command will start the managed server as a foreground process. This might be fine for development or debugging purposes, but to start the server in the background and to ensure that it continues to run after you have exited your session, start the server the following way:

```
[oracle@veridata bin]$ nohup ./veridataServer.sh start > veridataServer.log &
```

After a few minutes, the server should start. You can confirm server start by either checking the log file for a message similar to the following or by directly logging into the server:

```
<Notice> <WebLogicServer> <BEA-000365> <Server state changed to RUNNING.>
```

If the default address was not changed during setup, you should be able to get to the login splash page by using either of the following addresses:

```
http://192.168.56.203:8830/veridata
```

or

```
http://veridata.localdomain:8830/veridata
```

Before a login to the server will be successful, a user must be created and appropriate privileges assigned. Although the WebLogic administrator user can be used, this is not best practice. To create a user specific to Veridata, execute the following steps.

On the administration server Home Page, click Security Realm on the left ribbon menu. Once you access the Security Realm menu, a screen similar to the one in Figure 6-61 should open.

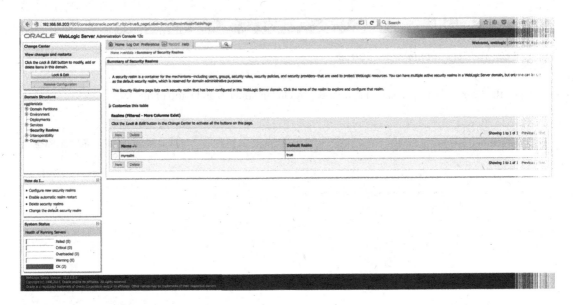

Figure 6-61. *WebLogic administration server*

Click myrealm to enter the security settings for the oggVeridata domain (Figure 6-62).

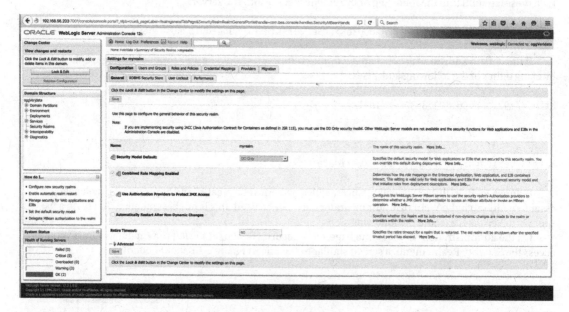

Figure 6-62. *WebLogic administration server*

Open the User and Groups page (Figure 6-63) by clicking the tab at the top of the page.

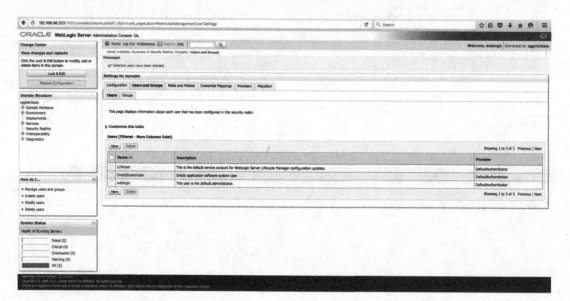

Figure 6-63. *WebLogic administration server*

Click New and proceed to enter the information required (Figure 6-64):

- *Name:* veridataadmin

- *Description:* Admin User for the Veridata Application Server

- *Provider:* Leave set to the default value of DefaultAuthenticator

- *Password:* Choose a password that best suits your environment

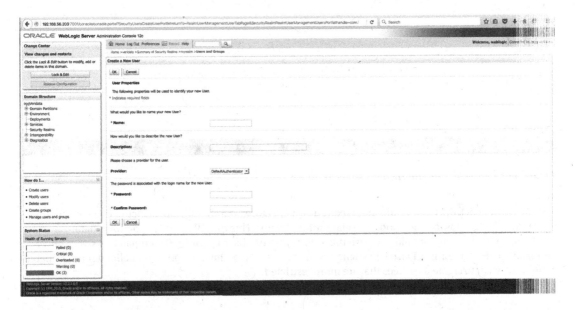

Figure 6-64. *WebLogic administration server*

Once all of the information has been entered, click OK to return to the Users and Groups page. Next, the appropriate roles must be assigned to the user. To begin this step, click the name of the user, and then click the Groups tab at the top of the page (Figure 6-65).

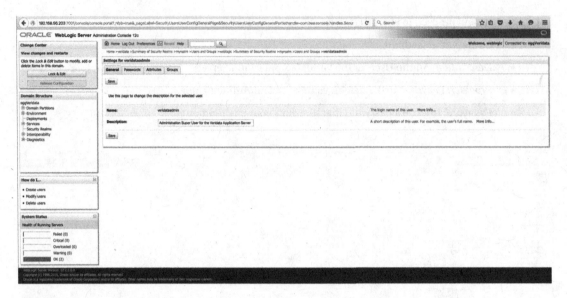

Figure 6-65. *WebLogic administration server*

When you click the Groups tab, the screen shown in Figure 6-66 should appear. Scroll to the bottom of the Available groups list and choose veridataAdministrator. This role allows you to perform data validation tasks; however, should you wish this user to also be able to perform data repair tasks, the role of veridataRepairOperator must also be assigned. You will notice that there are other predefined roles available should you wish to create user roles that are more restricted.

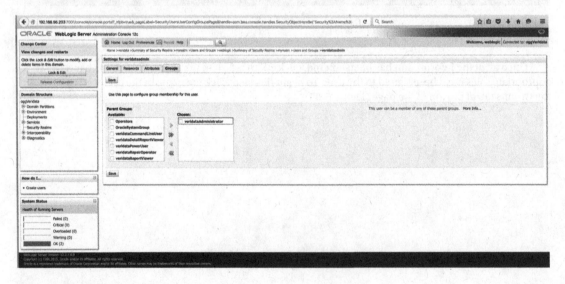

Figure 6-66. *WebLogic administration server*

Click Save to continue. Once again, you will be redirected to the main Users and Groups page. At this point you are ready to test logging into the Veridata application server. To do this, proceed to either of the following addresses:

http://192.168.56.203:8830/veridata

or

http://veridata.localdomain:8830/veridata

Once the page has loaded, you should see the login page shown in Figure 6-67.

Figure 6-67. *WebLogic administration server*

At this point, the user that was just created can be used to log in. After a successful login, you should see the page shown in Figure 6-68.

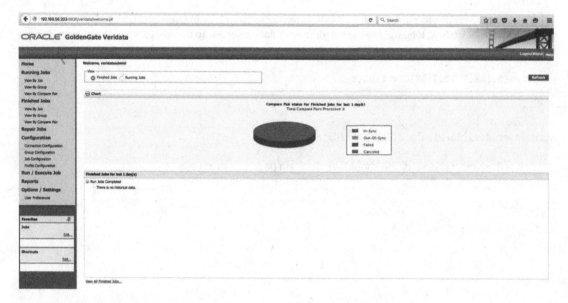

Figure 6-68. *WebLogic administration server*

You are now ready to begin your first data validation task.

Configure Veridata Data Validation Connections

Now that the tool is installed, and the application server and all agents are running, it is time to execute a data comparison task. Being able to execute this in an automated, unattended fashion is invaluable in a data replication scenario. The first step in this process is to define the source and target database connections. On the Veridata application server Home page, click Connection Configuration on the Configuration menu in the left menu ribbon (Figure 6-69).

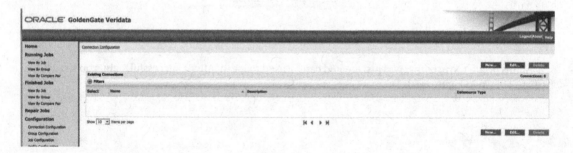

Figure 6-69. *Veridata application server: Define connection*

From there, click New to define a new connection (Figure 6-70).

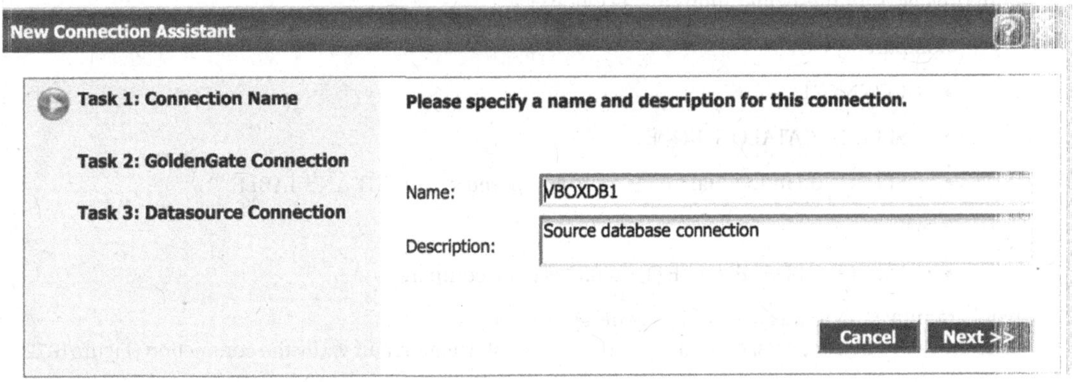

Figure 6-70. *Veridata application server: Define connection*

Once you have given the connection a name and description, click Next to move to the next step. This is where you will define the connection details to the agent (Figure 6-71).

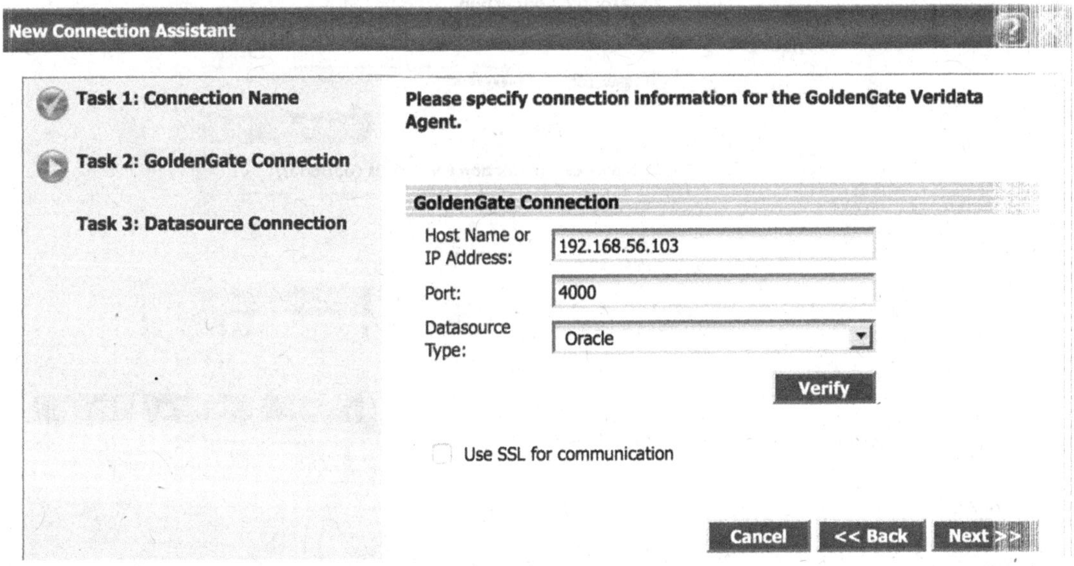

Figure 6-71. *Veridata application server: Define connection*

First, enter either the IP address or hostname. Then, enter the port number of the Veridata agent. In this configuration, it is 4000. At this time, choose what type of data source this represents. In this case, select Oracle. You can also observe here all of the possible data sources that Veridata can compare. It is important to note that in this example, we are using an IP address versus a hostname due to the virtual box configuration where there is no DNS server available; as a workaround, you can make an entry in the /etc/hosts file. It is advisable to always use a hostname versus an IP address.

Click Verify to check the validity of the connection. Once a successful check is obtained, click Next'to proceed. In the next dialog box, user information for the compare and repair operations is needed. The minimum privileges for these operations are as follows:

- Compare

  - CONNECT

  - SELECT_CATALOG_ROLE

  - SELECT on individual tables to be compared or SELECT ANY TABLE

- Repair

  - INSERT, UPDATE, DELETE on tables to be compared

Avoid granting DBA to this user, as it is generally unnecessary.

Once the dialog box appears, enter the pertinent user information and verify the connection (Figure 6-72).

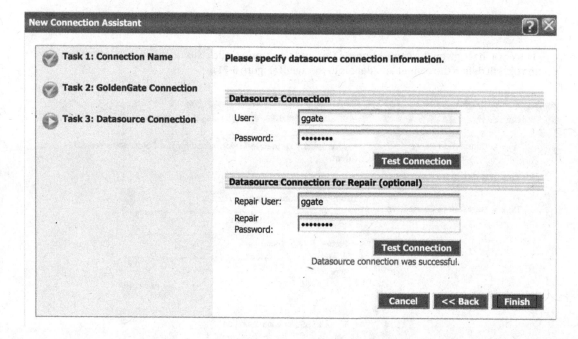

Figure 6-72. *Veridata application server: Define connection*

Click Finish to complete the definition and repeat the task for your target database.

Create Data Validation Job Group

Before we can actually create a job, we should define a job group. Groups are logical containers for one or more compare pairs. They help you to organize and partition large or diverse sets of data into more manageable units. Groups are linked to jobs when jobs are created. Any group can be linked to one or more jobs, allowing you complete control over how and when data are compared. Remember, before you can create a job group, the source and target connection you plan to use must be previously defined.

To begin, select Group Configuration from the Configuration menu on the left menu bar (Figure 6-73). The first dialog box you will see is where you will define the name of the group.

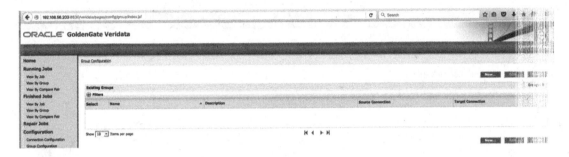

Figure 6-73. *Veridata application server: Create job group*

Click New to begin defining the group in the dialog box shown in Figure 6-74. Enter an appropriate name and description for the job group you would like to create. When the information has been entered, click Next to proceed.

New Group Assistant

● Task 1: Group Name	**Please specify a name and description for this group.**
Task 2: Connection Information	From: _____ ▼ **Browse...**
	Name: HR Comparison Group
	Description: HR Schema Comparison Group

Cancel **Next >>**

Figure 6-74. *Veridata application server: Create job group*

At this time, select the appropriate source and target connection information in the drop-down lists provided (Figure 6-75). Once the choices are made, click Finish to continue.

New Group Assistant

✓ Task 1: Group Name	**Please link datasource connections to this group.**
● Task 2: Connection Information	**Source And Target Connections**
	Source Connection: VBOXDB1 ▼ **Browse...**
	Target Connection: VBOXDB2 ▼ **Browse...**

Cancel **<< Back** **Finish**

Figure 6-75. *Veridata application server: Create job group*

Next a confirmation dialog box is presented with the ability to define the comparison pairs for the group. Ensure that the check box is checked and then click OK (Figure 6-76).

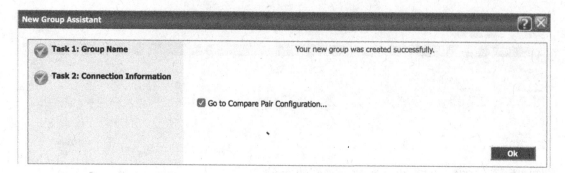

Figure 6-76. Veridata application server: Create job group

At this point, the Compare Pair Configuration screen is presented (Figure 6-77).

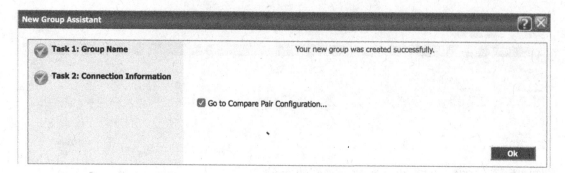

Figure 6-77. Veridata application server: Create job group

Click the Pattern Mapping tab and select the schema that will be compared on both the source and target. Because we know the two schemas to match definitions, there is no need to change any of the other settings. Even though none of the other selections are changed, you can see how flexible the tool is when it comes to matching objects for comparison.

Click Generate Mappings to continue. The next screen gives you one last opportunity to adjust mappings as appropriate (Figure 6-78).

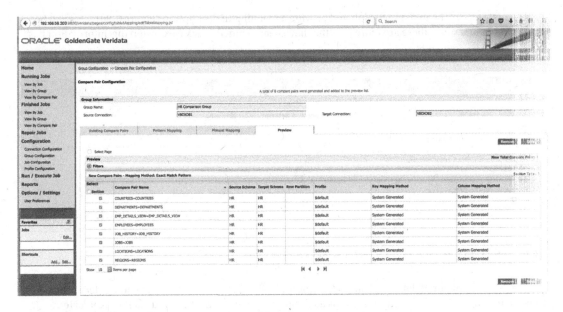

Figure 6-78. *Veridata application server: Create job group*

For example, there is no need to compare the EMP_DETAILS_VIEW, so that object can be removed from the mapping by selecting the check box to the left of the object name and clicking Remove on the lower right side of the grid. Once that object has been deleted, click Save to save the mapping and return to the Home page. At this point, it is time to define the comparison job.

Create Data Validation Job

After configuring the connections for a source and target database, the next task is to create and configure a validation job. On the Home page (Figure 6-79), click Job Configuration on the left ribbon to begin the task. Click New to create a new job.

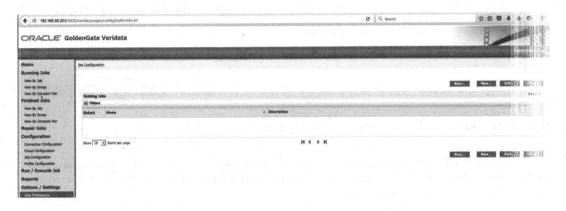

Figure 6-79. *Veridata application server: Create compare job*

The first step will be to name the job and provide a meaningful description (Figure 6-80). This will be useful in the future when there are more jobs that have been defined. Click Next when this information has been completed.

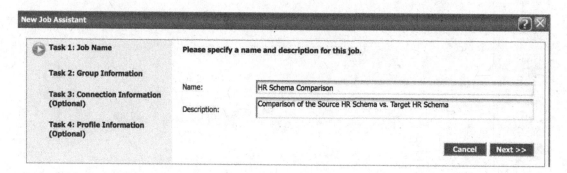

Figure 6-80. *Veridata application server: Create compare job*

If you have configured data verification groups, this is the dialog box where you could select those groups to be part of the job definition. Groups are helpful in a situation where you want to precreate groupings of connections that define a source and target database pair as well as a predefined comparison mapping (Figure 6-81).

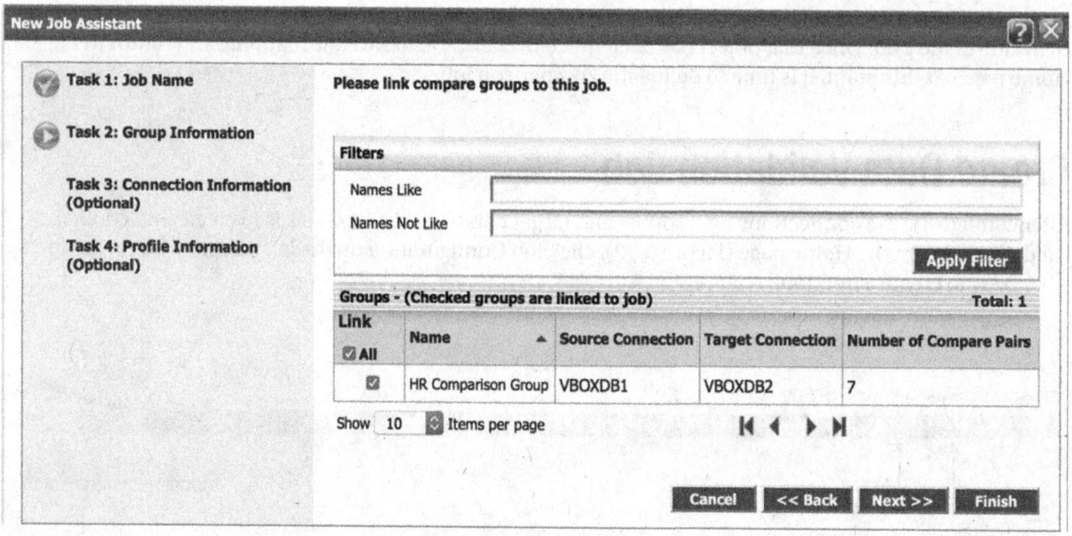

Figure 6-81. *Veridata application server: Create compare job*

Because there were groups defined, we are able to skip tasks 3 and 4 (Figure 6-82). If there were no groups defined, we would need to continue to tasks 3 and 4 and enter connection and profile information. Click Finish to complete configuration of the job.

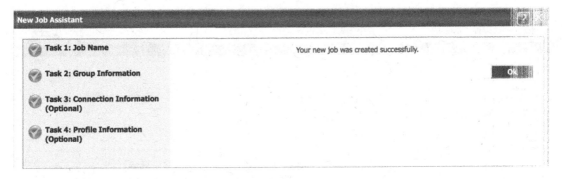

Figure 6-82. *Veridata application server: Create compare job*

The system is now ready to execute a simple data validation job.

Execute Veridata Data Validation

Now that the job has been defined, it is time to execute our first comparison task. To run the job, enter the appropriate menu by clicking Run/Execute Job on the left menu ribbon. This opens the Run/Execute Job dialog box shown in Figure 6-83.

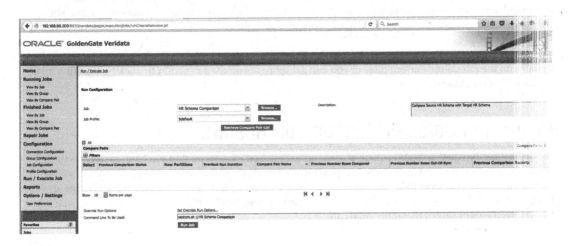

Figure 6-83. *Veridata application server: Execute compare job*

The first step is to select the job, which was just defined, from the Job drop-down list. You should notice that many other fields were filled in based on the job definition selected. However, before the job can be run, the retrieval of the pair list must be completed. To do so, click Retrieve Compare Pair List (Figure 6-84). Once the pairs are retrieved, a summary is displayed.

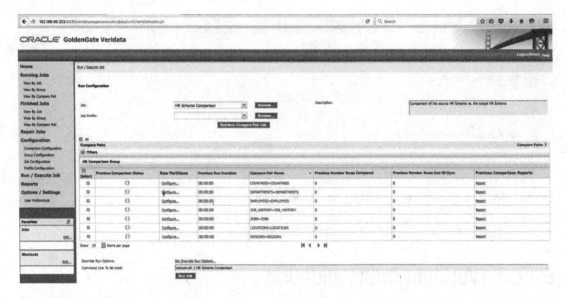

Figure 6-84. *Veridata application server: Execute compare job*

One additional item to notice is the text box at the bottom of the screen. Veridata provides the command to run to execute the comparison job directly from the command line. This is very useful should you not have access to the GUI or would like to configure scheduled run based on crontab or some other scheduling method.

At this point, the job can be executed, so click Run Job to proceed. The GUI will then present status updates on the job via the current page or you can get more detailed information by clicking Running Jobs on the left menu ribbon.

Reviewing Data Verification Job Results

Once the job is finished, a record will be placed in the Finished Jobs menu that can be accessed via the left ribbon menu. As shown in Figure 6-85, it appears that the last run of this comparison job was successful and found no differences in data. This is indicated by the green equals sign in the grid at the bottom of the screen. Additional details about the job run can be obtained by clicking the Report hyperlink, which is located on the right side of that individual run.

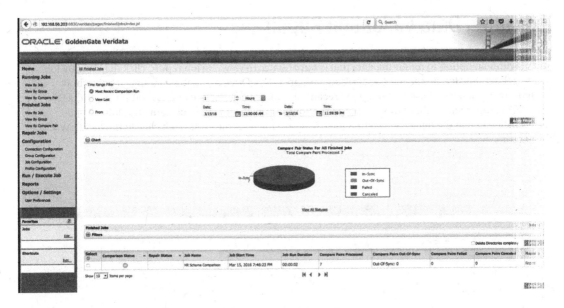

Figure 6-85. *Veridata application server: View compare job results*

Should you encounter a situation where Veridata finds a data inconsistency, there will be an indicator for that job as shown in Figure 6-86.

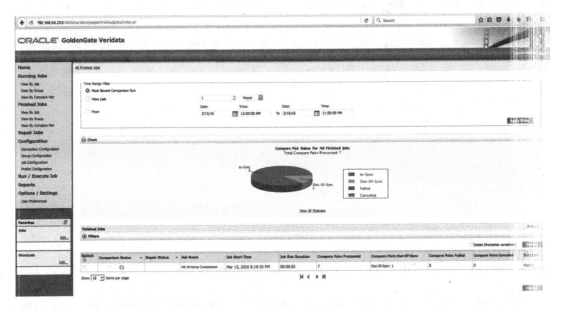

Figure 6-86. *Veridata application server: View compare job results*

Executing Data Validation Repair

When there is a data out of sync condition detected, Veridata application server reports the inconsistency and provides an option to repair the data that is out of sync. To view the job report, click the View By Job heading that is located on the left menu ribbon (Figure 6-87). Once there, the default will be to show the most recent job run. Based on our most recent run, we have a data out of sync condition for the HR. EMPLOYEES table. Details about this out of sync condition can be viewed by clicking the Out-of-Sync hyperlink located in the details about that job run. Once the hyperlink has been clicked the details will be displayed.

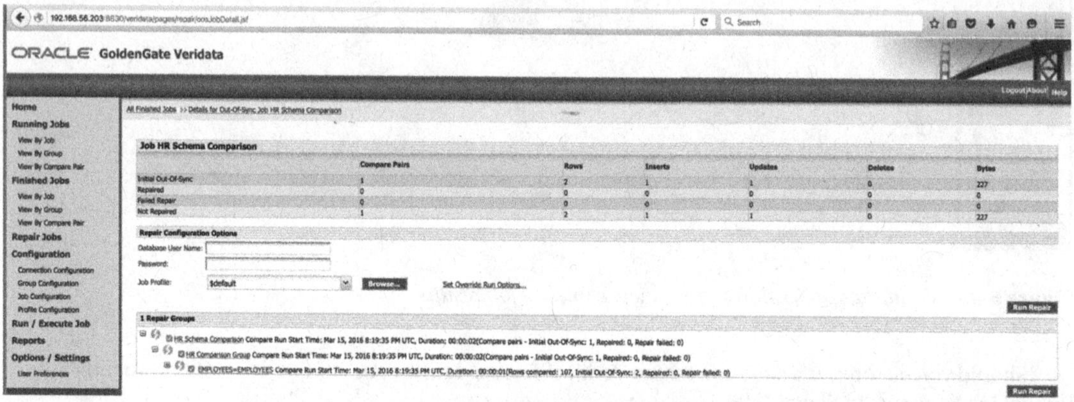

Figure 6-87. *Veridata application server: Execute data repair job results*

Veridata makes the task of repairing these data very simple. To see additional details about the data that are actually out of sync, click the + that is next to the table that shows an out-of-sync condition (Figure 6-88).

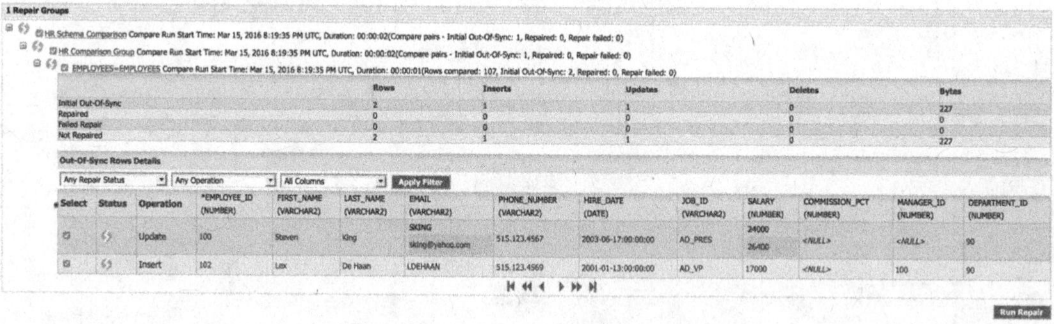

Figure 6-88. *Veridata application server: Execute data repair job results*

Veridata has detected that one row is missing from the target and another row requires an update to the data to become in sync. This screen also provides the opportunity to specify a database user and password that can be used to execute the repair. Because we defined the repair user as part of our connection configuration, the repair can be executed without specifying this information. At this point, click Run Repair.

Once the repair is completed, the system will return a report of what exactly was done, as shown in Figure 6-89. The green equals sign indicates that the rows are now in sync.

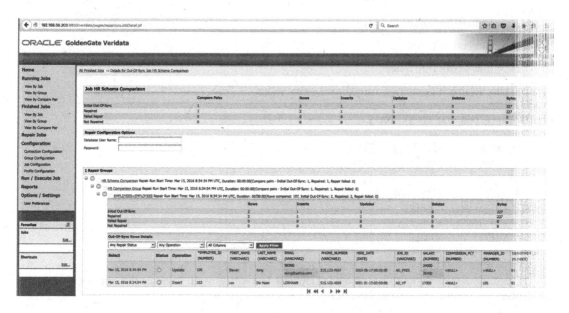

Figure 6-89. *Veridata application server: Execute data repair job results*

Notice that the rows that were repaired are still shown, as well as the proper and invalid data. If necessary, additional details can be found about the repair job by clicking Repair Jobs on the left ribbon menu and then drilling down into the appropriate job.

Alternative Methods of Data Comparison

If Veridata is not available for use for your implementation, there are a few other methods to compare data between a source and target database. Unfortunately, all of the other methods are not as accurate as Veridata. In most cases, though, these methods will provide a good indication that is something is awry with your data. In this section the following alternative methods are described:

- Row counts between schemas.

- DBMS_COMPARE package.

Although comparing row counts between schemas might seem a bit rudimentary, it is a good first step in determining if inconsistencies exist. Keep in mind that if a system is busy, row count differences could always exist; however, based on timestamps of when the count occurred and the typical GoldenGate heartbeat lag, a reasonable assumption can be made as to whether or not a true problem exists.

To start with this methodology, it is best to create a table in your target system GoldenGate schema (commonly defined within the GGSCHEMA parameter in the GLOBALS file). The table definition is very simple. The compare job will record the following metadata for each table:

- Table Owner

- Table Name

- Start Time

- End Time

- Source Row Count

- Target Row Count

- Row Count Difference

The table itself can be created using the following DDL:

```
CREATE TABLE OGG_ROW_COUNT_STATS
  (
    SCHEMANAME      VARCHAR2(30 BYTE),
    TABLENAME       VARCHAR2(30 BYTE),
    START_TIME      TIMESTAMP (6),
    END_TIME        TIMESTAMP (6),
    ROW_CNT_SOURCE NUMBER,
    ROW_CNT_TARGET NUMBER,
    CNT_DIFF        NUMBER
  );
```

To communicate with the source system, a database link will be used. To create this link, log in as the GoldenGate user and create the database link with the following DDL:

```
CREATE DATABASE LINK VBOXDB1 CONNECT TO GGATE IDENTIFED BY [PASSWORD] USING '(DESCRIPTION
= (ADDRESS = (PROTOCOL = TCP)(HOST = orcl-vbox1.localdomain)(PORT = 1521))(CONNECT_DATA =
(SERVER = DEDICATED)(SERVICE_NAME = VBOXDB1.localdomain)));
```

To run the row count check in a common fashion each time, a stored procedure is used. Each run of this procedure will insert or update a row for each table and record the count difference. A report can then be generated from the OGG_ROW_COUNT_STATS table to determine if there are differences that warrant further investigation. The stored procedure similar to the following can be used:

```
CREATE OR REPLACE PROCEDURE OGG_ROW_COUNT_STATS_SP(
    v_tgtschema IN VARCHAR2,
    v_srcschema IN VARCHAR2,
    v_dblink    IN VARCHAR2,
    v_tbl       IN VARCHAR2)
IS
  v_tgtcount NUMBER(16) := 0;
  v_srccount NUMBER(16) := 0;
  v_cntdiff  NUMBER(16) := 0;
  v_sqlstmt0 VARCHAR2(1000);
  v_sqlstmt1 VARCHAR2(1000);
  v_sqlstmt2 VARCHAR2(1000);
  v_begints  TIMESTAMP := systimestamp;
  v_endts    TIMESTAMP := systimestamp;
BEGIN
  FOR vtable IN
  (SELECT table_name
   FROM all_tables
   WHERE owner      = v_tgtschema
   AND table_name IN
     (SELECT table_name
      FROM all_tab_cols
```

```
      WHERE owner     = v_tgtschema
      AND table_name = v_tbl)
  ORDER BY 1)
  LOOP
    v_begints  := systimestamp;
    v_sqlstmt0 := 'select /*+ parallel('||vtable.table_name||',8) */ count(*) from '||v_
    tgtschema||'.'||vtable.table_name;
    EXECUTE immediate v_sqlstmt0 INTO v_tgtcount;
    v_sqlstmt1 := 'select /*+ parallel('||vtable.table_name||',4) */ count(*) from '||v_
    srcschema||'.'||vtable.table_name||'@'||v_dblink;
    EXECUTE immediate v_sqlstmt1 INTO v_srccount;
    v_cntdiff  := v_tgtcount - v_srccount;
    v_endts    := systimestamp;
    v_sqlstmt2 := 'update OGG_ROW_COUNT_STATS set row_cnt_source='|| v_srccount ||',
    row_cnt_target=' || v_tgtcount || ', start_time='''||v_begints||''', end_time='''||v_
    endts||''', cnt_diff='||v_cntdiff||' where schemaname='''||v_tgtschema||''' and
    tablename='''||vtable.table_name||''' and status=1';
    EXECUTE immediate v_sqlstmt2;
    IF (sql%notfound) THEN
      v_sqlstmt2 := 'insert into OGG_ROW_COUNT_STATS (schemaname,tablename,start_
      time,end_time,row_cnt_source,row_cnt_target,status,cnt_diff) values ('''||upper(v_
      tgtschema)||''','''||vtable.table_name||''','''||v_begints||''','''||v_endts||''','
      v_srccount || ',' || v_tgtcount || ', 1,'||v_cntdiff||')';
      EXECUTE immediate v_sqlstmt2;
    END IF;
    COMMIT;
  END LOOP;
EXCEPTION
WHEN OTHERS THEN
  DBMS_OUTPUT.PUT_LINE(SQLERRM);
END;
/
```

Once the procedure has been created, it can be run for each and every schema that needs to be compared. As mentioned earlier, due to the simple nature of this procedure, it might erroneously indicate row count differences simply due to the timing of replication that is actively occurring. Make sure that any lag is taken into account. Of course if the environment has been set up with FLASHBACK, you can use a FLASHBACK query along with GoldenGate lag statistics to get a more accurate indication as to what is occurring in the system.

Another alternative method to perform data validation is to use the DBMS_COMPARE package. Included as part of the base database install and originally used for verification of Streams replication, these packages can also be used to verify data replicated by GoldenGate. Keep in mind that although there are some built in optimizations, such as using hash methodology to compare data, the package executes the comparison on a row-by-row basis, which can be very slow, especially in the case of tables with very wide rows or tables with a large row count. The package does have some advanced features such as utilizing a sample size, but we do not discuss these features as part of this chapter.

Finally, there are some limitations to the package in that it is not able to compare LOB data types, nor is it able to compare tables without a primary key. For a full listing of the limitations of DBMS_COMPARE, please consult the Oracle documentation.

To use this package, just like with the row count stored procedure, a database link needs to be present. Because the creation of that database object has already been discussed, it is assumed that it is still present for this demonstration. The general steps to carry out the compare are accomplished in the following order:

1. Create a comparison task.

2. Execute the comparison task.

3. Address any inconsistencies.

For this demonstration, we compare the HR.EMPLOYEES table. First, create the task:

```
BEGIN
  DBMS_COMPARISON.CREATE_COMPARISON(
    comparison_name    => 'HR_EMPLOYEES_COMPARE',
    schema_name        => 'HR',
    object_name        => 'EMPLOYEES',
    dblink_name        => 'VBOXDB2.LOCALDOMAIN');
END;
/


PL/SQL procedure successfully completed.
Elapsed: 00:00:21.51
```

Now that the comparison definition has been created, we can execute a comparison task. To execute the comparison:

```
SET SERVEROUTPUT ON
DECLARE
  consistent    BOOLEAN;
  compare_info  DBMS_COMPARISON.COMPARISON_TYPE;
BEGIN
  consistent := DBMS_COMPARISON.COMPARE(
    comparison_name => 'HR_EMPLOYEES_COMPARE',
    scan_info       => compare_info,
    perform_row_dif => TRUE
  );
  DBMS_OUTPUT.PUT_LINE('Scan ID: '||compare_info.scan_id);
  IF consistent=TRUE THEN
    DBMS_OUTPUT.PUT_LINE('The table is equivalent');
  ELSE
    DBMS_OUTPUT.PUT_LINE('Tables are not equivalent… there is data divergence.');
    DBMS_OUTPUT.PUT_LINE('Check the dba_comparison and dba_comparison_scan_summary views for
    locate the differences for compare_id:'||compare_info.scan_id);
  END IF;
END;
/


Scan ID: 61
The table is equivalent
PL/SQL procedure successfully completed.

Elapsed: 00:00:00.40
```

So on this run, this package has determined that the data are the same in both tables. Let's run the comparison again after deliberately modifying data in the target system.

```
Scan ID: 62
Tables are not equivalent… there is data divergence.
Check the dba_comparison and dba_comparison_scan_summary views for locate the differences
for compare_id:62

PL/SQL procedure successfully completed.

Elapsed: 00:00:00.12
```

The package has detected data divergence. So how do we tell what rows are different? Oracle provides a few system tables that can be queried to tell what rows are different: DBA_COMPARISON, DBA_COMPARISON_SCAN_SUMMARY, and DBA_COMPARISON_ROW_DIF, among others. Using either SQL/Plus or SQL/DEVELOPER, let's look further into these tables to determine the different data (Figure 6-90). After querying DBA_COMPARISON_ROW_DIF, we can see that there is one row that is different. The package provides the ROWID of both the local row and the remote row that are different.

Figure 6-90. *DBMS_COMPARISON*

Now that we know the rows that differ, we can use a simple UNION statement to compare the data as in Figure 6-91.

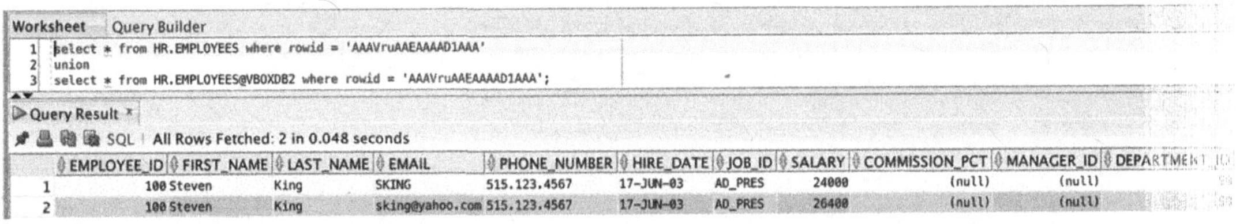

Figure 6-91. *DBMS_COMPARISON*

There are multiple ways to address the data divergence and that can be addressed as appropriate for the current situation.

Summary

This chapter took a very comprehensive look at Oracle Veridata from installing through data validation. You should now have a good understanding of how to use one of the best tools for verifying data in a GoldenGate environment. The next chapter looks at some of the advanced features of Oracle GoldenGate. Understanding and using advanced features, you will see how you can build out a robust Oracle GoldenGate framework.

CHAPTER 7

■ ■ ■

Advanced Features

To this point, you have been given a lot of information related to how Oracle GoldenGate can be installed, configured, run, verified and monitored. These are all great things to understand when running Oracle GoldenGate. Although these are the basics, Oracle GoldenGate also provides additional features to help you customize and make management a bit easier. These are the advanced features of Oracle GoldenGate.

Advanced features are used to help administrators customize, scale, and process transactions in a more robust way. This chapter takes a look at how to create and use macros, define and use tokens, and other advanced features of Oracle GoldenGate.

Macros

Macros are a powerful feature of Oracle GoldenGate. In the many deployments I have done, this seems to be the one feature that can prevent many mistakes within the environment. Macros provide a way to modularize the code base for the replication environment and make it easier to move replication settings between release environments. Many people, however, do not understand this simple time-saving technique.

Although macros are a timesaver, the question is where these modules of code should be stored for reuse. If you look at the subdirectories within the Oracle GoldenGate home, you will notice there is no directory named dirmac. This is normal because most people who use macros often put the macro files in the dirprm directory. I actually think this is bad practice because it doesn't provide a clear mapping of what is in the directory. To remedy this problem, you should create the dirmac" directory manually; then all the macros that you use within the environment can be called from a single location.

Creating a Macro

As discussed, macros are a very powerful tool to use within Oracle GoldenGate, as they provide the ability to modularize the GoldenGate environment. To use a macro, it first needs to be created and then set up to be used within the GoldenGate processes.

A macro is simply a code block that can be reused over and over again in the same environment or copied to other environments. The basics of a macro read similar to a PL/SQL code block. Listing 7-1 shows the basic components.

Listing 7-1. Basic Macro Code

```
MACRO <name>
BEGIN
<GoldenGate related information>
END;
```

© Bobby Curtis 2016
B. Curtis, *Pro Oracle GoldenGate for the DBA*, DOI 10.1007/978-1-4842-1179-3_7

In Listing 7-1, you see that the macro is created by simply editing a text file and adding lines that name the macro and define the beginning and the end of the macro. Everything in between the BEGIN and END calls of the macro are general GoldenGate commands that will be read when the GoldenGate process starts. To illustrate this functionality, Listing 7-2 shows what the macro rtables look like in my test environment.

Listing 7-2. Test Macro Example

```
MACRO #rtables
BEGIN
MAP SOE.ADDRESSES, TARGET SOE.ADDRESSES;
MAP SOE.CARD_DETAILS, TARGET SOE.CARD_DETAILS THREAD(2);
MAP SOE.CUSTOMERS, TARGET SOE.CUSTOMERS, THREAD(3);
MAP SOE.INVENTORIES, TARGET SOE.INVENTORIES, THREAD(4);
MAP SOE.LOGON, TARGET SOE.LOGON, THREAD(5);
MAP SOE.ORDER_ITEMS, TARGET SOE.ORDER_ITEMS, THREAD(1);
MAP SOE.ORDERENTRY_METADATA, TARGET SOE.ORDERENTRY_METADATA, THREAD(2);
MAP SOE.PRODUCT_DESCRIPTIONS, TARGET SOE.PRODUCT_DESCRIPTIONS, THREAD(4);
MAP SOE.PRODUCT_INFORMATION, TARGET SOE.PRODUCT_INFORMATION, THREAD(5);
MAP SOE.WAREHOUSES, TARGET SOE.WAREHOUSES, THREAD(1);
END;
```

■ **Note** The lines with THREAD(#) are related to a coordinated replicat.

Now that you have a macro that can be used to map tables, how do you use the macro in a parameter file? Like many programming languages that allow you to modularize code, an INCLUDE statement is needed to tell the GoldenGate process to read the associated file. Listing 7-3 shows how this is done using the replicat process.

Listing 7-3. Illustration of Including Macros

```
INCLUDE ./dirmac/rtables.mac
REPLICAT RSRC1
SETENV (ORACLE_HOME="/opt/app/oracle/product/12.1.0.2/dbhome_1")
SETENV (ORACLE_SID="rmt12c")
USERID GGATE, PASSWORD ********
ASSUMETARGETDEFS
REPORTCOUNT EVERY 5 SECONDS, RATE
DISCARDFILE ./dirrpt/RSRC1.dsc, append, megabytes 500
#rtables();
```

Executing a Macro

In Listing 7-3, you see that the INCLUDE statement is listed at the top of the parameter file. At the bottom of the parameter file, the macro that is desired is called. By providing these two pieces of information, you are telling GoldenGate that you want to read the macro and use it as part of the fundamental operation of the GoldenGate process.

When the GoldenGate process is started, the INCLUDE file is read (Listing 7-4) and the macro is executed to provide the process.

Listing 7-4. Execution During Startup of Process

```
INCLUDE ./dirmac/logon.mac
MACRO #logon_settings
BEGIN
USERID ggate, PASSWORD *****
END;
INCLUDE ./dirmac/rtables.mac
MACRO #rtables
BEGIN
MAP SOE.ADDRESSES, TARGET SOE.ADDRESSES;
MAP SOE.CARD_DETAILS, TARGET SOE.CARD_DETAILS THREAD(2);
MAP SOE.CUSTOMERS, TARGET SOE.CUSTOMERS, THREAD(3);
MAP SOE.INVENTORIES, TARGET SOE.INVENTORIES, THREAD(4);
MAP SOE.LOGON, TARGET SOE.LOGON, THREAD(5);
MAP SOE.ORDER_ITEMS, TARGET SOE.ORDER_ITEMS, THREAD(1);
MAP SOE.ORDERENTRY_METADATA, TARGET SOE.ORDERENTRY_METADATA, THREAD(2);
MAP SOE.ORDERS, #runrates(3);
MAP SOE.PRODUCT_DESCRIPTIONS, TARGET SOE.PRODUCT_DESCRIPTIONS, THREAD(4);
MAP SOE.PRODUCT_INFORMATION, TARGET SOE.PRODUCT_INFORMATION, THREAD(5);
MAP SOE.WAREHOUSES, TARGET SOE.WAREHOUSES, THREAD(1);
END;
REPLICAT RSRC1
SETENV (ORACLE_HOME="/opt/app/oracle/product/12.1.0.2/dbhome_1")
SETENV (ORACLE_SID="rmt12c")
#logon_settings()
USERID ggate, PASSWORD *****
ASSUMETARGETDEFS
REPORTCOUNT EVERY 5 SECONDS, RATE
DBOPTIONS NOSUPPRESSTRIGGERS
REPERROR (DEFAULT, EXCEPTION)
REPERROR (-1, EXCEPTION)
REPERROR (-1403, EXCEPTION)
REPERROR (-2291, EXCEPTION)
DISCARDFILE ./dirrpt/RSRC1.dsc, append, megabytes 500
#rtables();
MAP SOE.ADDRESSES, TARGET SOE.ADDRESSES;
MAP SOE.CARD_DETAILS, TARGET SOE.CARD_DETAILS THREAD(2);
MAP SOE.CUSTOMERS, TARGET SOE.CUSTOMERS, THREAD(3);
MAP SOE.INVENTORIES, TARGET SOE.INVENTORIES, THREAD(4);
MAP SOE.LOGON, TARGET SOE.LOGON, THREAD(5);
MAP SOE.ORDER_ITEMS, TARGET SOE.ORDER_ITEMS, THREAD(1);
MAP SOE.ORDERENTRY_METADATA, TARGET SOE.ORDERENTRY_METADATA, THREAD(2);
MAP SOE.ORDERS, #runrates(3);
MAP SOE.PRODUCT_DESCRIPTIONS, TARGET SOE.PRODUCT_DESCRIPTIONS, THREAD(4);
MAP SOE.PRODUCT_INFORMATION, TARGET SOE.PRODUCT_INFORMATION, THREAD(5);
MAP SOE.WAREHOUSES, TARGET SOE.WAREHOUSES, THREAD(1);
```

As you can see from the examples, it is easy to create a macro, include it in a parameter file, and have it execute. The examples showed here are very basic for demonstration purposes; however, the real power of a macro comes into play when you can nest macros withing macros to make a very modular configuration.

Tokens

Tokens are another advanced feature that can be used to capture and store data within the trail file's user token area. Data that are stored as tokens can be used to customize the way that Oracle GoldenGate delivers information. A few ways that tokens can be used are:

- Column mappings.

- Used in stored procedures that are called by SQLEXEC.

- User exits.

- Macros.

■ **Note**   There are two types of tokens: user-defined and GoldenGate-specific tokens (GGSToken). GGSTokens are used to store LOGSCN and TRANID, among other internal information.

Because tokens can be used in a wide range of GoldenGate areas, these bits of user-defined information can be powerful for defining specifics of a business rule or what is happening with the GoldenGate environment.

Defining Tokens

To define a token, you must define the token name and associate it with data that should be captured; this is normally environment-related information. The data that can be defined within a token can be any valid character data or values retrieved from an Oracle GoldenGate column-conversion function.

The record header of the trail file permits up to 2,000 bytes of data to be stored for user token information. The token name, length of data, and the data itself must all fit into the 2,000 bytes allocated in the record header.

You can define a token in the capture and pump processes of the GoldenGate environment. The TOKENS option is part of the TABLE parameter for the extract process. Listing 7-5 highlights the syntax needed for a token definition.

Listing 7-5. Token Definition Syntax

```
TABLE <table defined>, TOKENS (<token name> = <token_data> [, ...]);
```

The syntax for defining a token can be placed either directly into the parameter file for the extract or it can be defined in a macro for reuse.

Running Tokens

Now that you know how to define a token, putting them to use is the next step. As previously mentioned, tokens are defined as part of the TABLE parameter in the extract process. This allows you to define customer user tokens. To illustrate how to define a token in an extract, Listing 7-6 shows how this is done per table.

Listing 7-6. Defining Tokens in Extract Process

```
INCLUDE ./dirmac/logon.mac
--CHECKPARAMS
EXTRACT ESRC1
#logon_settings()
TRANLOGOPTIONS DBLOGREADER
SETENV (ORACLE_HOME="/opt/app/oracle/product/12.1.0.2/dbhome_1")
SETENV (ORACLE_SID="src12c")
EXTTRAIL ./dirdat/lt
WARNLONGTRANS 1h, CHECKINTERVAL 30m
WILDCARDRESOLVE IMMEDIATE
REPORTCOUNT EVERY 3 MINUTES, RATE
INCLUDE ./dirmac/heartbeat_extract.mac
TABLE SOE.ADDRESSES,TOKENS (
TK-OSUSER = @GETENV ('GGENVIRONMENT' , 'OSUSERNAME'),
TK-GROUP = @GETENV ('GGENVIRONMENT' , 'GROUPNAME'),
TK-HOST =  @GETENV('GGENVIRONMENT' , 'HOSTNAME'),
TABLE SOE.CARD_DETAILS;
TABLE SOE.CUSTOMERS;
TABLE SOE.INVENTORIES;
TABLE SOE.LOGON;
TABLE SOE.ORDER_ITEMS;
TABLE SOE.ORDERENTRY_METADATA;
TABLE SOE.ORDERS;
TABLE SOE.PRODUCT_DESCRIPTIONS;
TABLE SOE.PRODUCT_INFORMATION;
TABLE SOE.WAREHOUSES;
```

In Listing 7-6, notice that there are four tokens defined. These tokens start with the prefix TK-.

■ **Note** A token can be named anything you want to name it.

These are the names that will be used on the replicat side when reading the token from the trail file being processed. Also notice that the information being gathered is coming from the environment that GoldenGate is running in by using the @GETENV parameter. The information that is obtained from @GETENV is stored as the value of the token with the prefix of TK-. At a later point in the replication, this information can be retrieved by calling the token name.

■ **Note** Tokens can be populated with any type of information; if you need more information on the @GETENV function, you can find it at http://docs.oracle.com/goldengate/c1221/gg-winux/GWURF/column_conversion_functions015.htm#GWURF788.

Applying Tokens

With tokens being defined in the extract process and having your desired information captured in user tokens, you will want to have this information applied on the receiving end of replication. To do this, the replicat has to be told about the tokens and how they should be applied in the database.

To apply tokens, they need to be mapped to columns in the target table. The target table can either be the replicat table with additional columns for tokens or a separate table with columns that only map the tokens. Either way, the tokens have to be mapped to columns. In Listing 7-7, you will see how I map the table SOE.ADDRESS to a table that will only store the contents of the tokens.

Listing 7-7. Replicat Mapping with Tokens Via Macro

```
MACRO #rtables
BEGIN
MAP SOE.ADDRESSES, TARGET SOE.ADDRESSES;
MAP SOE.ADDRESSES, TARGET SOE.TOKEN_INFO, COLMAP(OSUSERNAME=@TOKEN('TK-OSUSER'),GROUPNAME=@
TOKEN('TK-GROUP'),HOSTNAME=@TOKEN('TK-HOST'),TABLENAME=@TOKEN('TK-TABLE'));
MAP SOE.CARD_DETAILS, TARGET SOE.CARD_DETAILS THREAD(2);
MAP SOE.CUSTOMERS, TARGET SOE.CUSTOMERS, THREAD(3);
MAP SOE.INVENTORIES, TARGET SOE.INVENTORIES, THREAD(4);
MAP SOE.LOGON, TARGET SOE.LOGON, THREAD(5);
MAP SOE.ORDER_ITEMS, TARGET SOE.ORDER_ITEMS, THREAD(1);
MAP SOE.ORDERENTRY_METADATA, TARGET SOE.ORDERENTRY_METADATA, THREAD(2);
MAP SOE.PRODUCT_DESCRIPTIONS, TARGET SOE.PRODUCT_DESCRIPTIONS, THREAD(4);
MAP SOE.PRODUCT_INFORMATION, TARGET SOE.PRODUCT_INFORMATION, THREAD(5);
MAP SOE.WAREHOUSES, TARGET SOE.WAREHOUSES, THREAD(1);
END;
```

The key thing to notice in this MAP statement is that the TARGET table is SOE.TOKEN_INFO. These tables are different in structure; however, the COLMAP option allows you to map what information is getting applied to what columns. In this case, I want to map all the tokens previously defined to the columns in the SOE. TOKEN_INFO table. If you mapped this out logically in a table, it would look similar to Table 7-1.

Table 7-1. Example of Column Mapping for Tokens

Column Name	Token Mapping
OSUSERNAME	@TOKEN=('TK-OSUSER')
GROUPNAME	@TOKEN=('TK-GROUP')
HOSTNAME	@TOKEN=('TK-HOST')
TABLENAME	@TOKEN=('TK-TABLE')

When the replicat begins to apply the information in the trail files to the database, the tokens will be mapped to the corresponding columns for SOE.TOKEN_INFO. After the apply process is complete, you can query the SOE.TOKEN_INFO table and verify that the token information has been applied to the table. Figure 7-1 shows the token information applied to the correct table.

```
select * from soe.token_info where tablename is not null;
```

	⬇ OSUSERNAME	⬇ GROUPNAME	⬇ HOSTNAME	⬇ TABLENAME
1	oracle	ESRC1	ggtest12c1.acme.com	SOE.ADDRESSES
2	oracle	ESRC1	ggtest12c1.acme.com	SOE.ADDRESSES
3	oracle	ESRC1	ggtest12c1.acme.com	SOE.ADDRESSES
4	oracle	ESRC1	ggtest12c1.acme.com	SOE.ADDRESSES
5	oracle	ESRC1	ggtest12c1.acme.com	SOE.ADDRESSES

Figure 7-1. *Token info in the table*

As you can see, the transactions that ran against the SOE.ADDRESSES table have presented the token information for the OS User who ran the GoldenGate process, the GoldenGate process group, the hostname where the token was defined, and the table that it was captured from.

Just like macros, tokens are a very powerful tool that can be used to customize the replication process. Tokens provide a way for you to define and capture custom or granular detail information from the source database and retain a record of it on the target side. Tokens also allow you to execute defined procedures using SQLEXEC depending on the contents of the token.

Heartbeat

Another feature that is part of Oracle GoldenGate is the ability to track the latency within the replication framework by using a heartbeat process. A heartbeat process is set of GoldenGate processes that are used to calculate the "true" lag within the network, from end to end. From an administration standpoint, this is a handy tool for validating the lag in the network.

Starting in Oracle GoldenGate 12c (12.2.0.1.0), there are two types of heartbeat processes. The first type is the traditional heartbeat, which is external to the existing GoldenGate processes. The second type is the integrated heartbeat, which is new in 12.2.0.1.0. Let's take a look at both processes so you can get an understanding of how they work.

Traditional Heartbeat

The traditional heartbeat is a process that was developed to measure lag between the source and target by using "heartbeat" tables. Although there are tables required for this heartbeat process, there are a few different parts that need to be configured to make the process work.

To successfully set the traditional heartbeat structure within a GoldenGate environment, there are a number of objects that need to be set up. Table 7-2 provides a brief breakdown of what needs to be added to the source and target database to run a traditional heartbeat.

Table 7-2. *Traditional Heartbeat Components*

Location	Component	Type
Source	HEARTBEAT	Table
Source	SEQ_GGS_HEARTBEAT_ID	Sequence
Source	HEARTBEAT_TRIG	Trigger
Source	<no name required>	Scheduler Job
Target	GGS_HEARTBEAT_HISTORY	Table
Target	SEQ_GGS_HEARTBEAT_HIST	Sequence
Target	GGS_HEARTBEAT_TRIG_HIST	Trigger
Target	TOTAL_LAG_HB	View

■ **Note** The component names in Table 7-2 can be changed when creating your heartbeat framework. The names are mostly taken from documentation and personal setup information.

The original heartbeat information provided by Oracle can be found in My Oracle Support Note ID 1299679.1.

As you can tell, there are a few things that need to be configured to make the traditional heartbeat work. When you first start configuring traditional heartbeats, the components in Table 7-2 are just the basics. These components do not contain anything that Oracle GoldenGate will need to replicate information. Table 7-2 only provides the framework from a database level. Let's take a closer look at this SQL framework before you dive into the specifics at the GoldenGate process level.

Source Database Configuration

The first thing that needs to be done is to set up the traditional heartbeat database components in the source database. These components consist of a table specific to heartbeat information, a sequence, a trigger, and a job scheduler configuration that fires the trigger. Let's take a look at each of these components.

Traditional Heartbeat Table

The traditional heartbeat table is just a standard table that you can create in any schema that you like. Traditionally, the heartbeat table should be created in the schema that will house your Oracle GoldenGate objects. Listing 7-8 shows the DDL for building out the table.

■ **Note** Your heartbeat table can be different from this framework.

Listing 7-8. Create DDL for Traditional Heartbeat Table

```
drop table &&ogg_user..heartbeat;

-- Create table statement
CREATE TABLE &&ogg_user..HEARTBEAT
(ID NUMBER ,
SRC_DB            VARCHAR2(30),
EXTRACT_NAME      varchar2(8),
SOURCE_COMMIT     TIMESTAMP,
TARGET_COMMIT     TIMESTAMP,
CAPTIME           TIMESTAMP,
CAPLAG            NUMBER,
PMPTIME           TIMESTAMP,
PMPGROUP          VARCHAR2(8 BYTE),
PMPLAG            NUMBER,
DELTIME           TIMESTAMP,
DELGROUP          VARCHAR2(8 BYTE),
DELLAG            NUMBER,
TOTALLAG          NUMBER,
thread            number,
update_timestamp  timestamp,
EDDLDELTASTATS    number,
EDMLDELTASTATS    number,
RDDLDELTASTATS    number,
RDMLDELTASTATS    number,
CONSTRAINT HEARTBEAT_PK PRIMARY KEY (SRC_DB)
)
/
```

Notice that the table will be used to keep track of key metric information and that the primary key is a standard number data type. This is due to the table being ideal for databases that are version 11g and below. If you build a heartbeat table in Oracle Database 12c, you can leverage the identity column features of the database as well. Now that you have an 11g version of the table created, you will need a sequence and a trigger to increment the information stored in the table. The parts of the traditional heartbeat can be created with the examples in Listing 7-9.

■ **Note**   The PL/SQL code presented here is a commented set of code that can be optained from an Oracle White Paper at http://www.ateam-oracle.com/wp-content/uploads/2013/04/OGG-Best-Practice-heartbeat-table-using-DBMS_SCHEDULER-V11_0-ID1299679.1.pdf.

Listing 7-9. Sequence and Trigger Required

```
DROP SEQUENCE &&ogg_user..SEQ_GGS_HEARTBEAT_ID ;

CREATE SEQUENCE &&ogg_user..SEQ_GGS_HEARTBEAT_ID INCREMENT BY 1 START WITH 1 ORDER ;

CREATE OR REPLACE TRIGGER &&ogg_user..HEARTBEAT_TRIG
BEFORE INSERT OR UPDATE ON &&ogg_user..HEARTBEAT
FOR EACH ROW
BEGIN
select SEQ_GGS_HEARTBEAT_ID.nextval
into :NEW.ID
from dual;
select systimestamp
into :NEW.target_COMMIT
from dual;
select trunc(to_number(substr((:NEW.CAPTIME - :NEW.SOURCE_COMMIT ),1, instr(:NEW.CAPTIME -
:NEW.SOURCE_COMMIT,' ')))) * 86400
+ to_number(substr((:NEW.CAPTIME - :NEW.SOURCE_COMMIT), instr((:NEW.CAPTIME - :NEW.SOURCE_
COMMIT),' ')+1,2)) * 3600
+ to_number(substr((:NEW.CAPTIME - :NEW.SOURCE_COMMIT), instr((:NEW.CAPTIME - :NEW.SOURCE_
COMMIT),' ')+4,2) ) * 60
+ to_number(substr((:NEW.CAPTIME - :NEW.SOURCE_COMMIT), instr((:NEW.CAPTIME - :NEW.SOURCE_
COMMIT),' ')+7,2))
+ to_number(substr((:NEW.CAPTIME - :NEW.SOURCE_COMMIT), instr((:NEW.CAPTIME - :NEW.SOURCE_
COMMIT),' ')+10,6)) / 1000000
into :NEW.CAPLAG
from dual;
select trunc(to_number(substr((:NEW.PMPTIME - :NEW.CAPTIME),1, instr(:NEW.PMPTIME - :NEW.
CAPTIME,' ')))) * 86400
+ to_number(substr((:NEW.PMPTIME - :NEW.CAPTIME), instr((:NEW.PMPTIME - :NEW.CAPTIME),'
')+1,2)) * 3600
+ to_number(substr((:NEW.PMPTIME - :NEW.CAPTIME), instr((:NEW.PMPTIME - :NEW.CAPTIME),'
')+4,2) ) * 60
+ to_number(substr((:NEW.PMPTIME - :NEW.CAPTIME), instr((:NEW.PMPTIME - :NEW.CAPTIME),'
')+7,2))
+ to_number(substr((:NEW.PMPTIME - :NEW.CAPTIME), instr((:NEW.PMPTIME - :NEW.CAPTIME),'
')+10,6)) / 1000000
into :NEW.PMPLAG
from dual;
select trunc(to_number(substr((:NEW.DELTIME - :NEW.PMPTIME),1, instr(:NEW.DELTIME - :NEW.
PMPTIME,' ')))) * 86400
+ to_number(substr((:NEW.DELTIME - :NEW.PMPTIME), instr((:NEW.DELTIME - :NEW.PMPTIME),'
')+1,2)) * 3600
+ to_number(substr((:NEW.DELTIME - :NEW.PMPTIME), instr((:NEW.DELTIME - :NEW.PMPTIME),'
')+4,2) ) * 60
+ to_number(substr((:NEW.DELTIME - :NEW.PMPTIME), instr((:NEW.DELTIME - :NEW.PMPTIME),'
')+7,2))
+ to_number(substr((:NEW.DELTIME - :NEW.PMPTIME), instr((:NEW.DELTIME - :NEW.PMPTIME),'
')+10,6)) / 1000000
into :NEW.DELLAG
from dual;
```

```
select trunc(to_number(substr((:NEW.TARGET_COMMIT - :NEW.SOURCE_COMMIT),1, instr(:NEW.
TARGET_COMMIT - :NEW.SOURCE_COMMIT,' ')))) * 86400
+ to_number(substr((:NEW.TARGET_COMMIT - :NEW.SOURCE_COMMIT), instr((:NEW.TARGET_COMMIT -
:NEW.SOURCE_COMMIT),' ')+1,2)) * 3600
+ to_number(substr((:NEW.TARGET_COMMIT - :NEW.SOURCE_COMMIT), instr((:NEW.TARGET_COMMIT -
:NEW.SOURCE_COMMIT),' ')+4,2) ) * 60
+ to_number(substr((:NEW.TARGET_COMMIT - :NEW.SOURCE_COMMIT), instr((:NEW.TARGET_COMMIT -
:NEW.SOURCE_COMMIT),' ')+7,2))
+ to_number(substr((:NEW.TARGET_COMMIT - :NEW.SOURCE_COMMIT), instr((:NEW.TARGET_COMMIT -
:NEW.SOURCE_COMMIT),' ')+10,6)) / 1000000
into :NEW.TOTALLAG
from dual;
end ;
/
```

After creating the components in Listing 7-10, the table needs to be primed to ensure that all the components are working. This is done by simply inserting into the table an initial record (Listing 7-10). Once this information is inserted, it should validate that the trigger fires and updates key information.

Listing 7-10. Insert Statement for Heartbeat

```
-- this assumes that the table is empty
INSERT INTO &&ogg_user..HEARTBEAT (SRC_DB) select db name from V$database;
commit;
```

Now that the source side of the heartbeat is configured, the next thing that needs to happen is to ensure this table is updated on a regular basis. To do this, you will need to set up a scheduler job that will fire the trigger every minute or on a defined timeframe that you are comfortable with. Listing 7-11 provides you with a scheduler job normally used for heartbeat tables.

Listing 7-11. Schedule Job Setup

```
grant select on v_$database to &&ogg_user;

BEGIN
    SYS.DBMS_SCHEDULER.DROP_JOB(job_name => '&&ogg_user..OGG_HB',
                                defer => false,
                                force => false);
END;
/

CREATE OR REPLACE PROCEDURE &&ogg_user..gg_update_hb_tab IS
v_thread_num     NUMBER;
v_db_unique_name VARCHAR2 (128);
BEGIN
SELECT db_unique_name
INTO   v_db_unique_name
FROM v$database;
```

```
UPDATE &&ogg_user..heartbeat
SET update_timestamp = SYSTIMESTAMP
,src_db = v_db_unique_name;
END;
/

BEGIN
SYS.DBMS_SCHEDULER.CREATE_JOB (
job_name => '&&ogg_user..OGG_HB',
job_type => 'STORED_PROCEDURE',
job_action => '&&ogg_user..GG_UPDATE_HB_TAB',
number_of_arguments => 0,
start_date => NULL,
repeat_interval => 'FREQ=MINUTELY',
end_date => NULL,
job_class => '"SYS"."DEFAULT_JOB_CLASS"',
enabled => FALSE,
auto_drop => FALSE,
comments => 'GoldenGate',
credential_name => NULL,
destination_name => NULL);

SYS.DBMS_SCHEDULER.SET_ATTRIBUTE(
name => '&&ogg_user..OGG_HB',
attribute => 'restartable', value => TRUE);

SYS.DBMS_SCHEDULER.SET_ATTRIBUTE(
name => '&&ogg_user..OGG_HB',
attribute => 'logging_level', value => DBMS_SCHEDULER.LOGGING_OFF);

SYS.DBMS_SCHEDULER.enable(
name => '&&ogg_user..OGG_HB');
END;
/
```

You will notice that this scheduler job will update the heartbeat table; however, the heartbeat table will have a few columns with NULL values (Figure 7-2). This is normal because the trigger doesn't have all the information needed. As the changes in the table are captured and replicated, the additional information will be provided on the target side.

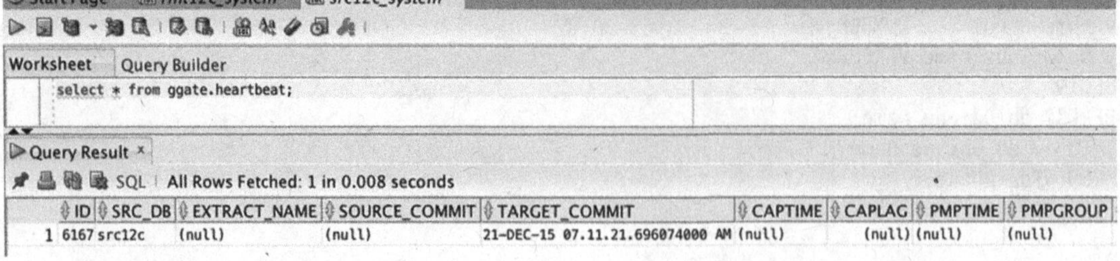

Figure 7-2. *Ouput of heartbeat table*

Target Database Configuration

With the source side set up, you need to set up the target side. The target side configuration has to be set up the same way using SQL. The components needed for the heartbeat to work are similar to those for the source side: a table, a sequence, and a trigger.

The table that needs to be created is a simple table to keep track of all the historical information for the heartbeat. Historical information provides a way to validate the lag over time. Listing 7-12 provides the DDL for the table.

Listing 7-12. Target Side Heartbeat Table

```
DROP TABLE &&ogg_user..GGS_HEARTBEAT_HISTORY;

CREATE TABLE &&ogg_user..GGS_HEARTBEAT_HISTORY
(       ID NUMBER ,
SRC_DB            VARCHAR2(30),
EXTRACT_NAME      varchar2(8),
SOURCE_COMMIT     TIMESTAMP,
TARGET_COMMIT     TIMESTAMP,
CAPTIME           TIMESTAMP,
CAPLAG            NUMBER,
PMPTIME           TIMESTAMP,
PMPGROUP          VARCHAR2(8 BYTE),
PMPLAG            NUMBER,
DELTIME           TIMESTAMP,
DELGROUP          VARCHAR2(8 BYTE),
DELLAG            NUMBER,
TOTALLAG          NUMBER,
thread            number,
update_timestamp  timestamp,
EDDLDELTASTATS    number,
EDMLDELTASTATS    number,
RDDLDELTASTATS    number,
RDMLDELTASTATS    number
);
```

You will notice that the table structure is the same as the source table. Like many other tables that are replicated in GoldenGate, having a matching table structure helps to simplify the replication requirements. Keeping this in mind, you will need to also create a sequence for the table to use (Listing 7-13).

Listing 7-13. Sequence Needed for Target Heartbeat Table

```
DROP SEQUENCE &&ogg_user..SEQ_GGS_HEARTBEAT_HIST ;
CREATE SEQUENCE &&ogg_user..SEQ_GGS_HEARTBEAT_HIST INCREMENT BY 1 START WITH 1 ORDER ;
```

Finally, you need to create the trigger that will fire when transactions happen against the table. This trigger, just like in the source table, will do a few calculations against the incoming data and calculate the lag from source to target. Listing 7-14 provides the DDL for the triggers.

Listing 7-14. Target Side Triggers

```
create or replace TRIGGER &&ogg_user.GGS_HEARTBEAT_TRIG_HIST
BEFORE INSERT OR UPDATE ON ggate.GGS_HEARTBEAT_HISTORY
FOR EACH ROW
BEGIN
select seq_ggs_HEARTBEAT_HIST.nextval into :NEW.ID
from dual;
select systimestamp into :NEW.target_COMMIT from dual;
select trunc(to_number(substr((:NEW.CAPTIME - :NEW.SOURCE_COMMIT ),1, instr(:NEW.CAPTIME -
:NEW.SOURCE_COMMIT,' ')))) * 86400
+ to_number(substr((:NEW.CAPTIME - :NEW.SOURCE_COMMIT), instr((:NEW.CAPTIME - :NEW.SOURCE_
COMMIT),' ')+1,2)) * 3600
+ to_number(substr((:NEW.CAPTIME - :NEW.SOURCE_COMMIT), instr((:NEW.CAPTIME - :NEW.SOURCE_
COMMIT),' ')+4,2) ) * 60
+ to_number(substr((:NEW.CAPTIME - :NEW.SOURCE_COMMIT), instr((:NEW.CAPTIME - :NEW.SOURCE_
COMMIT),' ')+7,2))
+ to_number(substr((:NEW.CAPTIME - :NEW.SOURCE_COMMIT), instr((:NEW.CAPTIME - :NEW.SOURCE_
COMMIT),' ')+10,6)) / 1000000
into :NEW.CAPLAG
from dual;
select trunc(to_number(substr((:NEW.PMPTIME - :NEW.CAPTIME),1, instr(:NEW.PMPTIME - :NEW.
CAPTIME,' ')))) * 86400
+ to_number(substr((:NEW.PMPTIME - :NEW.CAPTIME), instr((:NEW.PMPTIME - :NEW.CAPTIME),'
')+1,2)) * 3600
+ to_number(substr((:NEW.PMPTIME - :NEW.CAPTIME), instr((:NEW.PMPTIME - :NEW.CAPTIME),'
')+4,2) ) * 60
+ to_number(substr((:NEW.PMPTIME - :NEW.CAPTIME), instr((:NEW.PMPTIME - :NEW.CAPTIME),'
')+7,2))
+ to_number(substr((:NEW.PMPTIME - :NEW.CAPTIME), instr((:NEW.PMPTIME - :NEW.CAPTIME),'
')+10,6)) / 1000000
into :NEW.PMPLAG
from dual;
select trunc(to_number(substr((:NEW.DELTIME - :NEW.PMPTIME),1, instr(:NEW.DELTIME - :NEW.
PMPTIME,' ')))) * 86400
+ to_number(substr((:NEW.DELTIME - :NEW.PMPTIME), instr((:NEW.DELTIME - :NEW.PMPTIME),'
')+1,2)) * 3600
+ to_number(substr((:NEW.DELTIME - :NEW.PMPTIME), instr((:NEW.DELTIME - :NEW.PMPTIME),'
')+4,2) ) * 60
+ to_number(substr((:NEW.DELTIME - :NEW.PMPTIME), instr((:NEW.DELTIME - :NEW.PMPTIME),'
')+7,2))
+ to_number(substr((:NEW.DELTIME - :NEW.PMPTIME), instr((:NEW.DELTIME - :NEW.PMPTIME),'
')+10,6)) / 1000000
into :NEW.DELLAG
from dual;
select trunc(to_number(substr((:NEW.TARGET_COMMIT - :NEW.SOURCE_COMMIT),1, instr(:NEW.
TARGET_COMMIT - :NEW.SOURCE_COMMIT,' ')))) * 86400
+ to_number(substr((:NEW.TARGET_COMMIT - :NEW.SOURCE_COMMIT), instr((:NEW.TARGET_COMMIT -
:NEW.SOURCE_COMMIT),' ')+1,2)) * 3600
+ to_number(substr((:NEW.TARGET_COMMIT - :NEW.SOURCE_COMMIT), instr((:NEW.TARGET_COMMIT -
:NEW.SOURCE_COMMIT),' ')+4,2) ) * 60
```

```
+ to_number(substr((:NEW.TARGET_COMMIT - :NEW.SOURCE_COMMIT), instr((:NEW.TARGET_COMMIT -
:NEW.SOURCE_COMMIT),' ')+7,2))
+ to_number(substr((:NEW.TARGET_COMMIT - :NEW.SOURCE_COMMIT), instr((:NEW.TARGET_COMMIT -
:NEW.SOURCE_COMMIT),' ')+10,6)) / 1000000
into :NEW.TOTALLAG
from dual;
end ;
/
ALTER TRIGGER &&ogg_user..GGS_HEARTBEAT_TRIG_HIST ENABLE;
```

Now that the SQL components of the traditional heartbeat are in place, you will need to configure the GoldenGate processes for the heartbeat.

Heartbeat Configuration

To configure the heartbeat configuration is just like setting up normal replication; the only difference here is that the heartbeat table is the only object being replicated across the extracts and replicats. The design of this keeps the heartbeat as minimal as possible to prevent it from affecting existing replication and provide near real-time information on the network lag.

To do this, you will need to have three parameter files created, one parameter file for each of the processes needed in the heartbeat replication. Listing 7-15 provides a breakdown of the parameter files and their contents.

Listing 7-15. Heartbeat Parameter Files and Contents (Extract/Pump/Replicat)

Extract:

```
INCLUDE ./dirmac/logon.mac
--CHECKPARAMS
EXTRACT EXT_HB
#logon_settings()
TRANLOGOPTIONS DBLOGREADER
SETENV (ORACLE_HOME="/opt/app/oracle/product/12.1.0.2/dbhome_1")
SETENV (ORACLE_SID="src12c")
WARNLONGTRANS 1h, CHECKINTERVAL 30m
EXTTRAIL ./dirdat/h1
--WILDCARDRESOLVE IMMEDIATE
REPORTCOUNT EVERY 5 MINUTES, RATE
INCLUDE ./dirmac/heartbeat_extract.mac
```

Pump (Extract):

```
INCLUDE ./dirmac/logon.mac
EXTRACT PMP_HB
#logon_settings()
RMTHOST 10.10.1.12, MGRPORT 15000, COMPRESS
RMTTRAIL ./dirdat/h2
INCLUDE ./dirmac/heartbeat_pump.mac
```

Replicat:

```
INCLUDE ./dirmac/logon.mac
REPLICAT REP_HB
SETENV (ORACLE_HOME="/opt/app/oracle/product/12.1.0.2/dbhome_1")
SETENV (ORACLE_SID="rmt12c")
#logon_settings()
ASSUMETARGETDEFS
REPORTCOUNT EVERY 5 MINUTES, RATE
DISCARDFILE ./dirrpt/RSRC1.dsc, append, megabytes 500
DBOPTIONS NOSUPPRESSTRIGGERS
INCLUDE ./dirmac/heartbeat_replicat.mac
```

You will notice that in each of these parameter files, there is a call to a macro for its specific replication information. The macro for each process is specific to providing the tokens needed for replication of the heartbeat information. Listing 7-16 provides the information that is in these macros.

Listing 7-16. Macro Information for Heartbeat

Extract:

```
--Heartbeat Extract Macro
--Heartbeat Table
--Inital write - 12-21-2013 - BLC
table ggate.heartbeat,
tokens(
capgroup=@getenv('GGENVIRONMENT','GROUPNAME'),
captime=@DATE('YYYY-MM-DD HH:MI:SS.FFFFFF','JTS',@GETENV('JULIANTIMESTAMP')),
eddldeltastats=@getenv ('DELTASTATS', 'DDL'),
edmldeltastats=@getenv ('DELTASTATS', 'DML')
);
```

Pump (extract):

```
--Heartbeat Pump Macro
--Heartbeat Table
--Inital write - 12-21-2013 - BLC
table ggate.heartbeat,
tokens(
pmpgroup=@getenv('GGENVIRONMENT','GROUPNAME'),
pmptime=@DATE('YYYY-MM-DD HH:MI:SS.FFFFFF','JTS',@GETENV('JULIANTIMESTAMP'))
);
```

Replicat:

```
--Heartbeat Replicat Macro
--Tar_Heartbeat Table
--Inital write - 12-21-2013 - BLC
MAP ggate.HEARTBEAT, TARGET ggate.GGS_HEARTBEAT_HISTORY,
KEYCOLS (DELGROUP),
INSERTMISSINGUPDATES,
COLMAP (USEDEFAULTS,
ID = 0,
```

```
SOURCE_COMMIT=@GETENV ('GGHEADER', 'COMMITTIMESTAMP'),
EXTRACT_NAME=@TOKEN ('CAPGROUP'),
CAPTIME=@TOKEN ('CAPTIME'),
PMPGROUP=@TOKEN ('PMPGROUP'),
PMPTIME=@TOKEN ('PMPTIME'),
DELGROUP=@GETENV ('GGENVIRONMENT', 'GROUPNAME'),
DELTIME=@DATE ('YYYY-MM-DD HH:MI:SS.FFFFFF','JTS',@GETENV ('JULIANTIMESTAMP')),
EDDLDELTASTATS=@TOKEN ('EDDLDELTASTATS'),
EDMLDELTASTATS=@TOKEN ('EDMLDELTASTATS'),
RDDLDELTASTATS=@GETENV ('DELTASTATS', 'DDL'),
RDMLDELTASTATS=@GETENV ('DELTASTATS', 'DML')
);
```

With everything in place now, you can start create and start the extract, pump, and replicat processes associated with the heartbeat process. As the schedule job begins to update the table on the source side, the information will be replicated and applied to the target side. All the information captured in the tokens will be inserted into the table on the target side, providing you with near real-time information on the network lag. Figure 7-3 provides a view into the table on the target side.

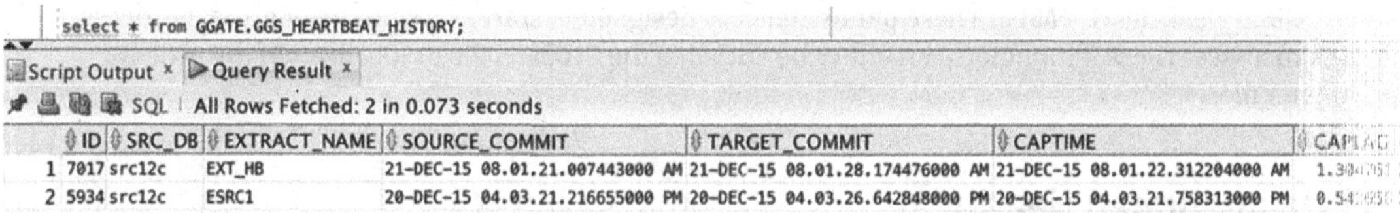

```
select * from GGATE.GGS_HEARTBEAT_HISTORY;
```

Script Output × ▷ Query Result ×

SQL | All Rows Fetched: 2 in 0.073 seconds

ID	SRC_DB	EXTRACT_NAME	SOURCE_COMMIT	TARGET_COMMIT	CAPTIME	CAPLAG
1 7017	src12c	EXT_HB	21-DEC-15 08.01.21.007443000 AM	21-DEC-15 08.01.28.174476000 AM	21-DEC-15 08.01.22.312204000 AM	1.30...
2 5934	src12c	ESRC1	20-DEC-15 04.03.21.216655000 PM	20-DEC-15 04.03.26.642848000 PM	20-DEC-15 04.03.21.758313000 PM	0.54...

Figure 7-3. *Output of the heartbeat process*

Another nice feature of the heartbeat process is that if you use the macros as pointed out here, you can then integrate the heartbeat into your existing GoldenGate processes. This provides you a way to calculate the lag on processes replicating your data. This approach is shown in Figure 7-3 as well.

Integrated Heartbeat

The heartbeat process has become such a main component of many GoldenGate environments, Oracle decided to take the process a step further and make it a core feature in the latest release of Oracle GoldenGate 12c. Starting with GoldenGate 12.2.0.1.0, the heartbeat process is now integrated into the core code base. This is both a good thing and a bad thing in my opinion. I say this because the new integrated heartbeat only solves the issue of the heartbeat in your existing processes; it does not allow you to monitor network lag like the traditional heartbeat can. In the end, the integrated heartbeat is a great feature if you want to quickly set up and monitor lag on your existing replication processes.

Parameters for Integrated Heartbeat

To set up the integrated heartbeat requires minimal configuration; however, like other aspects of GoldenGate, this setup requires adding a parameter within the configuration. If you want the parameters to take effect at the global level, the changes need to be made in the GLOBALS file. If the changes are to be localized to the process, they can be added to the individual process parameter files. The parameters that have to be used are the following:

- HEARTBEATTABLE <table_name>: This parameter allows you to define the heartbeat table you want to use; the default name will be GG_HEARTBEAT.

- ENABLE_HEARTBEAT_TABLE | DISABLE_HEARTBEAT_TABLE: These parameters are used to either start or stop the heartbeat-related items in the GoldenGate environment. (The parameters can be used in either GLOBALS, Extract, or Replicat to enable or disable the heartbeat.)

The HEARTBEATTABLE parameter tells GoldenGate where to build and look for the heartbeat table. This parameter is normally placed in the GLOBALS file so when it is built using the ADD HEARTBEATTABLE command, GoldenGate automatically builds the table. After the table is built, it will be referenced based on the information in the GLOBALS file.

The next set of parameters that is used with the integrated heartbeat table are ENABLE_HEARTBEAT_TABLE and DISABLE_HEARTBEAT_TABLE. These parameters are designed to start and stop the heartbeat process in the processes. These parameters can either be added to the GLOBALS file or localized in the process parameter files.

Set Up Integrated Heartbeat

Once you have decided where the parameters for integrated heartbeat should be located, the next step is to set up the heartbeat process. To do this, you need to see what options you have for creating the heartbeat table. Figure 7-4 provides the Command Summary that is used with GGSCI. You will notice that there is a HEARTBEATTABLE object with the commands for ADD, DELETE, ALTER, and INFO listed.

```
GGSCI Command Summary:

Object:           Command:
SUBDIRS           CREATE
DATASTORE         ALTER, CREATE, DELETE, INFO, REPAIR
ER                INFO, KILL, LAG, SEND, STATUS, START, STATS, STOP
EXTRACT           ADD, ALTER, CLEANUP, DELETE, INFO, KILL,
                  LAG, REGISTER, SEND, START, STATS, STATUS, STOP
                  UNREGISTER
EXTTRAIL          ADD, ALTER, DELETE, INFO
GGSEVT            VIEW
JAGENT            INFO, START, STATUS, STOP
MANAGER           INFO, SEND, START, STOP, STATUS
MARKER            INFO
PARAMETERS        EDIT, VIEW, SET EDITOR, INFO, GETPARAMINFO
REPLICAT          ADD, ALTER, CLEANUP, DELETE, INFO, KILL, LAG, REGISTER, SEND,
                  START, STATS, STATUS, STOP, SYNCHRONIZE, UNREGISTER
REPORT            VIEW
RMTTRAIL          ADD, ALTER, DELETE, INFO
TRACETABLE        ADD, DELETE, INFO
TRANDATA          ADD, DELETE, INFO
SCHEMATRANDATA    ADD, DELETE, INFO
CHECKPOINTTABLE   ADD, DELETE, CLEANUP, INFO, UPGRADE
WALLET            CREATE, OPEN, PURGE
MASTERKEY         ADD, INFO, RENEW, DELETE, UNDELETE
CREDENTIALSTORE   ADD, ALTER, INFO, DELETE
HEARTBEATTABLE    ADD, DELETE, ALTER, INFO
HEARTBEATENTRY    DELETE


Commands without an object:
(Database)        DBLOGIN, LIST TABLES, ENCRYPT PASSWORD, FLUSH SEQUENCE
                  MININGDBLOGIN, SET NAMECCSID
(DDL)             DUMPDDL
(Miscellaneous)   ! ,ALLOWNESTED | NOALLOWNESTED, CREATE SUBDIRS,
                  DEFAULTJOURNAL, FC, HELP, HISTORY, INFO ALL, OBEY, SHELL,
                  SHOW, VERSIONS, VIEW GGSEVT, VIEW REPORT
                  (note: type the word COMMAND after the ! to display the
                  ! help topic, for example: GGSCI (sys1)> help ! command
```

Figure 7-4. *GGSCI Command Summary*

To create the heartbeat table, you simply need to run ADD HEARTBEATTABLE if your heartbeat table name is listed in the GLOBALS file. If not, you will have to provide a schema and table name with the ADD HEARTBEATTABLE command. Listing 7-17 provides an example of the command structure if needed.

Listing 7-17. ADD HEARTBEATTABLE Without GLOBALS

```
GGSCI> dblogin userid [ gg user ] password ******
GGSCI> ADD HEARTBEATTABLE [ schema ].[ table name ]
```

After you have run the command for creating the heartbeat table, you will notice that GoldenGate creates all the items needed for the heartbeat process to work. Figure 7-5 provides a view of all the objects created.

```
GGSCI (wilma.acme.com) 7> dblogin userid ggate password ggate
Successfully logged into database.

GGSCI (wilma.acme.com as ggate@rcv12c) 8> add heartbeattable

2015-11-26 20:00:21  INFO    OGG-14001  Successfully created heartbeat seed table ["GG_HEARTBEAT_SEED"].

2015-11-26 20:00:21  INFO    OGG-14032  Successfully added supplemental logging for heartbeat seed table ["GG_HEARTBEAT_SEED"].

2015-11-26 20:00:21  INFO    OGG-14000  Successfully created heartbeat table ["GG_HEARTBEAT"].

2015-11-26 20:00:21  INFO    OGG-14033  Successfully added supplemental logging for heartbeat table ["GG_HEARTBEAT"].

2015-11-26 20:00:21  INFO    OGG-14016  Successfully created heartbeat history table ["GG_HEARTBEAT_HISTORY"].

2015-11-26 20:00:21  INFO    OGG-14023  Successfully created heartbeat lag view ["GG_LAG"].

2015-11-26 20:00:21  INFO    OGG-14024  Successfully created heartbeat lag history view ["GG_LAG_HISTORY"].

2015-11-26 20:00:21  INFO    OGG-14003  Successfully populated heartbeat seed table with [RCV12C].

2015-11-26 20:00:22  INFO    OGG-14004  Successfully created procedure ["GG_UPDATE_HB_TAB"] to update the heartbeat tables.

2015-11-26 20:00:22  INFO    OGG-14017  Successfully created procedure ["GG_PURGE_HB_TAB"] to purge the heartbeat history table.

2015-11-26 20:00:22  INFO    OGG-14005  Successfully created scheduler job ["GG_UPDATE_HEARTBEATS"] to update the heartbeat tables.

2015-11-26 20:00:22  INFO    OGG-14018  Successfully created scheduler job ["GG_PURGE_HEARTBEATS"] to purge the heartbeat history table.
```

Figure 7-5. *Objects created by ADD HEARTBEATTABLE*

If you are having a hard time reading the image in Figure 7-5, here is a list of all the database objects that the command creates for you.
Tables:

```
<heartbeat_table>_SEED (default GG_HEARTBEAT_SEED)
<heartbeat_table> (default GG_HEARTBEAT)
<heartbeat_table>_HISTORY (default GG_HEARTBEAT_HISTORY)
```

Views:

```
GG_LAG
GG_LAG_HISTORY
```

Stored Procedures:

```
GG_UPDATE_HB_TAB
GG_PURGE_HB_TAB
```

Scheduler Jobs:

```
GG_UPDATE_HEARTBEATS
GG_PURGE_HEARTBEATS
```

As you can tell, unlike the manual process of setting up the heartbeat process, Oracle has integrated all the steps and objects required into a single command. This provides a very effective way to use the heartbeat process within the GoldenGate framework.

Functions

The last advanced feature is how Oracle GoldenGate can be used to transform data while it is in transit. Oracle GoldenGate provides functions that allow data to be tested while in transit from the source system to the target system. These functions are executed on a column basis. Table 7-3 provides a summary of these functions for quick reference.

Table 7-3. *Oracle GoldenGate Functions*

Function	Category
CASE	Performance testing
EVAL	Performance testing
IF	Performance testing
COLSTAT	Handling missing columns
COLTEST	Handling missing columns
DATE	Dates
DATEDIFF	Dates
DATENOW	Dates
COMPUTE	Arithmetic calculations
NUMBIN	Strings
NUMSTR	Strings
STRCAT	Strings
STRCMP	Strings
STREXT	Strings
STREQ	Strings
STRFIND	Strings
STRLEN	Strings
STRLTRIM	Strings
STRNCAT	Strings
STRNCMP	Strings
STRNUM	Strings
STRRTRIM	Strings
STRSUB	Strings
STRTRIM	Strings
STRUP	Strings
VALONEOF	Strings
AFTER	Others
BEFORE	Others
BEFOREAFTER	Others

(continued)

Table 7-3. (*continued*)

Function	Category
BINARY	Others
BINTOHEX	Others
GETENV	Others
GETVAL	Others
HEXTOBIN	Others
HIGHVAL	LOWVAL	Others
RANGE	Others
TOKEN	Others

As you can tell, there are quite a few functions that can be used against data as it is being shipped. Many of these functions fit into six different categories, and every category can help in identifying what is happening with the data. To illustration how functions work, let's take a look at the IF function.

IF Function

The IF function belongs in the performance testing category and is helpful when you want to test data for conditions before the data arrive in the target database. This function operates just like a normal programming IF statement, by returning one of two values based on a defined condition as mapped in the COLMAP statement of the replicat. We take a closer look at this in a moment.

■ **Note** The @IF function can be used with other conditional arguments to test one or more exceptions.

To understand how the @IF functions work, the syntax is as follows:

@IF (condition, value_if_non-zero, value_if-zero)

To use the @IF function, you need to enable the replicat that is applying transactions to evaluate the data and make changes as required based on the values of the function. To do this, the MAP clause of the replicat parameter file needs to be updated. Listing 7-18 provides an example of a replicat parameter file using the @IF function in the MAP statement.

Listing 7-18. Replicat Using @IF Function

```
--CHECKPARAMS
REPLICAT REP
SETENV (ORACLE_HOME="/u01/app/oracle/product/12.1.0/db12cr1")
SETENV (ORACLE_SID="oragg")
USERID ggate, PASSWORD ggate
ASSUMETARGETDEFS
DISCARDFILE ./dirrpt/REP.dsc, append, megabytes 50
WILDCARDRESOLVE IMMEDIATE
BATCHSQL
map SF.ORDERS, target ATL.ORDERS
COLMAP (USEDEFAULTS, PRICE = @IF(PRICE>100, PRICE, 1000));
```

In Listing 7-18, you are saying to check the price column of the data coming in to see if the value is greater than 100. If the value is greater, then round the price to 1,000; otherwise, leave the price as the value being replicated.

Using conditional checking within Oracle GoldenGate, data can be evaluated and changed as it is replicated between environments. Doing these conditional checks during replication enables the administrator to quickly make changes to data as needed without spending a lot of time scrubbing data beforehand.

Summary

In this chapter, you have seen four types of advanced features that Oracle GoldenGate provides to help make configuration, running, transforming, and monitoring simpler. These features provide a rich framework for working with and around data that are being replicated. The next chapter builds on some of these features and how they relate to the security model of Oracle GoldenGate.

CHAPTER 8

■ ■ ■

Security

Chapter 7 looked at some the advanced features that Oracle GoldenGate provides for you to build a flexible and robust architecture. In this chapter, you expand on that knowledge by looking at the security items that Oracle GoldenGate provides to help keep your replication environment secure. For most organizations, security is a paramount concern and so the items discussed in the chapter are designed to help you understand what and how to use the security options.

Everyone knows that today's organizations are increasingly relying on data to make business decisions that affect daily operations and functions. Due to this criticality to business, the need to keep data secure is always increasing. Just keeping data secure while it is at rest is one approach. What does an organization do if the secure data have to be replicated to another location? In earlier chapters, you looked at the different architectures that can use Oracle GoldenGate for replication. You have also reviewed how to verify data once they have been replicated. A large area of review that has not been touched on yet is the security that Oracle GoldenGate provides.

The security that Oracle GoldenGate provides ranges from user security through how data are secured in the trail files and in transit to the targets defined. This chapter provides you with the different ways that Oracle GoldenGate can be secured.

User Security

For years, DBAs have been told to make sure their environments are secure. Organizations have gone as far as semiannual and annual audits to ensure these environments are secure; however, as hard as they, try environments are routinely left unsecure. This practice is then later passed on to their replication environment. If you are familiar with Oracle GoldenGate and as outlined in Chapter 3, you will need to create a GoldenGate user in the source and target database. This user naturally will have an encrypted password; this is a basic security approach. This becomes an issue, however, when you start configuring your parameter files for capture and apply processes.

With a database user created for Oracle GoldenGate, you can use this user in your parameter files for the capture and apply processes. In many parameter files, the user is defined as per Listing 8-1.

Listing 8-1. Unsecure Parameter File

```
EXTRACT EXT1
USERID ggate, PASSWORD ggate
TRANLOGOPTIONS DBLOGREADER
SETENV (ORACLE_HOME="/u01/app/oraprd/product/10.2.0/db_1")
SETENV (ORACLE_SID="src1")
WARNLONGTRANS 1h, CHECKINTERVAL 30m
EXTTRAIL ./dirdat/lt
WILDCARDRESOLVE IMMEDIATE
TABLE SCOTT.*;
```

© Bobby Curtis 2016
B. Curtis, *Pro Oracle GoldenGate for the DBA*, DOI 10.1007/978-1-4842-1179-3_8

You will notice in Listing 8-1 that the parameter file is passing the password for the GoldenGate user in clear text. This is a bad thing, and most audits will not catch this because they are not looking at the parameter files associated with GoldenGate. Because the password is stored in clear text, anyone with access to the system can quickly find the GoldenGate user password and access the database account.

To remedy this problem, Oracle has provided two solutions to address the clear text password issue. The first of these solutions is to encrypt the password in the parameter file. The second is to create and use a wallet for the password. Let's take a look at both of these approaches now.

Encrypting the User Password

The first solution for solving the clear text password issue is to encrypt the password in the parameter file. This is done by establishing an ENCKEY file that houses the encryption key that will be used to encrypt the password you want to use. This file is a standard ASCII file that is stored in the GoldenGate home directory and contains the key that will be used for encrypting the password. To create the ENCKEY file, you will need to use the keygen utility to produce the keys. Listing 8-2 provides an example of what you will see when you create the file.

■ **Note**   You can redirect the keys directly into the file as provided in Listing 8-2.

Listing 8-2. Generating the Keys Used for Encryption

```
$ ./keygen 128 1 > ENCKEY
$ cat ENCKEY
0xAA4944614E1FE06419CF1E755660514F
```

Now that the ENCKEY file has been created, it needs to be edited to provide a key name that can be referenced when you want to use it. In Listing 8-3, the key name being used is oldman. This is just a location indicator in the ENCKEY file.

Listing 8-3. Edited Output of ENCKEY File

```
$ cat ENCKEY
oldman 0xAA4944614E1FE06419CF1E755660514F
```

With the ENCKEY in place, you can now encrypt GoldenGate passwords using the ENCRYPT command from within GGSCI. After running ENCRYPT PASSWORD within GGSCI, you will be provided with the encrypted password that is needed for the parameter file. Listing 8-4 provides the syntax to encrypt the password.

Listing 8-4. Encrypting Password

```
$ ./ggsci
GGSCI> encrypt password [password][algorithm] encryptkey [key_name | default]
```

There are a few options you can provide to the ENCRYPT PASSWORD command. The first is the password you want to use for the GoldenGate user. The second of these options is the algorithms that the password will use for encryption. There are four types of algorithms that can be passed to the command. Table 8-1 provides the breakdown of these algorithms.

Table 8-1. *Algorithms for Password Encryption*

Algorithm	Description
AES128	Uses the AES-128 cipher, which has a key of 128 bits.
AES192	Uses the AES-192 cipher, which has a key of 192 bits.
AES256	Uses the AES-256 cipher, which has a key of 256 bits.
BLOWFISH	Uses Blowfish encryption with a 64-bit block size and a variable-length key size from 32 bits to 128 bits. Use AES if supported for the platform. Use BLOWFISH for backward compatibility with earlier Oracle GoldenGate versions, and for DB2 on z/OS, DB2 for i, and SQL/MX on NonStop. AES is not supported on those platforms.

The last piece to encrypting the password is providing a key that will be used to decrypt the password. A complete ENCRYPT PASSWORD command would look similar to Listing 8-5.

■ **Note** There is a default option that can be used as well, but the default is never a good thing use because of the widely available access to documentation.

Listing 8-5. Complete ENCRYPT PASSWORD Command with Output

```
GGSCI> encrypt password ggate aes128 encryptkey oldman
Encrypted
password: AADAAAAAAAAAAAFALGTARAXIRFBEJDGIOAWGLHRDBJKAOBRHKHLCDGIFEFVIIFFFQHEDAANEKDUDMFNF
Algorithm used: AES128
```

After running the command in Listing 8-4, GGSCI produces a password that can be copied into the parameter file for use as illustrated in Listing 8-6.

Listing 8-6. Secure Parameter File

```
EXTRACT EXT1
USERID ggate, PASSWORD
AADAAAAAAAAAAAFALGTARAXIRFBEJDGIOAWGLHRDBJKAOBRHKHLCDGIFEFVIIFFFQHEDAANEKDUDMFNF AES128
ENCRYPTKEY oldman
TRANLOGOPTIONS DBLOGREADER
SETENV (ORACLE_HOME="/u01/app/oraprd/product/10.2.0/db_1")
SETENV (ORACLE_SID="src1")
WARNLONGTRANS 1h, CHECKINTERVAL 30m
EXTTRAIL ./dirdat/lt
WILDCARDRESOLVE IMMEDIATE
TABLE SCOTT.*;
```

Now that the password has been encrypted, it can be stored in the associated parameter file. In looking at Listing 8-6, you will notice that you also have to provide the algorithm and key used to encrypt the password. Now ask yourself this: Is this a very secure approach to security? The answer to that question depends on the security you are trying to implement.

■ **Note**   In my professional opinion, having the algorithm and encryption key in the same file is a huge security issue because you can then decrypt the password if desired.

This brings up the concern of how to make this password encryption more secure than what was previously discussed. Oracle has addressed this by providing a credential store to use for passwords. Credential stores are kind of a wallet type approach to securing passwords. Let's take a look at this approach now.

Credential Stores

The next evolution in securing the Oracle GoldenGate password is to place the user ID and password into a credential store. By doing this, you can reference the user ID and password by using an alias. This simplifies your parameter file and makes your GoldenGate environment more secure.

To use a credential store, you have to let GoldenGate know by adding it to the environment. Listing 8-7 illustrates how to create a credential store.

Listing 8-7. Add Credential Store

```
$ ./ggsci
GGSCI> add credentialstore
```

Once the credential store is created, you can review the file that is created in the dircrd directory under the GoldenGate Home directory.

With the credential store created, user IDs and passwords need to be added to the credential store before they can be used by any process. To do this, the credential store has to be altered, as illustrated in Listing 8-8.

Listing 8-8. Adding a User ID and Password to the Credential Store

```
GGSCI> alter credentialstore add user ggate, password ggate, alias ggate
```

With the user ID and password stored in the credential store, it can now be referenced by the alias that was provided during its creation. To use the credential store in a parameter file you will need to use the parameter USERIDALIAS. This parameter tells GoldenGate to go and look in the credential store for the alias provided. Listing 8-9 provides an example in the parameter file reviewed earlier.

Listing 8-9. USERIDALIAS Used in Parameter File

```
EXTRACT EXT1
USERIDALIAS ggate
TRANLOGOPTIONS DBLOGREADER
SETENV (ORACLE_HOME="/u01/app/oraprd/product/10.2.0/db_1")
SETENV (ORACLE_SID="src1")
WARNLONGTRANS 1h, CHECKINTERVAL 30m
EXTTRAIL ./dirdat/lt
WILDCARDRESOLVE IMMEDIATE
TABLE SCOTT.*;
```

With the change in place for the user alias to be used, the process needs to be restarted. Once restarted, GoldenGate will log in to the database using the alias provided.

This provides a more secure approach to interacting with the Oracle GoldenGate environment without exposing the password. Using user ID aliases has an additional benefit because the alias that is stored in the credential store can also be referenced when you need to log in to the database from GGSCI. Listing 8-10 illustrates how to log in to the database using the USERIDALIAS.

Listing 8-10. Logging in to the Database

```
$ ./ggsci
GGSCI> dblogin useridalias ggate
```

Once you are logged in to the database, you can perform your normal GoldenGate administration routines.

GGSCI Command Security

At this point, you have walked through a few different ways to secure Oracle GoldenGate from a GoldenGate user perspective. There are more ways to secure Oracle GoldenGate, however; one of the ways of securing GoldenGate that you are going to look at is from the command line. This approach prevents anyone from accessing processes from GGSCI. This approach is GoldenGate Command Security (CMDSEC).

Implementing Command Security is pretty simple. The whole process consists of creating a text file called CMDSEC in the GoldenGate Home directory. This file will be used to store all the permissions that are granted to specific groups or administrators. The CMDSEC file allows defined users or groups of users to issue commands like INFO or STATUS while preventing the same users from issuing a START or STOP command. The syntax of the command security file is shown in Listing 8-11.

Listing 8-11. Syntax for Command Security Entries

```
Command_name Command_object os_group os_user { YES | NO }
```

Once the CMDSEC file is in place, the users defined in the file will be granted access to only the processes they can perform. This approach ensures that only registered administrators can interact with the GoldenGate environment.

Summary

This chapter took a quick look at a few different ways of securing an Oracle GoldenGate environment, with the most common way being securing the user at the parameter file level by using either the keygen utility or storing the password in a credential store. We then looked at how to secure Oracle GoldenGate from the GGSCI, where you can restrict users on a command basis. Throughout this chapter, you should have gotten a sense of how easy it is to secure an Oracle GoldenGate environment, so why not set up security for your critical replication environments?

The next chapter looks at how you can use Oracle GoldenGate to interact with your data. Oracle GoldenGate is a very flexible tool that can be used for simple data integration processes. Chapter 9 will help you get a basic understanding of the data integration processes you need to keep in mind.

CHAPTER 9

■ ■ ■

Data Integration

Previous chapters have looked at how Oracle GoldenGate is configured, tuned, and used for various architectures. This chapter looks at the flexibility of Oracle GoldenGate and how this powerful tool is used for various data integration processes.

The benefit of Oracle GoldenGate with a data integration process is seen not only with its ability to replicate transactional data, but the ease with which it can be used to capture data, transform, and apply those transactional data to a wide range of applications and platforms. This flexibility to provide data integration processes for capturing transactional data can be useful in many different environments, so Oracle GoldenGate is quite capable of many different data integration processes, including:

- Writing flat files.

- Generating native database loader files, such as Oracle SQL Loader.

- Using APIs.

- Big data interaction.

As you read through this chapter, you will notice that it is about the various ways that Oracle GoldenGate can be used to capture, transform, and provide data for data integration purposes. There are many different options that can be used from within Oracle GoldenGate for manipulating data.

Using Oracle GoldenGate to Create Flat Files

When the requirements for data integration require the data to be placed into a flat file for ingestion by other tools, Oracle GoldenGate can be used to generate the needed flat files The flat file and Java Messaging Service options, which are needed for flat file generation, are integrated to the core product starting in Oracle GoldenGate 12c. To keep the concepts simple to understand, we focus on the flat file option of Oracle GoldenGate.

■ **Note**   In previous versions of Oracle GoldenGate, 11g and earlier, there was a separate installation for flat file application. These files can be obtained from edelivery.oracle.com.

Types of Flat Files

There are two types of flat files that Oracle GoldenGate can generate as output files. The first of these files is known as a delimited separated file. The second of these files is known as a length separated file. The Oracle GoldenGate extract process can generate both types of files when properly configured. Let's take a look at both of these file types.

© Bobby Curtis 2016
B. Curtis, *Pro Oracle GoldenGate for the DBA*, DOI 10.1007/978-1-4842-1179-3_9

Delimited Separated Values Files

The first type of file is the delimited separated values (DSV) file. These files contain data extracted from the source database and formatted into a flat file separated by some delimited value. Typically this is a comma-delimited file, but the delimiter can be any value defined by the user. An example of a DSV file would be a flat file that contains company data for its employees. An example of a delimited separated file would look something like the data provided in Listing 9-1.

Listing 9-1. Delimited Separated Values

```
999, Heyward, Jason, St. Louis Cardinals
1000, McCann, Brian, New York Yankees
```

Later in this chapter, you will see how to write data out to a delimited separated formatted file in detail. Just understand that a delimiter is used when generating these type of files.

Length Separated Values File

Just like delimited separated value files, a length separated value file contains data separated by a specified length, such as a tab or spaces. The length of the data determines the space between the values in the record. An example of this would be an employee record in which each column has a fixed length of 30 characters. The length separated file would look something like the data in Listing 9-2.

Listing 9-2. Length Separated Files

```
999  Heyward   Jason    St. Louis Cardinals
1001 Freeman   Freddie  Atlanta Braves
```

In the next section, we look at how to generate a length separated file and a delimited separated file.

Generating Flat Files

Now that you know what kind of files you can generate using the flat file options for Oracle GoldenGate, you need to understand the parameters that go into generating these files. Just like anything you do in Oracle GoldenGate, there are parameters that support the process for generating the desired output. Table 9-1 lists four distinct parameters that can be used to generate a flat file in various formats. For now, we focus on the basic type of flat file that can be generated using Oracle GoldenGate 12c, the basic FORMATASCII type.

Table 9-1. *Extract Parameters to Write Flat Files*

Parameter	Description
FORMATASCII	Formats extracted data in an external ASCII format.
FORMATSQL	Formats extracted data into equivalent SQL statements.
FORMATXML	Formats extracted data into equivalent XML syntax.
NOHEADERS	Prevents record headers from being written to the trail file.

To generate a flat file using the FORMATASCII parameter, a separate extract needs to be created with a unique parameter file. This way the process does not interfere with any ongoing processing from other extract processes. The parameter file for this flat file extract is slightly different from a traditional extract parameter file. Listing 9-3 provides a view into what an extract for flat file writing should look like for a delimited separated flat file. Notice that this parameter file is setting up to write a text-based file instead of a trail file. By using the FORMATASCII parameter, you are telling Oracle GoldenGate that the flat file will be an ASCII file. The next line in the parameter file directs Oracle GoldenGate where to write the flat file, the name of the flat file, and the maximum size of the flat file. Finally, the parameter file is specifying from which table to extract the data.

Listing 9-3. Extract Parameter File for Delimited Separated File

```
--Your version of extract may vary –
EXTRACT EXTAF
USERIDALIAS aggate
FORMATASCII
EXTFILE ./dirdat/extaf_file.txt, megabytes 100 TABLE SF.CLIENTS;
```

With the parameter file created, the only thing left for you to do is add the extract to the Oracle GoldenGate environment and start the process. Once the process has been started, the extracted data will be written to the file specified in ASCII format. After the file is written out, the flat file can be used by any external data integration utility to view and manipulate the data in the file.

■ **Note**   The other parameters listed in Table 9-1 will generate data in flat files either as SQL statements that can be run against a database or XML that can be used for business applications.

All of these options are designed to ensure that the data captured can be easily integrated, either by text, SQL, or XML, into other systems. Let's take a look at how an extract is configured to provide these outputs.

Generate ASCII Formatted File

Using the FORMATASCII parameter will send transactions to a flat file rather than the normal canonical formatted trail file. Using this option, transactions can be output to a compatible format that can be used with most business integration tools that can read ASCII formatted files. Although this option provides a way to enable integration to other utilities, there are a few limitations that must be kept in mind when using flat file options:

1. Do not use FORMATASCII if the data will be processed by the replicat process.

2. Do not use FORMATASCII if FORMATSQL or FORMATXML are being used.

3. Do not use FORMATASCII if data contain large objects.

4. Do not use FORMATASCII if extracting from an IBM DB2 subsystem.

5. Do not use FORMATASCII if DDL support is enabled in Oracle GoldenGate.

6. Do not use FORMATASCII if PASSTHROU mode is enabled for a data pump process.

Depending on your purpose for using FORMATASCII or any of the other formatting options, it might be necessary to create a separate extract instead of updating the existing extract process.

Listing 9-4 shows an example of how the extract file needs to be configured to enable writing to an ASCII formatted file on the source side.

Listing 9-4. Extract Parameter File to Write ASCII Formats

```
--Your version of extract may vary -
EXTRACT EXTAF
USERIDALIAS aggate
FORMATASCII
EXTFILE ./dirdat/extaf_file.txt, megabytes 100 TABLE SF.CLIENTS;
```

Looking at Listing 9-4, we can see that we have an ASCII formatted file located in the `dirdat` directory of the Oracle GoldenGate 12c home. When we go and review extracted transactions in the ASCII file, by default the transaction is delimited by commas (,) (Listing 9-5).

Listing 9-5. ASCII Formatted File Output

```
B,2014-12-10:20:29:06.000000,1418261346,182,
I,A,SF.CLIENTS,CLIENT_CD,'ACE',NAME,'Ace Hardware',CITY,'Anniston',STATE,'AL'
C,
B,2014-12-10:20:29:38.000000,1418261378,182,
V,A,SF.CLIENTS,CLIENT_CD,NULL,STATE,'FL'
C,
```

Reviewing the data in the ASCII file, it is clear that commas separate the transactions; however, a single character that is not part of the transaction precedes each line of the file. These characters indicate what types of transaction are in the file. Just as canonical trail files indicate if a record is a before or after image of the transaction, these are indicated here as well. Values that can be seen in this ASCII file indicate that there are two before images, one of which is an insert and the other of which is an update. Table 9-2 provides a detailed explanation of how to identify these transactions.

Table 9-2. *Record Indicators in ASCII Files*

Record Indicator	Purpose
B	Beginning of record indicator on first line of the transaction.
C	Commit on the last line of the transaction.
B or A	Indicates if the transaction is a before or after image on the second line of the transaction.
I, D, U, V	Transaction type indicators: I = Insert D = Delete U = Update V = Compressed update

Use Oracle GoldenGate to Create Native Database Loader Files

To build on to the flat file option, Oracle GoldenGate flat file options can be used to create data files that can be used with native database loaders such as Oracle SQL Loader. This ability provides flexibility between environments that Oracle GoldenGate can support. There are three basic formats that Oracle GoldenGate can write out for usage by these native database loading tools. These formats are listed in Table 9-3.

Table 9-3. *Format for Database Loading Tools*

Parameter	Format Output
SQLLOADER	Oracle SQL*Loader utility output formatted with command file.
FORMATXML	Output provided in XML formatted file.
FORMATSQL	Output provided in the form of SQL statements.

For database loading utilities like Oracle SQL*Loader or Oracle Data Integrator to ingest data, data have to be in a formatted flat file. To ensure that the extract outputs the captured data in the format desired, the extract parameter file needs to be configured to output the file as desired. Let's take a look at how an extract parameter file should be formatted to provide the output expected.

■ **Note**   The placement of these extract parameters will have an effect on all extract files and trails files listed after them.

Extract for Database Utility Usage

Now that we understand how to write data to a flat file using the FORMATASCII option, it can be extended to enable length delimited value (LDV) files. One way to extend the FORMATASCII option is for use with Oracle SQL*Loader. Providing an option for SQLLOADER after the FORMATASCII parameter enables the extract to write LDV formatted data. The example (Listing 9-6) of the parameter shows how the flat file extract created earlier is modified to enable writing for SQLLOADER.

Listing 9-6. SQLLOADER Format

```
--Your version of extract may vary –
EXTRACT EXTAF
USERIDALIAS aggate
FORMATASCII, SQLLOADER
EXTFILE ./dirdat/extaf_file.txt, megabytes 100 TABLE SF.CLIENTS;
```

After starting the extract, the output is extracted in an LDV format for Oracle SQL*Loader to use (Listing 9-7).

Listing 9-7. LDV/SQL*Loader Formatted Output

```
DBNACE ^@^@^@^@^@^@^@^@^@^@^@^@^@^@^@^@^@^@^@^@^@^@^@^@^@^@^@^@^@^@^@^@^@^@^@^@^@^@^@^@^
@^@^@^@^^@^@^@^@^@^@^@^@^@^@^@^@^@^@^@^@^@^@^@
IANACE NAce Hardware    NAnniston    NAL
VAY    NAce Hardware    NAnniston    NFL
```

Using Oracle GoldenGate to generate flat files for different business applications or database load utilities can greatly save time when you need data in different formats and systems. Yet, this is only the beginning of data integration with Oracle GoldenGate.

Oracle GoldenGate User Exits

Another option that Oracle GoldenGate provides for data integration are user exits. User exits are custom routines that are written in C and called during capture (extract) or apply (replicat) processing. A called user exit interacts with a UNIX shared object or a Microsoft Windows dynamic-link library (DLL) while processing, allowing custom processing of transactions. Any custom-built user exit has to support four basic exit functions, which are summarized in Table 9-4.

Table 9-4. User Exit Functions

Parameter	Description
EXIT_CALL_TYPE	Indicates when, during processing, the routine is called.
EXIT_CALL_RESULT	Provides a response to the routine.
EXIT_PARAMS	Supplies information to the routine.
ERCALLBACK	Implements a callback routine.

Oracle provides a good number of example cases of using user exits with the core Oracle GoldenGate product. The examples can be found under the ./UserExitsExamples directory. Again, remember that user exits use C programs to interact between Oracle GoldenGate and the host operating system.

Testing Data with Oracle GoldenGate

With any data integration process the need to test the data coming in or being transformed is important. Oracle GoldenGate provides functions that allow data to be tested while in flight from source to target systems. These functions are executed on a column basis. Table 9-5 provides a summary of these functions for quick reference.

Table 9-5. *GoldenGate Functions*

Function	Category
CASE	Performance testing
EVAL	Performance testing
IF	Performance testing
COLSTAT	Handling missing columns
COLTEST	Handling missing columns
DATE	Dates
DATEDIFF	Dates
DATENOW	Dates
COMPUTE	Arithmetic calculations
NUMBIN	Strings
NUMSTR	Strings
STRCAT	Strings
STRCMP	Strings
STREXT	Strings
STREQ	Strings
STRFIND	Strings
STRLEN	Strings
STRLTRIM	Strings
STRNCAT	Strings
STRNCMP	Strings
STRNUM	Strings
STRRTRIM	Strings
STRSUB	Strings
STRTRIM	Strings
STRUP	Strings
VALONEOF	Strings
AFTER	Others
BEFORE	Others
BEFOREAFTER	Others
BINARY	Others
BINTOHEX	Others
GETENV	Others
GETVAL	Others
HEXTOBIN	Others
HIGHVAL | LOWVAL	Others
RANGE	Others
TOKEN	Others

As you can tell, there are a lot of functions that can be used. Many of these functions fit into six different categories. Every category can help identify what is happening with the data. For this reason, Oracle GoldenGate can be great in tool for implementing small data integration efforts along with replication of data.

Summary

This chapter has discussed Oracle GoldenGate and highlighted some of the features that can be used in a data integration process. These features are found in many different areas of the Oracle GoldenGate tool, enabling Oracle GoldenGate to be a flexible and reliable way of moving and manipulating data across platforms. To what end can Oracle GoldenGate be used in a data integration scenario? There appears to be no end in sight, making it one of the best data integration tools around.

CHAPTER 10

■ ■ ■

GoldenGate Utilities

Everything you have looked at in the previous chapters has been about how to configure and run Oracle GoldenGate. Besides the basics of building a GoldenGate environment, there are many utilities that come with the base product that allow you to work with data within the environment. These utilities are tools that allow you to either look up, replay, map, or trace different aspects of the Oracle GoldenGate environment. This chapter highlights some of the basic tools you will use to interact with your GoldenGate environment. At the end, you should have a basic understanding of what these tools look like and how to use them.

You might be wondering what utilities come with Oracle GoldenGate. Many of these tools can be found in the Oracle GoldenGate Home. The following is a list of utilities that are discussed in this chapter:

- Oracle GoldenGate Error (OGGERR)

- Logdump

- Definition Generator (Defgen)

- Check Parameters (checkprm)

- ConvChk

- Key Generation (keygen)

Oracle GoldenGate Error

Every now and then, Oracle GoldenGate throws an error. These errors are commonly known as Oracle GoldenGate errors (OGG errors). In the early days of Oracle GoldenGate, when these errors were thrown, users didn't know what they meant or even how to look them up. Fortunately, before and after the Oracle acquisition of Oracle GoldenGate, you could use a tool called oggerr to look up the error.

The oggerr utility resides in the Oracle GoldenGate Home directory and can be called from the command line. By simply calling the utility without any options, you will get a usage display (Listing 10-1).

Listing 10-1. oggerr Usage

```
$ ./oggerr
Usage: ./oggerr (-v | [OGG-code...])
```

Looking at the usage in Listing 10-1, you can see that the oggerr utility only has one flag option and then the OGG error code has to be provided. Listing 10-2 provides you with an example of how to look up an error.

© Bobby Curtis 2016
B. Curtis, *Pro Oracle GoldenGate for the DBA*, DOI 10.1007/978-1-4842-1179-3_10

Listing 10-2. oggerr Usage with Error Code

```
$ ./oggerr -v OGG-00001
00001, 00000, "Execution cannot continue - Program Terminating"
// *Cause:  This is a generic message that indicates a process failure.
// *Action: Look for other messages in the process report and error log that
//          provide more context for this failure. If you cannot determine and
//          resolve the problem, contact Oracle Support.
```

In the preceding example, you are asking for the verbose explanation of the error code provided. Using the –v flag, you are presented with detailed information about the error. Although some errors might not give you enough information when looking them up this way, it is still a good utility to use when you need a quick explanation of the error.

■ **Note**   You can find a list of all the error codes for Oracle GoldenGate in the reference guides at docs.oracle.com (http://docs.oracle.com/goldengate/c1221/gg-winux/GMESG/toc.htm).

Logdump

Of all the utilities that are discussed in this chapter, the most used utility is the logdump utility. Logdump allows you to look at the trail files that are generated on capture of data or before the data are applied to the target side. This utility is possibly the most used and largest of the tools provided by Oracle for GoldenGate.

The logdump utility is located directly in the root of the Oracle GoldenGate Home directory. This makes it simple to find and to use when needed to access trail files. Your trail files should be somewhere that you can access easily because the logdump utility requires you to open the trail file from within the utility. To start using logdump, you simply need to navigate to the Home directory for GoldenGate and execute the utility. Listing 10-3 illustrates this process.

Listing 10-3. Executing Logdump

```
oracle@wilma.acme.com:/home/oracle >cd $OGG_HOME
oracle@wilma.acme.com:/opt/app/oracle/product/12.2.0.0/oggcore_1 >./logdump

Oracle GoldenGate Log File Dump Utility for Oracle
Version 12.2.0.1.0 OGGCORE_12.2.0.1.0_PLATFORMS_151101.1925.2
Copyright (C) 1995, 2015, Oracle and/or its affiliates. All rights reserved.
Logdump 4 >
```

Once you have opened the logdump utility, there are a few things that need to be done before you can start reading trail files. There are quite a few options that can be used within logdump. To find out what these options are, you can type **help** at the logdump prompt. This generates a list of commands, shown in Listing 10-4, that can be used within logdump.

Listing 10-4. Logdump Help Output

```
Logdump 4 >help

FC [<num> | <string>]      - Edit previous command
HISTORY                    - List previous commands
OPEN | FROM  <filename>    - Open a Log file
RECORD | REC               - Display audit record
NEXT [ <count> ]           - Display next data record
SKIP [ <count> ] [FILTER]  - Skip down <count> records
     FILTER                - Apply filter during skip
COUNT                      - Count the records in the file
     [START[time] <timestr>,]
     [END[time] <timestr>,]
     [INT[erval] <minutes>,]
     [LOG[trail] <wildcard-template>,]
     [FILE <wildcard-template>,]
     [DETAIL ]
      <timestr> format is
        [[yy]yy-mm-dd] [hh[:mm][:ss]]
POSITION [ <rba> | FIRST | LAST | EOF ] - Set position in file
         REVerse | FORward           - Set read direction
RECLEN [ <size> ] - Sets max output length
EXIT | QUIT        - Exit the program
FILES | FI | DIR   - Display filenames
ENV                - Show current settings
VOLUME | VOL | V   - Change default volume
DEBUG              - Enter the debugger
GHDR  ON | OFF     - Toggle GHDR display
DETAIL ON | OFF | DATA - Toggle detailed data display
DECRYPT OFF | ON [KEYNAME key_name]. - Decrypt data encrypted with GoldenGate trail
encryption.
RECLEN <nnn>       - Set data display length
SCANFORHEADER (SFH) [PREV]  - Search for the start of a header
SCANFORTYPE   (SFT) - Find the next record of <TYPE>
     <typename> | <typenumber>
     [,<filename-template>]
SCANFORRBA    (SFR) - Find the next record with <SYSKEY>
     <syskey>               - syskey = -1 scans for next record
     ,<filename-template>
SCANFORTIME  (SFTS) - Find the next record with timestamp
     <date-time string>
     [,<filename-template>]
        <date-time string> format is
          [[yy]yy-mm-dd] [hh[:mm][:ss]]
SCANFORENDTRANS  (SFET) - Find the end of the current transaction
SCANFORNEXTTRANS (SFNT) - Find start of the next transaction
SCANFORMETADATA  (SFMD) - Find a metadata record
     [DDR] | [TDR]
     [NEXT] | [<Index>]
```

```
SHOW <option>        - Display internal information
     [OPEN]          - list open files
     [TIME]          - print current time in various formats
     [ENV]           - show current environment
     [RECTYPE]       - show list of record types
     [FILTER]        - show active filter items
BIO <option>         - Set LargeBlock I/O info
    [ON]             - Enable LargeBlock I/O (default)
    [OFF]            - Disable LargeBlock I/O
    [BLOCK <nnnn>]-  Set LargeBlock I/O size
TIMEOFFSET <option> - Set the time offset from GMT
     [LOCAL]                - Use local time
     [GMT]                  - Use GMT time
     [GMT +/- hh[:mm]]  - Offset +/- from GMT
FILTER SHOW
FILTER ENABLE | ON    - Enable filtering
FILTER DISABLE | OFF - Disable filtering
FILTER CLEAR [ <filterid> | <ALL> ]
FILTER MATCH      ANY | ALL
FILTER [INClude | EXCLude] <filter options>
    <filter options> are
         RECTYPE   <type number | type name>
         STRING [BOTH] /<text>/ [<column range>]
         HEX       <hex string>  [<column range>]
         TRANSID   <TMF transaction identifier>
         FILENAME <filename template>
         PROCESS   <processname template>
         INT16     <16-bit integer>
         INT32     <32-bit integer>
         INT64     <64-bit integer>
         STARTTIME <date-time string>
         ENDTIME   <date-time string>
         SYSKEY    [<comparison>] <32/64-bit syskey>
         SYSKEYLEN [<comparison>] [<value>]
         TRANSIND [<comparison>] <nn>
         UNDOFLAG [<comparison>] <nn>
         RECLEN    [<comparison>] <nn>
         AUDITRBA [<comparison>] <nnnnnnnn>
         ANSINAME <ansi table name>
         GGSTOKEN <tokenname> [<comparison>] [<tokenvalue>]
         USERTOKEN <tokenname> [<comparison>] [<tokenvalue>]
         CSN | LogCSN [<comparison>] [<value>]
    <column range>
         <start column>:<end column>, ie  0:231
    <comparison>
         =, ==, !=, <>, <, >, <=, >=  EQ, GT, LE, GE, LE, NE
X <program> [string]  - Execute <program>
TRANSHIST nnnn          - Set size of transaction history
TRANSRECLIMIT nnnn    - Set low record count threshold
TRANSBYTELIMIT nnnn   - Set low byte count threshold
LOG {STOP} | { [TO] <filename> } - Write a session log
```

```
BEGIN <date-time>      - Set next read position using a timestamp
SAVEFILECOMMENT on | OFF  - Toggle comment records in a savefile
SAVE <savefilename> [!] <options> - Write data to a savefile
    <options> are
    nnn RECORDS | nnn BYTES
    [NOCOMMENT]  - Suppress the Comment header/trailer recs, Default
    [COMMENT]    - Insert Comment header/trailer recs
    [TRUNCATE ]  - purgedata an existing savefile
    [EXT ( <pri>, <sec> [,<max>])] - Savefile Extent sizes on NSK
    [MEGabytes <nnnn>]           - For extent size calculation
    [TRANSIND <nnn>]             - Set the transind field
    [COMMITTS <nnn>]             - Set the committs field
USERTOKEN     on | OFF | detail - Show user token info
HEADERTOKEN   on | OFF | detail - Show header token info
GGSTOKEN      on | OFF | detail - Show GGS token info
FILEHEADER    on | OFF | detail - Display file header contents
ASCIIHEADER   ON | off          - Toggle header charset
EBCDICHEADER  on | OFF          - Toggle header charset
ASCIIDATA     ON | on           - Toggle user data charset
EBCDICDATA    on | OFF          - Toggle user data charset
ASCIIDUMP     ON | off          - Toggle charset for hex/ascii display
EBCDICDUMP    on | OFF          - Toggle charset for hex/ascii display
PRINTMXCOLUMNINFO  on | OFF     - Toggle SQL/MX columninfo display
TMFBEFOREIMAGE     on | OFF     - Toggle display of TMF before images
FLOAT   <value>                 - Interpret a floating point number
        [FORMAT <specifier>]    - sprintf format default %f
```

As you can tell, there are quite a few different commands, over multiple pages, that can be used within the logdump utility. Each command provides access to and a different outlook on the data contained within the trail files. Now that you have seen all the options that are associated with the logdump utility, let's take a look at accessing some data within a trail file.

Accessing Trail File Data

To access a trail file using the logdump utility, you have to explicitly tell logdump what trail file you wish to open. This is done by issuing the open command with the trail file you want to look at. Listing 10-5 illustrates this process.

Listing 10-5. Open a Trail File

```
Logdump 5 >open ./dirdat/rt000000000
Current LogTrail is /opt/app/oracle/product/12.2.0.0/oggcore_1/dirdat/rt000000000
```

■ **Note**   You can open a range of trail files by using wildcards.

Now that you have an open trail file, you want to look at some data. Before you can do that, you have to set up the environment to display what you want to see. To do this, you need to refer back to the list of commands in Listing 10-4. Although there are several commands to choose from, there are just a few common ones that will get you started. These common logdump commands are highlighted in Listing 10-6.

Listing 10-6. Common Logdump Commands

```
GHDR   ON | OFF    - Toggle GHDR display
DETAIL ON | OFF | DATA - Toggle detailed data display
USERTOKEN    on | OFF | detail  - Show user token info
HEADERTOKEN  on | OFF | detail  - Show header token info
GGSTOKEN     on | OFF | detail  - Show GGS token info
```

You might be asking yourself how to use these commands within logdump. It is quite simple. The commands can be entered at the logdump prompt to enable or disable the command you want to use. Use of these common commands can be seen in Listing 10-7.

Listing 10-7. Common Logdump Commands

```
Logdump 6 >ghdr on
Logdump 7 >detail on
Logdump 8 >detail data
Logdump 9 >ggstoken on
Logdump 10 >usertoken on
```

With the commands in Listing 10-7 executed, you now have a basic setup for reviewing a trail file established. The next thing you need to do is to start looking at the trail file and reviewing the data that it contains. By default you are positioned at the top of the trail file; that is, relative byte address (RBA) 0. All you need to do at this point is use the next (n) command to move forward in the file. Listing 10-8 shows you the contents of the trail file starting at RBA 0 when you click Next.

Listing 10-8. Trail File Header Information

```
Logdump 11 >n
2016/03/14 19:34:21.383.380 FileHeader          Len  1497 RBA 0
Name: *FileHeader*
 3000 0366 3000 0008 4747 0d0a 544c 0a0d 3100 0002 | 0..f0...GG..TL..1...
 0005 3200 0004 2000 0000 3300 0008 02f2 543e 2d1c | ..2... ...3.....T>-.
 82d4 3400 0043 0041 7572 693a 6672 6564 3a61 636d | ..4..C.Auri:fred:acm
 653a 636f 6d3a 3a75 3031 3a61 7070 3a6f 7261 636c | e:com::u01:app:oracl
 653a 7072 6f64 7563 743a 3132 2e32 2e30 3a6f 6767 | e:product:12.2.0:ogg
 636f 7265 5f31 3a50 4747 3132 4335 0000 4735 0000 | core_1:PGG12C5..G5..
 4300 4175 7269 3a66 7265 643a 6163 6d65 3a63 6f6d | C.Auri:fred:acme:com
```

All you see when you start at RBA 0 is the header of the trail file. The header tells you where the trail file came from, the version of GoldenGate being used, and what data pump process created the trail file. To get to an actual record in the trail file, you need to move forward in the trail file again using the next command.

After moving forward in the trail file a few times, you should come upon the first record that is stored in the trail file.

■ **Note** Starting in Oracle GoldenGate 12c (12.2.0.1.0) you will begin seeing table metadata in the trail files.

As part of the record, you will notice there are metadata for the table that was captured. This is new in Oracle GoldenGate 12c and helps with the mapping of data if columns are in different orders. Listing 10-9 shows you the header of the transaction header that corresponds to the metadata for the record that is coming through. Take a moment to review the header information.

Listing 10-9. Trail File Output (1)

```
Logdump 14 >n
```

```
Hdr-Ind      :     E  (x45)    Partition  :     .  (x00)
UndoFlag     :     .  (x00)    BeforeAfter:     A  (x41)
RecLength    :   281  (x0119)  IO Time    : 2016/03/14 20:27:28.773.265
IOType       :   170  (xaa)    OrigNode   :     2  (x02)
TransInd     :     .  (x03)    FormatType :     R  (x52)
SyskeyLen    :     0  (x00)    Incomplete :     .  (x00)
DDR/TDR Idx: (001, 001)        AuditPos   : 25851148
Continued    :     N  (x00)    RecCount   :     1  (x01)

2016/03/14 20:27:28.773.265 Metadata            Len 281 RBA 1707
Name: SOE.LOGON
*
 1)Name         2)Data Type       3)External Length  4)Fetch Offset      5)Scale
 6)Level        7)Null            8)Bump if Odd      9)Internal Length  10)Binary Length
11)Table Length 12)Most Sig DT   13)Least Sig DT    14)High Precision  15)Low Precision
16)Elementary Item 17)Occurs     18)Key Column      19)Sub DataType    20)Native DataType
21)Character Set  22)Character Length 23)LOB Type    24)Partial Type
*
TDR version: 1
Definition for table SOE.LOGON
Record Length: 134
Columns: 3
LOGON_ID      64     50       0  0  0 1 0    50      50     50 0 0 0 0 1     0
1    2    2        -1      0 0 0
CUSTOMER_ID   64     50      56  0  0 1 0    50      50     50 0 0 0 0 1     0
1    2    2        -1      0 0 0
LOGON_DATE   192     19     112  0  0 1 0    19      19     19 0 5 0 0 1     0
1    0   12        -1      0 0 0
End of definition
```

This example of a trail file header looks like Greek to the untrained eye. The information contained in the header is for the SOE.LOGON table. The cryptic header section provides information relative to the transaction that is coming through, such as record length, if it is a before or after transaction, the date the transaction occurred, and the number of records contained with the transaction.

The next section in this header provides details on the metadata for the SOE.LOGON table. The section that has the numbers that look like column headers is a key to help you decipher the specific information related to the columns provided just below that. Finally, the section below that area is information related to the record length and the definition of the table. This section lists the names of the columns in the record that is being sent. This helps with the mapping resolutions between the source and target metadata.

In the first section of the transaction header, you can see how the metadata are being passed in the trail file. In this portion of the trail file, you look at the same transaction, just more of the actual transaction. Just like the metadata header, the transaction has a header that specifies a lot of information for the transactions. Listing 10-10 provides this output for review.

Listing 10-10. Trail Output (2)

```
Logdump 15 >n
```

```
Hdr-Ind      :      E  (x45)     Partition  :      .  (x0c)
UndoFlag     :      .  (x00)     BeforeAfter:      A  (x41)
RecLength    :     54  (x0036)   IO Time    : 2016/03/14 20:27:20.008.002
IOType       :      5  (x05)     OrigNode   :    255  (xff)
TransInd     :      .  (x03)     FormatType :      R  (x52)
SyskeyLen    :      0  (x00)     Incomplete :      .  (x00)
AuditRBA     :      4814         AuditPos   : 25851148
Continued    :      N  (x00)     RecCount   :      1  (x01)


2016/03/14 20:27:20.008.002 Insert                  Len    54 RBA 2048
Name: SOE.LOGON   (TDR Index: 1)
After  Image:                                  Partition 12   G  s
 0000 000b 0000 0007 3239 3832 3938 3600 0100 0a00 | ........2982986.....
 0000 0637 3034 3737 3000 0200 1500 0032 3031 362d | ...704770......2016-
 3033 2d31 343a 3230 3a32 373a 3139              | 03-14:20:27:19
Column     0 (x0000), Len    11 (x000b)
 0000 0007 3239 3832 3938 36                     | ....2982986
Column     1 (x0001), Len    10 (x000a)
 0000 0006 3730 3437 3730                        | ....704770
Column     2 (x0002), Len    21 (x0015)
 0000 3230 3136 2d30 332d 3134 3a32 303a 3237 3a31 | ..2016-03-14:20:27:1
 39                                             | 9

GGS tokens:
 5200 0014 4141 415a 324a 4141 4841 4141 674d 2b41 | R...AAAZ2JAAHAAAgM+A
 4345 0001 7401 0000 4c00 0008 3235 3835 3835 3430 | CE..t...L...25858540
 3600 000a 322e 3235 2e32 3032 3137 6901 0002 0001 | 6...2.25.20217i.....
```

The header information provides the same information as was provided with the metadata. This includes the record length, before and after image information, and the date the transaction occurred. Along with this information, you will see just below the header a section with a date and timestamp. This line in the record provides information on the type of transaction that occurred, the length of the transaction, and the relative byte address. In the case of this transaction, it is an insert that had a length of 54 bytes located at the 2048 byte address.

■ **Note**   The RBA can be used to calculate a rough estimate of size between transactions. Additionally, you can use the count command to get a sense of how many transactions are being applied in a replicat environment.

Immediately after the header, comes the transaction-specific information. This section provides the binary and ASCII format of data. The binary section is to the left of the ASCII information that is displayed. The binary section also provides the column mappings for the data; however, it is not clear on the column names. This is where the metadata in the header are helpful. By marrying the two together, you can quickly see what columns are being mapped for the transaction.

This was a quick overview of running logdump and reviewing a trail file. Trail files are a good thing to take a look at to get a good understanding of what logdump can do for you. Logdump is one of the most powerful tools you can have in your GoldenGate toolkit when problems arise.

Definition Generator

Starting with Oracle GoldenGate 12c (12.2.0.1.0), Oracle is providing the metadata for tables in the trail files to make mapping of data between source and target a bit easier. Although this is provided now, the flexibility of Oracle GoldenGate allows for different version of GoldenGate to be used between each other and still replicat data. This means you can have an Oracle GoldenGate 11g replicating to an Oracle GoldenGate 12c environment and vice versa. So how would you successfully map data in such an architecture? If the table definitions are different or you are performing replication in a heterogeneous environment, you will need to use a definition file.

Definition files are generated by an Oracle GoldenGate utility called defgen, short for definition generator which comes bundled with the core product. The purpose of this utility is to provide a means of mapping the table structure while the data are actively replicated. Defgen allows for definition files to be created that supportthe defining of the table metadata structure on either the source or target side of the replication process. This section looks at how to use the defgen utility to map the source table to the target table.

When replicating data, the assumption made is that the metadata matches on both sides (source and target) of the replication environment. In some situations, this assumption is not accurate and leads to problems with processes abending due to mismatch structures. When this happens, the mapping between source and target metadata needs to be performed to ensure successful replication. This is where using the defgen utility will ensure successful integration of data on the target side.

■ **Note**   The defgen utility is installed in the Oracle GoldenGate Home directory.

Configure Defgen

Like anything in Oracle GoldenGate, before defgen can be used it needs to be configured. To configure a source-side mapping with the defgen utility, we need to create a parameter file. The following steps will create a parameter file called defgen.prm.

1.   From GGSCI, edit a parameter file called defgen.

```
edit params defgen
```

2.   Edit the parameter file with the parameters needed.

```
--Your parameter file will vary, this is an example only--
DEFSFILE ./dirdef/defgen.def
USERID ggate, PASSWORD ggate
TABLE sfi.clients;
```

3. Save and close the file.

4. Exit GGSCI.

After saving the parameter file, you will be ready to run the defgen utility to generate the definition file needed to ensure mapping of the source columns to the columns on the target side.

■ **Note** Parameters that can be used in the parameter file for generating a definition file can be found in Table 10-1.

The defgen utility has a few parameters that can be used when setting up the definitions, shown in Table 10-1. The parameters that are listed in Table 10-1 are to be used when configuring the parameter file for generating definition files.

Table 10-1. *Parameters for Defgen*

Parameter	Description
CHARSET character_set	Use this parameter to specify a character set that defgen will use to read the parameter file. By default, the character set of the parameter file is that of the local operating system. If used, CHARSET must be the first line of the parameter file.
DEFSFILE file_name [APPEND | PURGE] [CHARSET character_set] [FORMAT RELEASE major.minor]	Specifies the relative or fully qualified name of the data definitions file that is to be the output of defgen.
[{SOURCEDB | TARGETDB} datasource] {USERIDALIAS alias | USERID user, PASSWORD password [encryption_options]}	The datasource can be a DSN (Datasource Name), an SQL/MX catalog, or a container of an Oracle container database (CDB). If connecting to an Oracle CDB, connect to the root container as the common user if you need to generate definitions for objects in more than one container. Otherwise, you can connect to a specific container to generate definitions only for that container.
NOCATALOG	Removes the container name (Oracle) or the catalog name (SQL/MX) from table names before their definitions are written to the definitions file. Use this parameter if the definitions file is to be used for mapping to a database that only supports two-part names (owner.object).
TABLE [container.| catalog.] owner.table [, {DEF | TARGETDEF} template];	Specifies the fully qualified name of a table or tables for which definitions will be defined and optionally uses the metadata of the table as a basis for a definitions template.

Running Defgen

After you have built and saved your parameter file, the next step is to run the defgen utility to create the definition file. To run defgen, make sure that you are in the Oracle GoldenGate Home directory. The utility is run from the GGSCI prompt using the parameters that are defined in Table 10-2.

Table 10-2. *Parameters for Defgen Run*

Parameter	Description
PARAMFILE	Relative or full path name of the defgen parameter file.
REPORTFILE	Sends output to the screen and to the designated report file.
[NOEXTATTR]	Used to support backward compatibility with Oracle GoldenGate versions that are older than Release 11.2.1 and do not support character sets other than ASCII, nor case sensitivity or object names that are quoted with spaces.

To run the defgen utility that will create the definition file needed, the command is fairly straightforward. Listing 10-11 provides an example of running the command using relative paths.

Listing 10-11. Running Defgen Utility

```
$ defgen paramfile ./dirprm/defgen.prm reportfile ./dirrpt/defgen.rpt
```

After the definition file has been generated, the file needs to be copied over to the target system and specified in the replicat parameter file. To copy the definition file to the target system, any File Transfer Protocol (FTP) or Session Control Protocol [SCP] utility can be used as long as the transfer is done in binary mode. This ensures that the file is copied correctly between any platforms.

■ **Note** The definition file should be copied in binary mode to avoid any unexpected characters being placed in the file by the FTP utility.

Once the definition file is copied to the target system, the file is associated with the replicat parameter file using the SOURCEDEFS parameter. Listing 10-12 displays how a replicat parameter file would look with the definition file defined.

Listing 10-12. Replicat Parameter File with Definition File Defined

```
-- Example replicat parameter file. Your requirements may vary.--
REPLICAT REPI
SETENV (ORACLE_HOME="/u01/app/oracle/product/12.1.0/db12cr1")
SETENV (ORACLE_SID="oragg")
USERID ggate, PASSWORD <password>
ASSUMETARGETDEFS
DISCARDFILE ./dirrpt/REPI.dsc, append, megabytes 50
SOURCEDEFS ./dirdef/defgen.def
map SFI.CLIENTS, target ATLI.CLIENTS;
```

After configuring the replicat to use the definition file, data can be mapped between source and target without any errors. Notice, in Listing 10-12, that the MAP statement has an extract option after telling Oracle GoldenGate where the target table is. The DEF option that is an option for MAP is used to tell the replicat to use the definition file specified. Using a definition file allows table metadata to be different between source and target systems. This makes the process of integrating data between different systems easier and more flexible.

Check Parameters

Introduced in Oracle GoldenGate 12c (12.2.0.10) is a new way of validating parameter files, checkprm. The checkprm command is used to assess the validity of the specified parameter file. This utility can provide a simple PASS/FAIL or optional details about how the values of each parameter are stored and interrupted.

The checkprm command is a command-line tool that runs out of the Oracle GoldenGate Home directory. When you use the utility with no arguments, checkprm attempts to automatically detect extract or replicat and the platform and database of the installation. The syntax of the checkprm utility is provided in Listing 10-13.

Listing 10-13. Checkprm Syntax

```
checkprm <param file> [--COMPONENT(-C) <component name>]
         [--MODE(-M) <mode name>] [--PLATFORM(-P) <platform name>]
         [--DATABASE(-D) <database name>] [--VERBOSE(-V)]
```

As you can see there are a couple of different parameters that can be passed to the utility and it will provide a validation of the parameter file.

■ **Note**   Additional information on checkprm can be found in the Oracle Docs at http://docs.oracle.com/ goldengate/c1221/gg-winux/GWURF/non_ggsci_commands001.htm#GWURF1245.

Using Checkprm

Let's take a look at a few examples of using the checkprm utility against a replicat parameter file. These examples provide you with a quick understanding of how this utility can be used. In Listing 10-14, there are no parameters passed and the parameter file is strictly being tested for validity.

Listing 10-14. No Parameters Passed

```
oracle@wilma.acme.com:/opt/app/oracle/product/12.2.0.0/oggcore_1 >./checkprm ./dirprm/
rgg12c.prm

2016-03-16 21:15:46 INFO OGG-02095 Successfully set environment variable ORACLE_HOME=/opt/
app/oracle/product/12.1.0.2/dbhome_1.

2016-03-16 21:15:46 INFO OGG-02095 Successfully set environment variable ORACLE_SID=rmt12c.

2016-03-16 21:15:46 INFO OGG-10139 Parameter file ./dirprm/rgg12c.prm: Validity check: PASS.

Runtime parameter validation is not reflected in the above check.
```

In reviewing the output, you will notice that the utility successfully set the Oracle Home, set the Oracle SID, and verified the parameter file with a PASS. This means that the parameter file validated successfully and can be used within your environment.

Now, let's take a more verbose look at the same parameter file. We know that the parameter file passes validation, but you want to see what is contained in the parameter file and if everything is syntax validated. To do this, you would pass the verbose options. Listing 10-15 provides a sample of this output.

Listing 10-15. Verbose Checking with Checkprm

```
oracle@wilma.acme.com:/opt/app/oracle/product/12.2.0.0/oggcore_1 >./checkprm ./dirprm/
rgg12c.prm -V

2016-03-16 21:21:46 INFO OGG-02095 Successfully set environment variable ORACLE_HOME=/opt/
app/oracle/product/12.1.0.2/dbhome_1.

2016-03-16 21:21:46 INFO OGG-02095 Successfully set environment variable ORACLE_SID=rmt12c.

Parameter file validation context:

component(s): REPLICAT
mode(s)     : N/A
platform(s) : Linux
database(s) : Oracle 12c

GLOBALS

enablemonitoring                          : <enabled>
checkpointtable                           : ggate.checkpoint
ggschema                                  : ggate

./dirprm/rgg12c.prm

replicat                                  : RGG12C
setenv                                    : (ORACLE_HOME="/opt/app/oracle/product/12.1.0.2/
dbhome_1")
setenv                                    : (ORACLE_SID="rmt12c")
userid                                    : ggate
  password                                : ******
reperror                                  : <enabled>
  spec_option                             : default
    discard                               : <enabled>
assumetargetdefs                          : <enabled>
map                                       : SOE.*
  target                                  : SOE.*

2016-03-16 21:21:46 INFO OGG-10139 Parameter file ./dirprm/rgg12c.prm:  Validity check:
PASS.
Runtime parameter validation is not reflected in the above check.
```

Notice that in the verbose output, you can see what options have been enabled, the name of the process, what environment is set, and what the mappings are tied to. Just like before, the parameter file passes and can be used with your environment.

The last example shows how you can check to see if the parameter file and the associated parameters can be used between different modes of a process. The parameter file that has been used in the previous two examples has been from a classic replicat process. What if you wanted to take that same parameter file and convert to an integrated replicat? You can use the move option of checkprm to validate the parameter file before attempting the change. Listing 10-16 shows how you can validate the parameter for such a move.

Listing 10-16. Validating for Integrated Processes

```
soracle@wilma.acme.com:/opt/app/oracle/product/12.2.0.0/oggcore_1 >./checkprm ./dirprm/
rgg12c.prm -M Integrated Replicat

2016-03-16 21:24:17 INFO OGG-02095 Successfully set environment variable ORACLE_HOME=/opt/
app/oracle/product/12.1.0.2/dbhome_1.

2016-03-16 21:24:17 INFO OGG-02095 Successfully set environment variable ORACLE_SID=rmt12c.

2016-03-16 21:24:17 INFO OGG-10139 Parameter file ./dirprm/rgg12c.prm: Validity check: PASS.

Runtime parameter validation is not reflected in the above check.
```

From looking at the output, you can see that the current parameter file can be moved to an integrated replicat process without any issues. This is designed to help make your decision-making process easier and to check legacy environments before converting to newer Oracle GoldenGate standards.

ConvChk

In Oracle GoldenGate environments earlier than version 12.2.0.1.0, your trail files were limited to two-letter, six-digit names. Starting with Oracle GoldenGate 12c (12.2.0.1.0), the default name of a trail file is two letters with nine digits. This allows for long-running environments to have more distinct trail file names. If you are upgrading your Oracle GoldenGate environment to 12.2.0.1.0 or later, you will want to upgrade your trail file names as well. This is where the convchk utility comes in handy.

The convchk utility is used to upgrade your trail files from a six-digit checkpoint record for a given trail to a nine-digit trail name. The syntax for this utility is provided in Listing 10-17.

Listing 10-17. Convchk Syntax

```
convchk extrac trail [ seqlen_d | seqlen_6d ]
```

Key Generator

Oracle GoldenGate uses a user ID and passwords to interact with the database. These two critical pieces of information are stored in the parameter files in clear text. This means that the password for the user ID is stored in clear text. Does anyone else see a security violation here? If you are like 90 percent of the other administrators out there, you have a need to ensure that all passwords are secure and not passed in clear text. Oracle provides you a way to do this with the keygen utility.

The keygen utility is used to generate one or more encryption keys to be used with Oracle GoldenGate in the ENCKEYS files. The syntax for the keygen utility is illustrated in Listing 10-18.

Listing 10-18. Keygen Syntax

```
keygen key_length n
```

When using keygen without any options, the utility runs in an interactive mode. The key_length option is the length of the encryption key, up to 256 bits (32 bytes) and the n is the number of keys to generate to the screen. Listing 10-19 displays the output of running the keygen utility.

Listing 10-19. Keygen Output

```
oracle@wilma.acme.com:/opt/app/oracle/product/12.2.0.0/oggcore_1 >./keygen 128 5
0xB2BB5879131B52726615FD18668C116C

0x3DE1362B38DCB711E6A77F26F4AF924C

0xC706155D5C9D1D31663A023482D3132D

0x522CF30E805E8350E6CC844110F7940D

0xDC51D140A41FE96F665F074F9D1A166E
```

Now all you need to do is copy each of the encrypted keys to a file named ENCKEYS. Then the ENCKEYS file is shared between the needed Oracle GoldenGate environments. They can then be referenced in the parameter files instead of a clear text password.

Summary

This chapter looked at a few of the utilities that come bundled with Oracle GoldenGate. A few of these utilities are standard utilities that have been with GoldenGate from day one; there also are a few that are new as of Oracle GoldenGate 12c (12.2.0.1.0). All of these utilities are used to help you configure and manage your environments in the most efficient way possible.

At this point in the book, you have covered a wide range of items in the Oracle GoldenGate application from the command line. The next chapter looks at the next generation of building Oracle GoldenGate environments with the new Studio tool.

■ ■ ■

GoldenGate Studio and Oracle GoldenGate Monitor Agent

If you've made it to this chapter, then you have read about all the command-line options and how to use Oracle GoldenGate from the command line. If you are a graphical interface person, you might be thinking that GoldenGate is a great tool, but you do not want to work from the command line. If that is you, then you are in luck. Oracle has recently released a new tool that provides a graphical interface for Oracle GoldenGate, Oracle GoldenGate Studio.

Oracle GoldenGate Studio comes bundled in a new suite of tools called GoldenGate Foundation Suite. This suite of tools comprises the best tools used to work with GoldenGate, including the following:

- Oracle GoldenGate Studio

- Oracle Veridata

- Oracle GoldenGate Management Pack

With the addition of GoldenGate Studio, Oracle now provides an offering that will allow you to design and build Oracle GoldenGate architectures, validate data between environments, and monitor these environments from a central location. This is a huge step forward for the growing popularity of Oracle GoldenGate.

This chapter introduces you to Oracle GoldenGate Studio and some of the basic features that it provides.

Downloading Oracle GoldenGate Studio

Oracle GoldenGate Studio comes bundled with the OUI, which will walk you through installation. Before you can start installing Studio, you will have to download the software from OTN (http://otn.oracle.com) or from eDelivery (https://edelivery.oracle.com). Figure 11-1 shows you where you can find the GoldenGate Studio software on OTN.

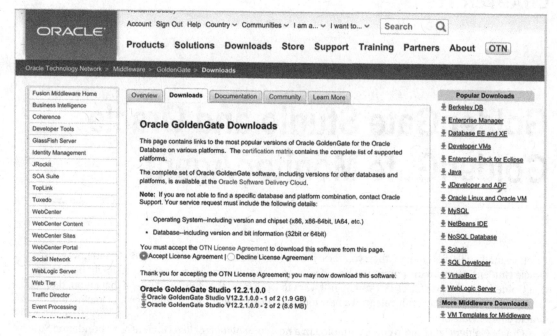

Figure 11-1. OTN location of Oracle GoldenGate Studio

You will notice that there are two files to download. These files are Java Archive (JAR) files that are compressed for download purposes. Both of these files are required for the installation. After you download the files, they need to be extracted in a location from which you want to run the installation.

■ **Note**   For the installation to work, there is a Java JDK 1.8 requirement. Java JDK 1.7 and earlier versions will not work with the JAR files for Studio. Java JDK 1.8 can be downloaded here at http://www.oracle.com/ technetwork/java/javase/downloads/jdk8-downloads-2133151.html.

Once the files are extracted, you are ready to install Oracle GoldenGate Studio.

Installing Oracle GoldenGate Studio

To begin installing Oracle GoldenGate Studio, you need Oracle Java JDK 1.8. Java JDK 1.8 should be in your path so the Java command can be called without issue. After you have access to the correct version of Java, starting the Oracle GoldenGate Studio installer is quite simple. Listing 11-1 shows you how to start the installer from the command line.

Listing 11-1. Starting the Installer

```
oracle@fred.acme.com:/home/oracle/Downloads >cd ggstudio/
oracle@fred.acme.com:/home/oracle/Downloads/ggstudio >ls -ltr
total 2035480
-rw-rw-r--. 1 oracle oracle 9023463 Dec 23 09:07 fmw_12.2.1.0.0_oggstudio_generic2.jar
-rw-rw-r--. 1 oracle oracle 2075303807 Dec 23 09:08 fmw_12.2.1.0.0_oggstudio_generic.jar
oracle@fred.acme.com:/home/oracle/Downloads/ggstudio >java -jar ./fmw_12.2.1.0.0_oggstudio_
generic.jar
Launcher log file is /tmp/OraInstall2016-01-23_01-11-27PM/launcher2016-01-23_01-11-27PM.log.
Extracting files.....................................
Starting Oracle Universal Installer

Checking if CPU speed is above 300 MHz. Actual 3192.107 MHz Passed
Checking monitor: must be configured to display at least 256 colors. Actual 16777216 Passed
Checking swap space: must be greater than 512 MB. Actual 12287 MB Passed
Checking if this platform requires a 64-bit JVM. Actual 64 Passed (64-bit not required)
Checking temp space: must be greater than 300 MB. Actual 35476 MB Passed
Preparing to launch the Oracle Universal Installer from /tmp/OraInstall2016-01-23_01-13-56PM/
Log: /tmp/OraInstall2016-01-23_01-13-56PM/install2016-01-23_01-13-56PM.log
```

■ **Note**   The java -jar command automatically combines the two JAR files to start the installer.

Once the installer performs a few prerequisite checks, the graphical portion of the installation will begin. If the graphical portion is unable to open the display, if you are using X-Term, then you will have to restart the secure shell session. If your display variable is correct, then you will see the initial load screen, which is displayed in Figure 11-2.

Figure 11-2. *Installer initial screen*

With the installer started, you are presented with an eight-step wizard for installing Oracle GoldenGate Studio. This wizard walks you through all the steps required to successfully install Studio.

Figure 11-3 shows the first page of the Installation Wizard. This page is just a general welcome screen that provides general information related to Studio. Click Next to move forward.

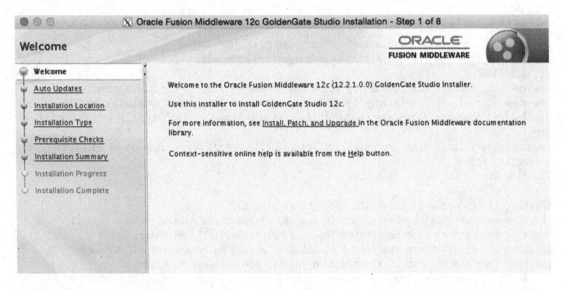

Figure 11-3. *Welcome page in Installation Wizard*

The next step in the wizard (Figgure 11-4) is to tell Oracle if you want to check for any updates to the software being installed. With this being the first release of Studio, you can select Skip Auto Updates and click Next.

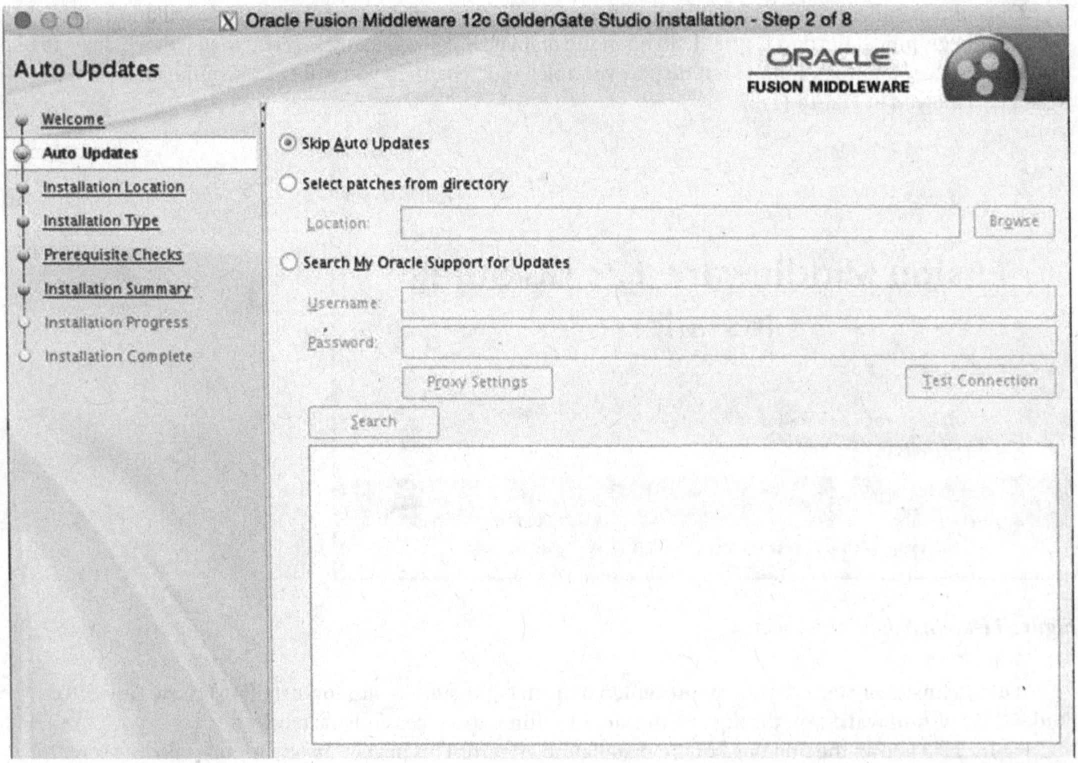

Figure 11-4. *Software update*

In the third step (Figure 11-5), you are presented with the opportunity to specify the location where you want to install Studio. This will be the Oracle Home directory of Studio. Specify the location as needed. There is a Browse button if needed, along with a button to show you the feature sets that are installed in that Home directory. With this being a new home, there will be no feature sets.

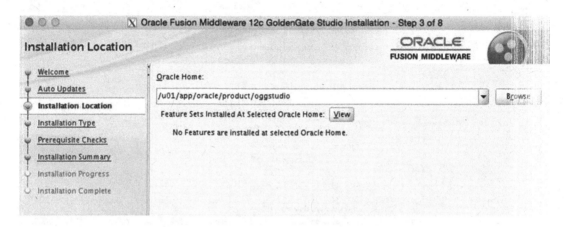

Figure 11-5. *Oracle Home location*

The fourth step in the wizard (Figure 11-6) provides you with the installation type. There is not much to pick from at this point. The only type of installation that can be performed is a complete install, which includes both the Studio software and the most recent version of the OPatch features.

Figure 11-6. *Installation Type page*

The fifth step of the installer (Figure 11-7) checks for prerequisites, which include checking the operating system and the version of Java used to run the installer. In Figure 11-7, you will notice that Java 1.8 is throwing a warning due to the version of Java that Studio is certified against. In installing this software, I'm using Java 1.8.0_40. When Studio was made generally available, it was certified against Java 1.8.0_51. This is not a huge difference, and it is something that should be corrected at a later time, after installation.

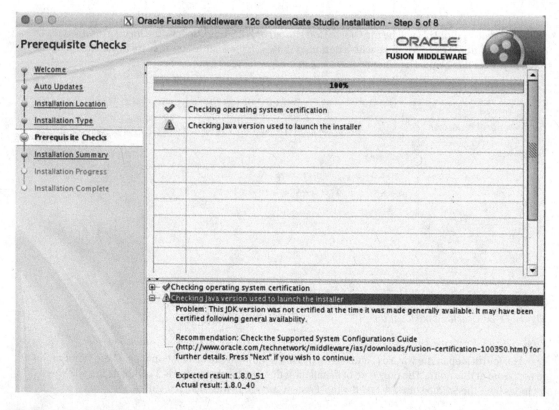

Figure 11-7. *Prerequisite Checks page*

After the prerequisites are checked, the wizard gives you a summary, as shown in Figure 11-8, of all the information you provided during installation. This page lists what will be installed, where it is installed, and how much disk space is required for the installation.

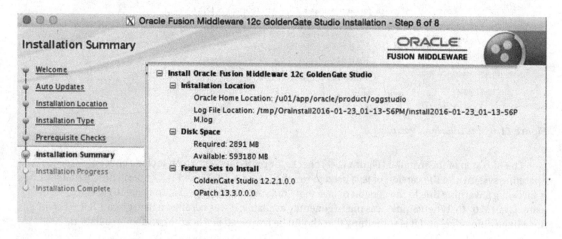

Figure 11-8. *Installation Summary page*

After you review the installation summary, click Install.The installer will begin to install Oracle GoldenGate Studio where specified (Figure 11-9). During the installation, you can keep track of the progress of the installation.

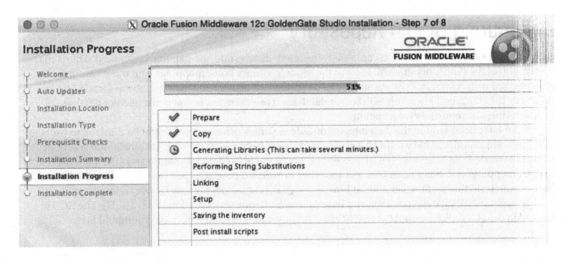

Figure 11-9. *Installation Progress page*

After completion of the installation, the wizard provides you with additional information needed to finish setting up Studio (Fiure 11-10). This information is listed in the Next Steps section on the Installation Complete page. Out of the two next steps, the most important one involves repository creation.

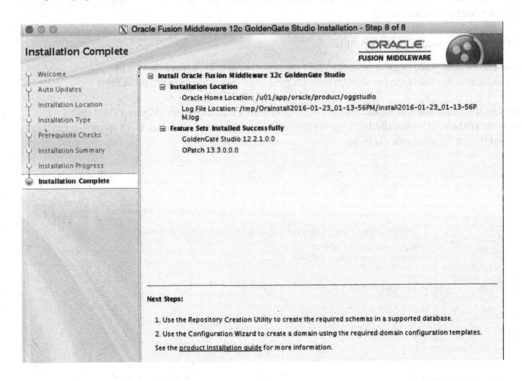

Figure 11-10. *Installation Complete page*

At this point, the Oracle GoldenGate Studio is installed, but you still need to create the repository that will be used for Studio. Let's take a look at that now.

Configuring Studio Repository

Before Oracle GoldenGate Studio is completely installed, there is one last step that is required. This is the installation of the repository that will hold all the models, connections, mappings, and other resources that are used within Studio. This repository can be configured against an Oracle database, Oracle MySQL database, IBM DB2, or a Microsoft SQL Server database. The end result is that it just needs a database in which to store the repository information.

If you have been around the data integration side of Oracle products, you might be thinking to yourself that this seems familiar. That would be a good assumption, because Oracle GoldenGate Studio was built using the Oracle Data Integrator (ODI) framework. Both Oracle GoldenGate Studio and ODI use a repository to store mappings and other resources. Because they are related products, you can use the one repository for both products. In this section, you look at how to install the repository for only Oracle GoldenGate Studio.

To begin installing the repository, you have to use the Repository Creation Utility (RCU). The RCU is located in the $OGGS_HOME/oracle_common/bin directory and is executed from the command line.

■ **Note** If you are on a Microsoft Windows machine, RCU will be in the same location and executed by double-clicking.

From a command prompt, you just need to be in the $OGGS_HOME/oracle_common/bin directory and execute rcu. This starts the graphical utility for creating the repository. Listing 11-2 provides a sample of the commands needed to execute the RCU.

Listing 11-2. Run Repository Creation Utility

```
oracle@fred.acme.com:/u01/app/oracle/product/oggstudio/oracle_common >cd bin
oracle@fred.acme.com:/u01/app/oracle/product/oggstudio/oracle_common/bin >./rcu
```

Much like the installation of Studio, the RCU starts off with a welcome page (Figure 11-11) that highlights what is about to be installed. On the welcome page, you can see there are eight steps that have to be performed before the repository is built.

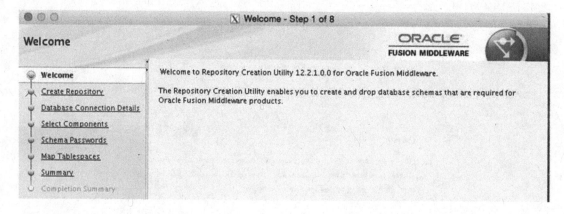

Figure 11-11. RCU Welcome page

The next step is to create the repository for Studio. On this page, shown in Figure 11-2, there are a few options for creating a repository. Because this is a simple installation, the default selections are fine; however, if you have additional requirements, you can use the other two options to have a DBA build the repository. Finally, if you need to delete a repository, this is the page where you can select that. If you delete a repository, the wizard will change a bit; because you are building a repository do not worry about that here.

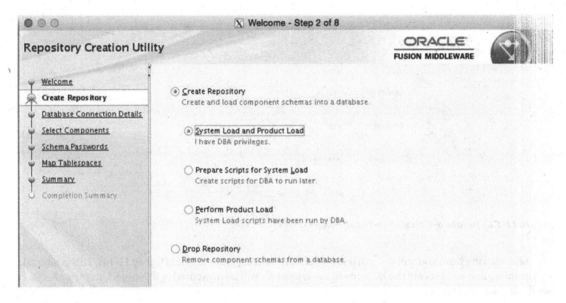

Figure 11-12. *Create Repository page*

The next step in creating the repository is to provide the connection to the database where the repository will be built (Figure 11-13). In the first drop-down list, Database Type, you can select the type of database that the repository will be built in. As mentioned previously, the repository can be built in Oracle Database, Oracle MySQL, IBM DB2, and Microsoft SQL Server databases.

After selecting the type of database where the repository is to be built, you will need to provide all the connection information for that database. For an Oracle database, this information would be hostname, port number, service name, username, password, and the role to which the user has access. Figure 11-13 shows what this screen would look like for an Oracle Database connection.

■ **Note**   By using service names, you can build out the repository in a pluggable database.

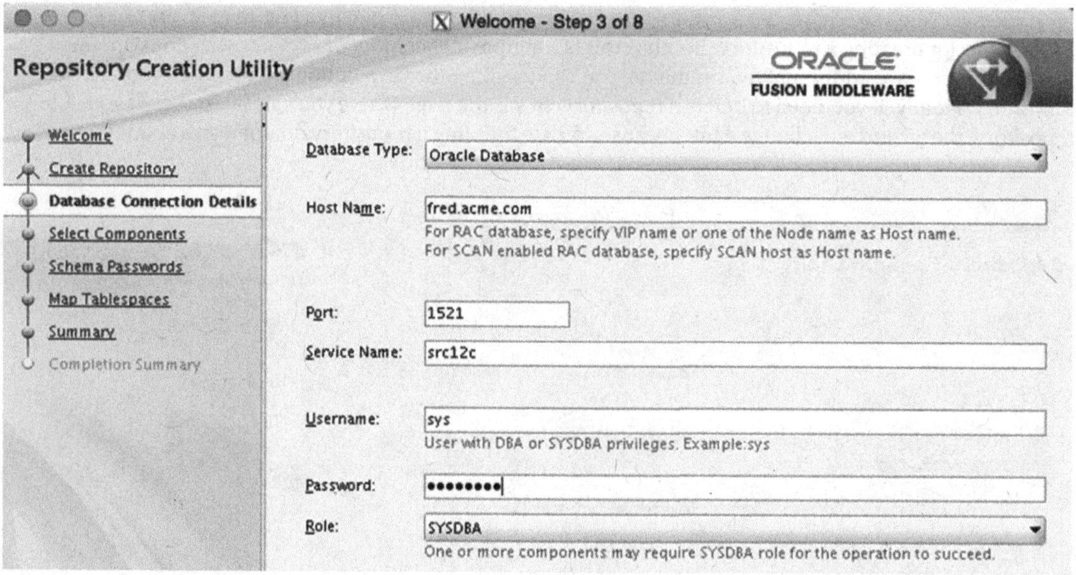

Figure 11-13. *Database Connection Details page*

After clicking Next, you will see a dialog box about checking prerequisites (Figure 11-14). This is normal, and anything that will prevent the building of the repository will be presented at this time. Once the checks are done, click OK to proceed.

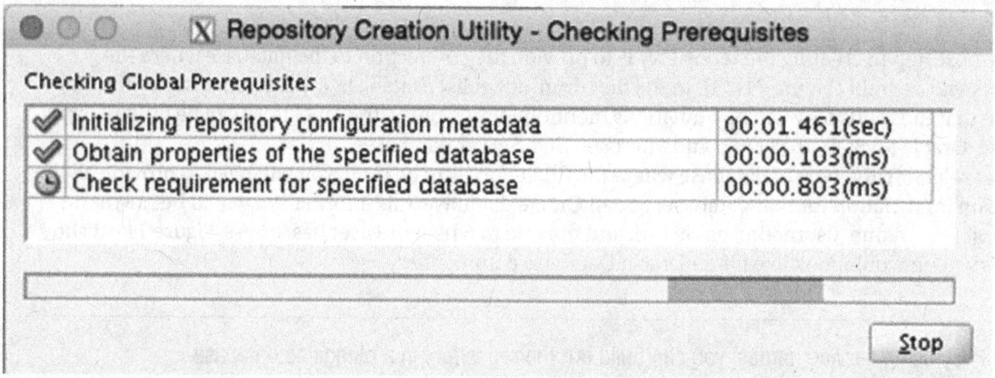

Figure 11-14. *Prerequisites check*

The next step in creating the repository is to select the components needed within the repository (Figure 11-15). These components will have a prefix associated with them so you can keep track of what is created for the repository. This prefix can be changed on this page as well. Select the Oracle GoldenGate check box. As you can see in Figure 11-15, there is an option for Repository to specify the repository for Studio. This will create associated schemas called DEV_STB and DEV_OGGSTUDIO_REPO within the database.

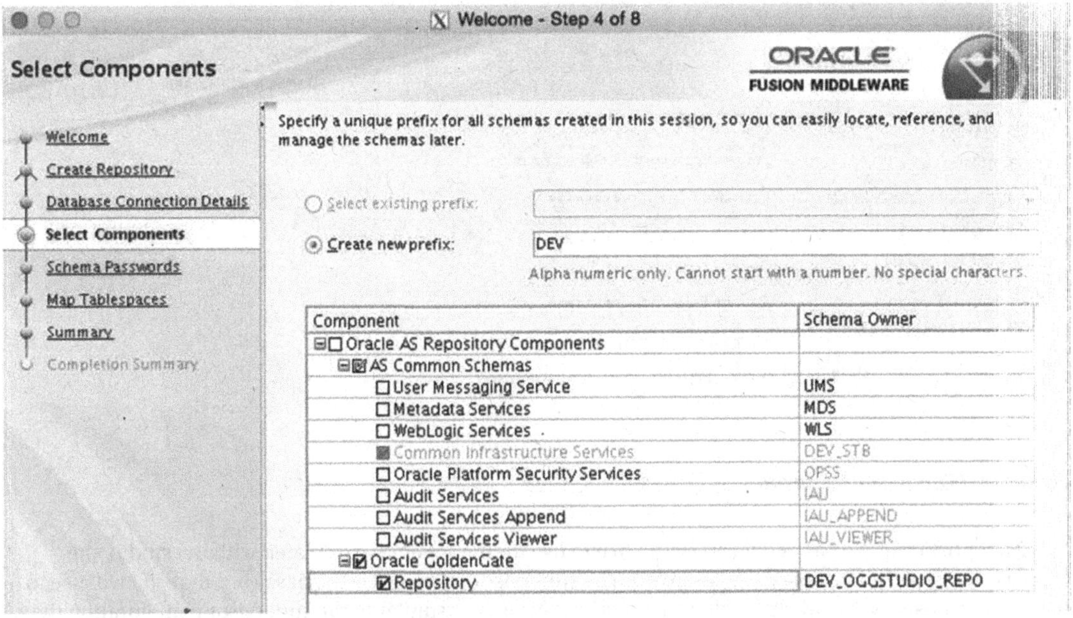

Figure 11-15. *Select Components page*

After you click Next, the Select Components page will run through a prerequisites check (Figure 11-16). This usually returns normal results and you just need to click OK to move forward with repository creation.

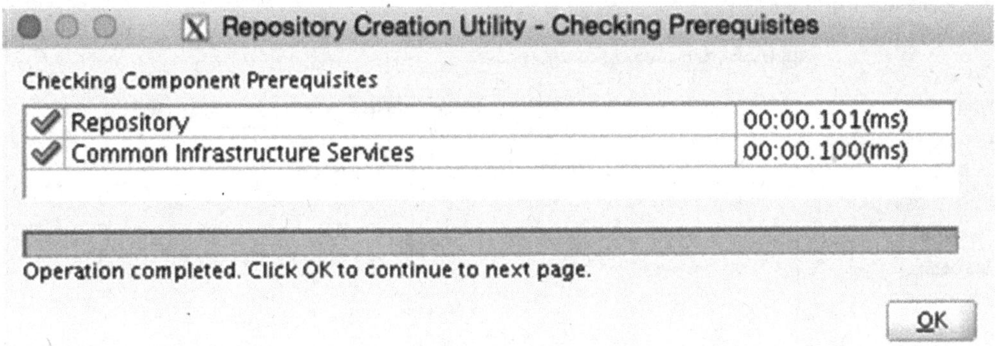

Figure 11-16. *Prerequisites check*

As with any schema being built inside a database, you will need to provide a password. The next step in the creation of the repository is to provide a password or define different passwords for all the schemas. To keep things simple in a test environment, it is best to use the same password for all schemas. Figure 11-17 illustrates this screen.

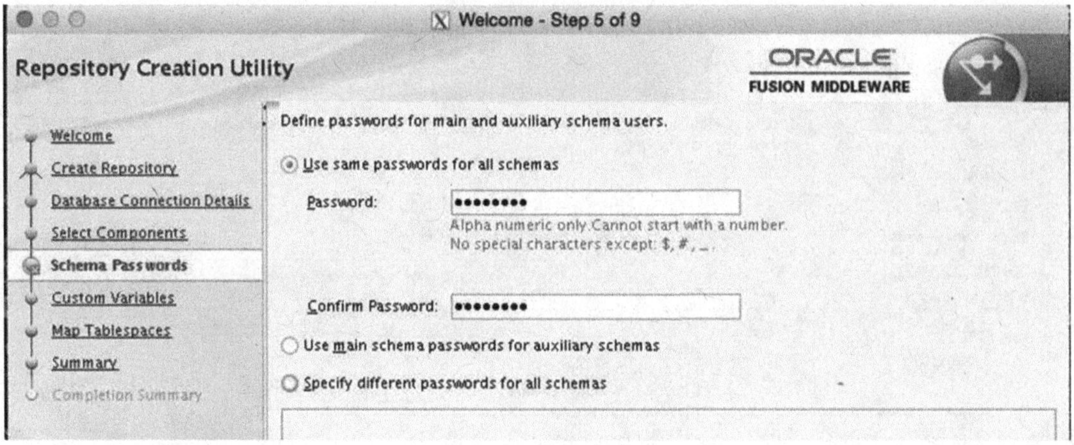

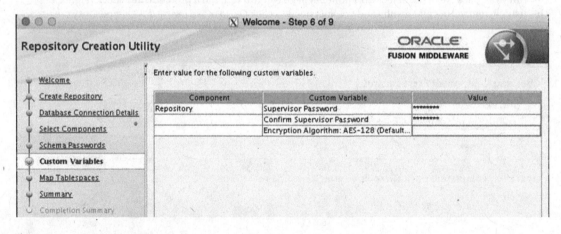

Figure 11-17. Provide password

After providing the password you would like to use for the schemas associated with the studio, the wizard will ask you for a supervisor password. The supervisor password is the password that you will use to access the repository for Oracle GoldenGate Studio. This is very similar to the supervisor configuration that you would use in Oracle Data Integrator. On the Custom Variables page shown in Figure 11-18, you need to provide the password you want to use for the supervisor in the first two fields. The field for Encryption Algorithm should remain blank.

Figure 11-18. Provide a supervisor password

■ **Note** If you provide an encryption algorithm value, you will break the installation. This is a known bug that was identified during beta testing.

The next step in repository creation is to map the tablespaces that are needed to store all the objects for Oracle GoldenGate Studio. By default, the utility adds predefined names for tablespaces. This information can be changed if desired. Figure 11-19 shows what the default settings look like using the schemas DEV_STB and DEV_OGGSTUDIO_USER.

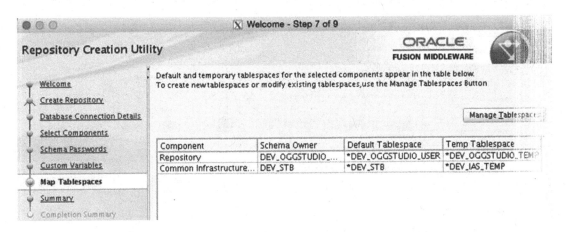

Figure 11-19. Create tablespaces

When you click Next, the wizard will check to see if the tablespaces you want for the schemas exist. If they do not exist, the wizard prompts you to verify the creation of the tablespace or to cancel and make other selections.

If you choose to create the tablespaces, then the utility provides a dialog box, shown in Figure 11-20, that will return the status of how long it takes to build the associated tablespaces.

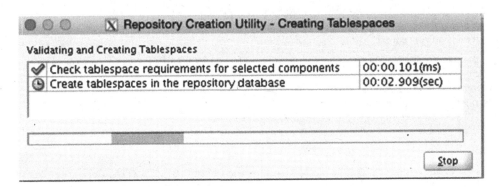

Figure 11-20. Tablespace creation

Once you reach the Summary page (Figure 11-21) in the utility, you can see all the information you provided before creating the repository. Once you click Create, the utility creates the repository needed for Oracle GoldenGate Studio.

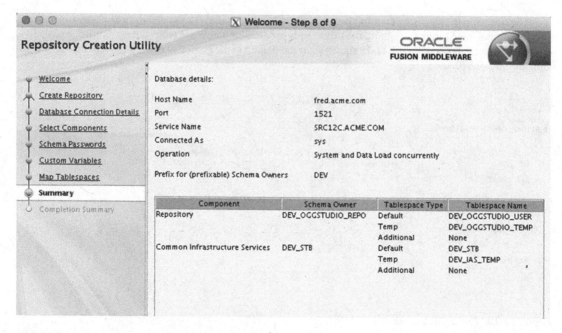

Figure 11-21. Repository Creation Utility Summary page

The creation of the repository (Figure 11-22) will take some time, depending on the database type and size of the hardware where the database is hosted. Once this step is finished, the repository will be completed and you will be able to access the repository from Oracle GoldenGate Studio.

Repository Creation Utility - System Load		
Repository System Load in progress.		
✔ Execute pre create operations	00:03.483(sec)	
🕐 Repository	00:00.702(ms)	
Common Infrastructure Services	0	
Execute post create operations	0	

Figure 11-22. Repository Creation Utility progress

The last thing the utility will provide once the repository is created is a summary of the events that were performed. On the Completion Summary page (Figure 11-23), you can clearly see the database details, log file locations, and what components were created. At this point, you can close the utility.

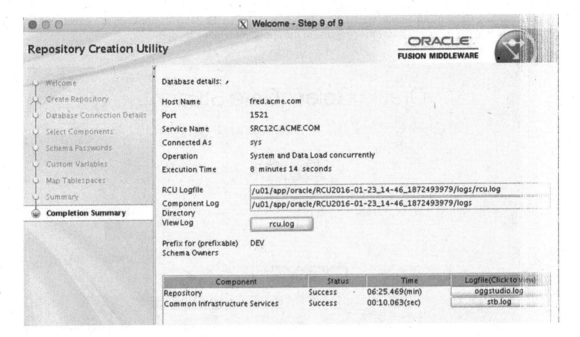

Figure 11-23. Repository Completion Summary page

With the repository created, you can begin working with Oracle GoldenGate Studio in mostly an offline capacity. I say offline because there is still one more component that needs to be installed before you can use Oracle GoldenGate Studio in an online status. Before we talk about that, let's take a look at Oracle GoldenGate Studio.

Starting Oracle GoldenGate Studio

With the binaries for Oracle GoldenGate Studio installed and the repository that is needed configured, it is now possible to start the Studio interface. To start Oracle GoldenGate Studio, you need to navigate to the $OGGS_HOME/oggstudio/bin directory and execute oggstudio. Listing 11-3 shows how this is done.

Listing 11-3. Directory to Start Oracle GoldenGate Studio

```
oracle@fred.acme.com:/u01/app/oracle/product/oggstudio >
oracle@fred.acme.com:/u01/app/oracle/product/oggstudio >cd oggstudio
oracle@fred.acme.com:/u01/app/oracle/product/oggstudio/oggstudio >cd bin
oracle@fred.acme.com:/u01/app/oracle/product/oggstudio/oggstudio/bin >ls
GG-SplashScreen.png oggstudio64.exe oggstudio.boot oggstudio.exe oggstudioW.exe
oggstudio oggstudio64W.exe oggstudio.conf oggstudio-logging-config.xml version.properties
oracle@fred.acme.com:/u01/app/oracle/product/oggstudio/oggstudio/bin >./oggstudio
```

■ **Note** You will notice in this directory there are other versions of Studio. These are for different operating system platforms.

Once Oracle GoldenGate Studio starts, the splash screen (Figure 11-24) will appear on the screen and provide a loading bar to let you know the progress of the application being loaded.

Figure 11-24. *Oracle GoldenGate Studio splash screen*

On the first use of Oracle GoldenGate Studio, you will be asked if you would like to import previous configurations (Figure 11-25). This is similar to other products provided by Oracle. In this case, because this is a fresh install, you can safely click No.

Figure 11-25. *Import preferences*

When the application is finished loading, Oracle GoldenGate Studio will start. Figure 11-26 shows you the interface without being connected to the repository.

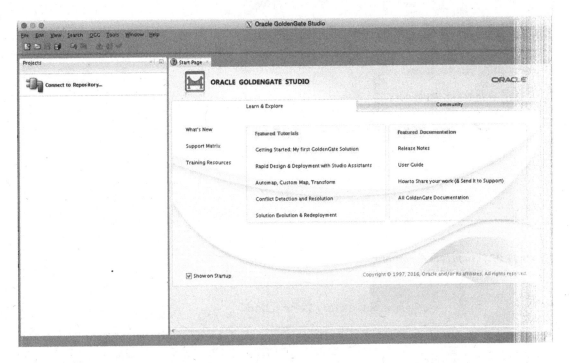

Figure 11-26. *Oracle GoldenGate Studio*

Now that Oracle GoldenGate Studio has been started, you can connect to the repository you created earlier in the chapter. Once you are connected to the repository, you can begin to design and build out your Oracle GoldenGate architectures.

Connecting to the Repository

With Oracle GoldenGate Studio running, you will want to connect to the repository database to begin building your diagrams and different architectures. To do this, you need to establish a connection to the repository, which is done simply from within the Studio interface.

On the left side of the Studio interface, you will see an icon that looks like a power plug. You will also see a similar icon just below the menu bar (Figure 11-27). Clicking on either of these icons opens a dialog box where you will need to define a profile for later access to the repository (Figure 11-28). Once you create the profile for accessing the repository, you will also be given the option for storing the password in a secure wallet.

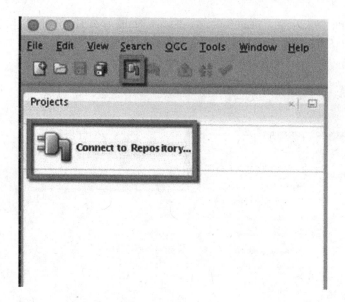

Figure 11-27. *Connect to Repository*

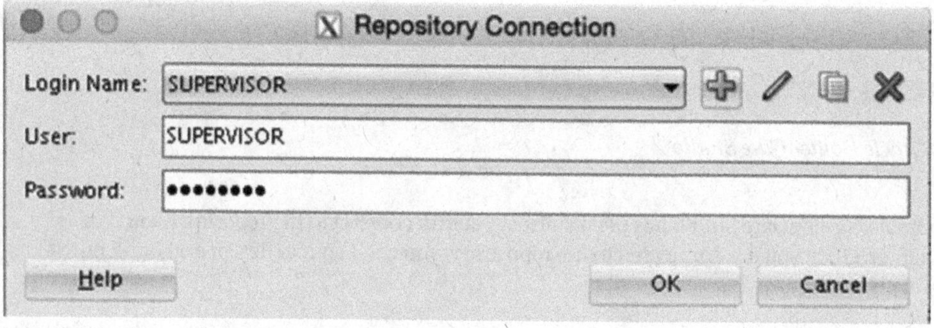

Figure 11-28. *Repository login*

After connecting to the repository, the interface for Oracle GoldenGate Studio changes to a more workable interface with windows for different components within the interface (Figure 11-29). At this point, take some time to explore the interface and figure out what you can do within it. Chapter 12 will familiarize you with the different components you can use within Oracle GoldenGate Studio.

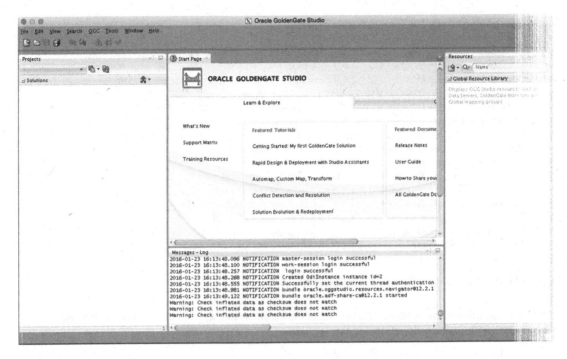

Figure 11-29. *Oracle GoldenGate Studio connected to the repository*

Disconnecting from the Repository

When you are finished working with Oracle GoldenGate Studio, you will want to disconnect from the repository before shutting down Studio. To do this, you need to click the power plug icon again. This time the icon will have a red X on it. Once you click this, you will be disconnected from the repository.

Oracle GoldenGate Monitor Agent

Earlier in the chapter as you were introduced to Oracle GoldenGate Studio, it was mentioned that you could use Studio in an offline fashion. Offline with Oracle GoldenGate Studio means that you have no way to connect your models to an existing GoldenGate environment. So what can you do if you want to work online? The answer is quite simple: You have to install the Oracle GoldenGate Monitor Agent, also known as the Java Agent (JAgent). This is not the same JAgent that comes bundled with the core Oracle GoldenGate product.

This version of the JAgent is provided with the Oracle GoldenGate Management Pack. Just like Oracle GoldenGate Studio, this product can be downloaded from OTN (Figure 11-30). This version of the JAgent provides more robust monitoring capabilities for Oracle GoldenGate, not only to be used with Studio, but with Oracle Enterprise Manager 12c and 13c as well.

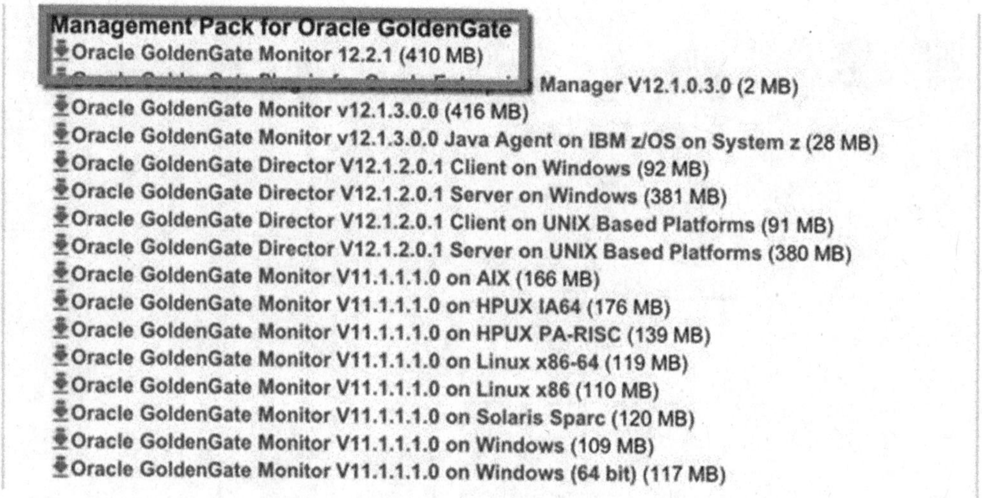

Management Pack for Oracle GoldenGate
⬇ Oracle GoldenGate Monitor 12.2.1 (410 MB)
⬇ ... Manager V12.1.0.3.0 (2 MB)
⬇ Oracle GoldenGate Monitor v12.1.3.0.0 (416 MB)
⬇ Oracle GoldenGate Monitor v12.1.3.0.0 Java Agent on IBM z/OS on System z (28 MB)
⬇ Oracle GoldenGate Director V12.1.2.0.1 Client on Windows (92 MB)
⬇ Oracle GoldenGate Director V12.1.2.0.1 Server on Windows (381 MB)
⬇ Oracle GoldenGate Director V12.1.2.0.1 Client on UNIX Based Platforms (91 MB)
⬇ Oracle GoldenGate Director V12.1.2.0.1 Server on UNIX Based Platforms (380 MB)
⬇ Oracle GoldenGate Monitor V11.1.1.1.0 on AIX (166 MB)
⬇ Oracle GoldenGate Monitor V11.1.1.1.0 on HPUX IA64 (176 MB)
⬇ Oracle GoldenGate Monitor V11.1.1.1.0 on HPUX PA-RISC (139 MB)
⬇ Oracle GoldenGate Monitor V11.1.1.1.0 on Linux x86-64 (119 MB)
⬇ Oracle GoldenGate Monitor V11.1.1.1.0 on Linux x86 (110 MB)
⬇ Oracle GoldenGate Monitor V11.1.1.1.0 on Solaris Sparc (120 MB)
⬇ Oracle GoldenGate Monitor V11.1.1.1.0 on Windows (109 MB)
⬇ Oracle GoldenGate Monitor V11.1.1.1.0 on Windows (64 bit) (117 MB)

Figure 11-30. Management Pack for Oracle GoldenGate

Next, you will see how to install this version of the JAgent as well as what needs to be configured to make it work with Oracle GoldenGate Studio.

Installing Oracle GoldenGate Monitor Agent

Just like Oracle GoldenGate Studio, the new Monitor Agent has to be installed. The requirements for installing the Monitor Agent include Java JDK 1.8 for the installation. After downloading and extracting the latest Oracle GoldenGate Management Pack, the associated JAR file has to be executed using Java. Listing 11-4 shows you how to execute the command to start the installer for the Monitor Agent.

Listing 11-4. Starting the Agent Installer

```
oracle@fred.acme.com:/home/oracle/Downloads >unzip ./fmw_12.2.1.0.0_ogg_Disk1_1of1.zip -d ./
ggmonitor122
Archive:  ./fmw_12.2.1.0.0_ogg_Disk1_1of1.zip
  inflating: ./ggmonitor122/fmw_12.2.1.0.0_ogg.jar
oracle@fred.acme.com:/home/oracle/Downloads >cd ggmonitor122/
oracle@fred.acme.com:/home/oracle/Downloads/ggmonitor122 >java -jar ./fmw_12.2.1.0.0_ogg.jar
Launcher log file is /tmp/OraInstall2016-01-23_04-36-44PM/launcher2016-01-23_04-36-44PM.log.
Extracting files....
Starting Oracle Universal Installer

Checking if CPU speed is above 300 MHz. Actual 3192.107 MHz Passed
Checking monitor: must be configured to display at least 256 colors. Actual 16777216 Passed
Checking swap space: must be greater than 512 MB. Actual 12287 MB Passed
Checking if this platform requires a 64-bit JVM. Actual 64 Passed (64-bit not required)
Checking temp space: must be greater than 300 MB. Actual 37064 MB Passed

Preparing to launch the Oracle Universal Installer from /tmp/OraInstall2016-01-23_04-36-44PM
Log: /tmp/OraInstall2016-01-23_04-36-44PM/install2016-01-23_04-36-44PM.log
```

Once the installer is started with the JAR file, you will see the initial splash screen (Figure 11-31) on the screen. Once you see the splash screen, the Installation Wizard will start.

Figure 11-31. *Splash screen*

You will notice that the splash screen says nothing about the agent. It only references that this is the installer for GoldenGate Monitor and GoldenGate Veridata. This is correct, as the latest Monitor Agent is bundled with these products and not with the core GoldenGate product.

With the installer started, you will be presented with the Welcome page (Figure 11-32). Just like the Oracle GoldenGate Studio installer, this provides you with information related to what you are going to be installing.

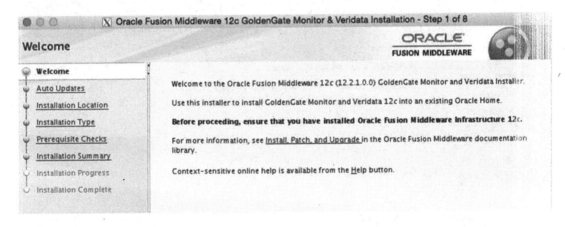

Figure 11-32. *Agent installation Welcome page*

On the Auto Updates page (Figure 11-33), you can select Skip Auto Updates. You should have downloaded the latest version of the Monitor Agent to use with Oracle GoldenGate Studio.

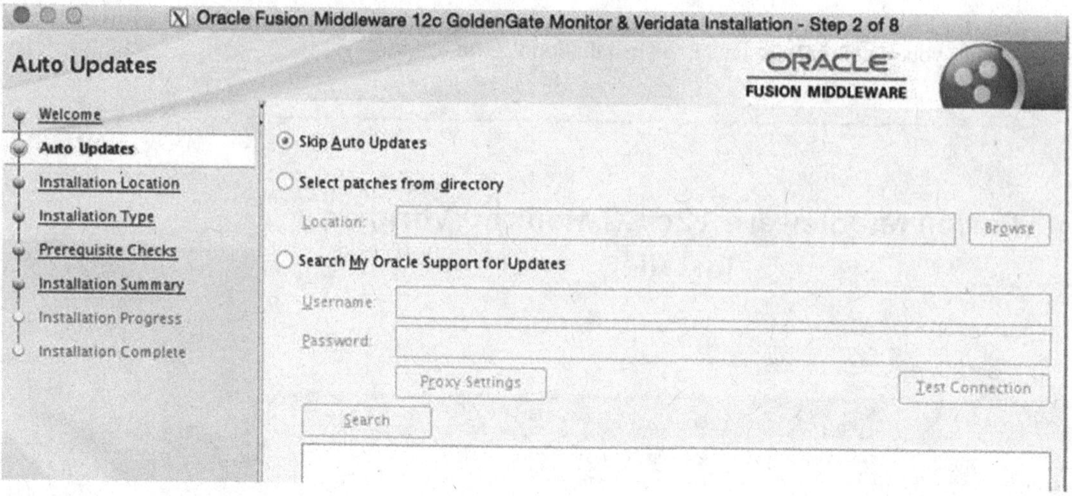

Figure 11-33. Auto Updates page

The next step is the Installation Location page (Figure 11-34), where you will install the Monitor Agent. If you look closely at the Oracle Home location, you will see that I'm still naming it JAgent. This is to keep it simple, but you can name it whatever you wish.

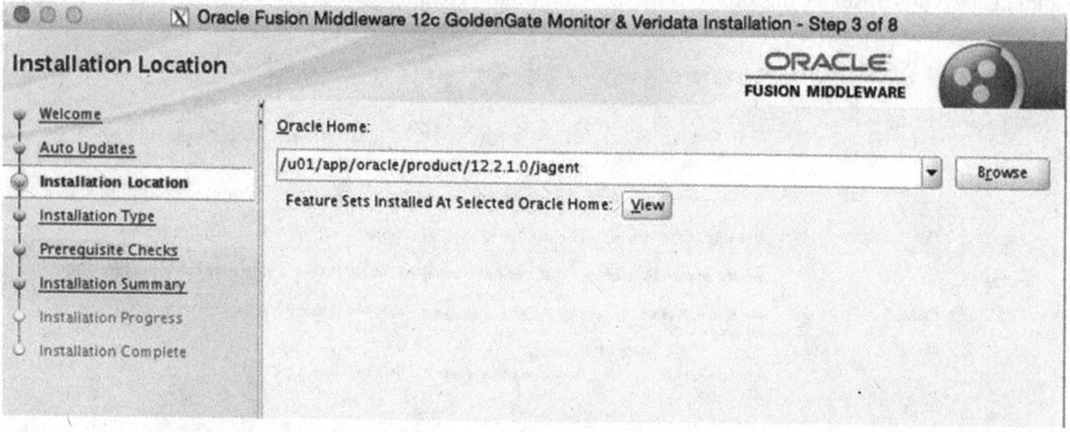

Figure 11-34. Installation Location page

You should now be on the Installation Type page (Figure 11-35). This is where you will select that you want to install the Monitor Agent. When you look at the page, the Monitor Agent is the sixth option down. This means that you will only install the binaries for the Monitor Agent.

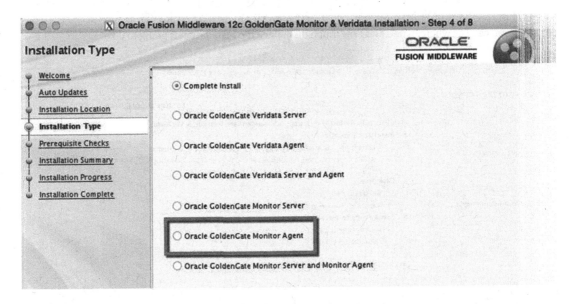

Figure 11-35. *Installation Type page*

After you select the option for installing the Monitor Agent only, the installer will move onto the the prerequisite checks (Figure 11-36). Just like the installer for Oracle GoldenGate Stuido, the installer is looking for Java 8 (1.8.0_51); however you can still install using a lower version of Java 8.

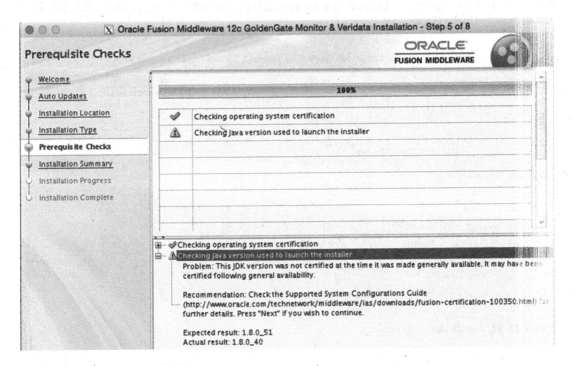

Figure 11-36. *Prerequisite Checks page*

After the prerequisite checks are done, the Installation Summary page (Figure 11-37) will be shown. On this page, you can see where, what, and how much disk space the installation is going to take.

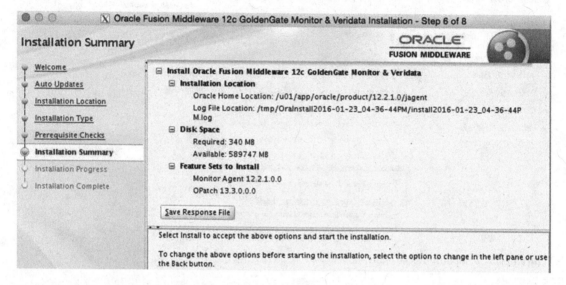

Figure 11-37. Installation Summary page

When you are satisifed with the installation settings, you can proceed to install the Monitor Agent (Figure 11-38). The installation will not take that long because you are only installing a subset of the binaries that are bundled in the JAR file.

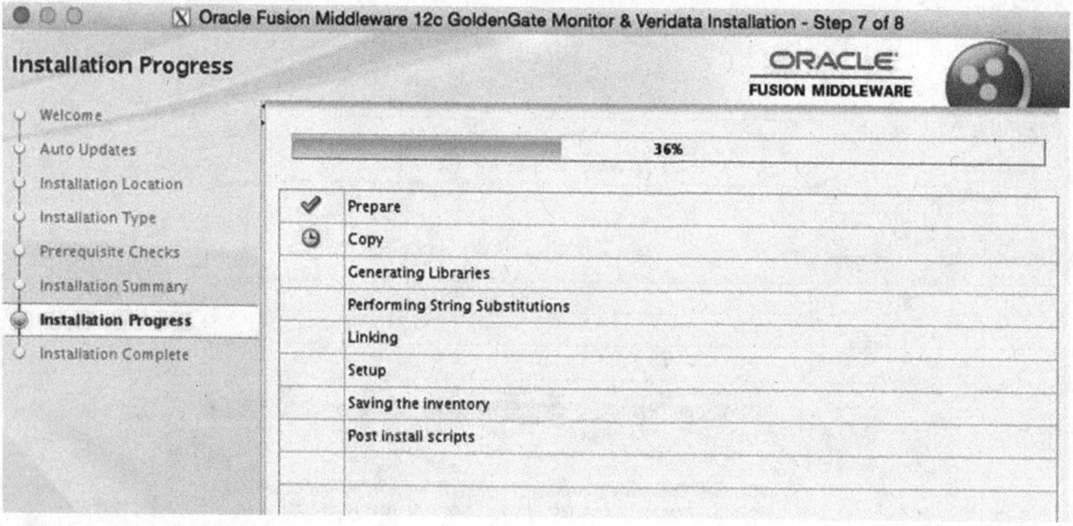

Figure 11-38. Installation Progress page

After the installation is complete, you will see the Installation Complete page (Figure 11-39), which provides all the information pertaining to the installation of the agent.

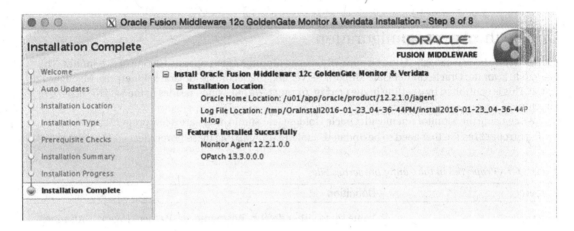

Figure 11-39. *Installation Complete page*

Now that the Monitor Agent is installed, you will need to configure it to be used with Oracle GoldenGate Studio. All of the configuration will be done at the command line because the agent is eventually controlled from within the GGSCI.

Configure Oracle GoldenGate Monitor Agent

Before you can start using the Oracle GoldenGate Monitor Agent, you need to configure the agent for the environment. This includes telling the agent where the Oracle GoldenGate installation resides and where you would like to install the actual agent process. To do this, you need to run createMonitorInstance.sh from the agent directory you created previously.

Create OGG Agent Instance

To execute the createMonitorInstance.sh script, you will need to change directories until you get to the $AGENT_HOME/oggmon/ogg_agent directory. Listing 11-5 illustrates this in my test environment.

Listing 11-5. Running createMonitorInstance.sh

```
oracle@fred.acme.com:/u01/app/oracle/product/12.2.1.0/jagent >cd oggmon/ogg_agent
oracle@fred.acme.com:/u01/app/oracle/product/12.2.1.0/jagent/oggmon/ogg_agent >./
createMonitorAgentInstance.sh
Please enter absolute path of Oracle GoldenGate home directory : /u01/app/oracle/
product/12.2.0/oggcore_1
Please enter absolute path of OGG Agent instance : /u01/app/oracle/product/12.2.1.0/jagent/
ogg_agent
Please enter unique name to replace timestamp in startMonitorAgent script
(startMonitorAgentInstance_20160123171554.sh) :
Successfully created OGG Agent instance.
```

Once this agent is created, you need to assign a password to the agent. This password will be stored in a wallet for later retrieval when needed on startup. This password will also be used to allow Oracle GoldenGate Studio and Oracle Enterprise Manager 12c or 13c to connect to the GoldenGate environment.

Update the Agent Configuration

As has already been established, the Oracle GoldenGate Monitor Agent operates in one of two modes. The first mode is for the Oracle GoldenGate Monitor Server and the second is for Oracle Enterprise Manager 12c or 13c. This is controlled by a setting in the Config.properties file, which resides in the $AGENT_HOME/cfg directory.

When using the Monitor Agent with Oracle GoldenGate Studio, there are a few properties in the Config.properties file that need to be updated. Table 11-1 highlights these properties.

Table 11-1. *Properties in the Config.properties File*

Property	Definition
Jagent.host	Value set to either default, hostname, or IP where JAgent is running.
Jagent.username	Set to JAgent username.
Jagent.rmi.port	Use default port or change to specific port.
Agent.type.enabled	Set to either OGGMON or OEM.
Jagent.backward.compatibility	Set to false.
Jagent.ssl	Set to false.

After you edit the Config.properties file, the values of this file would look similar to Listing 11-6.

Listing 11-6. Values Set in Config.properties

```
Jagent.host=localhost
Jagent.username=oracle
Jagent.rmi.port=5559
Agent.type.enabled=OEM
Jagent.backware.compatibility=false
Jagent.ssh=fasle
```

After saving the Config.properties file, you will be able to assign a password for the agent to use. Additionally, when monitoring for GoldenGate is enabled through the GLOBALS file, this information will be used to start the JAgent.

Assign Password to Agent Instance

The agent has to have a password assigned to it for external resources to access the information that is provided through the agent. To assign a password to the agent, you need to execute the pw_agent_util.sh script from the $AGENT_HOME/ogg_agent/bin directory. Listing 11-7 shows how this is done.

Listing 11-7. Setting Monitor Agent Password

```
oracle@fred.acme.com:/u01/app/oracle/product/12.2.1.0/jagent/ogg_agent/bin >./pw_agent_util.
sh -jagentonly
Please create a password for Java Agent: ********
Please confirm password for Java Agent: ********
Jan 23, 2016 10:49:38 PM oracle.security.jps.JpsStartup start
INFO: Jps initializing.
Jan 23, 2016 10:49:38 PM oracle.security.jps.JpsStartup start
INFO: Jps started.
Wallet is created successfully.
```

With the password set for the agent, you can now enable monitoring for GoldenGate and start the JAgent from GGSCI.

Enable Monitoring for GoldenGate

With all the settings configured in the Config.properties file and the password established for the JAgent, you need to enable monitoring from within Oracle GoldenGate. To do this, you have to place the parameter ENABLEMONITORING in the GLOBALS files under the $OGG_HOME directory. Once this parameter is in place, log out of GGSCI and start GGSCI again. At this time you should see an entry for JAgent (Listing 11-8).

Listing 11-8. GGSCI with JAgent Enabled

```
GGSCI (fred.acme.com) 3> info all

Program       Status      Group      Lag at Chkpt   Time Since Chkpt

MANAGER       RUNNING
JAGENT        RUNNING
EXTRACT       RUNNING     EGG12C     00:00:10       00:00:04
Description 'Integrated Extract'
EXTRACT       RUNNING     PGG12C     00:00:00       00:00:09
Description 'Data Pump'
```

After starting the JAgent, you can confirm that the JAgent has started with the correct properties file by checking the background processes. Once the JAgent is running, it can be used to interact with the GoldenGate environment from Oracle GoldenGate Studio along with Oracle Enterprise Manager 12c or 13c and Oracle GoldenGate Monitor.

■ **Note**   Java 8 (jdk1.8.0_51) is the best working version of Java to be used with the JAgent.

Summary

This chapter looked at how to install Oracle GoldenGate Studio, how to create the repository associated with Studio, and how to install the Oracle GoldenGate Monitor Agent. All three of these items are foundational building blocks to using Oracle GoldenGate Studio within any Oracle GoldenGate environment. This chapter should have provided you with the foundational knowledge of what and how to install Oracle GoldenGate Studio and the items needed to get it running. Chapter 12 dives deeper into Oracle GoldenGate Studio by showing you some of the functional tasks that can be done to ease the administration load of an Oracle GoldenGate administrator.

CHAPTER 12

■ ■ ■

Working with Oracle GoldenGate Studio

Now that you know how to install and configure Oracle GoldenGate Studio, you are going to need to know how to use this tool. In using Oracle GoldenGate Studio, there is a process for designing your environment with Studio. This process consists of five basic components:

- Creating resources.

- Creating projects.

- Creating solutions.

- Creating deployment plans.

- Creating mappings.

Each one of these components makes up the life cycle of an Oracle GoldenGate Studio design flow. In thinking of this design flow (Figure 12-1), it is easier to view it as a circular process that will be repeated time and time again depending on what you scope out for an architecture.

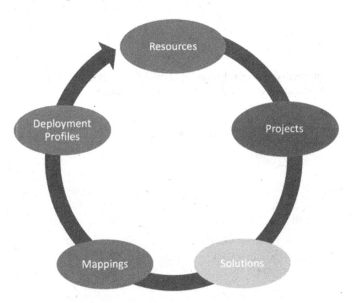

Figure 12-1. *Basic Oracle GoldenGate Studio life cycle*

B. Curtis, *Pro Oracle GoldenGate for the DBA*, DOI 10.1007/978-1-4842-1179-3_12

This chapter walks through this process to build out your Oracle GoldenGate environment.

Create Resources

With Oracle GoldenGate Studio installed, the repository created, and the associated Oracle Management Agent (JAgent) installed, you are now in a position where you can begin building out projects that will define your GoldenGate architecture. To begin defining your architecture, you need to first define the resources that will be used within the architecture. These resources consist of databases, Oracle GoldenGate instances, and any global mappings you might want to use.

■ **Note**   Global mappings are not discussed in this section.

After opening Oracle GoldenGate Studio, on the right side of the interface you will see a tab called Resources. This tab is where you can define the resources that will be used in your architecture. Once you open this tab, you see a space called Global Resource Library. All resources defined in Oracle GoldenGate Studio are items that can be used across all projects.

To begin creating a resource, use the icon that looks like a folder with a plus sign on it. This is the context menu for the resource that you will create (Figure 12-2).

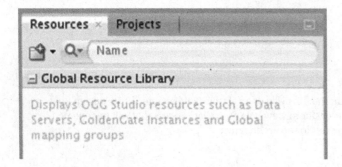

Figure 12-2. *Resources tab*

When opening the context menu, you are presented with a submenu that provides three options for global resources (Figure 12-3): Database, Global Mapping Group, and GoldenGate Instance.

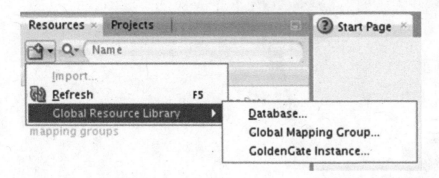

Figure 12-3. *Resource tab context menu*

Defining these global resources early in the design process will allow you to use these resources and name them correctly in your models. Let's take a look at how to create a database resource now. After creating a database resource, you will then review how to create a GoldenGate instance. The global mapping group is discussed later.

Defining a Database Resource

Database resources are connections to the databases you would like to use in your Oracle GoldenGate architecture. Oracle GoldenGate Studio allows you to define these databases as resources and then interact, by drag-and-drop interface, with them in the design view. To begin defining a database resource, open the Resources tab and then select Database from the Global Resource Library (Figure 12-4).

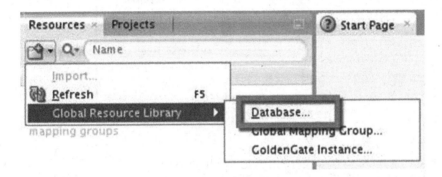

Figure 12-4. *Database option*

When you select the Database option, Oracle GoldenGate Studio opens a dialog box in which you will provide all the information needed to connect to the database (Figure 12-5). In this dialog box, you are provided the options to insert a name, connection type, username, password, user role, and connection information for the database. After providing all this information, you can test your connection setting to the database.

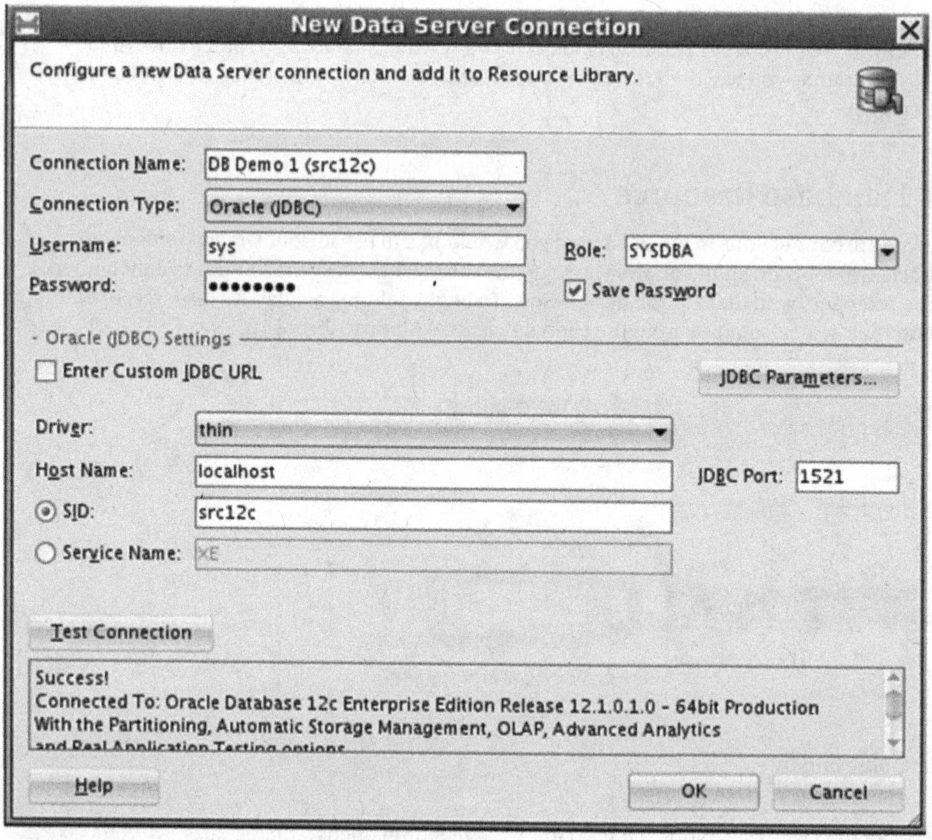

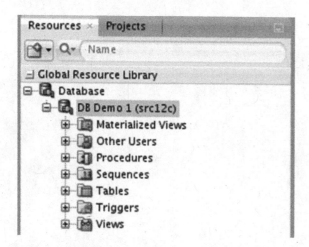

Figure 12-5. Data Server Connection dialog box

If your test connection is successful, you can click OK and then the database will appear on the Resources tab (Figure 12-6).

Figure 12-6. Resource Panel with Demo Database connection

The items listed under the database resource will be used in the mapping process later. Just know that you can create as many database resources as needed.

Defining GoldenGate Instance Resource

Another key resource that needs to be created is the GoldenGate instance resource. This resource interacts with the Oracle GoldenGate Monitor Agent. The name of the resource type is somewhat misleading, but this is really just the naming convention that Oracle is using to identify the resource in Studio.

To begin creating a GoldenGate instance resource, you will start in the same way you did with the Database resource. On the Resources tab, you will select GoldenGate Instance (Figure 12-7).

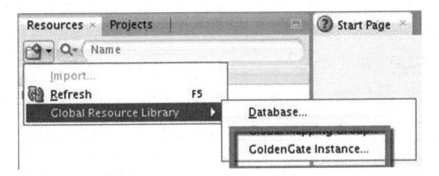

Figure 12-7. *Create GoldenGate instance*

Selecting GoldenGate Instance opens the dialog box for adding a new GoldenGate instance (Figure 12-8). This dialog box has quite a few fields and many of the values relate back to the Config.properties file.

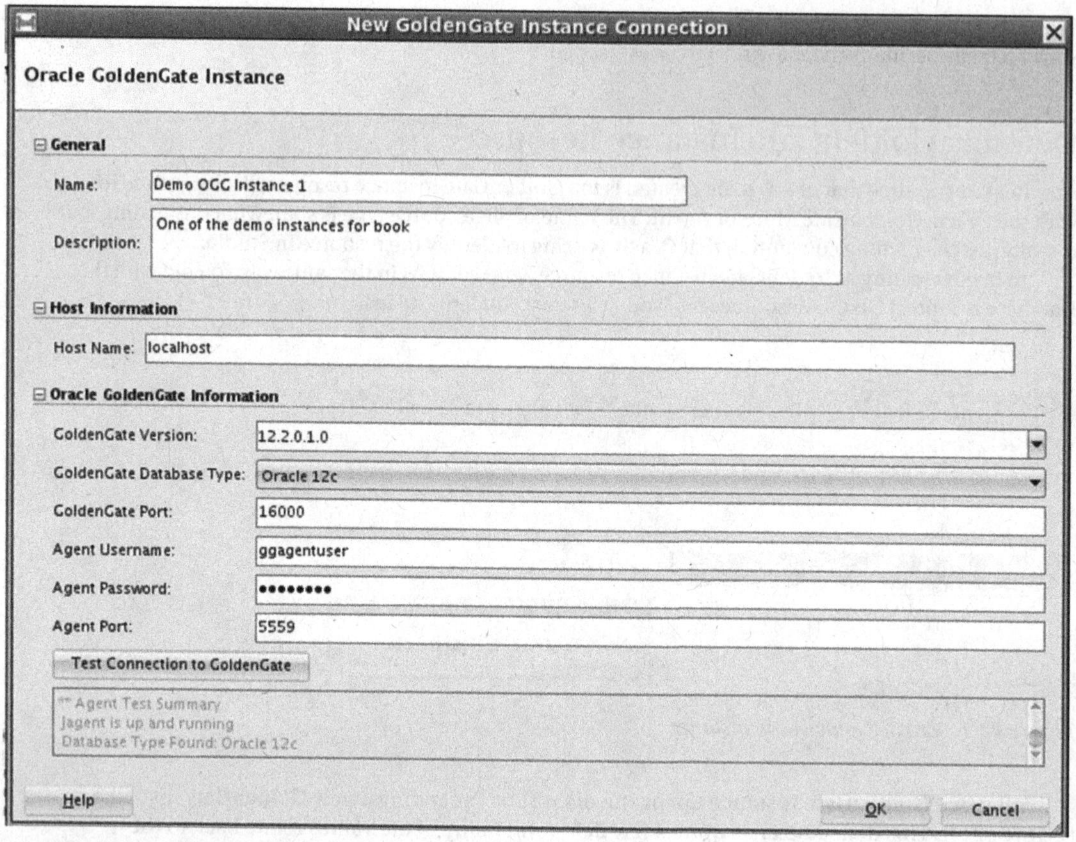

Figure 12-8. GoldenGate Instance dialog box

The fields in the GoldenGate Instance dialog box need to be filled in correctly so Oracle GoldenGate Studio will connect to the Oracle GoldenGate Monitoring Agent (JAgent). Once it connects to the JAgent, Oracle GoldenGate Studio can interact with the GoldenGate environment and perform the needed tasks.

■ **Note** Some of the titles in this dialog box seem to be confusing, but they all reference either the GoldenGate environment or the JAgent settings.

The dialog box allows you to provide a custom name for the instance you are working with, along with a description. In the Host Information section, you provide the name of the host where the GoldenGate instance is running. In the Oracle GoldenGate Information section, you provide all the connection information for the environment.

In the Oracle GoldenGate Information section, the first two fields are drop-down boxes that allow you to select the version of the GoldenGate instance and the database version you are running against. Next, you will provide the GoldenGate port number. This number is the port number that is provisioned when the GoldenGate Manager process is started. The last three fields in this section have to do with the JAgent itself. The information required can be found in the Config.properties file. The Agent Username and the Agent Port values are in the Config.properties file; however the Password value has to be established in the wallet during configuration.

Once this information is provided, you can perform a test to verify that the instance is connecting to the JAgent. Once a connection test is successful and you click OK, the GoldenGate instance you created will appear on the Resources tab (Figure 12-9).

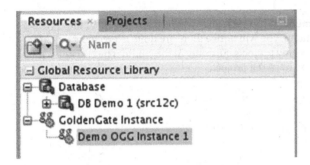

Figure 12-9. *Resources tab with GoldenGate instance*

You can create as many GoldenGate instance resources as needed. These types of resources are global in nature and will be used when you configure additional pieces in the architecture. Now that you have resources defined, you can begin creating your project and other items related to the GoldenGate environment you are building.

Create a Project

After creating Oracle GoldenGate resources, you are ready to start building out your Oracle GoldenGate environment. Every environment with Oracle GoldenGate Studio starts off by defining a project. A project in the Oracle GoldenGate Studio world is a logical container that allows you to separate environments from each other.

■ **Note** Depending on the repository database, you will have more than one project listed that you can be switch between.

To begin building your project, open the Projects tab within Oracle GoldenGate Studio. The Projects tab is one of the main tabs and will be visible by default. Figure 12-10 shows what the top of the Projects tab looks like.

Figure 12-10. *Projects tab*

On the Projects tab, you will notice there is an empty drop-down box. This drop-down box will display the name of the project once it is created. Additionally, it will allow you to switch between multiple projects. Just to the right of the drop-down box, there is a series of multicolored boxes. This is the context menu containing the command needed to create a project. To the right of that is a refresh icon, if needed once your project is created.

Returning to the multicolored boxes context menu, if you click on the little arrow next to it, the context menu will appear (Figure 12-11). On this menu, you will notice there are quite a few items that are unavailable. This is normal because you do not have any projects currently in the studio. The two items that are available allow you to create a new project and to import a project.

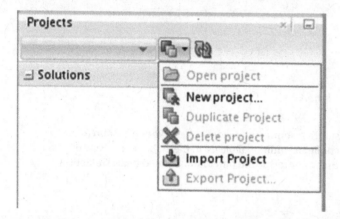

Figure 12-11. Project context menu

> ■ **Note** Oracle GoldenGate Studio allows you to export and import projects that you have created. This enables a collaborative approach to modeling GoldenGate environments between administrators, consultants, or both.

To create a new project, select New Project from the context menu (Figure 12-12). Once selected, that will open a dialog box that allows you name the project.

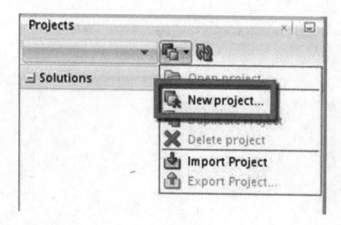

Figure 12-12. Selecting a new project

Notice in Figure 12-13 that there is a check box that tells the dialog box to open the Solution Wizard when you click OK. This is where Studio makes it easy for you to navigate to the next step in the project life cycle.

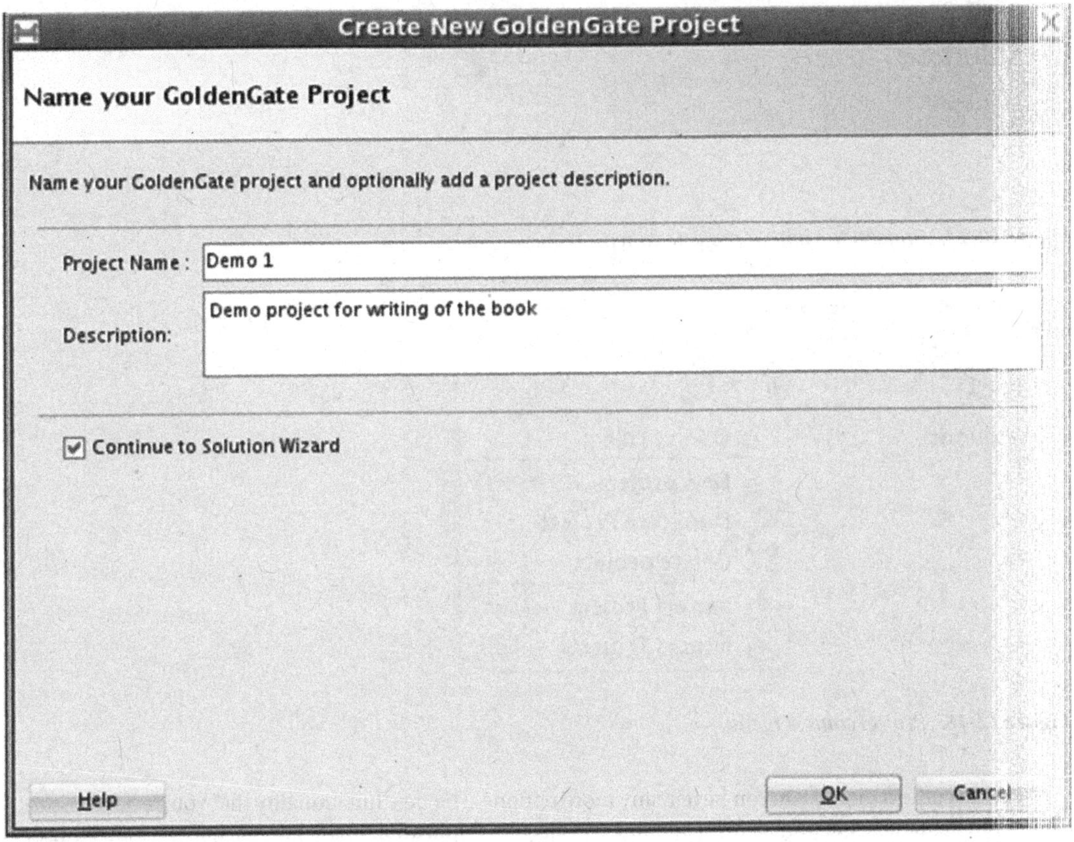

Create New GoldenGate Project

Name your GoldenGate Project

Name your GoldenGate project and optionally add a project description.

Project Name : Demo 1

Description:
Demo project for writing of the book

☑ Continue to Solution Wizard

Help   OK   Cancel

Figure 12-13. *Create a new project dialog box*

You can either leave the check box selected and start the Solution Wizard or clear it to only create the project. At this point in the demonstration, clear it before clicking OK.

Now that your project has been created, the drop-down box on the Projects tab will display the name of the project you are working with (Figure 12-14). If you click around, you will also notice that the context menu has changed to provide you the previously unavailable options for working with a project (Figure 12-15).

Figure 12-14. Projects tab with a project named

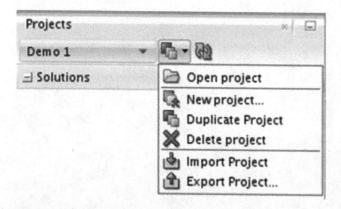

Figure 12-15. Project context menu

On the context menu, you can have many more options. The new functionality that you have access to allows you to manage the project from opening a project, to duplication of the project, and even deleting or exporting the project. Take a look around the context menu and see what you can do.

Creating a Solution

Solutions are the next step in the Oracle GoldenGate Studio life cycle. Once you have a project, the solution is the internal framework for your Oracle GoldenGate Studio project. A solution is where you will store the mappings and deployment plans for your project. Getting to the Solution Wizard is very similar to the process you used to create a project.

On the Projects tab, there is a little red puzzle piece. This icon indicates the Solutions context menu (Figure 12-16).

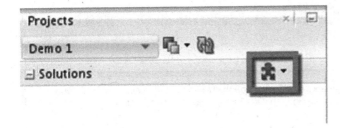

Figure 12-16. *Project puzzle piece icon*

On the Solutions context menu, you have the option to create a new solution or to import a solution (Figure 12-17).

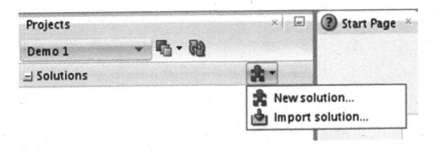

Figure 12-17. *Solutions context menu*

On this context menu, you want to create a new solution. When you do that, Oracle GoldenGate Studio opens a two-step wizard for creating a solution (Figure 12-18). In the first step of the wizard, you will be able to provide a name and description for the solution.

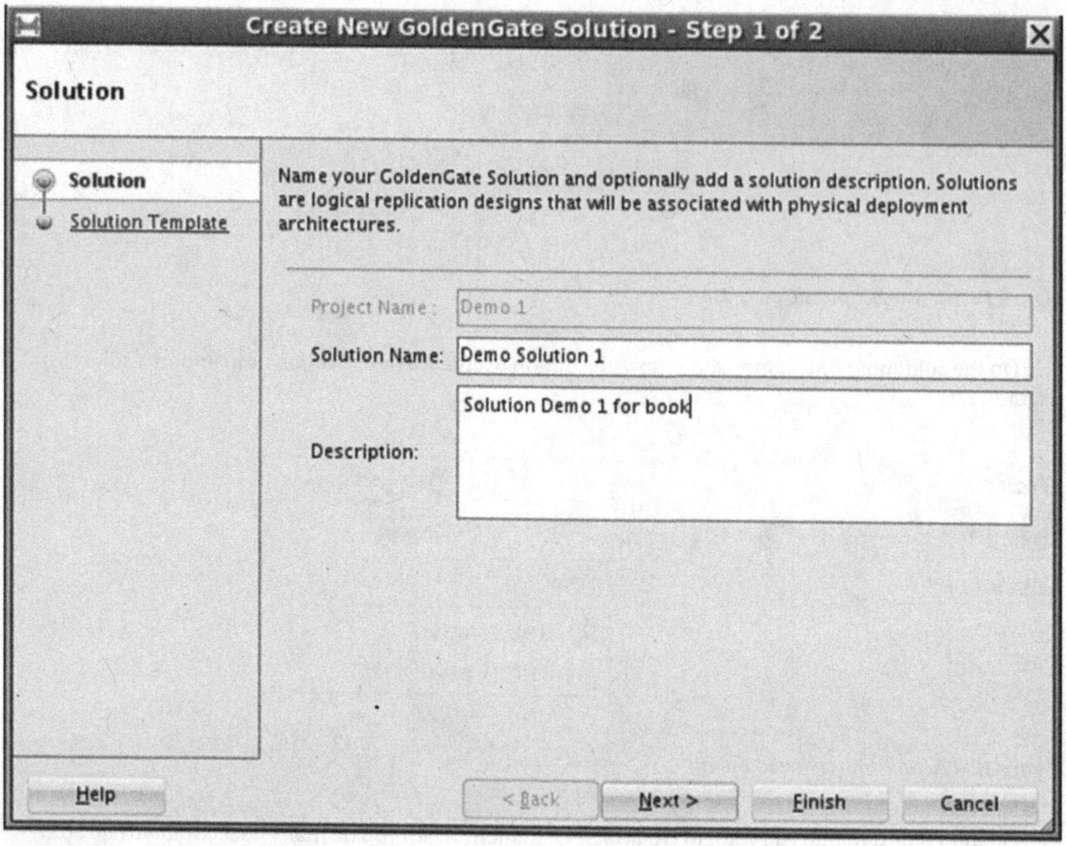

Figure 12-18. *Solution Wizard*

After providing the name and description for the solution, the wizard moves to the next step. In the second step, you can pick a basic architecture for your GoldenGate implementation (Figure 12-19). There are only three basic architectures that Oracle GoldenGate Studio provides at this time:

- Unidirectional
- Bidirectional
- Hub and spoke

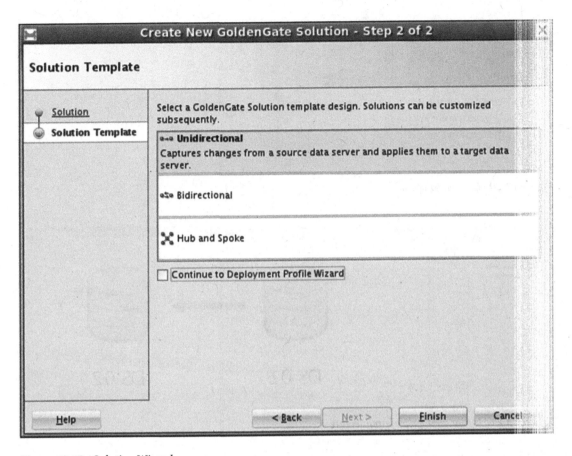

Figure 12-19. Solution Wizard

▪ **Note** There is a check box in this step that, if selected, takes you to the Deployment Profile Wizard once the solution is created.

On exiting the Solution Wizard, Oracle GoldenGate Studio updates the Projects tab will the solution or solutions associated with the project (Figure 12-20). Additionally, you will see the first rendering of your GoldenGate architecture in the main area of studio (Figure 12-21).

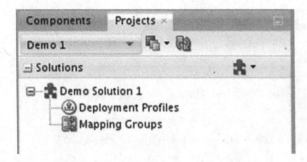

Figure 12-20. Created solution

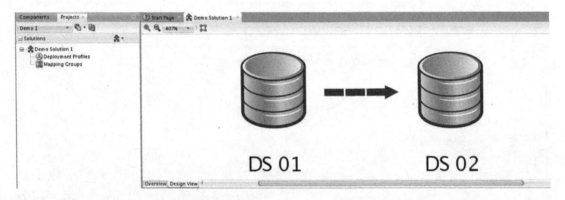

Figure 12-21. Initial rendering of architecture

Now that you have created a solution, take a look around before moving on to the next section. The solution that is created provides a lot of information. The naming of the database instances in the Design view can be changed if desired. In a later stage of the life cycle, you will assign these objects to a resource. For now, the important thing to know is that as long as you are in Design view, you can add components to the design and build out an Oracle GoldenGate architecture.

■ **Note**   The Components tab is opened after the solution is built. This tab normally opens next to the Projects tab.

Creating a Mapping

The next step in the life cycle is to create the mappings you want to use in the Oracle GoldenGate environment. Mappings are the tools that tell Oracle GoldenGate what data to capture and how to map it to the target side of the environment. This section looks at the different types of mappings, defining mappings, and how to include them in the design architecture.

Different Types of Mappings

Oracle GoldenGate Studio allows you to create two different types of mappings, global or local mappings. Each type of mapping does the same job; the only difference is that the global mappings are stored and used anywhere in the project, where as a local mapping is specific to that set of objects. Let's take a look at how to define both types of mappings.

Defining a Global Mapping

Global mapping groups are defined on the Resources tab, much like creating the resources you looked at earlier. To create a global mapping group, select that option from the Global Resource Library context menu (Figure 12-22).

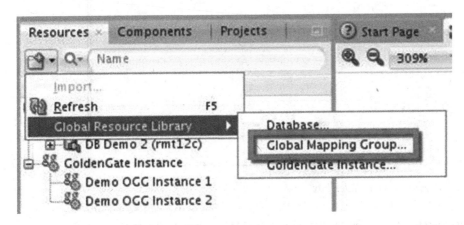

Figure 12-22. *Selecting a Global Mapping Group*

Once that option is selected, Oracle GoldenGate Studio opens a dialog box that allows you to name the global mapping group (Figure 12-23).

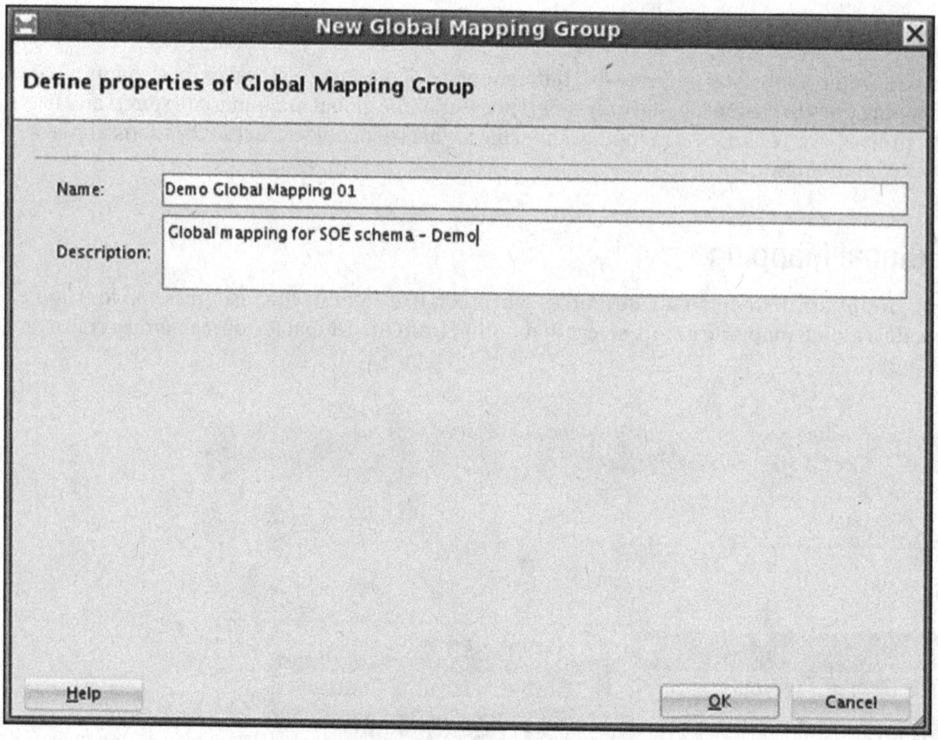

New Global Mapping Group   ✕

Define properties of Global Mapping Group

Name: `Demo Global Mapping 01`

Description: `Global mapping for SOE schema – Demo`

Help   OK   Cancel

Figure 12-23. *Global Mapping Group dialog box*

After you name your global mapping, the Resources tab will be updated with a mapping entry with the name you provided (Figure 12-24). When you double-click this entry, Oracle GoldenGate Studio opens a new tab in the main design area for you to begin working with the mappings (Figure 12-25).

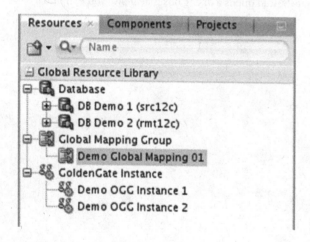

Figure 12-24. *Resources tab view*

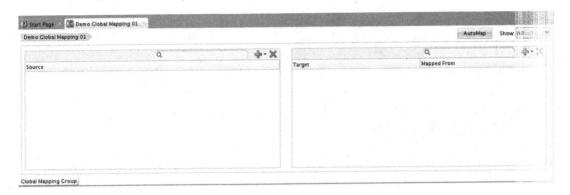

Figure 12-25. *Mapping in Design view*

At this point, you can start creating your mappings. You will learn about this in a later section.

Defining a Local Mapping

Much like a global mapping, a local mapping is used to map the tables you want to replicate between source and target. The difference is that the local mapping is defined within the project solution. This means a local mapping is created in the project itself and can only be used within the solution where defined.

To begin creating a local mapping, you need to look at the solution you defined earlier. Under the solution you will see an option in the tree called Mapping Groups (Figure 12-26) where you will define local mappings.

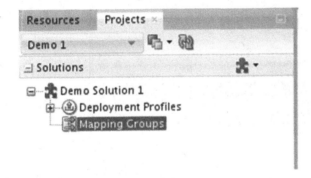

Figure 12-26. *Local mappings*

Right-clicking Mapping Groups on the Projects tab opens a pop-up menu (Figure 12-27). On this menu you will see options for creating a new mapping and importing a mapping. To create a new local mapping, select New.

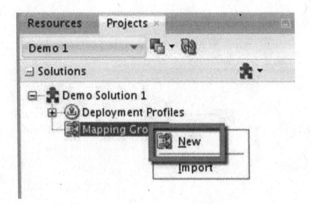

Figure 12-27. *Local mappings New option*

___

■ **Note**   If you try to right-click Mapping Groups without an open connection to the database, you will receive an error indicating this. This can also be seen if you leave Studio open for too long and connections time out (Figure 12-28).

___

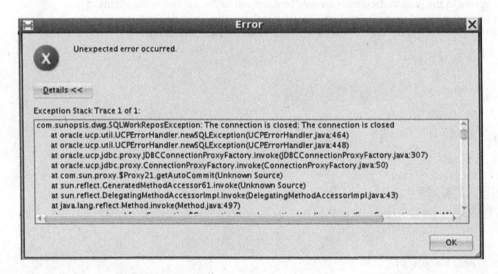

Figure 12-28. *Connection closed error*

After you select New, Oracle GoldenGate Studio opens a dialog box where you can name the local mapping (Figure 12-29).

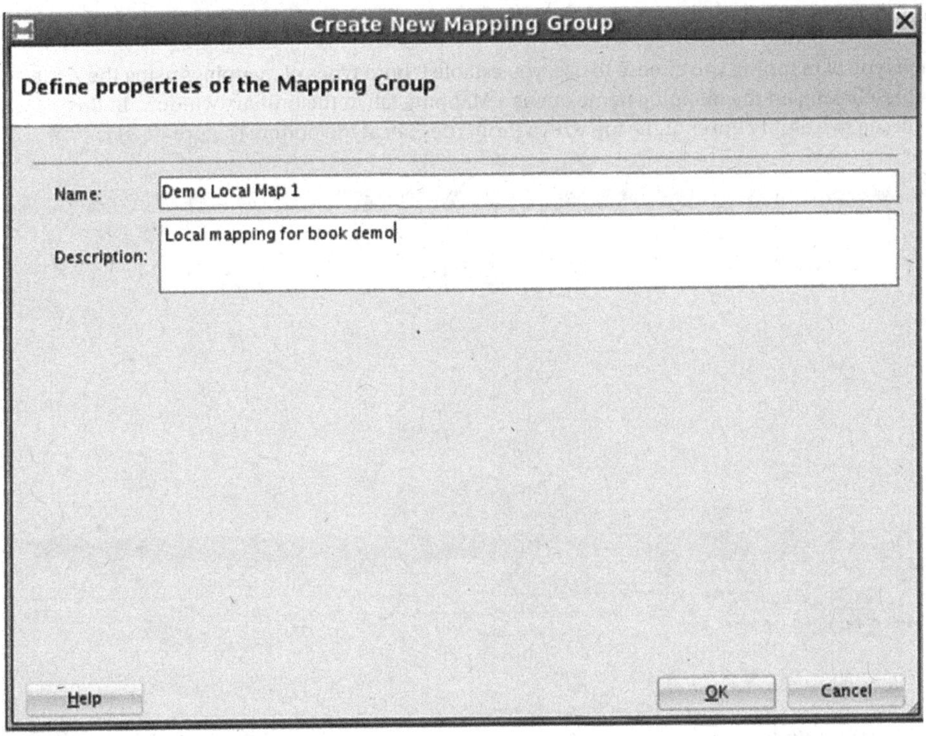

Figure 12-29. *Local mapping dialog box*

After you fill in the Name and Description fields, the mapping group will appear on the Projects tab under your solution (Figure 12-30). With the mapping appearing on the Projects tab instead of the Resources tab, this helps you identify that the mapping is a local mapping and is only for the project you are working in.

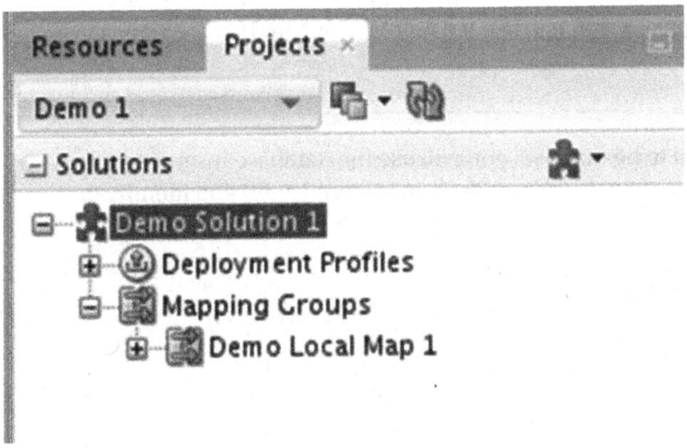

Figure 12-30. *Mappings on the Projects tab*

Establishing Mappings

No matter which type of mapping you choose to use, you establish both types of mappings using the same approach. Double-clicking on the mapping name opens a Mapping tab in the primary window. In this window, you will see two empty boxes at the top with a Properties tab at the bottom (Figure 12-31).

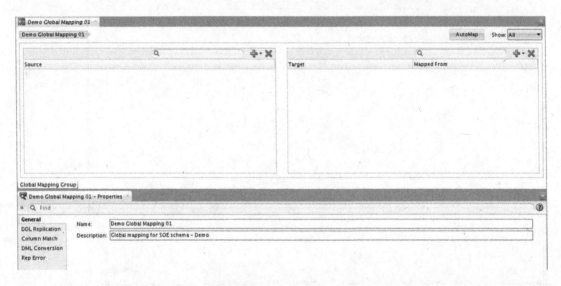

Figure 12-31. *Mapping window*

On this tab, you will define the schemas you want to map for replication purposes. The empty boxes at the top allow you to define mappings in a left-to-right manner. In the left box (Source) you define the tables from which you want to capture data. The right box (Target) is the box where you define tables to which data will be applied.

■ **Note** To make things a bit easier with mappings, you can use the AutoMap option. This button is above the Target box.

To identify and define the tables that need to be mapped, you will use the database resources you created earlier. On the Resources tab, open one of the databases defined (Figure 12-32) and identify the tables you want to map.

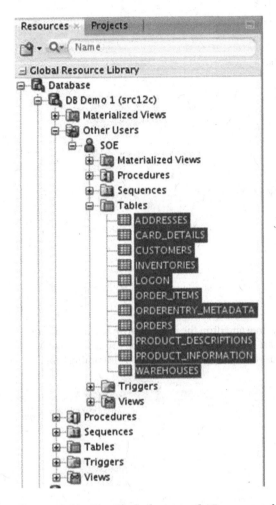

Figure 12-32. Identified schema on the Resources tab

Once you have identified the schema or tables, you can simply drag and drop the tables into the Source box, which will be populated with the items you selected (Figure 12-33).

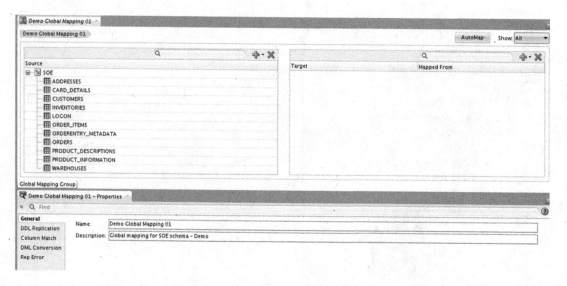

Figure 12-33. Global mappings

After the Source box is populated, you can manually drag and drop the individual tables into the Target box or you can use the AutoMap option. Once the tables are mapped to the Target box, you will notice there is a Mapped From column (Figure 12-34). This column just tells you where the mapping is coming from.

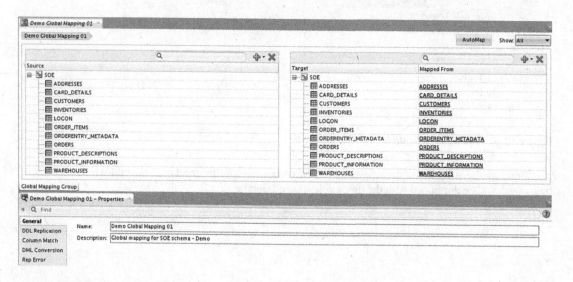

Figure 12-34. Completed mappings

At this point, you can save and use the mappings in your GoldenGate designs. If you need to ensure that DDL replication, Column Matching, DML Conversion, or Rep Errors are configured, these items can be found on the Properties tab (Figure 12-35).

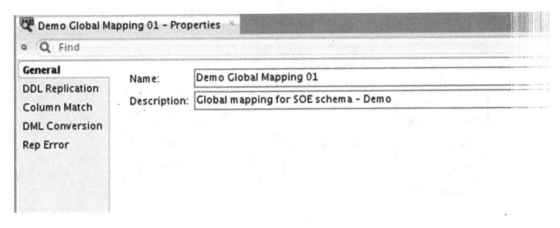

Figure 12-35. *Mapping properties*

Assigning Mappings

With a mapping defined, you will want to assign the mapping to a replication path. To do this, you will need to have your solution open in Design view. To do this, simply double-click the solution on the Projects tab. Once Design view is open, you will notice one or more black dashed arrow (Figure 12-36). These are the replication paths that have been defined based on the architecture you are building.

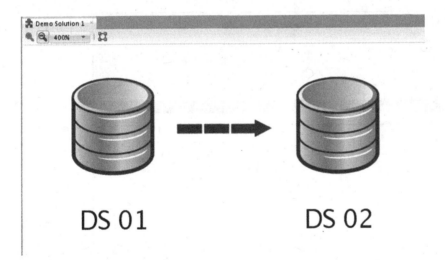

Figure 12-36. *Design view*

Once you select one of the black dashed arrows, it will turn red. Once the arrow is red, you can right-click it and select the option to assign mappings (Figure 12-37).

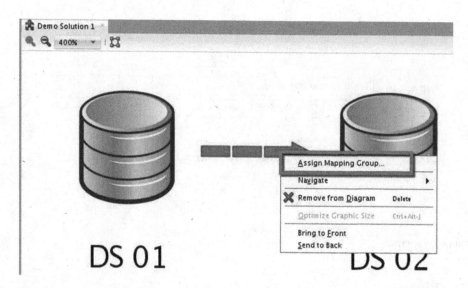

Figure 12-37. *Assigning mappings*

At this point, Oracle GoldenGate Studio opens a dialog box (Figure 12-38) that allows you to select whether you want to use a local or global mapping.

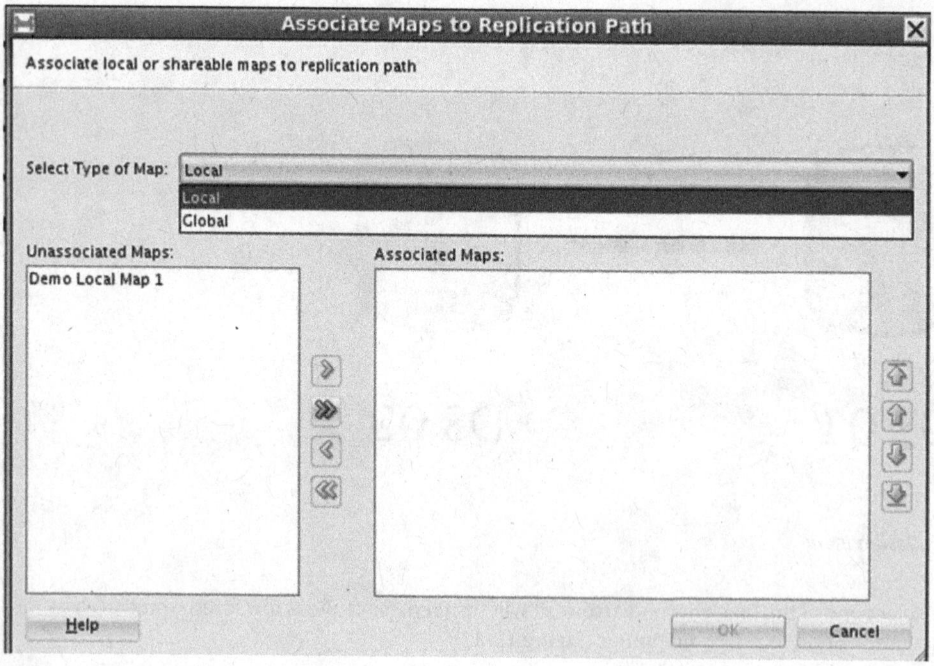

Figure 12-38. *Mapping dialog box*

After you select the type of mapping you want to use and Click OK, you will be prompted to confirm that mapping. If you are sure that is the mapping you want you use, the the arrow will turn into a solid red arrow (Figure 12-39).

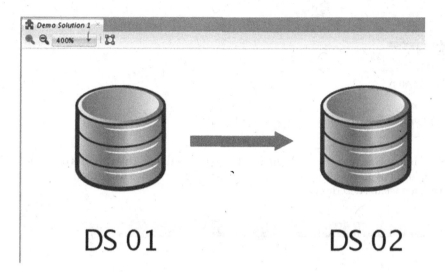

Figure 12-39. *Completed mapping*

Once you have solid (black or red) arrows, you have successfully mapped your desired replication path.

Up to this point, everything you have configured, mapped, and assigned has been leading you to the final step in the Oracle GoldenGate Studio life cycle, defining deployment profiles. Let's take a look at these now.

Creating Deployment Profiles

The final step in the Oracle GoldenGate Studio life cycle is the development and deployment of deployment profiles. These profiles define what and how you want to deploy Oracle GoldenGate. There are two types of deployments:

- Online deployment

- Offline deployment

You might be asking what the difference really is. For an online deployment, you have to have the Oracle GoldenGate Monitor Agent configured and running before you can push any changes to the GoldenGate environment. An offline deployment allows you to deploy your configuration changes to flat files that can later be manually deployed to the target system. With this simple understanding, let's take a look at how to perform each of these deployment methods.

Online Deployment

Up to this point in the life cycle, you have built all the needed pieces to deploy a GoldenGate environment. To begin deploying your GoldenGate process, you need to create a deployment profile. To do this, you need to have an open solution and right-click the Deployment Profile submenu. You will see with a context menu with a single entry: New (Figure 12-40).

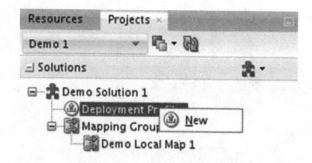

Figure 12-40. *Deployment Profile context menu*

When you click New, this launches the New Deployment Wizard (Figure 12-41). This wizard is designed to walk you through the deployment process. The first page of the wizard asks you for a name for the deployment profile and any associated description.

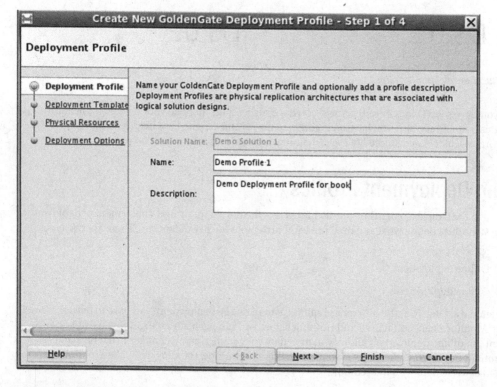

Figure 12-41. *New Deployment Wizard*

■ **Note**   Where needed, I point out in the wizard where you would do an offline deployment because the same wizard is used for that process.

The second step of the New Deployment Wizard asks you for what type of deployment you would like to build. This process is building off of the earlier selection you defined with the solution (Figure 12-42).

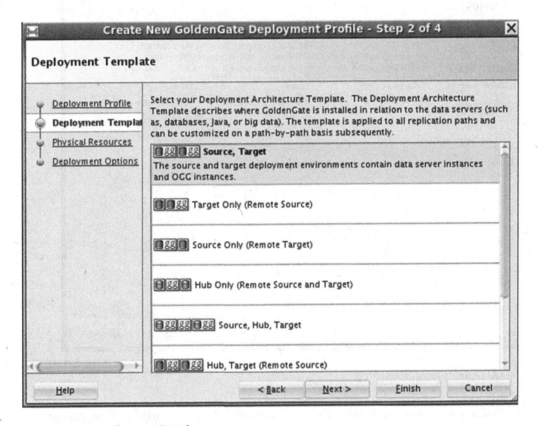

Figure 12-42. *Deployment Templates page*

These deployment architectures will describe what your solution will look like and where Oracle GoldenGate is installed. Once selected, the template will be applied to all replication paths in your solution. If there are any customizations that need to be done, this would be done on a path-by-path basis.

Progressing through the New Deployment Wizard, the next step is to define the resources that the environment will use. The resources that will be defined are the resources that you previously created on the Resources tab (Figure 12-43). You will provide a database and a GoldenGate instance resource for the replication paths you are defining.

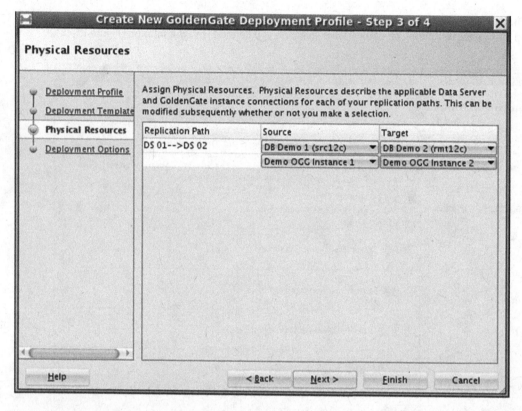

Figure 12-43. Defining physical resources

In the final step of the New Deployment Wizard, you will decide if you want to do an online deployment or an offline deployment. To make this decision, simply either leave the check boxes selected or cleared. If the check boxes stay selected, you are indicating that the New Deployment Wizard is going to create an online deployment. Clearing them does the opposite (Figure 12-44).

■ **Note**   Your decision to select or clear the check boxes will define the deployment provided and set up what files will be generated as well.

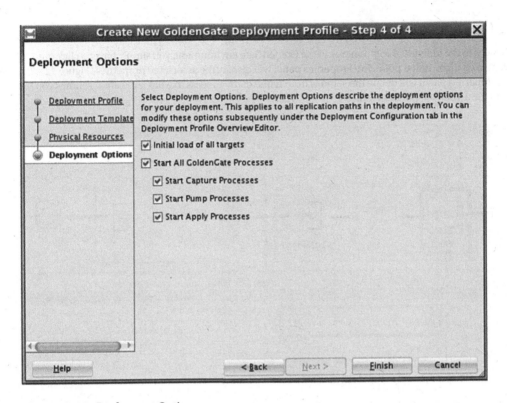

Figure 12-44. *Deployment Options page*

Once you finish setting up the deployment profile, Oracle GoldenGate Studio indicates that the profile has been created and opens the profile in Deployment view (Figure 12-45). This view is the physical display of the replication environment. At this point you can change physical attributes of the GoldenGate processes.

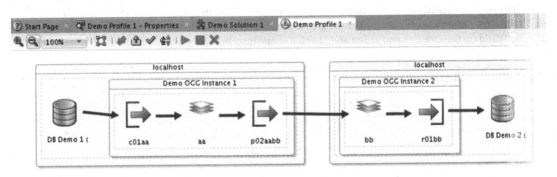

Figure 12-45. *Deployment view*

Making Changes

To make changes to the individual components of the GoldenGate environment, you simply have to click the item you want to change. At that point, the Properties panel will display the associated properties (Figure 12-46). Items in the Properties panel will define the settings from name of the process to what replication settings you want to use in the associated parameter files.

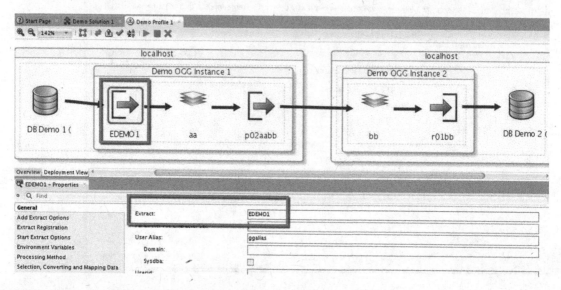

Figure 12-46. *Properties panel in Deployment view*

■ **Note**   In the Properties panel, you will see a category called Start Extract Options. In this section, there is a check box that is used to indicate if you want the extract started on deployment.

After you have spent some time configuring your environment, the changes you made need to be validated. To validate your changes, click the green check mark icon above the physical view (Figure 12-47). This will validate the changes you made and check if everything in the replication stream will work.

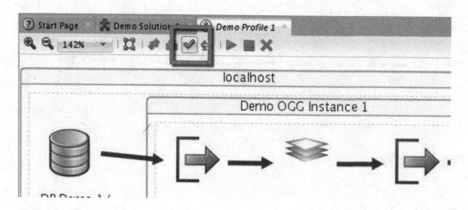

Figure 12-47. *Validation check mark icon*

Once you have validated your environment, you will want to deploy your settings. Here is where you have options for online or offline deployment. There are two options on either side of the validation check mark icon. One is a deployment option and the other generates your files for offline deployment. Figure 12-48 highlights the online deployment option. This option allows you to deploy your Oracle GoldenGate configuration to the target systems you have identified earlier in the environment setup. This also requires that you have the Oracle GoldenGate Management Agent installed and configured so GoldenGate Studio can connect to the systems and interact with the GoldenGate environment.

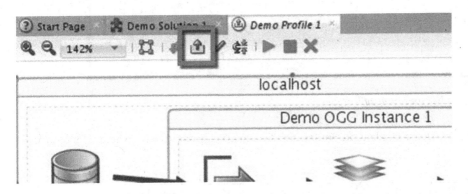

Figure 12-48. *Online deployment option*

■ **Note**   Any messages that are generated during the deployment process will appear in the messages panel.

Offline Deployment

Now that you understand how online deployment works, it is not a big step to generate the deployment files for offline deployments. Every step in this process is the same as for an online deployment, except for the button that you click. To generate offline files, you will need to select the option to generate your files. Figure 12-49 highlights where this button is.

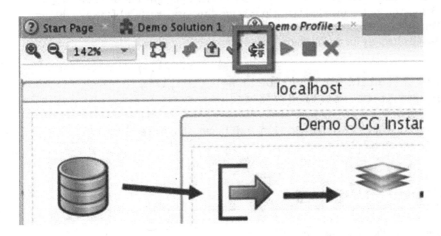

Figure 12-49. *Offline deployment button*

Once you click the offline deployment button, a dialog box to indicate where you would like to save the files is displayed (Figure 12-50). You can select anywhere you would like to save these files.

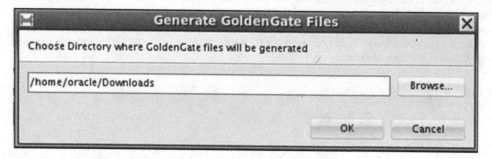

Figure 12-50. Dialog box for saving offline files

After you click OK, Oracle GoldenGate Studio provides you a dialog box showing where the files were saved (Figure 12-51).

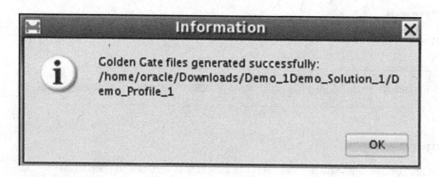

Figure 12-51. Dialog box for offline saved files

Once the files are saved offline, you can review what your parameter, obey, and any other files that are generated look like. Before you look at the files, take a look at the directory structure of the files that are created (Figure 12-52). You will notice that the offline process built a zip file for each GoldenGate instance and also created an unzipped directory for the instances.

```
[oracle@db12cgg Downloads]$ cd Demo_1Demo_Solution_1/
[oracle@db12cgg Demo_1Demo_Solution_1]$ ls
Demo_Profile_1
[oracle@db12cgg Demo_1Demo_Solution_1]$ cd Demo_Profile_1/
[oracle@db12cgg Demo_Profile_1]$ ls
Demo_OGG_Instance_1       Demo_OGG_Instance_2
Demo_OGG_Instance_1.zip   Demo_OGG_Instance_2.zip
[oracle@db12cgg Demo_Profile_1]$ █
```

Figure 12-52. Deployment files at the command line

Under each one of these directories you will notice there is a diroby and a dirprm folder. The diroby directory is for your obey files and the dirprm directory is for your parameter files. These folders contain all the files you need to manually deploy Oracle GoldenGate to an environment.

As you drill down into these directories, you will find the associated obey or parameter files. These files are generated by Oracle GoldenGate Studio in a top-down order. Figure 12-53 shows you the output of one of the parameter files. As you review the parameter files, you will notice there are a lot of comments added at the top. This is general information about the parameter file as well as the associated replication path.

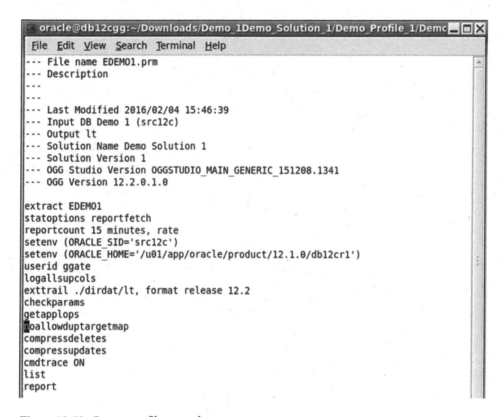

Figure 12-53. Parameter file example

Now that you have reviewed the complete life cycle of building an Oracle GoldenGate replication using Oracle GoldenGate Studio, you should have a good handle on how the Studio product works and what you can achieve with it.

Summary

This chapter looked at how Oracle GoldenGate Studio is used to build out a complete replication environment. You were given the basics of how Oracle GoldenGate Studio works and then provided with examples of how each one of the steps leads to a completed replication setup. Additionally, this chapter showed you how you can easily deploy your GoldenGate environments in a timely manner with just a few clicks.

Index

Get the eBook for only $5!

Why limit yourself?

Now you can take the weightless companion with you wherever you go and access your content on your PC, phone, tablet, or reader.

Since you've purchased this print book, we're happy to offer you the eBook in all 3 formats for just $5.

Convenient and fully searchable, the PDF version enables you to easily find and copy code—or perform examples by quickly toggling between instructions and applications. The MOBI format is ideal for your Kindle, while the ePUB can be utilized on a variety of mobile devices.

To learn more, go to www.apress.com/companion or contact support@apress.com.

 For the Complete Technology & Database Professional

IOUG represents the **voice of Oracle technology and database professionals** - empowering you to be **more productive in your business** and career by **delivering education,** sharing **best practices** and providing technology direction and **networking opportunities.**

Context, Not Just Content

IOUG is dedicated to helping our members become an #IOUGenius by staying on the cutting-edge of Oracle technologies and industry issues through practical content, user-focused education, and invaluable networking and leadership opportunities:

- *SELECT Journal* is our quarterly publication that provides in-depth, peer-reviewed articles on industry news and best practices in Oracle technology

- Our #IOUGenius blog highlights a featured weekly topic and provides content driven by Oracle professionals and the IOUG community

- Special Interest Groups provide you the chance to collaborate with peers on the specific issues that matter to you and even take on leadership roles outside of your organization

- COLLABORATE is our once-a-year opportunity to connect with the members of not one, but three, Oracle users groups (IOUG, OAUG and Quest) as well as with the top names and faces in the Oracle community.

Who we are...

... **more than 20,000** database professionals, developers, application and infrastructure architects, business intelligence specialists and IT managers

... a **community of users** that share experiences and knowledge on issues and technologies that matter to you and your organization

Interested? Join IOUG's community of Oracle technology and database professionals at **www.ioug.org/Join.**

Independent Oracle Users Group | phone: (312) 245-1579 | email: membership@ioug.org
330 N. Wabash Ave., Suite 2000, Chicago, IL 60611

Printed in the United States
By Bookmasters